CW00822445

# DICTIONARY OF THE
# SUPERNATURAL

# PETER UNDERWOOD

# DICTIONARY OF THE SUPERNATURAL

An A to Z of
Hauntings, Possession,
Witchcraft, Demonology
and Other
Occult Phenomena

Illustrated by Marion Neville

Harrap London

**For my wife**
**JOYCE ELIZABETH**
**with love and gratitude**

*First published in Great Britain* 1978
by GEORGE G. HARRAP & CO. LTD
182 High Holborn, London WC1V 7AX

© *Peter Underwood* 1978

ISBN 0 245 52784 2

*Filmset by Woolaston Parker Ltd, Leicester*
*Printed in Great Britain by offset lithography by*
*Billing & Sons Ltd, Guildford, London and Worcester*

# INTRODUCTION

The age of commercialism, computerization and control is still a wonderful period in which to live, for in every field – medicine, science, space, religion – barriers are being broken down and more and more is being accepted that was once dismissed as nonsense. Today almost any intelligent person is prepared to consider the evidence for hidden forces that would, not many years ago, have been dismissed out of hand; this state of affairs has probably come about because men of undoubted mental and scientific distinction have seriously investigated various aspects of the occult and the supernatural in recent years and are doing so today.

My object in compiling this book has been to cover not only the occult (that which is hidden) and the supernatural (that which is beyond our known laws), but the whole realm of psychic phenomena, including a few mythological figures whose reality has been accepted by necromancers in the past or by students of the occult today. I have endeavoured to include every element of the occult and the supernatural: its cults, sects and religions, its serious research and all its varied manifestations. Such a task is indeed formidable, and therefore this work is perhaps representative rather than comprehensive, though I have tried to include at least a brief mention of all important aspects of the vast world of the unexplained, including historical and contemporary material.

With limitations on the space available for these enormous and ever-growing subjects, it has been necessary not only to curtail some entries but also to omit many others, but I hope that I have not omitted any entry of great importance and that those I have included represent a fair cross-section of relevant information. In suggesting books for future reference, it has been necessary to limit these to two or three titles only at the end of each entry. In the main I have first sought to define the term or subject and then to confine myself to examining briefly the subject before suggesting references for further study;

exceptions are such important 'fringe' subjects as palmistry, numerology and cartomancy that merit longer entries.

The occult and the supernatural have always been mysterious regions, but gradually, and never more than during the latter part of the twentieth century, mankind is at last realizing that it is in the study of man himself, and particularly of his mind, that he will in all probability find the answer to many mysteries which have long seemed to have a supernatural origin, and those who venture into these exciting fields of exploration I have endeavoured to encourage with ideas for further reading and for practical investigation. The wonderful world of the occult and the supernatural is within the grasp of anyone who reaches out towards it.

I gratefully acknowledge the practical help and active encouragement that I have received from my wife and family and from such organizations as the Society for Psychical Research, the College of Psychic Studies, the Spiritualist Association of Great Britain, the British Museum and the Ghost Club.

Peter Underwood

The Savage Club
Berkeley Square
London

**NOTE**
A word in bold type within an
entry indicates that there is a
separate article for that subject.

# Ꭺ

## Aberdeen witches
Notorious victims, many undoubtedly innocent, of the sixteenth-century witch hysteria. Records of the Dean of Guild in the archives of the City of Aberdeen contain details of the trial (1596-7), which culminated in twenty-three women and one man being found guilty of witchcraft. All these were condemned to death, and were bound to stakes, strangled by the executioner and then burned to ashes. It is said that the black fumes and stench from the burnings hung over Aberdeen for weeks. The sentences were carried out 'between the hills', a grassy hollow that lay between Castle Hill and Heading Hill, an area that is now Commerce Street. Some of those accused had taken their own lives while in prison before being sentenced and their bodies were dragged through the streets of Aberdeen until no longer recognizable. A few, whose guilt was 'not proven', were branded on the cheek and banished from the city.

CONSULT: *Records of the Dean of Guild 1596-1597*, Aberdeen City Archives; Margaret Alice Murray, *The God of the Witches*, Sampson Low, Marston (1931).

## Abominable snowman
*See under* **animals and birds.**

## Absent healing
*See* **faith healing.**

## Acenesthesia
Sensation, sometimes found in certain types of paranoia, but also in mentally and physically fit people, the chief characteristic of which is that the person feels he has no material body; an experience often reported at the crisis of an illness. In extreme cases the feeling of

unreality and depersonalization become so extreme that the person concerned loses touch with reality and delusions and **hallucinations** bring the phenomena under the heading of hysteria.

CONSULT: D. H. Rawcliffe, *The Psychology of the Occult*, Derricke Ridgway (1952).

## Acupuncture
An ancient system of healing in which needles are inserted into the skin to a depth of about one tenth of an inch. Adherents of acupuncture maintain that there exist in the body dual flows of energy known as **Yin and Yang**, part of an overall concept of energy referred to as T'Chi or life-force. This vital energy circulates throughout the body along twelve main circuits known as 'meridians'; each being associated with a different body function or organ. The acupuncturist can ascertain the state of these meridians at the two radial pulses situated on the forearm just above the wrist; thereby receiving notification of the condition of Yin and Yang before any other signs or symptoms of the patient's health become apparent, total health being dependent upon the equilibrium of these energies within the body and within the universe.

Acupunture originated in China. More than 5 000 years ago it was noticed that occasionally soldiers who were wounded by arrows sometimes recovered from illnesses which had afflicted them for years. Experimentation seemed to establish that penetration of the skin at certain points cured certain illnesses. Later it was observed that the size of the wound was immaterial but the exact location and depth all-important. Armed with this knowledge the Chinese began to achieve results by artificially puncturing the skin, first with pointed wooden stakes, then with thorns, then bronze and iron needles followed by gold and silver needles. Today specially processed stainless-steel needles are used. Once it became apparent that certain specific areas on the skin affected and controlled certain organs in the body, needles were used to affect the organs concerned, and if they were diseased, to cure them.

The Chinese discovered about 1 000 points on the skin where stimulation by needles relieved or cured a disease. They divided these points into twelve systems, all the points belonging to any one system being connected by the invisible line called a meridian, each meridian being linked with a major organ of the body: heart, lungs, kidneys, bladder, etc. The meridian of the liver, for example, runs from near the liver to the inside of the leg and down to the big toe, and concentration

*Some of the ancient acupuncture points*

on any part of the line will affect the liver in some way. It is interesting that the heart meridian runs from the heart down the inside of the arm to the little finger: roughly the track along which pain is felt during a heart attack.

Today there are probably over 500 000 practitioners in China; some 50 000 in Japan; certainly over 5 000 in Europe (acupuncture is obtainable under the National Health schemes in France and Germany). There are also many acupuncture practitioners in the United States as well as in the Soviet Union, where needles are not used, but massage, ointments, weak electric shocks and lazar beams are employed instead. Acupuncturists have always been as much concerned with preventing disease as with curing it, and the emphasis on prevention rather than cure is reflected by the Chinese tradition that a doctor was only paid a fee when the patient was well and fees stopped when the patient fell ill; it was therefore in the doctor's interest to keep his patients fit. Before a patient is actually ill the body mechanism is slightly disturbed, though this may be too slight to be noticed by the patient himself; the acupuncturist, however, diagnoses the disturbance and seeks to halt its progress.

Treatment consists of diagnosis by pulse-taking with considerable sensivity. For the acupuncturist there are six pulses on the left wrist and six on the right making a total of twelve to correspond with the twelve meridians. Each pulse may have any of twenty-seven qualities, and depending on his interpretation of the pulse beats, the acupuncturist makes his diagnosis – often so intricate and delicate that he can not only describe the present condition of the patient but also past and future illnesses. Having diagnosed an affliction because the energy flows (Yin and Yang) are unbalanced, the illness is rectified by piercing the skin at certain points to facilitate or inhibit the energy flow, thereby restoring equilibrium to the whole body.

Recent years have seen the introduction of electro-acupuncture where a meter records the reduced skin resistance over the acupoints and a photo-electric cell signals the acupuncturist. The state of Yin and Yang having been assessed by electro-acupuncture, treatment is then applied prophylactically and therapeutically.

According to a *Which?* survey, most people who go to acupuncturists are medical rejects, yet over 70 per cent of these patients improve; a remarkable achievement. Acupuncture is being increasingly used in many areas of medical treatment, including childbirth (Britain's first acupuncture baby was born in June 1975), and since 1958 it is claimed that there have been over 600 000 successful operations using acupuncture as an anaesthetic.

A Chinese film on acupunctural anaesthesia shows several major operations with patients anaesthetized by acupuncture, usually in the ear, nose, face or extremities of the limbs. The patient remains fully conscious but feels only mild discomfort in the region of the operation, and the camera repeatedly shows the smiling faces of patients even as, in the same frame, separated from the patient's view by a raised sheet, the surgeon is at work with his knife. Advocates of acupuncture point out that this form of anaesthesia reduces post-operational discomfort and is ideal for operations performed in rural clinics and mountainous and isolated areas. It is also useful when normal anaesthetics might be harmful to a patient.

There are Berkeley Acupuncture Clinics is most major cities of Britain, and an Acupuncture Association at 2 Harrowby Court, Seymour Place, London W1.

CONSULT: Felix Mann, *Acupuncture: The Ancient Chinese Art of Healing,* Heinemann (1962); D. and J. Lawson-Wood, *Chinese System of Healing,* Health Science Press (1960).

## 'Adventure, An'
*See* **Versailles visions.**

## Aetherius Society

A modern society whose president is George King, a Western **yoga** master. The society holds meetings and discusses such subjects as **metaphysics**, flying saucers (*see* **unidentified flying objects**), **spirit healing**, **yoga**, **karma** and **reincarnation**. It believes that contact has been made with spiritually advanced beings on Venus, Mars and Neptune. Nineteen mountains throughout the world have been 'charged' with spiritual force by the 'cosmic beings' through the Aetherius Society. Address: The Aetherius Society, 757 Fulham Road, London SW6.

## Agrippa (1486-1535)

Heinrich Cornelius Agrippa von Nettesheim, real name Heinrich Cornelis. German writer, soldier, physician, medium, magician, traveller, linguist, omnivorous reader, endlessly curious adventurer, wandering scholar and natural mystic. Occasionally brilliant, Agrippa seems to have had an unfortunate life, although much of his career is shrouded in mystery. It is said that in 1525 he was visited at his alchemical laboratory in Florence by the legendary Wandering Jew. He was fascinated by the **Cabala** and long before his death became the centre of stories in which he figures as a black magician (*see* **black magic**). Goethe used some of these stories in *Faust*. Agrippa's major work, a defence of **magic**, is the three-volume treatise *De Occulta Philosophia* ('On Occult Philosophy') which he wrote at the age of twenty-four.

CONSULT: Henry Morley, *The Life of H. C. Agrippa*, Chapman & Hall (1856).

## Airlie 'drum of death'

A drumming sound is said to herald the deaths of heads of the ancient Scottish Airlie family, whose seat is Cortachy Castle, Kirriemuir, Angus. A former minister of Airlie, William Wilson, researched and published a fully documented history of the family and the 'drummer'. There is some evidence that the 'drum of death' was heard in 1881 only hours before the death of the then Earl of Airlie, and uncorroborated stories that it has been heard on many other occasions, before and after; it is a type of Scottish **banshee**.

CONSULT: Elliott O'Donnell, *Family Ghosts and Ghostly Phenomena*, Philip Allan (1933); Peter Underwood, *A Gazetteer of Scottish and Irish Ghosts*, Souvenir Press (1973).

## Aix-en-Provence

Beautiful French city in the department of Bouches-du-Rhône that early in the seventeenth century saw a terrible outbreak of **possession** at the Ursuline convent where Sister Madeleine de Demandolx saw **visions**, danced wildly, screamed madly, sang love songs, neighed like a horse, writhed in indecent postures and related stories of sodomy, cannibalism and sexual molestation.

In 1605 Madeleine had been admitted to a Ursuline convent but returned to her parents' home on account of bouts of severe depression. There, at the age of thirteen, she came under the influence of a thirty-four-year-old priest and friend of the family, Father Louis Gaufridi. His visits to the de Demandolx household became more and more frequent and prolonged, and for hours he and Madeleine were alone together. Perhaps inevitably, she decided that she was violently in love with him, and he did nothing to discourage these emotions. News of the protracted attachment reached the Ursuline authorities from the girl's mother and the priest was warned of a possible scandal.

Madeleine was now fourteen and she was admitted to the Ursuline convent under Mother de Gaumer, to whom the girl revealed for the first time the full story of her relationship with Gaufridi, which, she insisted, had included sexual intercourse since she had been thirteen. To avoid any possibility of further association with Gaufridi, Madeleine was transferred to the convent at Aix, and nothing more might have been heard of the matter had she not, two years later, when she was sixteen, suddenly fallen vicitim to apparent demonic possession. Her body was violently twisted and jerked into unnatural positions; she continually complained of being surrounded by hoards of **demons**; and during one spasm she destroyed a crucifix. The case proved obstinate; repeated **exorcism** did no good and only brought from the girl a flood of accusations against Gaufridi, including the charge that he was a worshipper of the **Devil** and that he had seduced her by means of a **charm** which he carried in a walnut. Father Gaufridi was questioned and insisted that his association with the girl had always been correct and respectable.

As the disturbances continued they began to affect other nuns, and especially Sister Louise Capeau, whose ravings and contortions rivalled even those of Madeleine. Father Romillon, who had conducted the abortive exorcisms, now sought the aid of a witch-hunter, Father Domptius, whose examinations of Madeleine produced blasphemous howls from the 6 666 evil devils that now apparently possessed the unfortunate girl, devils that included the mighty Beelzebub (*see under* **demonology**). She named twenty-four evil **spirits** that possessed her and said they entered her body in a string by the mouth and left it by the rear orifice. Father Gaufridi was ordered to exorcize Louise Capean but only succeeded in having himself denounced as a sorcerer and a cannibal. The inquisitors were unimpressed by his reply to these dangerous charges, and for a time he was imprisoned while the possessed nun Louise Capeau seemed determined to outdo Madeleine by repeatedly charging Gaufridi with every possible sexual perversion. Madeleine, meanwhile, continued to be terribly tormented in body and mind and the whole convent was in an uproar as the result of her obscene ravings and accusations.

The affair became the talk of France and a trial was inevitable. In court Madeleine seemed completely demented, at one instant retracting her accusations and pleading for a kind word from the unfortunate priest, and the next violently denouncing him as a devil-worshipper and a cannibal. At other times she was so overcome by lust that it was quite obvious from her convulsions and the movements of the lower part of her body that she was experiencing an orgasm before all the court. Twice she attempted suicide, and twice she was discovered to possess **devil's marks**, though these later mysteriously disappeared.

Gaufridi made a sorry figure in court, and his body too was shaven and searched for devil's marks, and some were found. To crown his defeat, a pact between Gaufridi and Satan was produced in court, signed in blood, that made all women subject to his will. In prison Gaufridi confessed that he had eaten babies, celebrated the **black mass** and exercised his magical powers over women, filling them with passion for him. It was a confession that he repudiated in court, saying that it has been obtained under torture; but his protests were in vain, and after further torture he was dragged through the streets for five hours and then strangled before his body was burned to ashes.

At the moment of his death Madeleine was suddenly set free from her tormenting devils. Thirty years later she had to defend herself against a charge of **witchcraft**, and received a sentence of perpetual imprisonment; she was released at an advanced age. Louise Capeau was less fortunate and seems to have been tormented by devils for the rest of her life.

CONSULT: Richard Cavendish, *The Black Arts*, Routledge & Kegan Paul (1967); Louis Coulange, *The Life of the Devil*, Knopf, New York (1929).

## Alchemy

A doctrine which claimed to penetrate the mystery of life, to procure the formation of inanimate substances and transmute base metals into gold and **silver**. A pseudo-science, it is the crude forerunner of chemistry; yet it is surprisingly difficult to dismiss all the evidence.

The theory of transmutation rests in the belief that all substances are composed of one primitive matter. The alchemist hoped, by taking away the various additions that had been imposed, to differentiate the resulting material, to reach and obtain the *prima materia*, and then to obtain the particular substance he required by the addition of different materials. Paracelsus, in the early sixteenth century, stated that the true object of alchemy was not the production of precious metals but the preparation of medicines; an observation that gave the subject a new and wider direction and dimension. Thereafter increasing attention was paid to investigation of the properties of substances and their effect on the human body.

Today we know that all materials in the universe are made up of protons and electrons and that the simple difference between gold and silver is that the former has seventy-nine protons in its centre and the same number of electrons circling round it while the latter has only forty-seven of each; and today transmutation of, say, mercury (or **quicksilver**) into platinum is possible but hardly practicable in view of the vast expense. To dismiss alchemy as so much nonsense – pre-scientific chemistry with overtones of **magic** – is to ignore circumstantial accounts of the subject and conclusions of such eminent authorities as Sir Isaac Newton and Robert Boyle. John **Dee** was also a leading advocate of the idea of alchemy, and Edward **Kelley** claimed to have discovered the **philosopher's stone**; he visited Prague and spent some time in the Street of Alchemists, which still exists.

The transmutation of baser metals into gold is a physical impossibility and any 'success' in making gold must therefore have been the result of trickery. One method was to use a crucible with a false bottom inside which a quantity of oxide of gold would be covered with a little powdered crucible, glued with wax. When the alchemist placed his various ingredients in the crucible and heat was applied, the false bottom would disappear and, at the end of the exercise, the gold in the crucible would seem to be the result of the operation. Other tricks included filling a hole in a piece of charcoal with oxide of gold and sealing the opening with wax; or stirring the mixture in the crucible with hollow rods that contained oxide of gold and producing gold nails by dipping them into the 'magic' liquid – an effect produced

*Ancient alchemists at work*

by using nails that were in fact one half gold and the other half iron, having coated the gold half with a substance that would be removed by dipping into the prepared liquid. A similar effect could be produced by whitening the gold half of a prepared half-gold and half-iron nail with mercury: when the gold half was dipped into a 'transmuting' liquid and the metal heated, the mercury disappeared, giving the impression that half the nail had been turned to gold; and, of course, such nails would be readily available for examination afterwards.

CONSULT: C. A. Burland, *The Alchemists*, Weidenfeld & Nicolson (1967); A. E. Waite, *The Secret Trading in Alchemy*, Stuart & Watson (1972 reprint).

## Alectoromancy

**Divination** by means of a white cockerel, popular in the seventeenth century. When a man desired to know the name of someone – a thief, his wife's lover, his successor, his enemy or some such person – he would mark a large circle on clear ground; divide and mark the circle into twenty-six compartments, one for each letter of alphabet; and place grains of wheat in each letter while reciting a 'magic' formula, preferably at sunrise. He would then take a perfectly white cockerel, cut its claws, place it in the centre and watch at which letters the bird chose to eat the grain. These letters, carefully noted, would reveal, it was believed, the answer to his inquiry.

## All Hallows' Eve
*See under* **festivals**.

## American Society for Psychical Research Inc. (ASPR)
Formed in 1885 as a result of a visit to the United States by Sir William
F. **Barrett**; Professor Simon Newcomb was its first President. In
1887 Dr Richard Hodgson became Executive Secretary, and the
organization later became a branch of the English **Society for
Psychical Research** until Hodgson's death in 1905. The American
Society for Psychical Research was then re-established with James H.
Hyslop as Secretary and Director. It was incorporated under the laws
of the State of New York in 1904 under the name of the American
Institute for Scientific Research for the purpose of carrying on and
endowing investigation in the field of **psychical research**, the stated
purpose and scope of the society being the investigation of **telepathy,
clairvoyance, precognition,** retrocognition, veridical **hallucinations, dreams, psychometry** and other forms of **paranormal**
cognition; of phenomena bearing upon the hypothesis of surviving
bodily **death**; of claims of paranormal physical phenomena such as
**telekinesis, materialization, levitation** and **poltergeists**; the
study of automatic writing (*see* **automatism**), **trance** speech,
**hypnotism,** alterations of personality and other subconscious
operations in so far as they may be related to paranormal processes; in
short, all types of phenomena called parapsychological, psychic or
paranormal. The society collects, studies and produces reports dealing
with such phenomena; maintains a library of books on psychical
research and allied subjects; and cooperates with qualified individuals
and groups who report their work to the society. Membership is
composed of Fellows, Patrons, Founders and Members, who all
receive the quarterly *Journal* (an affiliated publication of the
Parapsychological Association) and a *Newsletter*. The present (1975)
President is Dr Montague Ullman; and the society's address is 5 West
73rd Street, New York, NY10023.

## Amherst mystery, the great
Classic **poltergeist** case in 1878-9 at Amherst, Nova Scotia, that
centred around nineteen-year-old Esther Cox and followed an unsuccessful rape attempt by a boy, Bob McNeal, who drove her into
some woods and threatened her with a pistol. Eventually the boy drove
the terrified girl home, then fled the area. Esther had been fond of
Bob and the whole affair was a considerable shock; she cried herself

to sleep for seven nights, and then the curious happenings began.

Esther slept with her elder sister Jennie, and on the eighth night Esther suddenly screamed, said there was a mouse among the bedclothes and jumped out of bed. The bed was stripped and searched and nothing was found; but then movements were noticed within the mattress. The girls decided that the animal had made its way inside the mattress, and with commendable pluck returned to bed. Next night they heard movements from underneath the bed and saw a box containing patchwork jump up and down. Their screams brought help and the movements stopped. The following night Esther suddenly bounded out of bed into the centre of the room, dragging the bedclothes with her and screaming that she felt as though she was dying. Again the screams of Esther and Jennie brought the rest of the household to the girls' room, and there they found Esther in a very strange condition. Her hair was standing on end; her face was blood-red; her eyes were starting from their sockets; she was screaming with pain and she was visibly swelling all over! Suddenly there were four loud reports that seemed to shake the room, whereupon Esther instantly returned to her normal size and sank into a deep sleep.

Varied and typical poltergeist phenomena followed during the next twelve months: more swellings, loud banging noises, sudden 'deflations'; movement of objects, especially bedclothes. Messages, their characters nearly a foot high, appeared deeply scratched into the walls (including one which read 'Esther Cox you are mine to kill'); plaster and lighted matches fell on to the bed; a dress suddenly burst into flames; objects were thrown about; cold water bubbled and hissed like boiling water although its temperature was unaffected; voices were heard; physical violence was threatened and carried out – once Esther was stabbed in the back with a knife and another time pins were stuck into her body; chairs were piled up seven high. The disturbances were witnessed by the family doctor, two clergymen, many neighbours and Walter Hubbell (who went to the house as a sceptic and ended by writing a first-hand account of the disturbances) besides the Teed household where Esther lived. As with most **poltergeist** infestations, the troubles ceased as suddenly and as inexplicably as they had begun. Esther Cox later married and moved to Boston where she seems to have lived a normal, if hard, life. She was reluctant to talk about the terrible year afterwards because she was afraid the disturbances 'would come back'.

CONSULT: Peter Underwood, *Hauntings*, Dent (1977); Walter Hubbell, *The Great Amherst Mystery*, Saint John, N. B. (1879).

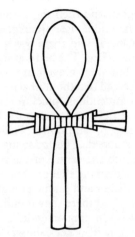

*Ancient Egyptian Sign of Life, the Ankl, a design that is still used as an amulet*

## Amulet

An object worn or carried that is alleged to have the power of protection against the **evil eye**, bad **luck**, **witchcraft** or disease; a **charm** that is magically endowed so that it has occult protective powers. Throughout history all races have had amulets and **talismans,** and amulets are as popular today as they were in the Middle Ages when 'pieces of the true cross' were held in especial reverence. They range from the **gris-gris** of Africa to the wishbones, **horseshoes** and rabbit's feet of Western man. Whereas an amulet has been likened to a shield, being essentially protective, a talisman has been compared with a sword since it is often used to perform a specific task.

CONSULT: William J. Fielding, *Strange Superstitions and Magical Practices,* Blakiston, Philadelphia (1945); Michael Howes, *Amulets,* Robert Hale (1975).

## Ancestor worship

The veneration of dead ancestors who are thought to be able to comprehend and influence events of earth; hence prayers and offerings are made by their descendants. Ancestor worship is still an important element in many religions of the world and is evident in a less religious context by the frequency with which foreign Communists pay their respects at the memorial to Karl Marx in Highgate Cemetery, London.

Ancestor worship has often been the reason not only for human **sacrifice** but also for offerings of food and weapons, of rare gifts of considerable value – goods and jewellery, of elaborate resemblances to help the dead person on his last great journey; and all in the hope that these sacrifices will in some way benefit the descendants. Even today the commemoration and attention given to our dead is an explicit recognition of our indebtedness and often enough a sort of insurance policy for those that are left; a kind of appeasement that is particularly apparent in embalming, or the 'eternal preservation' which is increasingly popular in the United States, reaching its zenith in the deep-freezing of corpses in the hope that science will find ways of curing **death** during the next 1 000 years that the deep-frozen body will be preserved. To a lesser degree funeral monuments (from those in any churchyard to Poets' Corner in Westminster Abbey), or such internments – laced with pomp and circumstance – as the Lenin Mausoleum and Napoleon's Tomb, emphasize man's continuing cult of the dead and the impulse to forge a link between the living and the dead; something that is never found in the animal kingdom.

Throughout the world, funeral ceremonies are full of customs that associate offerings to the dead while at the same time placating the ghost. In China and India the dead are believed to react with malevolence if they do not receive due reverence: in China by turning into **demons** and in India by haunting as aimless **ghosts**. In Japan the act of *hara-kiri*, often carried out during the course of funerals, was in the nature of an offering to the soul of the dead.

CONSULT: Jack Goody, *Death, Property and the Ancestors*, Tavistock Press (1962); Francis Hsu, *Under the Ancestors' Shadow*, Routledge & Kegan Paul (1948).

## Angelica
*See under* **trees and plants**.

## Angels of Mons
The legend that phantom armies assisted the English troops in the terrible retreat from the Belgian town of Mons in 1914, the first battle of the British Expeditionary Force in the Great War of 1914–18. Arthur **Machen** published the story in the *Evening News* on 29 September 1914, suggesting that ghostly bowmen from Agincourt helped the English to destroy 10 000 German soldiers against

overwhelming odds. During the early days of the First World War people were eager for a miracle, and they seized on Machen's story, insisting on believing that it was true. In his story, which he called 'The Bowmen', Machen says the German general staff decided that the English must have used shells containing an unknown poisonous gas since no wounds were discernible on the bodies of the dead German soldiers; he then quotes the testimony of an officer who reported that he and two colleagues saw 'a large body of horsemen' that inexplicably disappeared. After the story had been published confirmations began to pour in. Similar phantom armies were said to have been seen; Harold Begbie quoted soldiers' testimonies in his book *On the Side of the Angels*; a dying German prisoner revealed that his comrades had been reluctant to attack the English lines because of the thousands of men who should not have been where they apparently were. Then Machen confessed that he had invented the brief story that brought him more fame than anything he had ever done. In 1930 the mystery received fresh impetus when Friedrich Herzenwirth, a former director of German espionage, stated in his memoirs that the angels of Mons were motion pictures, projected by German flyers on to clouds, to make the English troops believe that God was on the German side.

CONSULT: Arthur Machen, *Tales of Horror and the Supernatural*, Richards Press (1949), which contains 'the Bowmen'; Harold Begbie, *On the Side of the Angels*, Hodder & Stoughton (1915).

## Animal ghosts
*See under* **animals and birds**.

## Animals and birds
Man has always sought an occult link between himself and creatures that he used, or feared, or admired for some particular reason. Sometimes he devised rituals of magical significance to obtain for himself special powers, and certain animals and birds, like man himself, came to be worshipped and elevated to the realms of the gods (*see also* **totems and totemism**). Folklore and mythology are full of talking animals and birds and fabulous creatures that mate with human beings.

Birds, their ability to fly bringing them into contact with the mysterious sky, and perhaps with the gods, have aroused man's envy, and so he has portrayed birds with a mixture of human and animal and supernatural attributes since time immemorial. One of the Stone Age cave drawings at Lascaux depicts a human figure wearing a bird mask – a theme treated in modern times by the Surrealist painter Max Ernst in his 'Robing of the Bride'. Most ancient religions employed bird-like creatures as symbols of higher power, and creation myths concerning birds' eggs abound in such widely separated place as Crete, Greece, Egypt, Peru, Hawaii, India and North America.

It is not surprising that birds have long been regarded as oracles and guides to future events (*see* **augury** and **omens**) and the **superstitions** concerned with birds are legion: in weather lore the call of the green woodpecker foretells rain; high-soaring swallows predict dry weather; seagulls inland mean a tempest at sea, as does an albatross flying around a ship at sea; a cuckoo seen on a bare bough foretells a bad harvest, on a bough bright with blossom a good harvest; and to sight eagles at any time means bad weather. The ancient Romans, it is interesting to recall, would often liberate an eagle over a funeral pyre to conduct the **spirit** of a loved one to the other world; some of the American Indians had the same idea, while the Yoruba tribe of West Africa sacrificed a fowl. Cambodian natives fasten ducks' feathers to the clothes of a corpse to enable it to cross streams and mountains on its journey to the lands of the dead; and Egyptian paintings and decorations repeatedly emphasize the belief that the soul takes wings at the time of **death**.

Good **luck** was once said to depend on whether you heard, for example, the cuckoo for the first time with a full stomach; whether you were born on the day a cuckoo was first heard; whether you heard the call from ahead of you or to the right; while its call at any time and from any direction, so Yorkshire folk say, means rain. Bad luck follows if an owl alights on the roof; if a robin enters a house; if an eagle flies low and utters shrill cries; if a dove is sighted over a colliery or over water; or if a raven croaks as a ship puts to sea. The eyeballs of an owl or the eating of the bird's crushed eggs enabled one to see in the dark; crushed owls' eggs are also said to cure drunkenness. Nightingales' tongues were eaten to improve the voice, and their flesh for wakefulness. The gall of an eagle, mixed with honey, remedied failing sight. Ravens' eggs gave the eater hair as glossy as the bird – but oil had to be held in the mouth or the teeth turned black! On hearing the cuckoo, Danish girls were in the habit of asking the bird how many years would pass before they would be married, but if the calls went on beyond seven or eight, the wise girls called the bird a mad cuckoo and refused to listen to him any further.

Bird symbolism includes the cocks on church towers that recall

Peter weeping as the cock crowed and so signify repentance. The common use of an eagle ('the bird that never grew old') as a lectern in churches owes its origin to the eagle being one of the four beasts which, according to Revelation, were round about the throne; the eagle was assigned to St John because his Gospel was considered to be the one which shows the most intimate knowledge of the mind of Christ and the eagle which flew up into the heavens was the symbol of inspiration: gradually the other three beasts of Revelation – the lion, the calf and the man – sank into disuse and the eagle of St John alone carried the Word of God on outstretched wings.

**Bats**, creatures of shadow and darkness, have a reputation for occult power, probably the result of their fluttering habit, their ability not only to fly and walk silently but also to hunt and find prey in total darkness, and their mysterious lethargic winter sleep; all have contributed to misunderstanding a much-maligned animal. Over the ages the bat has been associated with the bird, symbol of the soul, and with the **Devil**, dweller of darkness, and it is frequently encountered in folkore, **witchcraft**, **black magic**, **satanism** and **hauntings**. The bat is a symbol of death in Ireland and an embodiment of those already dead to the natives of West Africa; while in Britain a bat in a church at a wedding is a bad omen and a bat that flies round a house three times foretells a death in that house; in most of Europe, Asia and America the sudden entry of a bat into a house is thought to predict the death of an occupant.

Since it was believed to be magically powerful itself, the bat has also been used for protection and to induce favourable influences: in Germany the heart of a bat attached to the arm of a gambler by a red thread ensured him success, while Austrians used to believe that the possessor of a bat's eye could make himself invisible. Bats out early in the evening are still regarded as predicting fine weather in many parts of Europe; and a few drops of bats' blood in a loved one's drink was said to encourage his or her passion. Eliphas **Levi** used a bat which had been drowned in blood among his grisly ingredients for making a **magic circle**; bats' blood was also an important component in the witches' **flying ointment** since it was thought to aid nocturnal flights; it was also used in the celebration of the **black mass**.

In Africa, bats were regarded as manifestations of evil spirits that could enter the bodies of human beings, and Nigerian witchdoctors have been known to apparently extract bats and frogs from the mouths of patients afflicted in this way; while, in the southern United States evil spirits are similarly conjured out of human beings into the bodies of bats that then flit away into the darkness with their strange cargo. Today bats and bats' blood are still used in contemporary **magic**: a bat was transfixed with a **silver** pin on the chancel steps of a Yorkshire church in a ceremony of **sympathetic magic** not many years ago during a **vampire** destruction ceremony; and in 1962 New York outlawed the sale of '**voodoo** drugs' that included bats' blood.

*Bears* also hibernate, and their ability to progress either on all fours or in an upright position has caused them to be worshipped by Neanderthal man and to be the centre of European festivals to this day. Bear grease was an ancient cure for aches, pains and baldness and a preventative against blight in vegetables if rubbed on to garden tools; a cure for a child's whooping cough was a ride on a bear, and bear fur boiled in alcohol cured fits. The courage and strength of a bear could be transmitted to those who ate the heart of a bear; bear teeth are used to this day to assist babies in teething and as a charm against toothache, while backaches used to be thought curable by sleeping on a bearskin. There are many reported ghost bears, in America as well as in Britain, where Worcester Cathedral was once regularly haunted by such an **apparition**; there are others at the Tower of London and in Cheyne Walk, Chelsea.

The Indians of North America always apologized to the dead animal after they killed a bear, for the animal was believed to possess supernatural powers or to be a god in disguise, and a strict ritual covered the laying out of the bear's head, hide and bones. The Eskimoes believed that the soul of a polar bear remained for three days and nights close to the spot where it had been killed, and during that time they were careful to conform rigidly to the laws of **taboo** to avoid the swift punishment that came to those who had sinned against its soul. The Lapps, while glorying in the killing of a bear, which they consider to be the king of beasts, nevertheless regard all men who take part in its slaughter as unclean and require them to live apart for three days while they cut up and cook the bear's carcase.

On the principal that a real and substantial link existed between a name and an animal (in the way that a man might be affected by magic through his name, or his hair or nails, or other parts of his person) some Scandinavians, North Americans and Indians believed that as long as a bear was called by other than its proper name it would not attack; hence such euphemisms as 'the old man', 'grandfather' or 'golden feet' were used whenever a bear was referred to. Bear worship in Japan at one time involved bear cubs being nursed at a woman's breast before the animal was ritually strangled and 'sent away' to its spirit home.

*Cats* have been worshipped as gods and regarded as agents of the Devil; witches sometimes claimed that they could assume feline form and a cat, that was fed with its mistress's blood, was one of the common witches' **familiars**. There are numerous and often contradictory superstitions concerning the serene and mysterious cat who may be Satan incarnate or an unfailing weather forecaster or an independent friend of man.

*Crows*, and their relatives the *raven* and *rook*, are among the most highly developed of birds, and perhaps for this reason the crow had the reputation of being the confidant of the gods; it was therefore the emblem of prophecy. Through the ages the sinister air of the big bird and its sombre plumage has caused it to be associated with death and disaster. Cicero is said to have been awakened in his room by a raven on the day of his murder, and even today there are stories of great black birds tapping at windows to herald death, of death following a sick man hearing a raven croak, of a bird alighting on a house where death is imminent and of crows being the first birds to be seen after a death; small wonder that the bird was thought to possess knowledge and insight beyond that of other birds. Even today the ravens at the Tower of London are carefully fed and protected, for legend has it that when there are no ravens at the Tower, Britain will be doomed; it is also still believed that death will follow for anyone who causes the death of a Tower raven. In Greek augury sixty-four different crowings were recognized, each with its own significance. Sacred to Apollo and to the Ancient Egyptians and revered by the Norsemen who adopted it as their emblem, many a child in the north of England has been quietened with the dread words, 'the black raven will come'; a threat that was still in use two thousand years after the last Norseman sighted Britain.

*Eagles*, because of their size, strength and keen vision, together with their aristocratic bearing, ability to outsoar all other birds and their utter mastery of the air, have long been used as an emblem of divinity and kingship. Sacred to the Greek Zeus, the father of the gods and of man, and to the Roman Jove, the eagle was regarded with awe above all birds – was it not an eagle that carried the souls of the departed kings to join the immortals? Eagles were also among the birds used in augury, and they appear in the folklore of many countries, from the Ancient Egyptians, who believed that the human spirit took the form of an eagle after death, to the present-day Welshmen for whom Snowdon used to be called Caer Eryri ('the camp of eagles'), and who still regard the behaviour of any eagle on the mountain as significant, as is any sound that can be likened to the shrill cry of this majestic bird: a faraway cry, for instance, is regarded as an ill omen and death and disease are sure to follow.

Because there was a widely held and very ancient belief that the eagle never grew old, the flesh of the eagle, its eggs, its feathers and its blood have been used in witchcraft and occult practices, where its identification with the spirit of the air, its reputed renewal of youth, its supernormal eyesight and considerable strength and power have been used in rites of sympathetic magic: its feathers boiled to make broth, its body cooked and its blood drunk for medicinal and magical purposes, its heart used as a **love potion** and its 'marrow' as a contraceptive.

Representations of animals, especially *horses*, survive from man's earliest attempts at pictorial art on cave walls and cut into the turf or chalk to make hill figures. Indeed, the horse, worshipped as a Celtic goddess, Epona ('divine horse'), has been personified in stone and metal, attributed with psychic powers, worshipped and sacrificed for different reasons through the ages; even today the **horseshoe** is one of the most popular of lucky **charms.** In recent times several horses have been credited with human abilities, notably the **Elberfeld horses**.

The contrasting black and white plumage of the *magpie* has probably contributed to the somewhat sinister image and legends associated with the bird. Is it really a hybrid between the black raven and the white dove (two of the birds released from Noah's Ark) and therefore not baptized in the waters of the Flood? In Scotland the bird used to be regarded as 'the De'il's bird', and it was believed that its loud and raucous voice revealed a drop of Satan's blood on its tongue. It was also believed that magpies could learn to speak if the tongue of the bird was scratched and a drop of human blood introduced. Generally considered an unlucky bird, it was regarded as an ill portent should a magpie cross one's path, and particularly unlucky to kill one, although the bird has figured in satanic and occult rites. A well-known rhyme is still quoted by country folk who see the bird: 'One for sorrow, two for mirth, three for a wedding and four for a birth.' Other authorities assert that to see one magpie followed by others is unlucky; to see two at a time foretells a marriage or happiness; three, a successful journey; four, an unexpected piece of good news; and five, a fortunate omen. The bad omen could, it was thought, be averted by turning round three times or spitting three times.

*Pigs*, first domesticated by the Chinese, are still regarded as uncanny, psychic animals, and are often the subject of a taboo. While the whole of Northern Europe regarded, and in some respects still regards, pork as a food of delicacy and princely hospitality, the Jews and Arabs (for reasons now forgotten) consider the pig as unclean meat. Once sacrificed to the gods of Ancient Greece in elaborate ceremonies and worshipped in bygone Crete, the pig was regarded in Ancient Egypt as representing the spirit of Osiris at the time of sowing and of Seth (or Setekhy) at harvest time; it was only eaten by them at the great midwinter feast and it could only be sacrificed when the **moon** was full. The association of the pig as the personification of Satan is still occasionally recalled by present-day occultists, and while effigies of demon pigs can be seen in some English parish churches, the animal is also regarded as a good-luck token in China and many parts of Europe.

The Isle of Man is reputed to harbour fairy pigs and there are a number of spectral pigs throughout Britain. Another aspect of the pig echoed by contemporary magicians is the former practice of some Indonesian islanders whose chosen priest, after **sacrifice** of a pig at their festivals, would rush forward, thrust his head into the carcass and drink the warm blood; assistant priests would, after a few moments, drag him away, set him in a sitting position and listen to his prophetic utterences. A second feast of the pig's blood induced a second rush of predictions, and it was thought that the priest was inhabited, through the blood of the pig, by a spirit that possessed the power of prophecy.

The *rabbit*, noted for its extreme fecundity and great adaptability, has (like its cousin the *hare*) become the centre of many beliefs and superstitions and has long been associated with witchcraft. A rabbit's foot is probably the most popular of all lucky mascots or **charms**; it is considered to bring good luck if the first day of a new moon or a new month is greeted with the word 'rabbits' before any other word is spoken; good fortune also follows a rabbit crossing one's path ahead, but ill fortune can be expected if the rabbit crosses one's path behind. Miners always considered it unlucky to meet a rabbit on their way to the mine, and it is universally considered to be unlucky to dream of rabbits.

Hare-lips were thought to be the result of the child's mother having been startled by a rabbit or hare while pregnant. Easter rabbits are gradually replacing the Easter hare as the reputed producer of Easter eggs. Sorcerers have often used parts of rabbits in their practices, especially the ears, representing acute, almost supernatural, hearing, and the kidneys and genitals, representing the undoubted sexual potency of the animal. In witchcraft rabbits were a common familiar, and witches were reputed to be able to change themselves into rabbits or hares: there are many stories of such an animal being injured and next day a reputed witch being found with an identical injury.

The small, perky and popular **Robin**, with its bright eyes and conspicuous red breast, has long been associated with **fire** and **blood** in various legends and superstitions. A Candlemas ceremony in France used to consist of a robin being roasted on a spit of hazel, itself a magical tree (*see* **trees and plants**), which suggests some pre-Christian ritual; in Germany robins were thought to avert lightning; in Britain a robin entering a house foretold a death in the family and anyone who stole an egg from a robin's nest would shortly break a limb. There are many tales that purport to tell the origin of the robin's red breast: one tells of the fire in the stable where Christ was born being reduced to smouldering embers until a robin, then possessing a brown breast, fanned it into flames but burnt its breast in doing so; another tells of a robin plucking a thorn from the crown on Christ's head while he was on the cross, but the thorn pierced the robin's breast and thereafter all robins had red breasts.

Country folk believe that a robin singing in a hedge foretells rough weather while one singing on a roof-top portends fair weather. The inquisitiveness of the bird (it often keeps close to anyone digging – on the lookout for worms) and its liking for graveyards and open spaces has caused it to acquire a number of associations with death, including the belief that it would cover a dead body with leaves and moss; a possible reason for the occasional use and sacrifice of robins in magical and occult ceremonies.

**Serpents** are perhaps the commonest creatures in mythology in all parts of the world, including places where no snakes are found. Invariably they have been treated with awe and respect and often fear, from the idolatrous worship of the biblical Jews to the snake-handling religions of the present day. India, in particular, has been full of serpent worship since prehistoric times and the ancient snake cults were assimilated into the religion of the invading Aryans and have survived in the Hindu myths of semi-divine beings with serpent bodies, called Nagas, who mingle among and even marry mere mortals in numerous Hindu folktales; it is not surprising that snake worship continues in many part of the East up to the present day.

Greek mythology, too, is liberally sprinkled with stories of battles between the gods and serpents, while Egypt had a snake god, Japan a multi-headed serpent god, Scandinavia a giant serpent god, Polynesia a monster eel or snake and the Aztecs their plumed serpent. In many parts of the world, serpent deities were depicted as serpents with their tails in their mouth: the cosmic snake, representing an all-encircling force that protected and comforted its followers. Such a serpent god is Da or Dan of Dahomey in West Africa, a deity that travelled to the West Indies with the slave trade and became altered to Damballa or Damballah, the god of gods of **Voodoo** whose 'maid-servant' is a snake.

Certain American Indian tribes use venomous snakes in their magic rituals, as do white snake-handling Christian sects of the United States whose faith, they maintain, protects them. The reputed protective power of the snake may well account for the popularity of snake designs in tattooing, coupled with sexual symbolism. The unusual qualities of serpents, singular modes of progression, digestion, reproduction and growth have all helped to create an aura of mystery about these creatures which, together with its interpretation as a phallic symbol, has produced a curious atmosphere and association in the minds of many people – an influence that is exploited by the snake-charmer, the native witch doctor and modern sorcerers, black magicians and those who seek to practice the black arts.

There is considerable evidence to suggest that spontaneous apparitions of animals have been seen by responsible witnesses. The commonest are domestic animals: dogs, cats, horses (with and without riders), sheep, pigs and cattle; but there are also accounts of many ghostly wild animals – rabbits, hares, deer, birds and even apes, tigers, elephants and bears. Many animal ghosts are not true ghosts in the sense that they are the spirits of once-living creatures; often they are projections of the human minds concerned in the haunting or a type of atmospheric photograph; but there are also animal hauntings that seem to suggest the appearance of dead animals that return to the locality they have known during their lives.

Primitive societies had no doubt that animals had a future life; the ancient Egyptians mummified cats and other animals, and our own ancestors buried a warrior's favourite horse or dog with him so that he might have their company beyond the grave. If the appearance of a **ghost** is dependent upon psychic awareness, the fact that many animals seem to possess a consciousness of the supernormal more acute than most human beings would suggest that some animal ghosts are an objective reality, and, indeed, existing evidence is overwhelming in this respect.

Among the legendary and indistinct 'animals' of interest to the student of the occult and the supernatural are the Loch Ness Monster, the Bigfoot and the Yeti or Abominable Snowman.

The **Loch Ness Monster** is a reputed aquatic creature or family of creatures reported to have been seen, heard, recorded and photographed on and around Loch Ness in Scotland for many years. The affair was the great topic of 1933 when an AA Scout claimed that he had seen a serpent-like shape; a big-game hunter found a spoor in the shingle by the side of the loch; mutilated carcases of sheep were found on the shores of the loch and many of the Catholic monks of loch-side Fort Augustus said they had seen the 'monster' or been aware of reports for years. R. T. **Gould**, who had written a book, *The Case for the Sea Serpent* (Philip Allan), in 1930, studied the Loch Ness affair and became convinced that such monsters did indeed exist and had been seen more than two hundred times by about a thousand witnesses.

Over the years reports have continued to pile up, not only at Loch Ness but also at Loch Morar, on the west coast of Scotland. In 1970 a scientific team, based at London University, produced twenty-seven 'authenticated reports'; in 1961 the Loch Ness Phenomenon Investigation Bureau began a lengthy and exhaustive watch on the loch with powerful camera, and several sequences of film were obtained that contained material which defied 'ordinary explanation'; and Professor Tucker of Birmingham University sonar-recorded 'large objects behaving in an animate manner' at a depth of several thousand feet. Tim Dinsdale, a former aeronautical engineer, has already spent years in an endeavour to obtain conclusive and indisputable proof of the existence of the well-documented but camera-shy monster. Conducting his researches on the loch, in the loch, over the loch and around the loch, he has succeeded in obtaining a ciné film of something that could well be the 'monster'; certainly his film has been carefully examined by scientific and military bodies and found to be inexplicable in terms of known phenomena.

In 1975 Sir Peter Scott, the well-known naturalist and observer of wild life, declared his conviction that a family of a hitherto unknown species inhabited Loch Ness, and in the same year a Scottish schoolteacher obtained new and puzzling photographs of something in the deep waters of the loch.

The *Bigfoot* is the name given to America's 'abominable snowman'; they are said to be giant-sized man-like creatures, dwelling in the boreal forests of north-west America; it is the Sasquatch of the American Indians, 'the wild man of the woods'. Large footprints (the only material evidence) vary in length from about 42 cm. (16 in.) to a phenomenonal 56 cm. (22 in.), which, translated into terms of stature, suggests a creature between 279 cm. (9 ft) and 372 cm. (12 feet) in height. Over three hundred eye-witness reports; impressive travellers' tales and local legends all suggest that giant, hairy, half-human and half-ape creatures live in the vast and largely unexplored mountain ranges of British Columbia. The earliest reports of large and mysterious footprints in the area go back to 1811 when an explorer, David Thompson, reported coming across a track in deep snow that showed four toes, short claw marks and an indistinct heel.

In 1884 a gorilla-type creature was captured which had long, black, coarse hair all over its body, but otherwise resembled a man, although the forearms were noticably longer and the creature possessed extraordinary strength; the ultimate fate of this creature is unknown, though it was apparently exhibited by Barnum & Bailey at one time. Scattered reports have been collected every few years since 1901 right up to the present time, and photographs of varying quality and reliability have been produced. Three moving films purport to feature Bigfoot, the best, by Roger Patterson, showing a large and cumbersome creature walking upright through low brushwood. The film, allegedly shot at Bluff Creek Valley, Northern California, in the autumn of 1967, is now in the possession of the Northwest Research Foundation and has never been satisfactorily explained.

The *Yeti*, commonly known as the 'abominable snowman', is a supposed creature, half-human, half-animal, that haunts the vast wastes of the Himalayas. It is much feared by the local people, the Sherpas, and reports suggest a hairy, short creature that walks erect, swinging its arms, with red or light-brown and rather sparse hair on its head. Alleged scalps of the yeti and caps said to be made from yeti skin have been found to be made from the hides of known animals; huge footprints in the snow in deserted regions have been followed for miles; expeditions (including one led by Chris Bonington in 1974) have searched; and still the yeti remains a mystery.

Eric Shipton, veteran of five Everest climbs, faced with unmistakable evidence of clear, naked footprints of a creature that used well-developed toes for climbing, became convinced of the existence of a 'large, ape-like creature, either quite unknown to science or at least not included in the known fauna of Central Asia'; creatures that are neither bears nor human beings. In 1974, Lakpa Shepani, a 19-year-old Sherpa girl herder, reported that while grazing yaks in the Khonar area near Everest she was knocked unconsicous by a yeti. When she recovered consciousness she saw it kill five of her yaks. The girl said the creature was four to five feet tall, had thick black hair below the waist and brownish hair above. It had long nails and thick fingers and sometimes walked on all fours and sometimes on its two feet. Later the report was confirmed by the Nepalese police, who located giant footprints which were recorded by the police photographer. Sherpa folklore tells of a monkey king being converted to Buddhism and living as a hermit in the mountains. A female monster cohabited with the monkey king, and their first child, covered in hair and with a tail, was the first yeti. Another yeti-like creature is the Almas, which is said to inhabit the remote parts of the Caucasus and was the subject of a Soviet expedition in 1974.

Sightings and traces of apparently similar creatures have been reported for hundreds of years in widely separated parts of the world and some students think that primitive man-like creatures exist in remote and still-unexplored regions.

CONSULT: W. J. Brown, *The Gods Had Wings,* Constable (1936); Tim Dinsdale, *Project Water Horse,* Routledge & Kegan Paul (1975); John Napier, *Bigfoot: The Yeti and Sasquatch in Myth and Reality,* Jonathan Cape (1972).

## Anthroposophy
See **Steiner, Rudolf**.

## Apparitions
Supernormal appearances suggesting the real presence of someone distant or dead. Considerable evidence is available to suggest that men and women with sound minds and sound bodies do sometimes see apparitions of dead or distant persons in circumstances that rule out **illusion** or deception. Apparitions of the dying and recently dead have been seen by far-off friends and relatives; apparitions have spoken and imparted to living persons knowledge of facts previously unknown to them; apparitions of the dead have been seen by more than one living person at the same time; and altogether there is overwhelming

evidence that apparitions have objective reality, i.e. that they exist outside the minds of the people who see them and cannot be dismissed as merely projections from the subconscious of the viewer.

It is clear that apparitions differ from the purely subjective **hallucinations** that are the result of drugs or insanity, although some apparitions might correctly be called telepathetic hallucinations. 'Crisis apparitions' (*see also* **phantasms of the living**) (usually involving serious illness, extreme danger or **death**) have been studied by the **Society for Psychical Research**; as have 'post-mortem apparitions' – those that feature people who have been seen and recognized more than twelve hours after death (appearances which suggest a discarnate mind persists after death that is capable of conscious thought transference to a living person); 'haunting apparitions' consist of the same figure seen repeatedly in one locality (and occasionally at more than one locality) over a lengthy period of time; 'experimental apparitions' have been reported when a person has succeeded in 'appearing' to another person through conscious and deliberate effort of will. All may well be telepathetic in origin (*see* **telepathy**).

Apparitions have been reported from every age and culture since the beginning of recorded history: they are an integral part of folklore and religion, and it has been estimated that the chances of anyone seeing an apparition sometime during their lifetime is one in ten. Apparitions have been seen in old buildings, new buildings, mansions, cottages, theatres, railway stations, hospitals, hotels, public houses, ballrooms, flats and open spaces; they have been heard as well as seen, and occasionally photographs have been produced that, it is claimed, show apparitions. Domestic animals see them or behave as if they do. Britain probably has more reported apparitions than any other country in the world.

The evidence varies from the uncorroborated testimony of a person who briefly glimpses a recognized friend or relative who is later found to have died around that time, to the scores of people from all walks of life who claim to have seen the day-time **ghost** at Drury Lane Theatre. Apparitions seem to be especially prevalent in the vicinity of churches, and they usually appear to be completely solid and natural except that sometimes they make no sound and invariably disappear in circumstances that defy explanation. At **Borley Rectory** in Essex the apparition of a nun was repeatedly seen in the garden during more than fifty years, and after the destruction of the rectory it apparently transferred its activity across the road to the locality of the church where numerous people claim to have seen the same figure, usually in the churchyard.

CONSULT: Sir Ernest Bennett, *Apparitions and Haunted Houses*, Faber & Faber (1939); G. N. M. Tyrrell, *Apparitions*, Duckworth (rev. edition, 1953); Peter Underwood, *Haunted London*, Harrap (1974).

## Apports

Material objects that apparently defy accepted laws by materializing (*see* **materialization**) or penetrating matter in a way never satisfactorily explained. Apports, some of the more puzzling phenomena of **spiritualism**, vary in size and may be inanimate or living.

A considerable variety of objects has been reported as being apported over the past century and a half, varying from a bean or a button, a glassful of wine and a thirty-nine-inch snake to a plant in a pot over four feet high (the latter appeared in the presence of Professor Ernesto Bozzano) and an ape-like creature, during the mediumship of Franek Kluski. Magnetic power was at one time thought to be the explanation, and in 1844 Dr Larkin of Wrentham, Mass., stated (during a period when curious occurrences were taking place in the vicinity of the doctor's servant, a girl named Mary Jane), that on one occasion when the whole family were gathered around the bed of the magnetized and sleeping girl, all doors being shut, a heavy flat-iron from the kitchen suddenly appeared in their midst; and, at the request of Mrs Larkin, as suddenly disappeared and was found back in the kitchen, all the intervening doors have been closed at the time. Another theory is the existence of a **fourth dimension**, a higher form of space of which we have no real knowledge and into which the objects are lifted, conveyed to the desired place and there precipitated into our three-dimensional space – an exercise that has been equated with lifting something out of a circle and placing it elsewhere.

Apports do not appear to be any the worse for their strange journeys, and many spiritualists favour the idea that apports are disintegrated, conveyed to the required place and there reintegrated. **Séance**-room communications have maintained that the **spirits** can, by will-power, reduce the matter to be transported to its molecular elements without altering its form, and that in this way the object or matter can pass through intervening structures before being reconstructed by further concentration of will-power. René Sudre believed that a medium's mind could so influence the molecular construction of objects that disintegration or **dematerialization** and reintegration or rematerialization could take effect – a theory that suggests another, as yet unknown, aggregation of matter beyond the solid, liquid and gaseous state: a fourth, fluidic state in which matter becomes invisible, impalpable and malleable. It has been noticed that stone or metallic objects are often hot when they arrive; a fact recorded by Professor Johann Zöllner during his investigations of matter through matter, certain **poltergeist** cases and other psychic experiences.

Unfortunately the number of observations of apport phenomena under test or even strict conditions is very rare, though there exists an impressive number of reported instances of apportation and **asportation** from private sittings and home circles. Mediums who might be said to have 'specialized' in producing apports have included Mlle Stanislawa Tomczyk; Mme Elizabeth **d'Esperance**; Mrs Samuel Guppy; Mrs Maggs of Portsmouth; Lajos Pap; Eusapia Paladino. In 1930, Ernesto Bozzano, the Italian psychical researcher, produced a book on apports which dealt specifically with apports produced at the request of the experimentors present, apparently eliminating the possibility of surreptitious introduction of alleged apports which has proved to be the answer to some reported appearances.

CONSULT: Nandor Fodor, *Encyclopaedia of Psychic Science*, Arthurs Press (1934); Emma Hardings, *Modern American Spiritualism*, New York (1870).

## Aquarius
*See* **zodiac.**

## Aries
*See* **zodiac.**

## Arthame
*See* **Athame.**

## Ash
*See* **trees and plants.**

## Ashtoreth (plural Ashtaroth)
*See under* **demonology.**

## Asmodeus
*See under* **demonology.**

## Asportation

The reverse of apportation. Asports are objects that disappear from **séance** rooms and, apparently finding intervening solid structures no inconvenience, reappear at another place. As with **apports,** reliable first-hand testimony of asportation under test conditions is rare, though there is considerable evidence of this remarkable phenomenon at private sittings and home circles.

## Astarte, or Ashtoreth (plural Ashtaroth)

*See under* **demonology.**

## Astragalomancy

Native **divination** using knuckle-bones, small pieces of wood or stones. Each piece of wood, or bone or stone is marked with letters or symbols, and depending how the pieces fall when they are cast to the ground, so the diviner reads the answer to the question that has been asked. Australian aboriginals used bones of various sizes; American Indians stones of different shapes; North-West Africans used six pieces of wood, each bearing a different design.

The use of dice is a modern variation of this method of divination, two dice being used to give twenty-one possible combinations of numbers. From a list of thirty possible questions the seeker selects a question and, concentrating hard, throws the dice. From the resulting combination the diviner discovers the corresponding answer from a list of thirty possible answers.

## Astral body

An exact replica of the physical body, but composed of very delicate matter and having a shining and luminious appearance. The term is often used to describe the link between the physical nervous system and a theoretical cosmic reservoir of energy.

The astral body is the **double** or etheric body of **psychical research,** though the latter term is used in psychical research only when referring to the living. Students of **theosophy** would argue that the etheric body is quite different from the astral body, but the fact remains that in spiritualistic and allied literature the terms are often used indiscriminately. The astral body is apparently capable of separating itself from the physical body and moving through space and matter without any difficulty: a mode of locomotion known as **astral travel** (*see also* **out-of-the-body experiences**).

At **death** the astral body is said to leave behind the physical body and to continue to pursue an existence on the **astral plane**.

CONSULT: Robert Crookall, *The Study and Practice of Astral Projection*, Aquarian Press (1961); Celia Green, *Out-of-the-Body Experiences*, Institute of Psychophysical Research, Oxford (1968).

## Astral plane
The first of the **spheres** to which the **astral body** goes after bodily **death**; it is said to include the normal and everyday world, but to extend beyond it. There is much speculation as to whether such a place exists. Descriptive accounts obtained from mediums and other spiritualistic sources do not correspond to any great degree, and communication after death is not yet accessible to the majority of scientific researchers.

## Astral projection
The projection of the **astral body** for the purpose of **astral travel** has been recorded in many parts of the world, and is said to have been achieved in various ways. West Indian magicians utilize the singing of

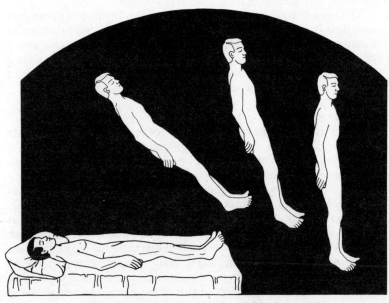

*Astral projection: the manner in which the astral or etheric body is said to leave the physical body*

special charm songs; students of **yoga** who have practised particular breathing exercises over many years have described apparent astral projection; Aleister **Crowley** advocated developing the astral body mentally as a separate entity; and, along similar lines, the American author Sylvan Muldoon believed that an intense desire for astral projection would always bring results. Projection is alleged to take place immediately above the recumbent experimentor, the astral body floating above the physical body and attached to it by an invisible 'elastic' cord linking the forehead of the physical body with the back of the 'head' of the astral body. The astral body then floats forward and away from the physical body and slowly assumes an upright position at the foot of the physical body to which it is still attached. At this point the astral body is unstable owing to the pull of the 'cord', and it either returns to the physical body or interiorizes when, according to some writers, the 'cord' returns to the physical body and the astral body can begin its travels. *See also* **out-of-the-body experiences**.

CONSULT: Robert Crookall, *The Techniques of Astral Projection*, Aquarian Press (1964); S. Muldoon and H. C. Carrington, *The Projection of the Astral Body*, Rider (1958).

## Astral travel

The experience of leaving one's physical body and travelling freely abroad has been reported by many people and often seems to be the result of concentration and determination. It is not uncommon for people to report the sensation of leaving their body and briefly looking at it from outside, but definite astral travel is usually deliberate and the result of conscious effort. There are accounts of astral travellers leaving behind physical evidence of their travels; of them being recognized and replying to questions put to them while undergoing such **out-of-the-body experiences**; and of some manifestation of a person's presence at his destination before he arrives there (known as a 'fore-runner' in Scotland). Astral travellers say that **astral projection** is not unpleasant, apart from the feeling of suspense in the mind, while moving parts of the **astral body** have been compared to the 'limbs' felt by amputees.

CONSULT: Robert Crookall, *The Study and Practice of Astral Projection*, Aquarian Press (1961); S. Muldoon and H. C. Carrington, *The Projection of the Astral Body*, Rider (1958).

## Astrology

The alleged art or science of judging the influence of the sun, the

**moon** and the planets upon human affairs. The theory of astrology is a logical and orderly explanation of heavenly behaviour, and therein lies its main attraction for many thinking people. The study of astrology (where, for convenience, the sun and the moon rank as planets) is said to owe its foundation to a sentence inscribed on an ancient tomb; the age-old magical theory of 'as above, so below'. In explanation of this theory, that 'that which is above is like that which is below and that which is below is like that which is above, to achieve the wonders of the one thing', it has been suggested that divine energy was evident in the movements of the sun, the moon and the planets, and that events on earth paralelled events in the heavens because both were controlled by the same power, the 'one thing'. It was therefore considered that a correct interpretation of the positions of the planets and other heavenly bodies was a kind of key to divine power, reconciling the opposites of 'above' and 'below' as two wheels are turned by one cogwheel.

As time passed, the fields of observation in astrology widened until they embraced every aspect and experience of human life and were seen to extend by the association of ideas to such variations as the parts of the human body and the days of the week. Astrology has always placed considerable importance on the apparent influence exerted by planets which are in ascendance at the time of a person's birth, the planet rising at that time being regarded as the most important (i.e. in the ascendant) for that individual or animal or nation, and ascendance was judged by the planet (or sign of the **zodiac**) which was nearest the eastern horizon at that precise moment of time.

Further study suggested that limitless information could be discovered concerning all aspects of the individual concerned, together with many precise details and approximate dates relating to events affecting the life of the individual. For this purpose a scientific diagram is built up showing the zodiacal positions of the planets, the presence of a planet or planets in one or other of the twelve areas or 'houses' and certain angular relationships between one or more planets, such a diagram being known as a **horoscope**. It is a sign of the enormous interest in astrology today that almost everyone in Western Europe and throughout the United States knows his or her zodiacal sign, the sector of the zodiac through which the sun was passing at their movement of birth, and most daily newspapers and many weekly and monthly periodicals print general predictions for each sign. Such daily or monthly prognostications must, by the law of averages, be fulfilled for a proportion of the readership concerned, but one of astrology's most interesting features is that it divides humanity into types based on astrological symbolism, and despite the obvious conclusion that the art – or science – should logically be disbelieved as a survival of ancient superstitious beliefs, the fact remains that 'scientific' analysing of a person's personality from their horoscope, and also the prediction of future events, is often remarkably accurate.

To produce a horoscope the astrologer must know the sex of the person involved and the place and exact time and date of birth – and whether the horoscope is for an animal or nation or whatever. Without doubt some remarkable predictions have been made. To quote just

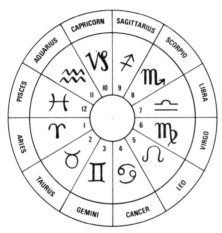

*Astrology: the twelve houses and their signs*

one: copy for a horoscope for the United States published in the November 1963 issue of *American Astrologer* (which came out in October) showed that planetary configurations were imminent that had in the past coincided with personal danger to the head of state and that November in particular was fraught with perils. President John F. Kennedy was assassinated on 22 November 1963. On the other hand, very few astrologers predicted or foresaw the onset of the Second World War.

Although there has probably never been a greater interest in the ancient and widely misunderstood subject than there is today, astrology has always been inextricably interwoven with occult and magical practices, with the most suitable days and times for performing various rites being calculated by resorce to the art: each planet was designated a particular scent or odour, colour and other attributes, and could be invoked by the sorcerer who used this knowledge. As with all occult practices, however, natural talent and carefully nurtured intuitive powers played a big part; some astrologers, for instance, produce astonishing results; while others, working with identical material, produce poor or inaccurate information. For the characteristics of those born under the various astrological signs, *see* **zodiac.**

CONSULT: Ronald C. Davison, *Astrology*, Arco (1963); P. I. H. Naylor, *Astrology*, Robert Maxwell (1967).

## Atavism

Reversion to an earlier type; recurrence of ancestral peculiarity or weakness; the idea that something frightening and primitive in the characterization can re-emerge after many generations. The term is used by occultists with reference to characteristics that they consider to constitute **reincarnations** or the embodiment of pre-human consciousness. Sometimes atavism appears to be the result of spiritual ecstasy, and sometimes it involves transformation. The artist Austin Osman **Spare** produced a number of disturbing pictures that, he claimed, were the result of the discovery of a formula (a combination of sexual ecstasy and magical visualization) which reached remote depths of the mind and featured elementals (*see* **elements and elementals**).

CONSULT: Austin Spare, *Earth Inferno*, printed privately (1906) (his pictures are scattered in various private collections); Frederick Kaigh, *Witchcraft and Magic of Africa*, Richard Lesley (1947).

## Athame, or arthame

The witch's black-hilted knife, allegedly endowed with magical properties, that is used by modern witches for drawing the **magic circle**, especially at initiation ceremonies; a use described in the **Key of Solomon** and other **grimoires** and textbooks on **magic.** The athame invariably has a black handle, and always has magic symbols or characters engraved on the one-sided blade; and not infrequently the handle is also decorated.

## Atlantis

The lost continent said to have been overwhelmed by the sea in the space of a single day and night; the legend of a lost paradise that has attracted romantic speculation for hundreds of years.

Plato (*c.* 428 – *c.* 348 B.C.) describes the island of Atlantis as a great sea power that sank beneath the waves in a natural cataclysm which also annihilated the Athenian army engaged in repulsing an attack on Greece and Egypt by this powerful continent that was larger than Asia Minor and situated just beyond the 'Pillars of Hercules', a term generally accepted as describing the Straits of Gilbraltar. There is no way of establishing whether the legend is the result of Plato's imagination or whether it is based on fact of which no record remains; but in his *Timaeus* and *Critias* we have the only written account of Atlantis – all later writings being expansions or fantasies that owe their origin to his account which describes Egyptian priests discussing the subject with Solon (*c.* 638 – *c.* 558 B.C.), a wise Athenian statesman, 9 000 years earlier. This dates the collapse of Atlantis to about 9600 B.C. and provides the great attraction for the credulous and the stumbling-block for those with a logical and scientific outlook.

However, it is possible that there was some confusion between 9 000 and 900 years, and this hypothesis immediately provides the possibility of an Atlantean civilization, especially when geophysicists and archeologists agree that there was a natural cataclysm around that date – one of the greatest volcanic explosions of all time, in fact, which overwhelmed the former island (now three islands) of Santorin, seventy miles north of Crete. Archaeological discoveries, as late as 1967, included Minoan remains deep under the pumice of Santorin, and strongly suggest that 'Atlantis', had it ever existed, was situated in the Mediterranean.

Occult research, on the other hand, which depends on the belief that a record of all past events exists on the **astral plane**, suggests that Atlantis was once in the middle of the Atlantic Ocean, perhaps a million years ago. Deep **meditation** and 'astral clairvoyance', pioneered in the 1890s by W. Scott-Elliot, has Atlantis peopled by giant black warriors whose ruler used **black magic** practices which ultimately brought retribution in the shape of the destruction of the whole continent, but not before a group of the ruling Toltecs emigrated from Mexico to Egypt, where their descendants designed and supervised the building of the pyramids (explaining why pyramids are also found in Central America) while another group engineered the building of Stonehenge in England.

CONSULT: A. G. Galanopoulos and E. Bacon, *Atlantis*, Nelson (1969); W. Scott-Elliot, *The Story of Atlantis*, reissued by Theosophical Society (1962).

# Augury

The art and practice of foretelling the future (originally discovering the approval or disapproval of the gods) by means of signs and **omens**; a portent or sign or the **prediction** that is made therefrom; the rite or ceremony conducted by an augur.

In ancient Rome, augurs were members of a college (an institution attributed to Romulus or Numa) who observed and interpreted the signs (auspices) of divine approval or disapproval in respect of all important undertakings. It is likely that the 'college' originally consisted of three members of whom one would be the king; later the number was doubled and increased by degrees until it was sixteen by the time of Julius Caesar, who appointed himself as chief priest. The life office of augur was much respected and sought after; the insignia consisting of the *lituus*, a staff free of any knots and curved at one end, and the *trabla*, a kind of toga with scarlet stripes and a purple border.

The signs were looked for in natural happenings, more particularly from the sky, so celestial and meteorological phenomena were carefully noted and the flight, song, feeding and behaviour of birds was regarded as especially significant (*see* **animals and birds**). Signs of divine will sought in the sky included thunder, lightning, moving comets, falling stars and eclipses; lightning from the left to right was favourable, for example, while from right to left it was unfavourable, but its mere appearance from any direction usually saw the suspension of public assemblies for the day. Birds were observed with reference to the direction of their flight, and of the singing and other sounds; some birds, notably the eagle and the vulture, were especially important, as, to a lesser extent, were the owl, the crow and the raven. Certain birds indicated good or bad luck simply by appearing; others were associated with specific persons or events. The manner in which birds ate grain provided was considered to be significant, and such trivia as whether a particle of grain fell from the bird's mouth were eagerly watched for since this was a sign that the gods looked favourably upon the enterprise in hand.

Warnings of ill-luck or bad fortune consisted chiefly of unusual noises such as the fall of a stick in a temple; the spilling of salt; sneezing; the squeak of a mouse; an unexplained 'crack' or 'bang'; the sudden squeak or squeal of an animal. There were no fixed places for augury and the ceremonies were carried out at a convenient spot or one relevant to the matter under consideration; preferably between midnight and dawn of the day fixed for the proposed undertaking. The

Roman augur would pitch his tent, mark out with his staff the *templum*, or consecrated space, either on the ground or in the air, within which his observations were to be made. At the appropriate time he would cover his head, offer a prayer and a **sacrifice**, ask the gods for a sign of either approval or disapproval and then await a reply. An unexpected noise or an object inadvertently dropped were interpreted as unfavourable signs, while the augur, looking south, had the east, the lucky quarter, on his left, and therefore signs on the left side were considered to be favourable and those on the right unfavourable. In Greece the practice was reversed, and there the observers looked towards the north so the signs on the right were regarded as fortunate and those on the left as unfavourable.

Other means of discovering the gods' pleasure or displeasure included the casting of lots, **oracles** of Apollo and the examination of the entrails of animals and birds killed for sacrifice. The position which the entrails fell into and any abnormality were highly significant, and public augury remained important in official and military matters until a few years B.C., when it became apparent that the rules of augury and **divination** had become so complicated and the conditions required for favourable omens so numerous that it was almost impossible to conduct an augury that led to a favourable result. So the practice fell into neglect and 'the foreknowledge of the truth that is to be' became – as far as augury was concerned – a thing of the past.

CONSULT: W. J. Brown, *The Gods Had Wings*, Constable (1936); Cicero, *On Divination*: various editions, but *Complete Works* edited by C. F. W. Muller and others (1869–96).

## Auldearn witches
A coven of thirteen led by Isabel **Gowdie**, whose trial, perhaps the most remarkable of all Scottish **witchcraft** trials, took place before the sheriff of Auldearn, Nairn, in 1662.

## Aura
Ethereal emanation or luminous appearance said to surround every human body and perhaps every living thing; an effluence of life force that may be electro-magnetic. Sometimes called od, odyle or **odic force**, it is related to the 'halo' surrounding the heads of figures in religious art.

Belief in the existence of auras is very old, and medieval occultists and mystics recognized four different types: the 'nimbus', the 'halo', both issuing from the head; the 'aureola', which issues from the whole body; and the 'glory', a combination of the two. Theosophists (*see* **theosophy**) distinguish five auras: the health aura, the vital aura, the Karmic aura, the aura of character and the aura of spiritual nature. Clairvoyants and many mediums often claim to be able to see the human aura, and from its colour and appearance deduce information concerning the character and emotional state of the person. A bright-red aura indicates anger and force; one that is middle red, passion and sensuality; a brown aura denotes a greedy and miserly personality; a rose-coloured aura reveals affection; yellow, a high intellectual activity; purple, spirituality; blue, religious devotion; green, deceit and jealousy; and dark green, sympathy; while a very dark aura heralds the approach of **death**.

In the nineteenth century, Baron Karl von **Reichenbach** con-tended that the human body (especially the fingertips) gave off rays or an 'aura' which could be seen under certain conditions. In 1874 an American, Francis Gerry Fairfield, published the results of his researches, which convinced him that all organic structures have a special form of nerve-aura. He recounts that epileptics, in the build-up to a fit, 'appeared to be enveloped in a sensitive and highly excited nerve-atmosphere' followed by the fit – or a state of **trance**. He deduced that the 'nerve-aura' was a form of ether, at once a force and a medium, 'suspectible of control by the will of the operator and capable of sensory impression': an atmosphere that could take shape and dissolve, move in any direction and through all obstacles; in fact in the nerve-aura Fairfield saw the explanation of the manifestations of physical mediums (*see* **apports; materialization**) and, possibly, of spontaneous **apparitions**.

Dr Walter J. **Kilner** (1847–1920) of St Thomas's Hospital, London, developed a dicyanin screen (a solution of coal-tar sealed hermetically between two pieces of glass) which apparently enabled the aura to be seen by anyone. A recumbent man, naked, viewed in a dim light *after* looking through the screen in daylight, had three distinct radiations. The first, dark and colourless, that closely surrounded the whole body, Kilner called the 'etheric body'; the second, the 'minor aura', followed the contours of the body at a distance of about 76 cm. (30 in.); and the third, the 'outer aura', surrounded the body at a distance of about a third of a metre (1 ft). During the course of many experiments, Kilner discovered that the depth of the aura could be influenced by a magnet, and that it was sensitive to electric currents to the extent that it could be made to vanish completely or increase by 50 per cent; it was also affected by vapours of various chemicals and lost brilliance when the subject was hypnotized. Illness, impairment of mental powers, and nervous diseases were found to affect the aura, and suggested that the higher brain centres were closely concerned in the production of the aura, the apparent connection being emphasized by experiments that showed the aura shrinking with the approach of death and no trace of it whatever around a corpse.

Other doctors have drawn inferences and reached conclusions and based medical diagnoses on the condition of the aura and changes in auric colour. Dr Charles Féré of the Asylum Bicêtre; Professor Enrico Morselli, Professor of Psychiatry at Genoa University; Professor Theodor Flournoy, Professor of Psychology at the University of Geneva; Dr Gustave Gelley; Dr Hereward Carrington; Dr Paul Joire; Professor F. Cazzamalli; Dr O'Donnell of the Chicago Mercy Hospital; and Dr Drysdale Anderson in West Africa have all conducted experiments relating to the aura – or odic force; the meeting-ground between this phenomenon and **psychical research**, it has been said, is the human body.

CONSULT: O. Bagnall, *The Origin and Properties of the Human Aura*, Routledge & Kegan Paul (1957); Walter J. Kilner, *The Human Atmosphere or The Aura Made Visible*, Redman (1911).

## Automatism

Involuntary action; the state of being automatic; functions not controlled by the conscious self; the state or condition accompanying self-motivated phenomena.

F. W. H. **Myers** postulated that automatic phenomena were either active, involving the movement of the limbs, head or tongue beyond the conscious will; or passive, the externalization of perceptions in inner vision or audition; the origin of both being either the subconscious self or a discarnate intelligence. Automatism includes automatic drawing and painting, both attempts at artistic expression without control of the conscious self. Many mediums and others have succeeded in producing drawings and paintings of considerable complexity at great speed and with artistic and perceptive skills quite beyond their capacity in a normal state; flowers of intricate spiral forms and architectural designs of balance, vision and originality have been repeatedly produced. In some cases, visions are presented to the automatist, who proceeds to sketch or paint the idea; at other times, the drawing or painting is produced entirely spontaneously and without any conscious effort on the part of the person concerned. Such works are often produced at great speed and sometimes in total darkness.

*The position of the hands for obtaining automatic or
inspirational information*

Psychologists regard automatic painting and drawing as belonging
to a range of phenomena which are manifestations of layers of
personality that are subconscious or dissociated from the conscious
mind; phenomena which include loss of memory, sleep-walking,
multiple personality and **mediumship**. Automatic writing is executed without the conscious control of the person whose hand produces
the script and is a very common form of mediumship, often a source of
self-delusion, but, when reliable, perhaps a valuable aid to apparent
contact with life after **death**.

Some automatic writers experience something resembling an
electric shock running through their arm or hand: a tingling, aching
sensation that produces a numb feeling which extends to the finger
tips; others have no feeling except a sensation of remoteness from
their writing hand, as though it did not belong to them or had a life of
its own. In most cases the pen or pencil is held very lightly (sometimes
merely resting on the hand), and then proceeds to write, sometimes in
a minute hand, sometimes so large that half a dozen words fill a quarto
page; but invariably the writing is quite different from the automatist's
normal handwriting. The 'messages' are often rambling, unpunc-
tuated and joined together in a continuous sprawl; others may be neat,
separate and easily deciphered. Occasionally they are in a language or
dialect unknown to the automatist in his or her normal state. Many
automatic writers are completely normal in all other respects.

Most psychologists and psychical researchers regard automatic writing, drawing and painting as genuine in its automatic and unconscious spontaneity, but the result of subconscious activity on the part of the mind. The planchette and **ouija board** are contrivances that take the place of the hand in the production of such automatic phenomena. The execution of music and dance that is subliminally initiated, such as the **whirling dervishes**, is also an example of automatism, as are inexplicable impulses which, when acted upon, result in the prevention of some tragedy; some psychical researchers also regard **telekinesis**, table tilting and **table turning** as representations of automatic behaviour, while mixed automatism has been regarded as an indication of previous incarnations (*see* **reincarnation**).

CONSULT: Rosalind Heywood, *The Sixth Sense*, Chatto & Windus (1959); Anita M. Mühl, *Automatic Writing*, Dresden and Leipzig (1930).

# B

## Ballechin House

An alleged haunted house in Perthshire that has been the subject of controversy since 1897 and at one time featured in the correspondence columns of *The Times* for nearly a month. In 1892, John, 3rd Marquess of Bute, heard about the haunting from a Jesuit priest, and after making lengthy inquiries rented the mansion and arranged for two researchers, Colonel Lemesurier Taylor and Miss A. Goodrich-Freer (Mrs Hans Spoer), to move in and conduct an investigation. In a subsequently published report, *The Alleged Haunting of B— House*, strange and apparently inexplicable noises – voices, footsteps, bangs, thumps and knockings – were reported; coherent messages were received during experiments with an **ouija board**, and one of the experienced investigators reported seeing a nun-like figure several times. The case is a puzzling one. In some ways it is a classic case among **hauntings**, in other respects it is unconvincing; and the recent assessment of Miss Goodrich-Freer by J. L. Campbell and T. Hall sheds little light on the Ballechin mystery.

CONSULT: J. L. Campbell and T. Hall, *Strange Things*, Routledge & Kegan Paul (1968); A. Goodrich-Freer and John, Marquess of Bute (editors), *The Alleged Haunting of B— House*, George Redway (1899; rev. edition, 1900).

## Bamberg

Cathedral city in central Germany that achieved a great reputation for the suppression of **witchcraft** and, between 1609 and 1633, reportedly saw 900 executions. The archives of the municipal library contain records of one of the most famous trials in the history of European witchcraft: that of the burgomaster himself, Johannes Julius. He was but one of five burgomasters to be burnt at the stake, together with a chancellor of the diocese and his wife and child, and a number of town councillors. A letter from Julius to his daughter, dated 24 July 1628, is preserved and reveals that his 'confessions' were obtained under torture and were 'all falsehood and invention . . . They never cease to torture until one says something.' Bamberg, from 1623 to 1632, was ruled by a fanatical witch-hater, Prince-Bishop Gottfried von Dornheim, known as 'the witch-bishop', who set up special prisons for the interrogation and torture of those suspected of witchcraft, the most notorious establishment being the *Hexenhaus* or 'Witch House'.

CONSULT: Alan C. Kors and Edward Peters, *Witchcraft in Europe 1100–1700*, Philadelphia (1972); Charles Williams, *Witchcraft*, Faber & Faber (1941).

## Bangs sisters

Lizzie and May Bangs of Chicago were mediums who specialized in types of **automatism** – 'spirit' or slate writing, paintings and drawings – and who impressed a number of people until they were exposed. Sealed envelopes brought by the sitters were placed between a pair of slates and held while the medium sat on the opposite side of the table. After an interval that varied between a few moments or half an hour, raps announced that the 'message' had been received and answered.

Admiral William Usborne Moore had many sittings with the Bangs sisters, and once, on the advice of Sir William **Crookes**, added lithium citrate to ink which he took to the sitting. He duly obtained an eight-page message and spectrum analysis later established the presence of lithium in the ink used for writing the message – thus seeming to prove that his own ink had in some way been used in the preparation of the message in the sealed envelope between the admiral's slates. In addition, he had placed his visiting card on top of the plates, tearing off one corner for identification, and this card found its way into the sealed envelope. On the other hand, Dr Hereward Carrington addressed a letter to 'Dearest mother, Jane Thompson' (a fictious name) and received a reply signed 'devoted mother, Jane Thompson'.

The 'spirit' portraits, which the sisters produced in colour and in daylight before the sitters' eyes, seemed to be an even more mysterious phenomenon. Sitters were required to bring with them a photograph of the dead person whose portrait they wished to have, but they did not have to produce the photograph. A locked box or curtained-off space was used and the portraits were often produced in about eight minutes. Two identical paper-mounted canvases in wooden frames were held up, face to face, against the window in the box or curtained-off space, the lower edges of the frames resting on a table with each of the two mediums holding one side. A short curtain was hung on either side and an opaque blind was drawn over the canvases. With light behind the canvases it was possible to watch shadowy outlines appear and disappear as if an invisible artist was making a preliminary sketch; and then the picture grew at a tremendous rate. When the frames were separated, a portrait was found on the paper surface of the canvas closest to the sitter. The paint, greasy to the touch, left no stain or mark on the paper surface of the other canvas. The final portrait was not a copy of the concealed photograph which the sitter had brought but rather a facial resemblance or imitation. Sometimes the tones in the portrait deepened and became richer after exposure to the air. Admiral Moore has stated that on occasions he took his own frames, sealed the window himself, searched the rooms and closely watched every movement in the room, yet the pictures were still produced.

Other apparent phenomena produced by the sisters, sometimes in front of many people in public halls, included **apports** and the disappearance of objects, and such chemical effects as changing ink into water. One witness of slate-writing with Lizzie Bangs, A. B. Richmond, stated that he heard a faint noise that seemed to come from the direction of the slates although it did not sound like writing, more like the noise of an insect trapped between the slates, followed by three raps: the signal that a message had been completed. Opening the slates, Richmond found two messages written in Morse, one signed by a deceased person who in life could neither read or write telegraphy and the other from a former prominent jurist. Later Richmond obtained three communications between two screwed-together slates, one being in the same handwriting as another 'spirit' message he had obtained, apparently emanating from the same deceased person, a year before with another medium.

Another witness of Lizzie Bangs's 'spirit writing' described the use of a typewriter which continued typing messages with the aid of a materialized hand when the machine was held high in the air by four of the male sitters. Dr Hereward Carrington, the distinguished American psychical researcher, exposed the sisters by means of a small hand-mirror which he held beneath the table. He found that under cover of a writing-pad the slates were wedged open, the letter inside extracted and dropped on to a frame which lay on the floor from where it was drawn back beneath a door into the next room where the other sister presumably steamed open the letter and answered it. In both 1880 and

1891 the sisters were seized while masquerading as materialized 'spirits', and in 1890 a charge of fraud in slate-writing was, after searching inquiry, upheld by Dr Richard Hodgson, a keen, intelligent and critical investigator for the **Society for Psychical Research**.
CONSULT: David P. Abbott, *Spirit Portrait Mystery: Its Final Solution*, Chicago (1913); A. B. Richmond, *What I Saw at Cassadaga Lake*, Boston, Mass.(1888).

## Banshees
From the Gaelic, *bean si* ('fairy woman'); a loud mournful wailing sound said to be heard at night-time before a death of some member of the household visited; a death **omen**. The banshee is common in Celtic folk literature, and, especially in Ireland and the West Highlands of Scotland, there are still today many who believe that a female fairy makes her presence known by shrieks and wailings to give warning of a death in a family over whom she is supposed to exercise a kind of guardianship. Records of Irish banshees suggest that they are limited to ancient families of pure descent. First-hand and apparently reliable accounts of banshee wailing are not infrequently encountered. The **Airlie 'drum of death'** is one example of a banshee.
CONSULT: Elliott O'Donnell, *Family Ghosts and Ghostly Phenomena*, Philip Allan (1933); W. Wirt Sikes, *British Goblins*, Low (1879).

## Baphomet
*See* **demonology**.

## Baptism
Ritual **initiation** by splashing or immersion in water that is of great antiquity, from long before the Christian era, and probably owes its origin and significance to the fact that no living thing can survive without water, which also washes away such worthless things as dirt. The ancient Egyptians, Greeks and Babylonians believed that water was the source of life, and the idea of water as a life-giving substance and its use as a purificatory rite is to be found in many religions, often linked with repentance of sins and with the doctine of original sin which held that a newborn child, while not guilty of actual sin, nevertheless was subject to God's wrath since it was part of the inherited sin of mankind; so a baby that died unbaptized (with the **Devil** still within) was condemned to a kind of **hell**; and it was thought that the Devil remained inside a child that did not cry during the rite. Today Christian baptism symbolizes acceptance of membership and

initiation into a Christian community, with the Roman Catholics retaining a more elaborite ritual.

CONSULT: L. Duchesne, *Christian Worship*, S.P.C.K. (1931); J. D. C. Fisher, *Christian Initiation: Baptism in the Medieval West*, S.P.C.K. (1965).

## Barrett, Francis

Author and student of **magic** and **occultism** whose fame rests on the publication in London in 1801 of *The Magus, or Celestial Intelligencer; Being a Complete System of Occult Philosophy*. This contains vivid portraits of **demons** drawn by the author, about whom very little is known, though he probably taught a form of **ritual magic** to people who later influenced a group headed by Bulwer Lytton. *The Magus* includes sections on the reputed magic power of animals, herbs and stones; on **alchemy, numerology, talismans**, the **Cabala** and ceremonial magic. Francis Barrett claimed to have caused 'terrible rains and claps of thunder' by using magic words, and there are grounds for suspecting that he created and ran a magic circle at Cambridge.

CONSULT: Francis Barrett, *The Magus* (Intro. by Timothy d'Arch Smith), University Books, New York (1967).

## Barrett, Sir William Fletcher (1844-1925)

Physicist, and one of the distinguished early psychical researchers; born in Jamaica and educated in Manchester; was Professor of Physics at the Royal College of Science, Dublin, from 1873 to 1910. He discovered 'Stalloy', a silicon iron used by electrical engineers during research on alloys; he also studied mesmerism and **hypnotism, divination, telepathy** and most branches of **psychical research**.

In January 1882, Barnett called a conference at the offices of the British National Association of Spiritualists and the **Society for Psychical Research** was born. During a visit to the United States in 1885 he was instrumental in founding the **American Society for Psychical Reseach Inc**. In 1876 he submitted a paper based on his researches into the physical phenomena of **spiritualism** to the British Association for the Advancement of Science: a paper that revealed his conviction, based on his experiences, that telepathy had been proved to exist, though he was inclined to attribute the more spectacular physical phenomena of spiritualism, ranging from **levitation** and fire immunity to **hallucination**. He did, however, maintain that he had witnessed 'paranormal' raps in broad daylight and out of doors in conditions which completely eliminated trickery.

Later on Barnett abandoned his hallucination hypothesis with regard to physical mediums after finding mediums among his personal friends who were above suspicion and who produced phenomena under his conditions in daylight. By the time he contributed a paper, 'Some Reminiscences of Fifty Years of Psychical Research', to the SPR *Proceedings* in 1924, he considered that there was evidence for the existence of a spiritual world, for survival after **death** and for occasional communications with the dead.

CONSULT: W. F. Barrett, *Psychical Research*, Williams & Norgate (1911); and *The Divining Rod* (with Theodore Besterman), Methuen (1926).

## Basil
*See under* **trees and plants**.

## Bathory, Countess Elizabeth (1560-1614)
The 'Blood Countess' who lived at Castle Csejthe (or Csej) in north-west Hungary. Married at fifteen years of age, she appears to have been introduced to the Black Arts by a servant and her old nurse. Aided and abetted by them and by local witches, she began torturing the young servant girls for fun: an exercise which became an earnest undertaking when she decided that fresh human **blood** had a unique value for conditioning, restoring and beautifying the skin. Before long the countess was literally bathing in the blood of the unfortunate girls who went to work at Castle Csejthe - and were never seen again.

For ten years the savage blood-letting continued until the authorities received information on what was happening, and, in 1610, the king of Hungary ordered the castle to be raided. One girl was found, recently dead and completely drained of blood; others were just alive, their bodies pierced with holes for blood-letting; and in the cellars the bodies of fifty more girls were discovered. Elizabeth Bathory was charged and arrested, but her family still had great influence and she was never convicted of any crime, though all those who had assisted in her ghastly activities were beheaded and cremated. The countess was walled up in her bedchamber at the castle with only a single small space for food to be passed in to her, and there she lived alone with her thoughts and desires and memories of several hundred girls who had died horrible deaths at her bidding. Four years later, in 1614, the guards found her dead.

CONSULT: T. McNally and Radu Florescu, *In Search of Dracula*, New English Library (1973); Valentine Penrose, *Erzébet Bathory, la Comtesse sanglante*, Paris (1962).

*Elizabeth Bathory, 'the blood countess'*

## Bats
*See under* **animals and birds**.

## 'Bealings Bells'
A small book published in 1841. The full title is *Bealings Bells. An account of the Mysterious Ringing of Bells at Great Bealings, Suffolk, in 1834*. The author is Major Edward Moor (1771–1848), a Fellow of the Royal Society, and his account of paranormal bell-ringing at his home, Bealings House, Great Bealings, near Woodbridge in Suffolk, has become known as a classic **poltergeist** infestation. The disturbance, nothing more than inexplicable bell-ringing, persisted from 2 February to 27 March 1834. The nine bells that had hung in the kitchen for twenty-eight years rang seemingly by themselves scores of times, and were heard and seen by Major Moor, his son, his grandson and all of the six servants. At least once he saw the bells ringing in the kitchen when all the servants were present, though it may be significant that Major Moor never describes an occasion of the ringing when *every* member of the household was under surveillance; at the end of the fifty-four days the ringing ceased as abruptly as it had begun

and no satisfactory explanation for it was ever discovered. The author mentions in his book some twenty other cases of apparently **paranormal** bell-ringing and states that he is thoroughly convinced that the ringing is 'not by human agency'. The same bells, now disconnected, still hang at Great Bealings House.

CONSULT: Edward Moor, *Bealings Bells*, Woodbridge (1841); Harry Price, *Poltergeist Over England*, Country Life (1945).

## Bears
*See under* **animals and birds**.

## Beech
*See under* **trees and plants**.

## Beelzebub
*See under* **demonology**.

## Bell, book and candle
Ancient form of ceremonial excommunication where the officiating priest closes the book from which he has read the malediction or **curse**; a bell is tolled for the dead, and candles are extinguished to signify that the soul of the offender has been removed from the sight of God. A modified form of 'Bell, book and candle' ritual is also used occasionally for **exorcism**.

## Bells
Hollow, metallic, percussion instruments, usually resembling an inverted cup and sounded either by striking with a hammer or swinging to move a suspended clapper inside. Hand-bells were used by the Ancient Egyptians at the festival of Isis and in the worship of Cybele, the Great Mother of the Gods; Jewish high priests wore golden bells; the Greeks used bells in their camps and the Romans to announce the hours of their hot baths, their marketing and their processions. In Japan, where bells were introduced *c.* A.D. 650, there is a bell hanging at Todaiji Temple in Nara that was cast in 752; it weighs about thirty tons and each New Year's Eve is rung 108 times to release the listeners from the 108 worldly passions.

Bells have always been associated with ceremonies of a sacred character, and in some religions they are consecrated, anointed and receive names; once they were baptized, sprinkled with holy water, clothed in rich garments and decked with flowers. Inscriptions on bells reveal the idea that bells were believed to have power over evil **spirits** and to dispel storms and end famines. The ringing of bells on Christmas Day and at other festivals is derived from the bell-ringing that once heralded the arrival of emperors, bishops and other people of importance. Passing bells were rung to terrify evil spirits and drive them from the dying; pardon bells were used in association with the forgiveness of sins; the curfew bell (first enforced by William the Conqueror) was a signal for all lights and fires to be extinguished; the pancake bell, rung on Shrove Tuesday, was originally a summons to confession; the harvest bell called labourers to their work; the oven bell denoted to his tenants that the lord of the manor's oven was ready to bake their bread; the market bell was a sign for bidding and selling to begin; burial bells were rung after funerals to frighten away evil spirits; and so forth.

In Scotland in the eighteenth century there was a bell belonging to the Chapter of St Fillan that had a considerable reputation in the curing of mad people. The night before the ceremony, during which such persons were to be dipped in the Saint's Pool, the bell was bound with ropes and placed in the chapel; when the time came the bell, 'of some mixed metal and about a foot high', was set upon the heads of the afflicted.

It was popularly believed that should a bell be stolen it would return by itself, to the place where it belonged, ringing all the way. The bell of St Mura, long preserved at the Abbey of Mabian near Innisbowen, Co. Donegal, was said to have descended from heaven, ringing loudly, but when it neared the earth the tongue detached itself and returned to heaven; this bell was regarded as beneficial in a number of ways, but especially in mitigating the pains of childbirth. The great bell at the Abbey of Saint-Germain in Paris was believed to cause thunder and lightning to cease when it was rung, as was St Adhelm's bell at Malmesbury Abbey, Wiltshire; in both instances the bell-ringing was thought to disturb the bad spirits that caused the thunder and lightning.

**Superstitions** concerning bells are legion. They were thought to have great affection for the churches to which they belonged, and when a bell was removed it was sometimes supposed to make a nightly visit to its old place of residence unless secured by a rope or chain. Bad luck followed the couple for whom the church bells rang before their wedding ceremony was concluded; **death** followed for anyone who heard a bell tolling when no one touched it (modern superstition has modified this and it is now thought that bad news follows the tinkling of a telephone when there is no cause). A good harvest was assured if the local church bells rang at the time of reaping.

Bells that are used as good-luck **charms** date from the ancient Eastern idea of summoning the supreme spirit; bells attached to domestic animals not only indicate the whereabouts of the beasts but also afford protection against evil spirits and the **evil eye**. Stuttering was thought to be cured by drinking from a bell, and a bell attached to the girdle of a pregnant woman helped in the delivery of the child and protected it from evil spirits. The head of a corpse in Scotland would be pillowed on a bell to protect the soul from the **Devil**. People born at the chime hours of three, six, nine and twelve o'clock were thought to be blessed with the gift of **second sight** and able to see **ghosts**; a ship's bell was regarded as the ship's soul, and it was said that however tightly the bell might be secured, it would ring if the vessel sank. Ghost lore is also full of allusions to bells from the tolling bells of buried churches to reported death knells in some haunted houses. Ringing the bells backwards was a warning in times of peril and distress and is now sometimes used in **witchcraft** ceremonies.

*See also* '**Bealings Bells**'; **bell, book and candle**.

CONSULT: T. North, *English Bells and Bell Lore*, T. Mark, Leek (1888); G. S. Tyack, *A Book About Bells*, Andrews (1898).

## Bermuda Triangle

A stretch of the Atlantic ocean bounded by Bermuda, Florida and Puerto Rico, also known as the 'Triangle of Death', the 'Magic Rhombus', the 'Hoodoo Sea' and the 'Graveyard of the Atlantic'; an area that is thought to have been responsible for the mysterious disappearance of more than 1 000 people and over a hundred aeroplanes between 1945 and 1975.

Although the 'triangle' lies in one of the most frequented parts of the Atlantic, ships, boats and aeroplanes have, it is said, disappeared here without leaving the slightest trace of their fate. Radio messages from pilots stating that they cannot see land and do not know where they are, have been followed by silence and their inexplicable disappearance. Seaplanes sent to search for missing craft have themselves disappeared. In 1945, says one account, a general alert resulted in dozens of aeroplanes and more than two hundred boats and ships scrutinizing the whole area for six missing aeroplanes, but these were never found and their disappearances never explained. In 1948, says another report, two airliners disappeared; in 1949, three tankers, a four-engined transport plane and a trawler.

There are various theories: a hole in the sea or in the sky; alien civilizations; fireballs that explode and destroy ships and aeroplanes; kidnapping by extra-terrestrial beings using spacecraft; sudden and giant tidal waves caused by earthquakes; attacks by sea monsters; a passage into the **fourth dimension**; a gap in time that shifts pilots, sailors and vessels into the future – or the past; electrical interaction between the sea and the sky in what may be an exceptionally magnetic area of the earth; the periodic production of unknown chemical compounds that annihilate the will and the senses; a kind of oceanic metabolism that gives rise to chemical reaction of an unknown kind of organic decomposition. We do not yet know whether the answer to the enigma of the Bermuda Triangle lies in one of these fantastic theories – or does the answer lie in the love that mankind has for mysteries: the will to believe and the wrong interpretation that has been put upon inaccurate facts?

CONSULT: Charles Berlitz, *The Bermuda Triangle*, Souvenir Press (1975); Lawrence David Kusche, *The Bermuda Triangle Mystery – Solved*, Harper & Row, New York (1975).

## Bernadette, St

Marie-Bernarde Soubirous, commonly known as Bernadette, was the fourteen-year-old girl who, in 1858, saw the figure of a girl of her own age at a grotto at **Lourdes**: an **apparition** that stated, 'I am the Immaculate Conception.' Bernadette was described by the Curé of Bartres, where the girl stayed for several months, as 'attentive, devout and unassuming', and it may be significant that girls in puberty not infrequently demonstrate apparent psychic power, see **visions**, experience **hallucinations** and attract **poltergeist** phenomena. Bernadette was canonized in 1933.

## Besant, Annie (1847-1933)

British theosophist, socialist, freethinker, humanitarian; pupil of Madame Helene **Blavatsky**; President of the Theosophical Society (*see* **theosophy**); advocate of Indian Nationalism; gifted lecturer and organizer and indefatigable student of the occult.

Annie, the daughter of William Page Wood, married the Rev. Frank Besant in 1867, but they were legally separated six years later. From 1874 to 1888 she worked with Charles Bradlaugh and was co-editor of the *National Reformer*, taking a prominent part in politics, free thought and radical movements. She met George Bernard Shaw and joined the Fabian Society, and before long was a member of its executive committee; in 1889 she met Madame Blavatsky and joined the Theosophical Society, becoming President eighteen years later. As a devoted pupil of Madame Blavatsky, she became absorbed in Indian matters and politics, founding the Central Hindu Girls' College at Benares, establishing the Indian Home Rule League and becoming President of the Indian National Congress.

Madame Blavatsky once remarked that Annie Besant was neither psychic nor spiritual: rather was she all intellect. Yet, when she was alone, she heard a voice, saw a light and recognized a voice: these belonged to 'one of the two greatest Tibet-based Mahatmas or Great Souls, Master Moyra', whose disciple Annie Besant was to become. On Madame Blavatsky's death in 1891, Annie Besant emerged as the leader, not only of the British but also of the American and Indian theosophists (with the exception of one American section); though the struggle for leadership had damaging effects, not the least being a revelation that some of the letters supposedly written by the Mahatmas were spurious.

In 1910 Annie Besant associated herself with Jiddu Krishnamurti, whom she and C. W. Leadbeater, an ex-Anglican clergyman, believed to be the new world teacher; the Order of the Star was formed and Annie Besant and the new Messiah travelled widely, she urging Krishnamurti's claims rather more vehemently than he wished. When they returned to India she was involved in a lawsuit with the boy's father, saw her protégé renounce all pretentions to spiritual leadership and herself had to withdraw much of what she had claimed. Nevertheless, as an Englishwoman, this many-sided and strong character, with her devouring passion for the unseen world, held for a time a unique position as leader of a Hindu political movement. During her association with Leadbeater advanced occult experiments were conducted which resulted in several books, notably *Man: Whence, How and Whither* with chapters on 'Black Magic in Atlantis' and on past incarnations (*see* **reincarnation**) of theosophists and other personalities.

CONSULT: Annie Besant, *An Autobiography*, T. Fisher Unwin (1893); A. H. Nethercot, *The First Five Lives of Annie Besant*, Hart-Davis (1961).

## Bibliomancy

**Divination** from a book, usually but not always the Bible; from the Greek, *biblion* = 'book' and *manteia* = 'prophecy'. The usual procedure is for the person seeking information to open the book at random and, with eyes shut or head turned away, place a forefinger on a page: the sentence or passage thus indicated, the first to meet the eye, is believed to foretell the future or to indicate the course to take. The Romans used the Sibylline Books (Sibyl being the priestess who prophesied under direct inspiration from Apollo); *see also* **Sibyls**. In the Middle Ages, Virgil's *Aeneid* and Homer's *Iliad* were often used; the process then being termed *sortes Virgilianae* and *sortes Homericae* respectively. Moslems frequently use the Koran for the same purpose.

CONSULT: H. Diels, *The Sibylline Oracles* (trans. by M. S. Terry) (1890).

## Bigfoot
*See under* **animals and birds**.

## Birch
*See under* **trees and plants**.

## Birds
*See under* **animals and birds**.

## Black Box
Device invented by an American, Dr Albert Abrams, and later adopted in England by George **de la Warr**: a radionic 'machine' for use in **radiesthesia**, where it was supposed to measure the disharmony of electronic oscillation in a patient from a drop of blood. After a British court case in 1960, 'radionic' devices fell into disfavour, and it seems likely that any results obtained by using the Black Box were attributable to the patient's conviction that the apparatus worked. Certainly the box itself, with its meaningless circuits and impressive appearance, was quite senseless from an electronic point of view.

CONSULT: Christopher Evans, *Cults of Unreason*, Harrap (1973); A. Mermet, *The Principles and Practice of Radiesthesia*, Stuart (1959).

## Black magic
The working of **magic** which involves blood **sacrifice** for evil purposes. Rites of black magic always include **sympathetic magic**, which is said to act between a person or animal or object and its likeness or representation; for example, a clay or wax figure was often made in the form of a particular person, incorporating a bodily secretion, or a hair, or a nail paring of that person to make it

particularly potent; it was then thought (as in **witchcraft**) that any injury symbolically and ritually performed upon the image would be experienced by the person. Thus a pin thrust into the body of the figure would produce internal body pains; a pin thrust into an eye would cause eye trouble; breaking a limb would cause a similar injury; and slow burning and burial of the remains would cause **death**.

In the Dark Ages, black magic was rife throughout Europe and permeated every aspect of daily life. The simplest activity could bring danger or provide material for black magic to be worked, and with only **talismans** and counter-spells to help them, people lived in constant dread of the unknown. All activity was governed by **spells** and the consultation of **oracles** and **divination** of every description. **Grimoires** or black books were compiled that contained information on such subjects as calling up the dead, casting spells, invoking **spirits**, making oneself invisible or changing one's form, subjecting **demons** to **exorcism** and generally using occult powers.

The **Black Mass**, with its worship of the **Devil**, was said to be an essential part of black magic, and involved the sacrifice of a new-born child with the naked body of a woman forming the altar. In the light of black candles, surrounded by inverted religious symbols and the skulls and bones of criminals, and amid blasphemous incantations and sexual abominations, the ultimate in magic ceremonies could, it was said, prolong life or cause death. Forms of black magic have always been practised by primitive tribes, and in civilized countries repeated thefts from churches, desecrations of graves, occasional confessions and periodic traces of black-magic rites indicate that the temptation to dabble in the black arts is by no means dead.

CONSULT: Rollo Ahmed, *The Black Art*, John Long (1936); J.-K. Huysmans, *Down There (Là Bas)*, Transatlantic Book Service (1958).

## Black mass

A magical ceremony and inversion or parody of the Catholic Mass that was indulged in ostensibly for the purpose of mocking God and worshipping the **Devil**; a rite that was said to involve human **sacrifice** as well as obscenity and blasphemy of horrific proportions. The origin of the belief in the Black, or Satanic, Mass goes back to medieval **magic** and **witchcraft**, yet no one really knows the early history of this magical act, for there exists no single reliable, first-hand description; there is a detailed description in J.-K. Huysmans's novel *Là Bas (Down There)*, and it is possible, if unlikely, that, as he claimed, Huysmans had attended a Black Mass. A witch who said she was present described a Black Mass at a **sabbath** in France in 1594; she claimed that the ceremony had taken place on St John's Eve in a field with about sixty people present. The celebrant wore a long black cloak devoid of the customary cross, and his assistants were two girls; while a slice of turnip, black (either stained or putrid), was used instead of consecrated bread.

Other stories of the Black Mass include mention of black triangular or hexagonal hosts and a black chalice; of mocking screams of 'Beelzebub! Beelzebub!' of wine that may be either urine or **blood** drunk from a human skull; or celebrants naked beneath sleeveless vestments decorated in brilliant colours with such subjects as a naked and spreadeagled woman, a rampant pig or bear or goat; of sacramental wafers (incorporating menstrual blood and semen) being burnt or stabbed, and consecrated wine being poured contemptuously on to the floor; of missals bound in wolfskin or even human skin; of feasts on roasted human flesh; of frenzied sexual orgies and new-born children being crucified alive or baptized in holy oil, strangled and offered as a sacrifice to **Satan**; of naked bodies being used as altars; of young boys' throats being cut to provide blood for the chalice; of Christian prayers being said backwards; of black candles made from human fat; of parts of the Mass being read backwards; of 'Satan' being substituted for 'God' and 'evil' for 'good'; of crosses being tattooed on the soles of the feet so that the symbol of Christ is continually trodden underfoot. Eric Maple, a leading authority on witchcraft, goes so far as to assert that the Black Mass is an illusion, fostered by the press, that never played any part in English witchcraft.

The Abbé Boullan (1824–93), a defrocked Catholic priest who believed that he was a reincarnation of John the Baptist, is reported to have celebrated a Black Mass in vestments on which an inverted cruifix was embroidered, with a **pentagram** tattooed at the corner of his left eye (the left being the side of evil). He recommended the ceremonial sacrifice of a child at the high point of the Mass, and the use of consecrated hosts being mixed with faeces as a cure for nuns who complained they were tormented by devils!

CONSULT: Richard Cavendish, *The Black Arts*, Routledge & Kegan Paul (1967); H. T. F. Rhodes, *The Satanic Mass*, Rider (1954).

## Blake, William (1757–1827)

English mystic, poet and artist whose father was a disciple of **Swedenborg**, who had prophesied that 1757 (the year of Blake's birth) would be the beginning of a new world.

As a child, Blake had seen visions, conversed with angelic beings and been himself influenced by the doctrine of Swedenborg. Blake's early drawings of monuments in Westminster Abbey (used in Gough's *Sepulchral Monuments*) probably also had a profound influence on his mind, and for the rest of his life he regarded the Gothic style as the ideal and 'living form'. After an apprenticeship in engraving he set up on his own and executed many commissions for booksellers and publishers; he also began (1780) to exhibit at the Royal Academy, and, in partnership, started a print shop, though this did not succeed. However, he earned a living by engraving and in 1787 devised a new method of printing from etched copper-plates, later maintaining that the secret of this process was revealed to him in a **vision** by the **spirit** of his brother Robert, who had himself shown great promise as an artist before he died at the age of twenty-five, having been nursed by William.

As William Blake's creative output increased, and his work as both artist and poet was prodigious, his health suffered, perhaps inevitably, and he experienced periods of mental and physical exhaustion and began to see visions ceaselessly. He began to live a double life, on the surface attending to his work and home life quietly and attentively, but in secret depending more and more on his mystical and visionary faculties to inspire his engravings, water-colour paintings and poetry. In later years some acquaintances regarded him as insane, but his more intimate friends had no doubt either of his sanity or his genius. Samuel Palmer, a close friend for many years, considered him 'the most practically sane, steady, frugal and industrious' man he ever met.

Blake was a creator of myths and his world one of imagination; its gods, their sons, daughters and emanations, have been labelled archetypes and self-portraits of the instinct. The vivid mental patterns or images that Blake perceived deep within the orderliness of his mind he called the collective unconscious wherein all Deities resided, since he believed that all religions were one. His visions seem to have been both a penetrating insight into his own unconscious mind and a vivid discernment of nature. Much of his poetry he felt to have been dictated and inspired by people who were dead, and this conviction and the esoteric and occult aspects of Blake's work have suggested to W. B. **Yeats** and others that Blake was a true **Rosicrucian**. Certainly paraphrases of some of Blake's poetry and phraseology were included in the rituals of the Hermetic Order of the **Golden Dawn**, a magical society with Rosicrucian overtones.

Blake's own books include *Songs of Innocence* (1789); *The Book of*

*Thel* (1789); *The Marriage of Heaven and Hell* (1790); *The Gates of Paradise* (1793); *America* (1793); *The Visions of the Daughters of Albion* (1794); *Songs of Experience* (1794); *Europe* (1794); *The Book of Urizen* (1794); *The Song of Los* (1795); *The Book of Ahaniah* (1795); *Jerusalem* (1804) and *Milton* (1804); and his mythology – Satan = the self-ego; the Saviour = the god within man; Jerusalem = the soul – permeates all his work and affords endless speculation and opportunities for exploration into a world of imagination that Blake considered to be the world of eternity.

CONSULT: A. Blunt, *The Art of William Blake*, Oxford (1959); G. W. Digby, *Symbol and Image in William Blake*, Oxford (1957).

## Blavatsky, Madame Helena Petrovna (1831-91)

Enigmatic theosophist who astounded the world with her esoteric writings and prophecies; for a while, assistant to the celebrated medium D. D. **Home**; co-foundress of the Theosophical Society whose Esoteric Section of the Blavatsky Lodge (an inner circle specializing in the occult) included Annie **Besant** and W. B. **Yeats** (*see also* **theosophy**).

Helena Blavatsky was raised in an atmosphere of superstition and fantasy in Russia, and as a child declared that she had **invisible playmates**; her sister has related that she frequently suffered from somnambulism and often talked aloud as she sleep-walked. She repeatedly frightened the rest of the household by running in terror from glaring eyes that she said she saw in inanimate objects as well as in phantom forms. Her will-power, even as a child, was such that she could cause **hallucinations** in playmates by her vivid story-telling. After marrying a man much older than herself at seventeen years of age, and leaving him three months later (she subsequently endured a second unsuccessful marriage), Mme Blavatsky, with her passionate curiosity for the mysterious and the unknown, travelled widely in Europe, Asia, North and South America, Africa, India and Tibet, from whence she returned to annouce that she had been initiated into esoteric **Buddhism** and was able to perform supernormal feats with the aid of her 'Mahatmas' or spiritual teachers. Certainly raps, whisperings, movement of objects and other manifestations of some strange power seemed to follow her.

In 1867 she fought under Garibaldi as a man and was left for dead after the battle of Mentana. In 1871 she founded the Societé Spirité in Cairo: a dubious venture which did her no good and soon folded amid mounting accusations of fraud and embezzlement. In 1873 she associated with prominent people investigating **spiritualism** in the United States, and demonstrated her apparent ability to produce similar phenomena without the aid of **spirits**. The Theosophical Society was founded in 1875, and two years later her first book was published: *Isis Unveiled*. This contained original and surprising theories on the evolution of humanity and the subject of religion. Her later books included *The Secret Doctrine* (1887–97); *The Key to Theosophy* (1889); *The Voice of the Silence* (1889); and *The Theosophical Glossary* (1892).

Blavatsky visited India again in 1879, and with Colonel Henry Steel Olcott reorganized the Theosophical Society and established headquarters at Madras. While in India, she produced, amid some opposition and scepticism, many apparently paranormal manifestations and effects, though Dr Richard Hodgson, sent to India to investigate reports of startling phenomena being produced in her presence, witnessed nothing but fraud and credulity and accordingly produced an adverse report; while the Coulombs (who had also been associated in the Societé Spirité fiasco) confessed that they had manufactured, in collaboration with Blavatsky, a number of 'miracles', and revealed the secret sliding panels of the Shrine in the Occult Room through which 'astral' letters appeared. Nevertheless, by the time she died Mme Blavatsky had approaching 100 000 acknowledged followers throughout the world.

CONSULT: A. Trevor Barker, *The Complete Works of H. P. Blavatsky*, Rider (1833); A. P. Sinnett, *Incidents in the Life of Madame Blavatsky*, Redway (1886).

# Blood

Long associated with life, the soul, strength and virility, blood is regarded with awe by magicians, who use it in many ways: as one of the products of the body to work harm against a person; in rituals to force the magician's will on **demons**; in image magic (*see* **sympathetic magic**) to mix with the wax, or to use to write the name of the person who is to be bewitched; as protection against disease and misfortune; to write **names of power**; for drowning a bat and staining a girdle in making certain **magic circles**; to drink as part of a magician's consecration and in rites and pacts of **black magic**. The Countess **Bathory** believed that regular bathing in virgins' blood preserved her skin and beauty; Gilles de **Rais** used blood for conjurations that he thought would bring him wealth and power; the Aztecs offered blood to the sun god in the form of human **sacrifice**. Because blood is assumed to possess inherent and mysterious qualities, there are many stories of ineradicable bloodstains in places where violent happenings have taken place, as at Glamis Castle in Scotland.

CONSULT: Richard Cavendish, *The Black Arts*, Routledge & Kegan Paul (1967); B. Seeman, *The River of Life*, Museum Press (1962).

### Bond, Rev. Frederick Bligh (1864-1945)

Ecclesiastical architect and archaeologist who carried out extensive excavation at **Glastonbury** based on automatic writing (*see* **automatism**), usually received by John Alleyne and Mrs Hester Dowden, with Bligh Bond supplying a kind of mental contact; he also conducted experiments in **psychic photography**, produced his own inspirational writings and considered that survival writings and the survival beyond **death** of mind, memory and personality was proved beyond doubt. His books include *The Gate of Remembrance* (1918), *The Hill of Vision* (1919) and *The Company of Avalon* (1924).

CONSULT: W. W. Kenawell, *The Quest of Glastonbury, a Biography of Frederick Bligh Bond*, Helix Press, New York (1965).

### Borley Rectory

The best-known haunted house of modern times, perhaps the most famous of all haunted houses: a rambling, red-brick monstrosity of a house that stood opposite the little church of Borley in Essex (a few miles from Long Melford in Suffolk) and was known as 'the most haunted house in England' long before Harry **Price** or any other investigator went there.

Borley Rectory was built in 1863 by the incumbent, the Rev. H. D. E. Bull (1833–92), on the site of a previous building, the Herringham rectory, and there is no doubt that Henry Dawson Bull (Rector of Borley, 1862–92) and his family were well aware of apparently ghostly happenings and of the date 28 July when the ghost-nun is reputed to always appear. Henry Bull was succeeded in the living by his son the Rev. Henry ('Harry') Foyster Bull (1863–1927; Rector of Borley, 1892–1927), followed by the Rev. Guy Eric Smith, Rector 1928–30; the Rev. Lionel Algernon Foyster, 1930–35; and the Rev. Alfred Clifford Henning, Rector 1936–55. It seems indisputable that all these successive rectors, their wives, families, servants and many friends and visitors, encountered strange happenings that convinced them that Borley was a very haunted place.

During the incumbency of the Rev. H. D. E. Bull (1862–92), he, his

*Borley Rectory, known as the most haunted house in England*

wife and their fourteen children knew all about the phantom nun; they accepted the mysterious footsteps, bell-ringing and other noises, unexplained figures and various disturbances as part and parcel of their normal life. The Rev. 'Harry' Bull built a summer house in the garden and spent hours there 'communing with the spirits'; he claimed to have seen the 'nun' many times, and to have seen and heard a phantom coach-and-horses that vanished in front of him; and both he and his wife heard footsteps and bell-ringing and experienced a wealth of strange happenings similar to those reported from his father's time.

In 1900 the well-known apparition of the 'nun' was reported on 28 July by four of Harry Bull's sisters. Three of them were returning from a garden party one afternoon, and as they entered the rectory garden they all saw the dark figure of a nun gliding along one edge of the lawn – a path that became known as the 'Nun's Walk'. One of the sisters ran to the house and fetched a fourth sister, who also saw the figure but refused to believe there was anything strange about it, and moved to intercept it, whereupon the **apparition** vanished. Two of the sisters who saw this figure lived on until 1961 and 1963 and recounted their story to a number of investigators.

The Rev. G. Eric Smith and his wife, 'intelligent, much-travelled and sceptical people', as well as their servants experienced such a mass of apparently inexplicable phenomena, including whisperings, bell-ringing, footsteps, strange lights, shadowy forms and shapes, unaccountable figures, the ghost nun, the phantom coach-and-horses, movement of objects, and so forth, that in 1929 they appealed to a national newspaper for help, with the result that psychical investigator Harry Price went to Borley, little thinking that he would write two books on the subject and be occupied with the Borley case, on and off, for the rest of his life.

The Smiths soon moved out of the haunted rectory, which then stood empty for six months until the Rev. Lionel Foyster was appointed to the living in 1930, and he and his wife Marianne and a little adopted daughter moved into the rectory, where they stayed for five years while the alleged phenomena reached a hitherto unparalleled intensity and variety. During this period bottles were apparently materialized and hurled about the house, **bells** rang violently, doors were mysteriously locked and unlocked, articles appeared and disappeared, messages were scratched on walls and written on scraps of paper that appeared all over the house, heavy footsteps sounded, voices were heard, figures were seen, strange smells encountered, fires were started and just about every other activity ever experienced in a haunted house was reported; not once but many times.

The many visitors to the rectory during the occupancy of the Foysters included Sir George and Lady Whitehouse and their son Edwin (later Dom Richard Whitehouse); Mrs Kathleen M. Goldney, M.B.E.; Mr W. H. Salter (a later president of the **Society for Psychical Research**); François d'Arles; Professor Cook of Cambridge; Guy P. L'Estrange, J.P.; and most of them had some strange happening to report afterwards. The rector kept a kind of diary of events which he used to send round periodically among his family at the time when the events were occurring, and he later condensed these reports into a book-length manuscript. The Rev. Lionel Foyster relinquished the living because of ill-health in 1935, and died in Suffolk ten years later. His wife Marianne, apparently the nexus of much of the alleged phenomena during the years they were at Borley, and often suspected of being consciously or unconsciously responsible for some of the incidents at this period, had a chequered marital career and now lives quietly in a small American town.

When the ecclesiastical authorities decided that Borley rectory was no longer suitable as a habitation for clergy, Harry Price succeeded in renting the place for a year, and by means of an advertisement in *The Times* (25 May 1937) sought to enlist the help of responsible, critical, intelligent and unbiased persons to form a rota of observers. People like Sidney Glanville, a consulting engineer who was to become one of Price's leading associates in the investigation; Mark Kerr-Pearse, later British Pro-Consul at Basra; S. J. de Lotbinière, head of the BBC's Outside Broadcasting Department; Major H. Douglas-Home; John Snagg and C. Gordon Glover from the BBC; Dr C. E. M. Joad; Flight-Lieutenant R. Carter Jonas, later Air Commodore Jonas, C.B.E.; and A. P. Drinkwater of Longmans, Green, the publishers, came forward, and many of them spent a night in the rectory. The results of that twelve-month investigation are included in Price's first book on the case, '*The Most Haunted House in England*'. In 1939 the rectory was gutted by fire, one of its few remnants being the Great Bell which now hangs at the Hampshire home of Peter Underwood. But still curious happenings were reported and Price produced a second volume, *The End of Borley Rectory* (1946), and had plans for a third book on the case when he died in 1948.

After Price's death considerable controversy surrounded an apparent reappraisal of this unique case of haunting. Three members (at the time) of the Society for Psychical Research (SPR) (an organization with which Price had never enjoyed the best relationships) produced a curious volume entitled, enigmatically, *The Haunting of Borley Rectory*. The authors were Eric John Dingwall, Kathleen M. Goldney and Trevor H. Hall, and the book was published by Duckworth under the auspices of the SPR in 1956; in it the authors sought to discredit the Borley case in general and Harry Price's reputation in particular. Other members of the SPR eventually succeeded in obtaining publication by the society of a rebuttal of the allegations against Price, and 'An Examination of the "Borley Report" ' by Robert J. Hastings (Pt 201, vol. 55, of the SPR *Proceedings*) seems to go some way towards vindicating Harry Price and to look at the case in a way that manages to be both non-partisan and civilized.

From 1948 to the present day, the **hauntings** seem to have continued on the site of the rectory, in the former coach house that has housed successive owners of the rectory site, and in the vicinity of the little church just across the road. The full story of the early and later history of the Borley haunting was published for the first time in 1973 when Peter Underwood and Dr Paul Tabori produced *The Ghosts of Borley*; a volume that may well prove to be the definitive book on the case, including, as it does, an abundance of new and important evidence; the story of digging and excavation at Borley; a chronological account of the whole story; and, for the first time, photographs are reproduced of the chief actors in this remarkable and apparently continuing drama.

CONSULT: Harry Price, '*The Most Haunted House in England*', Longmans, Green (1940); Peter Underwood, *The Ghosts of Borley* (with Dr Paul Tabori), David & Charles (1973).

## Breath and breathing

Breathing is the first activity of a human being, and the last before **death**; and so air, one of the four elements, with its life-giving properties, has often been identified with the essence or soul of man, and the control of breath has meant the control of life. Still today the control of breathing is the basis of many paths said to lead to spiritual enlightenment and fulfilment.

Some early peoples believed that the last breath of a dying person released the soul from the body; and since it was desirable for the soul to re-enter another body rather than become lost, the Ancient Romans, for example, were among those who observed the custom of entitling a near relative to inhale the last breath of a dying kinsman. The Ancient Egyptians portrayed air, the companion of the dead on its journey to the underworld, as a bird with a human head. In Hinduism, *prana*, the breath or life-current, is considered to be identical with the mind, and control of breathing forms the basis of **yoga** techniques, in particular of **hatha yoga**. Rhythmic breathing is also the basis of **sex magic**, and Eliphas **Levi** maintained that if a man breathed in a certain way on the nape of a woman's neck, she would come under his complete control. The last breaths of a Tibetan are carefully controlled to ensure that they are intact to await re-birth in a form appropriate to spiritual development.

In **mediumship** deep and rapid breathing is often noticed in association with the manifestations of both mental and physical mediums, and in apparent regressions to a previous life, under **hypnosis**, by reincarnationist subjects (*see* **reincarnation**). **Swedenborg** professed his belief that a system of respiration was responsible for his psychic gifts; Hindu teachings suggest that controlled breathing can counter gravitation and cause **levitation**, an exercise investigated by Baron von **Schrenck-Notzing**; while Camille

Flammarion noticed a correlation between **séance**-room phenomena and the breathing of the sitters.

CONSULT: Hereward Carrington, *The Story of Psychic Science*, Rider (1930); Camille Flammarion, *Mysterious Psychic Forces*, Boston (1907).

## Brocken Spectre

The name given to the giant shadow cast on clouds or fog by someone standing on a mountain pass or peak. The name originates from the fact that the phenomenon is reputed to occur frequently on the Brocken, the highest peak of the Herz Mountains in East Germany; a place long famous for witches' revels on Walpurgis Night (30 April), and, in 1932, the scene of an experiment by Harry **Price** into the 'Bloksberg Tryst', a fifteenth-century magical formula for turning a goat into a handsome young man. To emphasize the futility of ancient **ritual magic** under twentieth-century conditions, Price, accompanied by Professor C. E. M. Joad, followed minutely all the instructions (in the presence of forty photographers, seventy newspapermen and a movie camera!), and, not surprisingly, the goat remained a goat! The full story is recounted by Harry Price in his *Confessions of a Ghost-Hunter* (1936).

CONSULT: W. H. Murray, *Undiscovered Scotland*, Dent (1951) (contains a good photograph of a 'Brocken spectre').

## Broomstick

Originally made from the stalk of the broom plant, the broomstick or besom is particularly associated with witches who are said to have travelled astride broomsticks, flying through the air to the **sabbaths**, though there are in fact a remarkably small number of witches on record as confessing to having done so. The idea probably arose from the fact that witches danced with a stick between their legs, jumping high into the air, and one convicted witch, Guillaume Edelin, said in 1453, that the **Devil** had given her a stick 18 inches (45 cm.) long and a jar of ointment. She would grease the stick, put it between her legs, say, 'Go, in the Devil's name, go,' and at once rise into the air and be carried to the sabbath. Today, when the flying of witches is regarded as having been **hallucination**, the broomstick survives as a symbol of **magic** in such performances as the Mummers' plays, the broomstick dance of the Fens, the broomstick wedding of the gipsies, and, transformed into a **wand**, in modern witch **covens**.

CONSULT: Margaret A. Murray, *The Witch-Cult in Western Europe*, Oxford University Press (1967 reprint); Montague Summers, *A History of Witchcraft and Demonology*, Routledge & Kegan Paul (1965 reprint).

## Brown, Rosemary

English housewife who believes that she obtains music inspired by such long-dead musicians and composers as Liszt, Beethoven, Chopin, Schubert, Brahms and Debussy.

With limited musical experience and ability, Rosemary Brown has convinced experts that the music she produces is genuinely inspired. She first 'saw' Liszt when she was a seven-year-old girl, and 'he' told her that he would come back and give her music when she grew up. In 1964 Liszt returned, and she found that he guided her hands over the piano keys and she played 'beautiful music' without any effort. Since then Liszt has brought other musicians and she has produced hundreds of compositions, songs, piano pieces, string quartets, the beginning of an opera and parts of concertos and symphonies. Rosemary Brown herself is a modest and reserved person who accepts that the music which comes to her in a dozen different styles originates in the world of spirit and that the purpose behind it all is to prove immortality. Her undoubted sincerity and the remarkable virtuosity and varied styles have impressed such people as Sir George Trevelyan; Leonard Bernstein; Richard Rodney Bennett; Professor W. H. C. Tenhaeff, the Director of the Institute of Parapsychology at the State University of Utrecht; Professor Ian Parrott of the Department of Music at the University of Wales; and Hephzibah Menuhin.

The spiritualists have claimed that Rosemary Brown's **mediumship** is a breakthrough in spirit communication, and the Bishop of Southwark has stated that he believes the most likely explanation is a psychic one; but some psychical researchers are less enthusiastic and feel that Rosemary Brown's subconscious mind may be responsible. The *Rosemary Brown Piano Album* has been published by Paxton, and some of the music is available on a long-playing record, 'Rosemary Brown's Music', issued by Philips.

CONSULT: Rosemary Brown, *Immortals at my Elbow*, Bachman & Turner (1974); Peter Underwood, *Deeper into the Occult*, Harrap (1975).

## Buddhism

Founded in India five hundred years before Christ, Buddhism is today widely practised not only in India and the surrounding area but also in China and Japan; and it has penetrated to a modest extent in the West.

Siddhartha Gautama, the founder (the Buddha or 'Enlightened One'), was born in Nepal *c.* 563 B.C., presented his first sermon near Benares in *c.* 530 B.C. and died *c.* 485 B.C. Buddhists do not accept a personal creator of the universe or an immortal soul; they do believe that until a man achieves liberation or enlightenment (the prime and essential aims of the religion) he is fated to be reborn over and over again, 'transmigrating' in never-ending **reincarnation**; they also accept the doctrine of **karma** – both concepts being an offshoot from the much older Hindu religion. Through **meditation**, concentration and contemplation, the Buddhist attains serenity, awareness and wisdom. Buddhists believe in many wicked **demons** and guardian **spirits** and that the fruits of their life-style bring  psychic powers, including projection of the mind, **clairaudience, clairvoyance**, mind-reading and memories of previous lives. The adherents of Buddhism worship, together with the Buddha and the Sangha (Community), the Dharma (Doctrine); and in the representation of the Wheel of the Dharma in India's flag they see the beginning of the religious universalism of Buddhism.

CONSULT: E. Conze, *Buddhist Thought in India*, Allen & Unwin (1962); R. H. Robinson, *The Buddhist Religion*, Dickenson, Los Angeles (1969).

# C

## Cabala, or Cabbala, or Kabbalah, or Qabalah

The true knowledge, inner wisdom and secret lore that is, in fact, a body of occult and magical doctrine, originally Jewish, that became universally accepted in **occultism** from about the fifteenth century A.D. Basically the Cabala is a philosophical system that believes that the ultimate spirit somehow 'fell' into a much lower state – in fact, fell through ten whole planes, and that the human world in which we find ourselves is supposed to be the lowest of the ten. However, a kind of ladder, known as the Tree of Life, stretches upwards through the ten planes, and Cabalists believe that man can, theoretically, clamber upwards through them; they picture the Tree of Life stretching upwards through the ten different planes, and a kind of path wandering up the tree from one plane to the other – not straight, like a fireman's pole, but moving from side to side more like the snake in a game of Snakes and Ladders.

Such occultists as Eliphas **Levi**, MacGregor **Mathers** and Aleister **Crowley** have been much influenced by this mystifying and obscure system, with its principles of unity and divinity within everyone; its pattern involving numbers and the planets; and, in particular, the idea that it is possible for man to develop to a degree where he controls the entire universe. The 'hidden wisdom' of the Cabala was, it is claimed, originally revealed by God to Abraham, and has since been passed on from generation to generation of wise men. The ten spheres or emanations of supreme power are revealed in a Tree of Life which combines Ayin (or Kether), the crown of God, with male gods of wisdom (Hokhmah or Reshith), love and mercy (Hesed) and endurance (Netsah) and with the female understanding and intelligence (Binah), power (Din or Geburah) and majesty (Hod), which, together with beauty (Tifereth) and active force (Yesod), combine in the kingdom or universe (Malkhuth or Shekhinah). These names have been used by occultists because they are said to be reservoirs of power which the magician can harness when using them in certain elaborate rituals.

CONSULT: Richard Cavendish, *The Black Arts*, Routledge & Kegan Paul (1967); S. A. Hirsch, *The Cabbalists*, Heinemann (1922).

## Cagliostro, Count Alessandro (1743-95)

Probably born Guiseppe Balsamo, an imposter and prince of charlatans who became an enigmatic magician, adventurer and wonder-worker, and combined Catholicism, freemasonry and **magic** with remarkable results.

Thomas Carlyle called him the 'King of Liars'; Lewis Spence referred to him as 'one of the great occult figures of all time'. The truth probably lies somewhere between these extreme views. Talented at drawing, possessing **second sight**, healing powers and **clairvoyance** to a degree, Cagliostro was always attracted to **occultism**, to **alchemy** and to **astrology**; and while he seems to have been party to a number of disgraceful intrigues and forgeries, he was nevertheless a true wizard or magician who claimed to evoke the **ghosts** of the dead and compel them to answer questions. Widely travelled, he was well versed in **love potions** and magic cures, secret initiations and practices, cabalistic (*see* **Cabala**) formulas, magic numbers and names, **crystal-gazing**: his art of philosophical and mystical persuasion carried him along – together with the proceeds of his 'elixir of immortal youth' – to the gullible society of the day, until events (including the affair of a diamond necklace in 1785) overwhelmed the 'bull-necked forger' and he died (probably strangled by his jailer) in a fortress prison while undergoing a sentence of perpetual imprisonment.

CONSULT: F. Ribadeau Dumas, *Cagliostro – Scoundrel or Saint?*, New York (1967); W. R. H. Trowbridge, *Cagliostro: the Splendour and Misery of a Master of Magic*, Chapman & Hall (1910).

## Cancer
*See* **zodiac**.

## Capricorn
*See* **zodiac**.

## Cards
*See* **cartomancy; divination; Tarot**.

## Cargo cults

Modern systems of belief among natives of islands in the Pacific Ocean which seek to attract, by magical means, cargo-laden ships and aeroplanes to benefit the inhabitants.

A strange and persistent religious manifestation, practically confined to the Melanesia Islands, cargo cults are probably a reaction to white domination and an impractical dream. A leader talks of salvation in the form of the imminent arrival of a ship or aeroplane loaded with luxury goods for distribution among the islanders provided that various ritual preparations are observed and preparation made by distributing worldly goods and money, observing sexual abstinence and passively accepting the belief in the arrival of a cargo. The ritual may take the form of a skeleton jetty or a magical airstrip in preparation for the arrival of the expected cargo; or a wooden cross painted red to draw back the Red Cross planes with their loads of medical supplies and succour for the ravished islanders during the Second World War; or a crude model aeroplane or ship for, since like attracts like (as in **sympathetic magic**), these images, it is thought, will draw the cargo-laden vehicles to the islands. If a day is named for the arrival of the long-awaited cargo and nothing happens, some plausible story is concocted to defer the arrival to a later, unspecified date, and so the cult continues.

The belief in imminent redemption is, of course, common to many religions, but the cargo cults can as well be explained as attempts to organize social change within a religious framework; they are also a confused mixture of the Melanesians' traditional beliefs and the white man's Christian ideas, and of frustration and disappointment at the exploitation of their lands by traders, colonizers, missionaries and soldiers.

CONSULT: Peter Lawrence, *Road Belong Cargo*, Manchester University Press (1964); Peter Worsley, *The Trumpet Shall Sound*, MacGibbon & Kee (1957).

## Cartomancy

From the Italian *carta* = 'card', and the Greek *manteia* = 'divination'. Cartomancy is the art of **divination** or fortune-telling by means of cards, either by normal playing cards or by **Tarot** cards. Students of the practice maintain that they can read the past, present and future from the order in which the cards fall (each has a qualified meaning to the card-reader), their proximity to other cards and the general pattern presented.

One of the most popular methods of telling cards is known as the 'Wheel of Fortune'. At the beginning of the sitting the fortune-teller removes from the pack the card that most resembles the client – in the case of a dark-haired, married woman the Queen of Clubs will be separated – and this card is placed face upwards between the card-reader and the client. After the rest of the cards have been thoroughly shuffled, the client is invited to reshuffle them and at the same time think about his or her hopes, fears, wishes and aspirations, so that these may become absorbed by the cards. The client then cuts the pack of cards into three piles with the left hand and places the piles face down in front of the fortune-teller, who then proceeds to turn each pack face upwards and gains the first general impression of the reading from the cards revealed. The cards are then reshuffled and dealt into nine piles representing such aspects of the client's life and fortune as the good or evil currently hanging over him or her; good and bad times in the past and in the future; confirmation or refutation of hopes or fears; and predictions for the near or distant future. Perhaps the most sinister card in the whole pack is the Ace of Spades, often known as the 'Death Card', but its appearance is always influenced by those cards close to it and its general position.

The cards of the mysterious and ancient Tarot pack are usually regarded as the best for fortune-telling, and many students believe that, with experience, they reveal many hidden mysteries. There are various methods of using the seventy-eight cards to reveal the present and predict the future, and it is a general rule that while one lay of the cards gives a good indication, three separate readings give a more comprehensive and detailed result; the first lay dealing solely with the past, the second with the present and the third with the future. As with a normal set of playing cards, the Tarot cards should first be shuffled by the fortune-teller and then by the client. Ten packs, each of seven cards, are then constituted, and the balance of the cards discarded. One popular lay-out is known as the 'Tree of Life' and is indicated in the sketch on page 340. Turning each card face upwards one at a time, and proceeding from stack to stack, each card is read separately and also in conjunction with others as they are revealed until the final Tree of Life is shown as a complete story.

The individual packs themselves are usually interpreted as follows: pack 1, the sacred and holy; pack 2, fatherhood; pack 3, motherhood; pack 4, compassion; pack 5, power and victory; pack 6, sacrifice; pack 7, love; pack 8, skill; pack 9, health; and pack 10, worldly things. The order in which the packs are laid out is regarded as resembling a tree with the central trunk representing harmony, the left-hand branches discipline, and the right-hand branches love; while the four packs that form the stem of the tree also represent, individually, reading from the top down (with the base nearest the fortune-teller) and affected by the cards near by: the spirit, reason, intuition and the earth. Each card has several related meanings for the experienced reader, and always each card is influenced by its position in the pack, in the tree as a whole and in relation to the other cards near by or turned up at the same time. For example, the Sun card can mean enlightenment or happiness, or light on some mystery or problem, a freeing of the mind from conventional wisdom and orthodox ideas, or joy, a renewal of life, a good fortune, honour or fame, all qualified or exaggerated or conditioned by other cards in close proximity.

The standard significance for the numeral cards applicable to each suit is as follows:

*Hearts* (normal playing cards) or *Cups* (Tarot cards): 1, love and marriage; 2, friendship; 3, enjoyment; 4, change; 5, a legacy; 6, cause or originality; 7, luck; 8, companionship; 9, fulfilment of a wish; 10, personal life, the home.

*Diamonds* or *Pentacles*: 1, a promise or engagement; 2, bad luck; 3, friendship; 4, an inheritance; 5, an assignation; 6, pardon or forgiveness; 7, wealth or money; 8, good fortune; 9, misfortune; 10, gain in money matters.

*Clubs* or *Wands*: 1, success; 2, enterprise; 3, kindness; 4, joy; 5, a lawsuit; 6, good news; 7, a conquest; 8, deceit; 9, expectation; 10, a journey.

*Spades* or *Swords*: 1, death; 2, deception; 3, a parting; 4, peace; 5, a burial; 6, good fortune; 7, modesty; 8, a quarrel; 9, bad health; 10, a loss.

The twenty-two major trump cards, or Greater Arcana, of the Tarot pack can be used by themselves for simple readings with the client calling slowly five numbers below twenty-two. The remaining cards are continually shuffled, and as the five cards are selected they are laid out in the form of a cross. The card in the centre is said to represent the combining element; the card to the left is the card of affirmation, representing the forces working in the client's favour; the card to the right, the card of negation, representing the forces working against the client; and the card above, the card of argument, represents the discussion of the problem; the card below, the solution.

Considerable speculation has surrounded the origin of the Major

Arcana cards with their characters of Fool (concerned with folly and foolishness), the Juggler (representing a gamble or choice), Wisdom (representing wisdom or judgement), the Empress (ruling woman or action), the Emperor (ruling man, intelligence or will-power), the Pope (inspiration and influence), the Lovers (affection, passion or choice), the Chariot (travel, movement, guidance), Justice (fairness or a settlement), the Hermit (shrewdness, secret knowledge), Strength (courage and inner knowledge), the Hanged Man (catastrophe or sudden change), the Skeleton (death or certainty), Temperance (moderation or reason), the Devil (temptation, inducement or evil), the Tower Struck by Lightning (alteration, giving up or repudiation), the Star (hope, the prospect of success), the Moon (danger and approaching catastrophe), the Sun (happiness, good fortune), the Day of Judgement (progress and improvement), the World (gain and spiritual attainment) and the inevitable Wheel of Fortune (representing destiny, fate and inevitability).

The validity of cartomancy has to be decided by each individual for himself; to some it is an amusing pastime, to others a serious method of divination. Serious students sometimes recommend the practice of selecting a card at random each day and concentrating on its significance and implications as the day progresses. The sceptic will point out that any attempt at divination demands the acceptance of a preordained future and the disturbing acknowledgement that there is no random element in anything we do.

CONSULT: K. Martin, *Fortune Telling with Cards*, Macmillan, New York (1971); B. I. Rakoczi, *Fortune Telling*, Macdonald (1970).

## Cats
*See under* **animals and birds**.

## Catoptromancy
**Divination** by **mirror**.

## 'Census of Hallucinations'
Valuable and important work on **ghosts** undertaken by the **Society for Psychical Research** in 1889; it includes evidence for such phenomena as **telepathy**, **apparitions**, **illusions**, death-coincidences and **premonitions**. The first major work to be conducted under the auspices of the SPR, it formed most of Pt XXVI, vol. 10, of the society's *Proceedings* (1894). Some 17 000 people were questioned and 1 684 claimed to have seen apparitions.

CONSULT: *Ghost or Illusion, A Census of Psychical Experiences,* Society for Psychical Research (n.d.); G. N. M. Tyrrell, *Apparitions,* Duckworth (1943).

## Charms

A form of words or an object that contained **magic** power, especially good **luck** and prevention of illness. Such objects – or **amulets** – vary from the four-leafed clover, pieces of metal and precious stones, old bones and teeth to images and rings. Charms, sometimes in the shape of magic words or the magical arrangement of letters, could also be used against the **evil eye**, to preserve the devotion of a loved one or to protect valued objects, articles and livestock.

*See also* **talisman.**

CONSULT: William J. Fielding, *Strange Superstitions and Magical Practices,* Blakiston, Phil. (1945); Sirdar Ikbal Ali Shah, *Occultism, Its Theory and Practice,* Rider (1952).

## 'Cheiro'

Pseudonym of Count Louis Hamon (*c.* 1860–1936), seer, palmist and prolific author of such books as *Cheiro's Book of Numbers,* a lucid exposition on **numerology**; *Cheiro's World Predictions; True Ghost Stories; Cheiro's Guide to the Hand; Cheiro's Life, Love and Marriage; Palmistry for All; The Language of the Hand; You and Your Hand;* and *Mysteries and Romances of the World's Greatest Occultists.* In his *Confessions of a Modern Seer,* 'Cheiro' reveals interviews with King Edward VII, Queen Alexandra, King Leopold of Belgium, King Humbert of Italy, the Tsar of Russia, the Shah of Persia, Pope Leo XIII, Pope Pius X, Lord Kitchener, Mata Hari, Mark Twain and many other public figures. Oscar Wilde wrote in his visitors' book: 'The mystery of the world is the visible, not the invisible, to Cheiro.' In *Cheiro's World Predictions,* published in 1931, five years before Edward VIII abdicated, Cheiro wrote: 'It is well within the range of possibility, owing to the peculiar planetary influences to which he is subject, that he will in the end fall a victim of a devastating love affair. If he does, I predict that the Prince will give up everything, even the chance of being crowned, rather than lose the object of his affection.' 'Cheiro' never lived to see his prediction proved correct. After many years residence in England, he had moved to the United States, where he died two months before the abdication.

CONSULT: 'Cheiro' (Count Louis Hamon), *Confessions of a Modern Seer,* Beacon Library edition, Jarrold (1937).

## Chirographology
The study of hands and handwriting; **graphology**.

## Chiromancy
*See* **palmistry**.

## Christmas
*See under* **festivals**.

## Circle, magic
*See* **magic circle**.

## Clairaudience
Clear hearing: the psychic ability to hear voices and other auditory phenomena not present to ordinary hearing. Such voices may be subconsciously generated and externalized in auditory perception, or they may be objective but pitched on such an auditory scale or vibration as to be inaudible to most people. Clairaudients have been known throughout the ages since biblical times (II Kings 6); the enigmatic **Joan of Arc** began her mission in response to voices heard by her alone; while the voices that William Cowper, the eighteenth-century poet, heard his in later years, affected his life and influenced his poetry. Clairaudience can be either spontaneous or experimentally induced, and in **parapsychology** the ability is regarded as part of **extrasensory perception**. Books have been produced that are apparently received and dictated entirely by clairaudience. *See also* **spiritualism** and **clairvoyance**.

## Clairvoyance
Clear seeing: the psychic ability to see or sense people and things not present to those with ordinary sight. Such perception, which results in a visual image being presented to the conscious mind, may pertain to the past, the present or the future.

Clairvoyant experiences may be spontaneous or experimentally induced – by auto-suggestion or **hypnotism**. So-called 'X-ray clairvoyance' is the name given to the apparent faculty to see into closed rooms, boxes or envelopes; medical clairvoyance was the early name given to clairvoyant diagnosis of illness (both the clairvoyant's and other peoples'), but diagnosis was soon followed by the apparent ability to heal and 'medical clairvoyance' is now an accepted part of **spirit healing**. Travelling clairvoyance, in effect **astral travel**, consists of the clairvoyant visiting distant places and describing scenes, and actions presently being enacted; spontaneous travelling has been reported in addition to induced travelling, freely exercised by the shamans (see **shamanism**) and medical men of many primitive peoples.

Clairvoyance is often noticed in children, only to disappear at an early age. It is possible that clairvoyance can be explained in terms of **thought-forms**, and it is interesting to note that the taking of alcohol and drugs often enhances clairvoyance. This may be because alcohol and drugs lower inhibitions, reasoning and attention, and thereby increase the power of the subconscious.

Clairvoyance, a supernatural mode of perception, is apparent to many people in such activities as **dreams** or sleep-walking. Even the instant attraction or dislike of a person on first meeting may be a form of clairvoyance. Certainly it is a faculty that is independent of normal eyesight and is exercised by the mind without the assistance of the senses; placing the hands over the eyes makes no difference to clairvoyant visions, though turning the head away often causes the pictures to disappear. Often the clairvoyant describes the images as resembling a small card that seems to appear somewhere about the middle of the forehead. In **parapsychology** the ability is regarded as a part of **extrasensory perception**. *See also* **clairaudience** and **spiritualism**.

CONSULT: T. Fukuai, *Clairvoyance and Thoughtography*, Rider (1931); Upton Sinclair, *Mental Radio*, T. Werner Laurie (1930).

## Cock Lane ghost

Famous case of apparent **haunting** and **poltergeist** infestation at a small terraced house (long vanished) in Cock Lane, London, in 1762. The alleged ghost of a former resident, Mrs Kent, apparently returned to assert that she had been murdered by her husband. Raps and movements of objects were reported in the vicinity of a twelve-year-old girl, Elizabeth Parsons, daughter of the then occupant of the house, but when an investigating committee which included Dr Samuel Johnson and several clergymen spent some hours in the house, nothing happened. Other visitors to the 'house of mystery' included Horace Walpole, Oliver Goldsmith and the Duke of York accompanied by Lady Northumberland, Lady Mary Coke and Lord Hartford. When the child was frightened by threats, she resorted to trickery and was immediately exposed, but by no means all the reported incidents were so easily explained.

CONSULT: Douglas Grant, *The Cock Lane Ghost*, Macmillan (1965); Andrew Lang, *Cock Lane and Common-Sense*, Longmans, Green (1894).

## College of Psychic Science

*See* **College of Psychic Studies**.

## College of Psychic Studies

Founded in 1884 as the London Spiritualist Alliance by, among others, the Rev. Stainton Moses and Alfred Russel Wallace. Later it was known as the College of Psychic Science. The college is not a religious or spiritualistic organization, but rather encourages a spirit of free inquiry into the realm of **psychical research**. Its members are uncommitted and each is free to express his or her own views and to reach their own conclusions. The college does not conduct examinations or confer certificates; it does conduct lectures and can arrange sittings with mediums. For a time the **Ghost Club** held its meetings at the college, which has an excellent library of some 11 000 volumes and issues a quarterly journal, **Light**, and College Papers twice a year. It offers study courses; **meditation** and consciousness-training workshops. The President (1975) is Paul Beard. Address: 16 Queensberry Place, London SW7.

## Colour therapy

The idea that colour can affect a person to the extent of improving health and happiness and achieving an inner sense of tranquillity. Coloured light has been used successfully in the treatment of mental disorders, and occultists believe that since disease is a vibratory disorder, and colour therapy affects the vibrations, a diseaseless future will eventually be possible for mankind. The colours of the spectrum are usually considered to rise from the lowest, red, through orange, yellow, green, blue and indigo to the highest, violet, and the qualities of the respective colours have been detailed as follows. Red: strength and wrath, mastery; orange: pride, life force associated with the physical state; yellow: prudence, intelligence; green: temperance, the link between nature and the supernatural (the middle of the spectrum); blue: justice, perfection; Indigo: love, spiritual mind and intellect joined to the soul; violet: hope, the working of inner forces. Students of the **aura** place similar characteristics on these colours.

## Control

Term used in **spiritualism** and **psychical research** to denote the invisible 'personality' which purports to communicate through a medium (*see* **mediumship**); perhaps a secondary personality separate from the normal consciousness of the medium, where the voice, handwriting, character and whole identity are quite different from those of the medium. Such a communicator is also known as a **guide** when a distinct and continuous personality uses a medium to deliver or relay messages to sitters and to 'control' entities wishing to communicate; to keep away undeveloped or evil entities; and to instruct and help benign entities to use the medium's body to communicate direct. Many controls purport to be American Indians, while others profess to be children, Chinese, doctors and friends and relatives of the medium concerned.

CONSULT: Maurice Barbanell, *This is Spiritualism*, Herbert Jenkins (1959); E. W. Wallis, *Mediumship Explained*, J. Burns (1885).

## Cook, Florence (1856-1904)

British **materialization** medium. *See under* **spiritualism**.

## Cook, Katie (1859-1923)

Sister of **materialization** medium Florence Cook (*see under* **spiritualism**), and a medium in her own right.

## Corn dollies

Figures and other shapes made from the last sheaf of corn that used to be kept at the farm throughout the winter to ensure the success of the following year's harvest. They probably have their origin in the ancient cultivation of corn (some 7 000 years old in some parts of the world) that gave rise to the concept of a corn spirit or goddess who had to be kept alive during the winter period when corn did not grow, the last sheaf cut containing the spirit of the corn. Sometimes a few ears of corn would purposely be left standing in a field; in other districts they ceremoniously cut the last handful of corn, decked it with ribbons and left it in the field; but more usually the last sheaf was plaited into a traditional shape and preserved within the farmhouse. Modern corn dollies are produced in some country districts for ornamentation, and even as baby rattles.

CONSULT: George Ewart Evans, *Ask the Fellows Who Cut the Hay*, Faber & Faber (1966); Sir James George Frazer, *The Golden Bough*, Macmillan (1913 edition).

## Cosmic ice, or glacial cosmology

Theory invented by Hans Hörbiger (1860–1931), an Austrian engineer who was prompted by the appearance of a comet in 1882 to consider the possibility that the comet was made of ice – an idea reinforced by a **vision** he saw some years later. By 1906 he had completed a complex theory and was well on the way to convincing Philipp Fauth, an astronomer, who, in particular, studied the **moon**. Six years later the two men published *Glazialcosmogomie* in which they expounded such suggestions as that the universe was filled with light gases which, in cosmic form, exist as ice; that a block of cosmic ice plunging into a hot star creates a stellar system; that everything evolves in a spiral towards the sun; and that the present moon will inevitably crash into the earth with cataclysmic results, as had happened during such previous events as the biblical flood and the disappearance of **Atlantis**.

Professor Hermann Wirth also embraced Hörbiger's theories, adding that the original Aryan master race had arisen in Atlantis; and before long Hitler, Himmler and other later members of the Nazi movement accepted Hörbiger's theories and ideas which, in 1937, became Nazified with the publication of an official pamphlet (one of a series of handbooks that were compulsory reading for the German SA) on Cosmic Ice. In Britain, Hörbiger's disciple, Hans Schindler Bellamy, produced several books linking Cosmic Ice with Atlantis and South American archaeology.

CONSULT: H. S. Bellamy, *Moon, Myths and Man*, Faber & Faber (1936); James Webb, *The Occult Liberation*, Alcove Press (1973).

## Cottingley fairies

Remarkable case of fairy sightings by two girls of sixteen and nine years old respectively in 1917, who produced a series of photographs to 'prove' that the **fairies** they often played with near their home at Cottingley, near Bradford, actually existed. Sir Arthur Conan **Doyle** investigated the case at the time and was satisfied that the girls' story was true. In 1971 a television team explored the story and interviewed many of the people concerned. Today (1975) both still maintain that they saw and photographed the fairies.

CONSULT: Arthur Conan Doyle, *The Coming of the Fairies*, Hodder & Stoughton (1922); Peter Underwood, *Deeper Into the Occult*, Harrap (1975).

## Coven

Group or band of people of both sexes, possibly thirteen in all, who gather to practice **witchcraft**. Evidence in witchcraft trials suggests that covens were always so organized: twelve members and the **horned god**; in small districts there would be a single coven, in larger districts several covens. All covens met at weekly **esbats** and the quarterly **sabbaths** at which all believers were welcome.

CONSULT: Christina Hole, *Witchcraft in England*, Batsford (1945); Margaret A. Murray, *The God of the Witches*, Sampson Low, Marston (1931).

## Crandon, Mrs L. R. G., 'Margery' (1887-1941)

Controversial American physical medium who maintained that table-tilting and raps began to take place in her presence after she attended a **séance**. Later, her dead brother Walter is said to have communicated through her by **direct voice**; moving lights were also reported, and the **materialization** of objects; phantom hands appeared to exude from her vagina – hands that rang bells and even left thumb-prints in wax.

In December 1922, the *Scientific American* magazine announced that it would present $2500 to any medium producing 'a visible psychic manifestation' under test conditions to be imposed by a committee that included the psychologist, Professor William McDougall, F.R.S., the prominent psychical researcher Hereward Carrington, PH.D., and the magician and illusionist Harry **Houdini**. In April 1924 the magazine invited 'Margery' to participate in the tests; she did so and a number of séances were held. In general, the committee was sceptical of the phenomena it witnessed, and Houdini denounced her as a fraud. Arguments and disunion between members of the committee and 'Margery' and her husband, Dr Le Roy Goddard Crandon, led to the break-up of the investigating committee, and 'Margery' never received the award. However, she continued to practise her mediumship, and indeed extended it to include automatic writing (*see* **automatism**) in several languages, **apports, telekinesis, clairvoyance, cross-correspondence** tests and the production of wax 'spirit' gloves and materialized 'ectoplasmic' forms (*see* **ectoplasm**).

At one séance in London, in the presence of Harry **Price**, Professor F. C. S. Schiller, Dr William Brown, Lady Florence Barrett (a gynaecologist), Sir Ernest Bennett and Lord Charles Hope, 'Margery' was secured by the ankles, wrists and neck to a chair, and in darkness 'Walter', 'Margery's' control, took charge and a high-handled floral basket 'appeared' and wax finger-prints were produced. At the end of the séance Harry Price noted that the medium's wrists were swollen as though from exertion. For a long time the thumb-prints, purporting to be those of the spirit-control 'Walter', were a puzzling point for critics of the 'Margery' mediumship, until, in 1932, a former officer of the **American Society for Psychical Research** had the bright idea of asking everyone who had ever sat with 'Margery' to supply him with prints of their thumbs, whereupon it transpired that the prints were those of a dentist friend of 'Margery', a visitor at some of her séances and still in the land of the living!

'Margery' has been repeatedly described as a very attractive blonde, with a charming personality and an excellent figure; she also had what has been described as 'an amorous disposition', and there is no doubt that she charmed many of the researchers who investigated her **mediumship**, many manifestations of which appeared to emanate from interesting parts of her body. The 'Margery' case is one of the most interesting, complex and controversial instances of apparent physical mediumship in the whole history of **psychical research**; there is no doubt that it was also a most ingenious, persistent and fantastic fraud.

CONSULT: Malcolm J. Bird, *'Margery' the Medium*, John Hamilton, Boston, Mass. (1925); Paul Tabori, *Pioneers of the Unseen*, Souvenir Press (1972).

## Croiset, Gerard (b. 1906)

Dutch clairvoyant known as 'the wizard of Utrecht', 'the man with the X-ray mind' and 'the miracle man of Holland'.

Gerard Croiset has astounded many sceptics, and his successes in **clairvoyance**, especially in finding lost people, has made his name a household word throughout Europe and in the United States. Professor W. H. C. Tenhaeff, with whom Croiset has worked for over twenty years at the University of Utrecht, coined the word 'paragnost' to describe Croiset's remarkable powers. Since 1946, Croiset has been tested, controlled, documented, interpreted and investigated in many ways by researchers from many parts of the world. He has worked with the police in many countries, including Britain, Holland and the United States, and has solved crimes of theft and murder, found missing persons, located lost objects and animals and helped scholars to trace and identify old manuscripts and historical objects. The precise manner in which Croiset 'sees' the past, present or future has never been satisfactorily established. He does not use **crystal-gazing**, an **ouija board** or a **dowsing** rod, **trance** or **hypnotism**, but he does talk incessantly, and when he talks he sees and often immediately 'knows' a person through handling an object or article of clothing that once belonged to that person. It is a kind of thinking in images: a practice that ancient man and the American Indians used to take for granted.

CONSULT: Brian Branston, *Beyond Belief*, Weidenfeld & Nicolson (1974); Jack Harrison Pollack, *Croiset the Clairvoyant*, W. H. Allen (1965).

## Crookes, Sir William (1832–1919)

Distinguished scientist who investigated the phenomena of **spiritualism** and fearlessly published his findings over many years. His versatility and meticulous investigations as a chemist and physicist, and his work and success as the discoverer of thallium, the inventor of the radiometer, spinthariscope, Crookes tubes, etc., brought him world-wide renown.

Knighted in 1897, Crookes had been awarded the Royal Gold Medal in 1875 and the Davy Medal in 1888; he received the Sir Joseph Copley medal in 1904 and the Order of Merit in 1910. Elected to the Royal Society at the early age of thirty-one, he became its President from 1913 to 1915, other societies of which he was also president at different times including the Chemical Society, the Institution of Electrical Engineers, the British Association, the **Society for Psychical Research** and the **Ghost Club**, whose members were privileged to glimpse the more personal side of his nature with its many lovable traits.

Crookes had many personal experiences with D. D. **Home**, of whom he always spoke with the greatest respect, and those **séances** are among the best documented on record. He also attended many séances with Kate Fox and with Florence Cook – séances that apparently convinced his scientific mind beyond any shadow of doubt that he had witnessed **levitation** of objects and human beings; **paranormal** sounds; and the **materialization** of partial and complete human forms. He undoubtedly attended more séances than any scientifically qualified investigator before or since. Unfortunately most of Crookes's records of psychical experiences were destroyed after his death, but luckily a wealth of published material is extant, his contemporary papers having been collected and published in book form in 1874.

While some later psychical researchers are sceptical of the more extreme phenomena accepted by Crookes and believe that he was deluded, there is no doubt that he did a great service by bringing his scientific mind to bear on the phenomena of spiritualism in its Victorian heyday. Sir Oliver **Lodge** said of Crookes: 'It is almost as difficult to resist the testimony as it is to accept the things testified.' Perhaps his unlikely memorial is that his recorded researches became the foundation stone of modern spiritualism.

CONSULT: William Crookes, *Researches in the Phenomena of Spiritualism*, Two Worlds (1926 editions); R. G. Medhurst and K. M. Goldney, 'William Crookes and the Physical Phenomena of Mediumship', *Proceedings of the Society for Psychical Research*, vol. 54 (1964).

## Cross-correspondence

Concordant **automatism**; allusions to the same topic received at approximately the same time through different mediums (*see* **mediumship**). Cross-correspondence was devised by F. W. H. **Myers** in an attempt to eliminate the hypothesis of **telepathy** from apparent spirit communication.

Simple forms of cross-correspondence have been noticed in many accounts of mediumship, but the most famous, extensive and complex involved distinguished members of the **Society for Psychical Research**, including F. W. H. Myers himself, Edmund Gurney, Professor Henry Sidgwick – all deceased – and the automatists Mrs Verrall, a lecturer in classics at Newnham College, Oxford; her daughter, Helen Verrall; Mrs Fleming (known in the reports as 'Mrs Holland'), a sister of Rudyard Kipling; and Mrs Coombe-Tennant (known in the reports as 'Mrs Willett'), a British delegate to the Assembly of the League of Nations. Over 2 000 relevant scripts were produced and carefully transcribed, to reveal many instances of cross-correspondence. Including, as they do, a wealth of complicated classical and literary allusions, the tests called for considerable knowledge and ingenuity on the part of those involved, and careful study of the published records, which some people consider to be irrefutable evidence of survival after **death**, is extremely rewarding.

Criticism of those cross-correspondence experiments include the suggestion that the pattern and design of the messages were illusory and that conclusions were made to fit the theory of the origin and nature; also it was pointed out that since Mrs Verrall was a classical scholar, it was perhaps possible that in some unknown way her **subliminal** mind was responsible for passing fragments of classical information to her fellow automatists. The latter criticism would appear to be overcome by the fact that the cross-correspondence phenomena did not cease after Mrs Verrall died, and dummy cross-correspondence experiments have found no evidence to suggest that the other main criticism of this curious and important phenomenon is valid. The impressive material on the subject of cross-correspondence suggests some kind of perception between living minds and discarnate entities.

CONSULT: H. F. Saltmarsh, *Evidence of Personal Survival from Cross Correspondences*, Bell (1938); G. N. M. Tyrrell, *Science and Psychical Phenomena*, Methuen (1938); and various *Proceedings of the Society for Psychical Research* from 1906 (vol. 20) onwards.

## Crossroads

Long regarded as ominous and dangerous places. Ancient peoples often built their altars at crossroads and their human **sacrifices** formed part of the ritual that led to these locations being regarded as execution grounds. Later on, criminals and suicides were buried at crossroads at night-time so as to assimilate their funeral rites to those of pagans and to confuse their **ghosts** should they choose to walk. In Japan and Pompeii, phallic symbols at crossroads protected passers-by; in India, the god Rudra, who ruled ghosts and evil **spirits**, was placated by offerings at crossroads; in Russia and Hungary, **vampires** were thought to haunt crossroads and to attack late travellers; in Western Europe today crossroads are still favourite midnight meeting places for certain occult and **witchcraft** groups. Even in mythology, Hecate, chief goddess of the **magic** arts, visited crossroads, accompanied by ghosts and hell-hounds, on the last day of the month, to accept offerings of eggs and fish, black puppies and black female lambs; her three bodies, set back-to-back, enabling her to look all ways at once from her sacred crossroads.

CONSULT: Sir James George Frazer, *The Golden Bough*, Macmillan (1913 edition); Richard Cavendish (ed.), *Man, Myth and Magic*, Purnell (1970–72).

## Crow

*See under* **animals and birds**.

## Crowley, Aleister (1875–1947)

Magician, occult practitioner, author and poet, mountaineer, artist and drug addict; self-styled 'the **Great Beast**'; the most celebrated and dedicated student of **magic** in recent times; originator of secret societies who reviled the Christian God and took as his creed and code:

'Do what thou wilt shall be the whole of the law'; also known as the Earl of Boleskine, Count Syareff and Prince Chioa Khan.

After education at Malvern, Tonbridge and Cambridge (Trinity), Crowley soon became absorbed in the study of ceremonial magic, drugs and sex; subjects that were to engage him for the rest of his life and eventually to consume him. During his life he conducted a **black mass** many times; organized and took part in sexual orgies (as manifestations of **sex magic**); propagated a new religion; founded his own magical association; saw his first and second wives die in lunatic asylums and at least five of his mistresses commit suicide.

Crowley genuinely believed that he was a channel of communication for occult intelligences, and he travelled widely in Mexico, Hawaii, India, the United States, France, Germany, North Africa and studied and practised **yoga, Tantrism, Buddhism,** the **I Ching, cartomancy** and other magic and mystical arts and practices. His *Book of the Law,* containing the heart of Crowley's magic, was apparently the result of astral communication received by his wife Rose (sister of the painter Sir Gerald Kelly, later President of the Royal Academy) while they were on their honeymoon in Egypt in 1904. His book *Magick in Theory and Practice* has been described as a city within a city, a complex juxtapositioning of the vast subject of magic, **phallic worship** and Crowley's thoughts, fantasies and actual experiences.

In 1920 he founded his Abbey of Thelema on Sicily, intending it to be a centre for the study of his kind of **occultism,** but within two years was expelled by the other members. He spent the rest of his life promulgating his 'magick', acting as the grand master and revealer of mysteries, talking of establishing a magical colony or community where his disciples could call forth the awesome powers he had once had manifested to him, publishing endless books and pamphlets – including his last work *The Book of Thoth,* a reinterpretation of the **Tarot** cards – and finally peddling **love potions**. He died at Hastings and was cremated at Brighton, where his old friend Louis Wilkinson recited his *Hymn to Pan,* and the Gnostic Requiem Crowley had written himself was sung for the departed spirit of 'the wickedest man in the world'.

CONSULT: Kenneth Grant, *Aleister Crowley and the Hidden God,* Muller (1973); John Symonds, *The Great Beast,* Rider (1951); and *The Magic of Aleister Crowley,* Muller (1958).

## Cryptesthesia

Term to denote a hidden sensibility: a perception of things by a method of which we have no knowledge but are conscious of by its effects. Cryptesthesia is an all-inclusive psychic sense that includes such phenomena as **clairvoyance, premonition, psychometry, dowsing** and **telepathy**. The term was coined by Professor Charles Richet to account for such faculties as these without the necessity of a hypothesis that includes the intervention of **spirits** of the dead.

## Cryptomnesia
Unconscious memory; sometimes noticed in **trance** and in subjects under **hypnotism**, and a possible explanation for unusual and unexpected information. It is, apparently, spontaneous in certain circumstances.

CONSULT: Cesare Lombroso, *After Death – What?*, T. Fisher Unwin (1909).

## Crystal-gazing
Ancient method of **divination**, also known as **scrying**; a form of **clairvoyance** induced by gazing into a small sphere of crystal that may be white, blue, green or transparent, the effect being to bring about a state of partial self-hypnosis when events at a distance, in the past or in the future apparently show themselves in the crystal ball as pictures or symbolic images. Many psychical researchers consider crystal-gazing to be a form of **automatism** by which the subconscious self sends messages in the form of pictures to the conscious self. Crystal-gazing, like **hypnotism**, produces facts not in the conscious knowledge of the participants (such as locating lost objects); it revives forgotten memories, and preserved perceptions may be retrieved by its means. It has also been used, with varying success and total unreliability, to communicate with '**spirit** entities' in haunted houses; as it was used in the sixteenth century by Edward **Kelley** and John **Dee** for spirit communications.

CONSULT: Theodore Besterman, *Crystal Gazing: A Study in the History, Distribution, Theory and Practice of Scrying,* Rider (1927); John Melville, *Crystal-Gazing and the Wonders of Clairvoyance,* Weiser, New York (1970 reprint).

## Cummins, Geraldine (1890-1969)
Remarkable automatic writer (*see* **automatism**) who received alleged communications from Phillip the Evangelist, Cleophas, F. W. H. **Myers**, Colonel Fawcett and others.

Her **mediumship** began in 1923 and lasted until her death; she never studied theology or visited Egypt or Palestine, yet her first book, *The Scripts of Cleophas* (1928), contained detailed and relevant information about the early history of Christianity and in fact supplemented the Acts of the Apostles and the Epistles of St Paul in a historic narrative apparently conveyed from the world beyond **death**, recounting the work of the Apostles from immediately after the Crucifixion to St Paul's departure from Berea to Athens. This work was succeeded by *Paul in Athens* and *The Great Days of Ephesus,* volumes that gave new meaning to obscure passages in the Bible and appeared to show close contemporary acquaintanceship with the apostolic circle.

*The Road to Immortality* (1932) purports to be a series of communications with the spirit of F. W. H. Myers and presents what could be the progression of the human **spirit** through eternity. Her other books (fifteen of her twenty-two published works she regarded as 'transmitted') included *When Nero was Dictator* (1939); *Beyond Human Personality* (1935); *The Fate of Colonel Fawcett* (1955); *Mind in Life and Death* (1956) and *Swan on a Black Sea* (1965) which Dr R. H. Thouless, sometime President of the **Society for Psychical Research**, regarded as 'of absorbing interest . . . the strongest evidence for a real communicator that I have ever seen'; while Professor C. D. Broad – also a former President of the SPR – said he believed the scripts were 'a very important addition to the vast mass of such material which *prima facie* suggests rather strongly that certain human beings have survived the death of their physical bodies and have been able to communicate with certain others who are still in the flesh'.

CONSULT: Geraldine Cummins, *Unseen Adventures,* Rider (1951); and *Mind in Life and Death,* Aquarian Press (1956).

## Curse

**Invocation** of destruction or evil; a profane oath. It is part of the accustomed armoury of the magician and there are many accounts of harm and even **death** resulting from a curse, especially in primitive societies where a curse remains a power to be reckoned with even in the 1970s.

A curse is, in fact, the product of inner tension, which it relieves, and it often achieves its purpose of bullying others into compliance; in less enlightened societies a curse can still be a very potent force; in recent years an aborigine died in a hospital because he knew a death curse had been placed on him, and a West African spent years of misery and unhappiness in London, convinced that nothing would go well with him because he had been cursed by his brother.

There is a cursing well near Colwyn Bay where curses were a flourishing trade little more than a hundred years ago, and it is still possible to locate people who believe they have been cursed, especially those who have disturbed the rest or possess a relic of the Ancient Egyptians who were renowned for their powerful curses. During the excommunication ceremony known as **Bell, book and candle**, a curse is read from a book which is then slammed shut. The 'Curse of the Chains' is used by magicians on disobedient **spirits**, condemning them 'into the depths of the Bottomless Pit, there to remain in unquenchable fire and brimstone until the Day of Wrath . . .'.

Although most curses were intended as punishment until the recipient made amends, the epitaph on Shakespeare's tomb at Stratford-on-Avon reminds us that a curse was considered potent enough in Elizabethan times to prevent a grave from being disturbed, and the curse of death and/or misfortune for future generations is by no means unknown in this day and age; indeed, there are many curious cases of curses, especially by gipsies, that do appear to have worked. One possible explanation is the 'tape recording' theory – that somehow, thought or feeling can imprint itself on an object or person in such a way as to be picked up by other people; if the thought is malevolent, then the effect can be unpleasant.

CONSULT: J. Middleton (ed.), *Magic, Witchcraft and Cursing*, Natural History Press, New York (1967); Peter Underwood, *Deeper Into the Occult,* Harrap (1975).

# D

## Damballa
The god of gods of **voodoo**. *See also under* **animals and birds**.

## Dance of death
An allegorical attitude to the final crisis in human life. **Death** as a grotesque skeleton leading all men and women to the inevitable grave was a popular theme of medieval art, and there are many European woodcuts and frescoes showing him capering with various people of all classes before enticing or leading them away to unavoidable doom; while the *danza macabra* of Spain is depicted as a quadrille of skeletons carrying a scythe, a clock and a banner.

CONSULT: J. M. Clark, *The Dance of Death in the Middle Ages and the Renaissance*, Jackson, Glasgow (1950): and *The Dance of Death by Hans Holbein*, Jackson, Glasgow (1949).

## De Demandolx, Sister Madeleine
*See* **Aix-en-Provence**.

## de la Warr, George (1904-69)
English radiesthesist and advocate of the **Black Box**, originally devised and manufactured by an American physician, Albert Abrams (1863-1924); also the inventor of strange camera-like devices designed to produce 'etheric photographs' from blood spots.

The theory of **radiesthesia** enjoyed something of a vogue in the late 1940s and 1950s, but after a court case in which a woman purchaser of a de la Warr box sued the de la Warr laboratories for the return of her money on the grounds that she was unable to obtain any satisfactory results, serious interest in the idea subsided, possibly on account of the judge's comments on the de la Warr camera. Although the woman lost her case, simply because de la Warr honestly believed in his wares and

*The Dance of Death*

had no fraudulent intentions, the scathing summing-up on the matter left little room for argument: 'The totality of the evidence suggested that the camera was completely bogus and that the photographs were fakes.'

In those cases where de la Warr's radionic devices produced results it seems likely that the driving force was a belief in their efficiency to begin with. Certainly from an electronics viewpoint, the circuits used in the Black Box seemed quite irrelevant and without meaning.

CONSULT: Longston Day, *Matter in the Making,* Vincent Smith (1966); L. Day and G. de la Warr, *New Worlds Beyond the Atom,* Stuarts & John Watkins (1956).

## Death
The end of life; the greatest psychical experience when, according to

spiritualist belief, the human personality moves on to other **spheres**: the final mystery; the last enemy.

Death has frightened, fascinated and puzzled man ever since he began to think. In art, death is variously depicted: as a reaper with a scythe or hour-glass, as a fearful devouring monster, as a terrible and avenging angel, as an animated skeleton capering with all classes in the **Dance of Death**, and as a swordsman on a white horse – as in William **Blake**'s depiction of the Fourth Horseman of the Apocalypse, 'Death on a Pale Horse'. **Spiritualism** and **psychical research** abound with references to death, and, especially just before and just after death, supernormal phenomena have often been reported. **Apparitions** of the recently dead are common, and it is not unusual for a dying person to talk of seeing forms about them not (usually) visible to others present. Certain families have traditional **omens** and apparitions that appear whenever there is a death in that family, sometimes foretelling the death in the form of a **premonition** or a **banshee**, and at other times imparting news of death to a distant relation or loved one in an accepted form, as, for example, the **Airlee 'drum of death'**.

Death, in the form of **sacrifice**, has dominated religions, cults, customs in all parts of the world throughout the ages and is reflected in burial rites, past and present.

*See also* **reincarnation**.

CONSULT: S. G. F. Brandon, *The Judgment of the Dead*, Weidenfeld & Nicolson (1967); Sir James George Frazer, *The Golden Bough*, Macmillan (1913 edition).

## Dee, John (1527-1608)

English scholar, mathematician, scientist, astrologer and magician, born at Mortlake.

A Fellow of Trinity College, Cambridge (where he was accused of sorcery when he invented and produced a realistic beetle for a stage production of Aristophanes' *Peace*), Dee spent two years studying and lecturing in Belgium and France, making a particular study of **magic**; the dividing line between science and the occult always fascinated him. He is said to have learned much from Cornelius **Agrippa**. Receiving a pension from the youthful King Edward VI, he promptly exchanged it for the living of Upton-on-Seven. Early in the succeeding reign his talent for casting **horoscopes** attracted the attention of the court of Queen Mary, and he produced horoscopes for both the queen and her prospective bridegroom, Philip of Spain; but at the same time he rather unwisely sought and developed a close association with the

Princess Elizabeth, then in semi-captivity at Woodstock near Oxford (his horoscope for Elizabeth is preserved in the British Museum). He was charged with making an attempt on the life of Queen Mary by poison or **black magic**, and imprisoned for nearly two years, though acquitted of the charge. With the death of Mary in 1558, Elizabeth had him cast a propitious date for her coronation, and from then onwards he enjoyed the favour of the new queen.

The year 1563 saw the appearance of his abstruse and controversial book, *Monas Hieroglyphica*, with its secret of the relationship of numbers to natural magic (*see* **numerology**), produced in code and symbols, only intelligible to Dee and those he initiated into the mystery. In 1581 he began his collaboration with Edward **Kelley** who claimed to have discovered the **philosophers' stone** and to be able to raise **spirits**; and in the same year he became deeply interested in **crystal-gazing** or **scrying**. He possessed more than one 'magic glass', and, indeed, showed one to Queen Elizabeth, who visited him for the express purpose of seeing his wonderful **mirror**: possibly the 'speculum' or 'magic glass' (acutally a piece of pink-tinted glass about the size of an orange) reputed to have belonged to Dee that is preserved in the British Museum.

Dee had many strange **dreams** and **visions** and made careful notes of his conversations with angels – some of these are also in the British Museum. He depended on others to scry for him, and he depended greatly on Kelley (a man of highly dubious reputation) who would relate to Dee the spirits he saw and the information and instructions they imparted. Once, to the horror of Dee and his family, Kelley related that a spirit had counselled the Dees and the Kelleys to share all things, including their wives, and in due course a document was drawn up and signed by John Dee, Edward Kelley and their respective wives, swearing obedience to the 'angelic commands'. After several journeys abroad, where he was the guest of the King of Poland and the Emperor Rudolph II of Bohemia, and was offered a handsome salary and great honours by the Tsar of Russia, Dee returned to England, but never again enjoyed the Queen's favours. He became warden of Christ's College, Manchester, until 1604; suffered the rejection of his petition to James I seeking the removal of the imputation of magician, then retired to Mortlake, where he meted out an existence as a common fortune-teller before dying in great poverty.

There is some evidence to suggest that Dee had acted as an official spy for Queen Elizabeth; at all events, he was a sincere searcher after knowledge (though sometimes unlucky or imprudent in his choice of friends). He was a mystic with a scientific outlook, and in some respects a pioneer in scientific research. He produced forty-nine books on scientific subjects.

CONSULT: R. Deacon, *John Dee*, Muller (1968); Peter J. French, *John Dee: The World of an Elizabethan Magus*, Routledge & Kegan Paul (1972).

## Déjà vu

The feeling that it has all happened before, that you are in a place doing something which you have already done on a previous occasion; a common feeling that varies from a vague disquiet to a specific and detailed conviction. It has been supposed that déjà vu ('seen previously') is evidence for belief in **reincarnation**, but more likely it is the working of the subconscious mind triggered off on a particular course by an insignificant detail which escapes our conscious senses; and thus, reminding our unconscious mind of a similar incident or situation, persuading us that other details and happenings are also remembered. We are telling ourselves we were aware of what was about to take place, though in reality it was not until after the happening took place that we thought of it as a re-occurrence.

CONSULT: Raymond Buckland, *Guide to the Supernatural*, Universal-Tandem (1970); Nandor Fodor, *Between Two Worlds*, Parker Publishing Company, New York (1964).

## Dematerialization

The dissolving and disappearance of a materialized or physical body (*see also* **materialization**). There is evidence for the dematerialization of part of a medium's physical body (including Mme Elizabeth d'Esperance, and other examples to be found under **spiritualism**) and many reports of the dematerialization of materializations produced at physical **séances**. Such materializations are alleged to be composed of **ectoplasm** exuded from one of the natural orifices of the medium's body, whence it returns when dematerialization takes place, apparently causing distress, discomfort and pain if it returns too quickly, as is likely in the event of a sitter attempting to touch the materialized form without permission from the medium. Some evidence suggests that the medium's body within the cabinet is partly or wholly absorbed in the production of materialized forms, or **apparitions**, that are seen by the sitters outside the cabinet. *See also* **apports**.

## Demonology

Study of **demons** and the **superstitions** concerning them; a branch of religion dealing with evil **spirits** and demons and other superhuman beings apart from gods; the practice of worshipping evil forces. In demonology, Satan and his fallen angels are the subject of reverence, and at one time heathen nations and their gods were considered to be demonic since they were opposed to the Christian God and his angels or good spirits.

*Great magic circle for evoking demons*

**Asmodeus** is a demon of rage and lust, probably identical with Aeshma, one of the seven archangels of Persian mythology who visited heaven every day to eavesdrop on the conversations of the angels. In Jewish tradition he was King of the Demons; a spirit of the storm and personification of rage that belonged to the order of Seraphim (*see* **seraphs**), from whence he fell to fill mens' hearts with anger and revenge and so inspire them with lust that they would betray their wives; his especial delight was to plot against the newly married, preventing intercourse between them, and to encourage adultery.

Asmodeus is the demon who unwittingly helped to build King Solomon's Temple. When the Temple was under construction, Solomon heard about a demon that was molesting one of his favourite wives and prayed for a day and a night that he might gain power over the demon. At length the archangel Michael appeared to the king and presented him with a magic ring inscribed with a powerful pentacle (*see* **pentagram**) that enabled its owner to have command over all spirits. Thus King Solomon was not only able to defeat Asmodeus, but was also able to summon other demons to help him in the building. Asmodeus had his revenge, however, when he tricked Solomon into lending him the ring, which he then hurled to the bottom of the sea.

One magical textbook or **grimoire** (*The Lemegeton*) describes Asmodeus as the third demon to be conjured up and as appearing to human beings as riding a dragon, carrying a spear, having the tail of a serpent and having three heads: those of a ram, a bull and a man (all traditionally lecherous creatures); also as having large wings and the feet of a cock, a bird noted for its indiscriminate sexual vigour. Magicians always summon Asmodeus bare-headed as a mark of respect, for, according to medieval writers, this demon knew the secrets of geometry and astronomy, could discover buried treasure and had the power of invisibility.

*Astarte* (or Ashtoreth, plural Ashtaroth) is the great nature goddess; the principal female divinity; the goddess of love and fruitfulness; the moon-goddess, identified with Selene, Artemis and Aphrodite and corresponding with the male Baal. Solomon was among those who built temples to the goddess, and the popularity of her cult is evident from the many biblical references and from the many representations of the deity that have been discovered, especially clay plaques dating from 1700 to 1100 B.C., probably worn to promote fertility. The worship of Astarte became, to quote one authority: 'the most impure and revolting that can possibly be imagined and it was celebrated in shady groves – proverbial as scenes of the most degrading lust and debauchery' (John Eadie, *Biblical Cyclopaedia*, fifth edition, 1855).

Astarte, sometimes called 'Asherat of the Sea', is said to have been the wife of the supreme god, El ('the god'), and by him to have been the mother of seventy deities; the worship of Astarte was basically a fertility rite of **sympathetic magic**. After denunciation as an enemy of the Christian God, Astarte became Ashtoreth, somewhat strangely a *male* demon, recognized by his fetid breath. When summoned by magicians, the demon appears in human form, but half-black and half-white; he knows all secrets and can reveal events of the past, present and future. Ashtoreth was among the demons who possessed some of the **Aix-en-Provence** nuns, and in 1673 Madame de Montespan (at one time possessor of the **Hope diamond**) sacrificed children to the same 'god' in her attempt to utilize **black magic** to influence Louis XIV's affections.

Ashtoreth has been described as the 'great treasurer' of hell, where he has command over forty legions; a fallen angel who is sloathful and idle, he ranks as a powerful grand-duke of hell and it is said that he can only be invoked on Wednesdays between the tenth and eleventh hours of the night.

*Baphomet* was the deity worshipped by the **Knights Templar**, and in black magic as the source and creator of evil; the Satanic goat of the witches' **sabbath** and one of the names adopted by Aleister **Crowley**. The word is probably a combination of two Greek words meaning 'absorption into wisdom', with the implication that wisdom is the knowledge of the god who really created the universe and of whom Christ was an evil enemy. The word has also, however, been regarded as a corruption of Mahomet; but at all events, the Templars performed appropriate rites, ceremonies and initiations in front of a huge idol of Baphomet.

The physical appearance of this demon has been described in different and contradictory ways: as an idol with a human skull, a head with two faces, with three faces, with or without a beard, with the heads of a cockerel, a man and a goat, and with the head of a goat and the body of a man but with wings and cloven feet. Certainly the idol was worshipped as a symbol of lust, generation and wisdom. As illustrated by Eliphas **Levi**, Baphomet had the head of a he-goat, the upper part of the body of a woman (symbol of maternity), cloven feet, a pair of wings, a lighted torch on the forehead (symbol of revelation) and combining male sexual potency with the four elements and human intelligence. Goya produced a painting representing a materialization of Baphomet the Goat God surrounded by his followers.

*Beelzebub* (also spelt Beelzebul, Baalzebub or Belzebub) is the prince of demons, the idol of the Philistines, a god that was probably worshipped as the patron deity of medicine and accordingly thought to have power over other demons. The name is most likely derived from the Hebrew *baal* = 'lord', and *zebub* = 'flies', hence 'Lord of the Flies', i.e. the god who could bring or send away flies. The Greek New Testament gives the spelling 'Beelzeboul', meaning 'dung god', which some authorities have suggested may have been changed by the Jews to show contempt for heathen divinities; Beelzebub was without doubt one of the chief heathen gods, and so becomes the prince or chief of devils.

Another possible derivation is from Baal-Zebul, 'lord of the high house'; the title 'Lord of the Flies' has also been said to have its origin in the fact that the idol of the god, dripping with sacrificial blood, must have attracted many flies in a land where flies were specially prevalent. Medieval demonologists have described the god as of prodigious height and seated on a gigantic throne with a band of fire encircling his forehead, cavernous nostrils, two large horns and great bat-like wings, ducks' feet, a lion's tail and covered all over with thick black hair. Beelzebub was another acknowledged lord and master at witches' sabbaths, and it was in his name that Jesus Christ was denied, and at the end of the ceremonies it was said to be Beelzebub who copulated with all the participants present to signal the frenzied orgy that invariably ended such gatherings. Beelzebub was one of the demons that apparently possessed the nuns at Aix-en-Provence, especially Sister Madeleine de Demandolx, causing the nun to have visions of sodomy and cannibalism and to writhe on the ground and expose her genitals.

Beelzebub is one of four powerful demons, named in a manuscript in the British Museum, whose help is needed to compel other demons to appear; so powerful a demon, magicians say, that should he be conjured up without a carefully and correctly prepared **magic circle** being formed beforehand, the death of the magician can result.

*Lilith* is one of the ten evil sephiroth and chief of the demonesses who preyed on newly born children, throttling them, and on men to seduce them in their sleep (like the **succubi**) and suck their blood. Protection against attacks by Lilith (probably successor of the Assyrian *lilitu*, a demoness with wings and long hair) was a magic circle drawn on the wall of the bedroom containing the words, 'Adam and Eve, barring Lilith', which is interesting in view of the legend that Lilith was Adam's first wife, created by God out of mud and filth, and that Adam's offspring by her were demons. She is said to have left Adam to consort with lascivious demons and to have given birth to demonic children called *lilin* at the rate of a hundred a day while God created Eve to comfort Adam. King Solomon is supposed to have suspected the Queen of Sheba of being Lilith because of her hairy legs, and without doubt Lilith fills the bill as the 'terror by night' of Psalm 91.

*Lucifer*, meaning 'Light Bearer', was the name the Romans gave to the morning star; it became one of the names for Satan, the **Devil** himself, who was thought to be an archangel who tried to make himself the equal of God. Lucifer, son of the morning, has always been called upon by sorcerers and dabblers in the black arts, for, as chief of devils and lord of the darkness, Lucifer was summoned for worship and service unobtainable from any other demon. Witches often talked of meeting Lucifer and making pacts with him, or worshipping him with obscene rites and submitting to his terrible lusts. Demonology in an extreme form becomes **Satanism**.

CONSULT: Richard Cavendish, *The Black Arts*, Routledge & Kegan Paul (1967); Edward Langton, *The Essentials of Demonology*, Epworth Press (1949); Victoria Hyatt and Joseph W. Charles, *The Book of Demons*, Lorrimer (1974).

## Demons
Evil **spirits**, originating from the Greek *daimon* = 'daemon', meaning a spirit, good or bad; but Christian dogma decreed that all pagan spirits were under the command of the **Devil**, and so demons came to be associated with evil, an association that has continued ever since. *See also* **Demonology**.

CONSULT: Victoria Hyatt and Joseph W. Charles, *The Book of Demons*, Lorrimer (1974); Edward Langton, *Supernatural*, Rider (1934).

## Dermography
Skin writing, a phenomenon comparable to **stigmata** but less durable. In the early days of **spiritualism** there were mediums who specialized in dermography, some of whom were undoubtedly fraudulent since letters or figures traced on sensitive skin by any blunt instrument, even finger nails, will often reappear after a few moments. That suggestion also played a part in such demonstrations has been evident from experiments where mediums have successfully reproduced on their own skin a mentally communicated word or image. Sir Arthur Conan **Doyle** was among those who drew attention to the possibility that concentration by an invisible entity may have an effect on a medium which is similar to the self-concentration of religious ecstatics who produce stigmata.

CONSULT: Nandor Fodor, *Encyclopaedia of Psychic Science*, Arthurs Press (1934).

## Dervishes, whirling
Distinguished from the 'howling' dervishes by the silence of their whirling movement or 'dancing'. The dervish is a Mohammedan and usually a holy man: a member of a religious fraternity that follows a form of Sufism whose philosophical systems and physical exertions are designed to improve and enhance the operations of the human mind.

*Whirling dervishes controlled by the semazenbashi keeping watch by the sheik's post*

The whirling of the dervishes is executed to induce ecstasy in which communication with God grows easier, and in so doing the practitioners' perceptions and capacities extend beyond those of ordinary men: power for healing, immunity from pain, telepathic powers and other apparent miracles. Regarded by the rest of the world as strange and fanatic, even insane perhaps, because of the seemingly mad dancing consisting of a monotonous whirling round and round, dervishes as they circle and turn in apparently endless rhythmic movements are attempting to so improve the quality of the mind (sometimes with and sometimes without a religious context) that self-realization will achieve the perfected man – or woman.

Their *sema*, or whirling dance, begins with the Sultan Veiled Walk, the dervishes parading three times around the *semahane*, or hall, wearing black cloaks which represent the tomb and worldly attachment. Once the dance commences the left foot of the whirler should never leave the floor, but sometimes the whirler is carried away by an experience of ecstasy when both his feet may leave the ground. One *semazenbashi*, or dancing master, who by his movements and position during the *sema* (or whirling dance) controls the pace of the ceremony, has said, 'I can teach how to turn in three months, but it can take the rest of one's life to learn to turn.' At the conclusion of each selam, the dervishes stop abruptly and bow towards the sheik's post; their billowing skirts wrapping round their legs. 'It is not ordinary music, this dervish music, it is music you drink with your whole body, your whole being, and you live this music' - Nezih Uzel.

CONSULT: John P. Brown, *The Dervishes*, Frank Cass (1968); Ira Friedlander, *The Whirling Dervishes*, Wildwood House (1975).

## D'Espérance, Madame Elizabeth (1855-1919)
Private medium whose real name was Elizabeth Hope, later Mrs Reed. *See under* **spiritualism**.

## Devil
Satan, supreme spirit of evil, foe of God and man; also minor·evil **spirit**, **demon** or wicked person. Primitive philosophy ascribed all phenomena to personal agencies: the good things were gifts from the gods, the bad the works of demons or devils; and since a fundamental belief in the world of spirits never seems to be entirely eradicated from man's consciousness, belief in the Devil (although it has declined in proportion to belief in God) is still alive and a force to be reckoned with. Devil worship, with and without human **sacrifice**, was practised by Gilles de Rais in the middle of the fifteenth century when the Devil was enjoying his heyday; it has been practised all over the world at various times and in different guises, and undoubtedly is still practised in secret today (*see* **satanism**). Pictures and representations of the Devil abound in churches and in old manuscripts where, as befits the Prince of Darkness, he is often depicted as a dark man in dark clothes: the man in black whose influence on man in the past has been enormous. In the present his 'reality' is questioned by many, but he is still believed in and worshipped by a few.

*See also* **demonology**.

CONSULT: M. D. Conway, *Demonology and Devil Lore*, Chatto & Windus (1874); J. Charles Wall, *Devils*, Methuen (1904).

## Devil's hoofmarks
Name given to a mysterious trail of prints on untrodden snow that appeared in south Devon on 8 February 1855. Resembling the hoofmarks of a donkey - except that they were in a single line - they stretched for nearly a hundred miles around Exmouth, Dawlish and Teignmouth, over ground, roof-tops and on both sides of walls and haystacks; all perfectly spaced about eight inches apart. Theories have

included a trailing balloon cable, a sea slug of unknown variety and a visit from the **Devil** himself. Commander Rupert T. **Gould** made a study of the subject.

CONSULT: Rupert T. Gould, *Oddities,* Bles (1928).

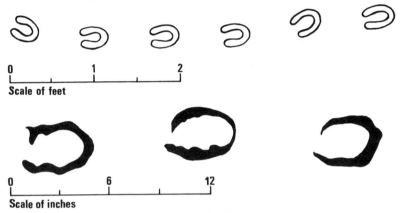

0    1    2
Scale of feet

0    6    12
Scale of inches

*The 'Devil's hoofmarks'*

## Devil's mark

A **witchcraft** term for places on the body that were said to be insensitive to pain. The discovery of the 'devil's mark' was indisputable evidence of a witch, so suspected witches and warlocks were stripped naked and prodded in every part of the body by enormous pins or lancets; and since it was often the practice to stab one area of the body causing sharp pain, and then immediately afterwards, using the blunt end of the instrument, to touch the victim lightly elsewhere, causing little or no reaction, it was exceedingly rare for no 'devil's mark' to be located. The examiners often spent many hours taking turns at the examination, which was always thorough, especially if the suspected person was young and female.

## Dickens, Charles

*See* **Mystery of Edwin Drood, The**.

## Dieppe Raid case

In August 1951 two young married women who were sisters-in-law were staying for a couple of days near Dieppe. Their room faced the direction of the sea and the house they occupied had been used by

German Troops during the Second World War. Very early on Saturday, 4 August, when it was still dark, one of the women, referred to as 'Agnes Norton' in the records of the **Society for Psychical Research**, heard a series of 'unusual noises' from the direction of the beach, noises which she described as cries of men heard as if above a storm. She listened to the noises for about fifteen minutes and then got out of bed to leave the room. Her sister-in-law asked her to switch on the light, which she did. When 'Agnes' returned to the bedroom she asked 'Dorothy' whether she had heard anything. She had, and she thought the sounds had started suddenly, and she likened the noise to a storm rising at sea. She was certain that she had been awake before the sounds started and that she had heard the noise for about twenty minutes before 'Agnes' had got out of bed.

The two women lay in the dark, listening to the roaring sounds that ebbed and flowed; and they also heard, quite distinctly, the sounds of cries and shouts and gunfire. They put on the light again and checked the time; it was 4.20 a.m. The noises still continued and they both went out on to the balcony where they could look down towards the beach but could not see the sea. As they stood there the sounds seemed to intensify, according to 'Agnes', and then they seemed to be a mixture of gunfire, shellfire, dive-bombers, landing-craft and mens' cries. 'Dorothy' agreed that the noises came from the direction of the sea in 'rolls of sound', and that there was a separate sound of cries, dive-bombing and guns firing. Often the two women heard the sound of a shell bursting at the same moment.

At 4.50 a.m. both women agreed that all the noises ceased. They began again abruptly a few minutes after five o'clock (5.05 according to 'Dorothy', and 5.07 according to 'Agnes'). Again the noises became intense and so loud that the two women were amazed that they did not awaken the rest of the household and other people in the vicinity. Dawn began to break and birds started to sing. Both women heard a single rifle shot from the direction of the hill above the beach. They noticed again sounds of dive-bombing, mens' cries and shouts, and the noise, coming in waves as before, was very loud at times. At 5.50 both women heard planes overhead and mens' voices and then the sounds grew fainter and the two women, tired from their disturbed night, finally went to sleep again between 6.30 and seven o'clock.

Next day both women wrote notes of their experiences and posted them to the SPR with a letter asking whether the society had received any similar reports. The case is particularly interesting in view of the remarkable coincidence between the times of the noises of battle heard by the two ladies on 4 August 1951 and the actual Dieppe Raid of 19 August 1942, when 4 963 Canadian troops attempted a landing and only 2 211 returned, almost 1 000 dying on the beaches. The first wave of landing craft had touched down at Puys at 5.07 hours in the face of heavy fire, the landing being seventeen minutes later than scheduled; at 5.12 a destroyer had started to bombard Dieppe.

No one else apparently heard the noises, and there seems little doubt but that the ladies experienced a collective auditory **hallucination**. The SPR were impressed by the care with which the ladies prepared independent reports, their prompt action in sending the reports to the society, their candor in answering questions, their well-balanced characters and their lack of exaggeration or any tendency to 'flights of fancy'. Guy Lambert, a former President of the SPR, considered the experience to be a genuine psychic phenomenon 'of which little or nothing was derived from previous normally acquired knowledge'.

CONSULT: Lucille Iremonger, *The Ghosts of Versailles*, Faber & Faber (1957); SPR *Journal*, May-June 1952, vol. XXXVI, No. 670.

## Dill
*See under* **trees and plants**.

## Direct voice
Phenomenon associated with certain mediums, i.e. direct-voice mediums; an isolated voice without evident source of origin or agency; a 'spirit' voice that speaks directly at **séances** to sitters without apparently using the vocal chords of the medium – indeed it has been suggested that an independent 'voice-box' is materialized (*see* **materialization**), composed of **ectoplasm**, a kind of artificial larynx that may or may not be visibly attached to the medium's ear or nostril; a voice that appears to issue from a **trumpet** that sails about the séance room in darkness and may or may not itself be visibly attached to the voice-box. Direct-voice mediumship dates back to the early days of **spiritualism**, and while it can be a very dramatic manifestation, the ease with which it can be produced fraudulently has always made it suspect; and while there is a wealth of evidence for the phenomenon, some is good, some bad and much indifferent.

CONSULT: Maurice Barbanell, *They Shall Be Comforted*, Psychic Press (1936); Leslie Flint, *Voice in the Dark: My Life as a Medium*, Macmillan (1971).

## Divination

The professed exploration of the unknown or the future by means of **scrying, automatism, dreams, omens, astrology, cartomancy, palmistry, tasseography, phrenology, graphology, dowsing, radiesthesia, numerology,** the **I Ching** and so forth. Any system, it has been suggested, is good for the man with supernormal powers, and any system is bad for the man who is not so gifted. To divine is to 'find by intuition', **magic** or inspiration, and although the history of divination is riddled with unfulfilled prophecies and inaccurate diagnosis, human nature is such that it continues to rely to a considerable extent on information that originates from an unknown source.

Man has always looked for supernatural guidance, and the role of primitive soothsayer, augur (*see* **augury**) or medicine man was taken up by the priest or the prophet, then the astrologer, the gipsy and the village wise-man or wise-woman; and today professional clairvoyants in every city in the world meet the never-ending demand of clients from all walks of life – and who can say whether the hope and encouragement they give does not outweigh the disappointments?

CONSULT: Richard Cavendish, *The Black Arts*, Routledge & Kegan Paul (1967); A. M. Miall, *Complete Fortune Telling*, Greenberg, New York (1950).

## Divining

*See* **dowsing or divining**.

## Dixon, Jeane

Contemporary American clairvoyant (*see* **clairvoyance**) and prophet who uses **crystal-gazing, astrology, numerology** and **cartomancy**. Unwilling to submit to any scientific examination, her powers are treated with some reserve by **parapsychology** researchers, although her claims are widely accepted by the general public and there is no doubt that she has some remarkable abilities. Perhaps her most celebrated prediction was that President Kennedy would be assassinated while serving his term of office, and in 1963 she begged him not to go to Dallas. Jeane Dixon regards her powers of **extrasensory perception** in the field of **precognition** as a divine gift and many of her messages are relayed as spirit messages while she is in church. In 1966 the *Christian Century Magazine* (dated 10 August) carried an eye-witness account that she had dematerialized during Mass at St Matthew's Cathedral, Washington; and later materialized in her own home (*see* **dematerialization; materialization**).

CONSULT: Jeane Dixon, *My Life and Prophecies*, Morrow, New York (1969); Ruth Montgomery, *A Gift of Prophecy*, Morrow, New York (1965).

## Doppelgänger
German name for the **wraith** or **apparition** of a living person; the **double**.

## Double
The exact counterpart of the physical body; the etheric replica; the **astral body**: the subtle body – the bilocation of the Church of Rome which recognizes such a 'duplicate' that can become detached from the physical body in which it normally resides. While there exist thousands of reports of people seeing their doubles, convincing experimental evidence is rare, though evidence does exist to demand serious consideration. To see oneself in this way is regarded as an **omen of death**. *See also* **Doppelgänger**; and for projection of the double, *see* **astral travel**.

CONSULT: Nandor Fodor, *Encyclopaedia of Psychic Science*, Arthurs Press (1934); Celia Green, *Out-of-the-Body Experiences*, Institute of Psychophysical Research, Oxford (1968).

## Dowsing or divining
The art of using a divining – or dowsing – rod, a V-shaped twig, usually about a third of a metre long, preferably of hazel or rowan wood, wire, whale-bone or metal. If the two ends are held firmly, one in each hand, by someone with the gift (about one in ten of the population), the apex end of the twig will inexorably move downwards to denote running water, metal or precious stone, according to what is being sought. Modern dowsing rods incorporate a small compartment to take a sample of whatever is being sought, and some dowsers find this helpful. Some practitioners of the art of **rhabdomancy** can dowse over maps and locate water, metal or oil without ever having visited the area themselves (*see also* **radiesthesia**); other dowsers need to work on the spot. Many people have a degree of ability to dowse, and with a little practice can locate springs and underground streams. Scientific experiment suggests that the explanation lies beyond unconscious muscular action and may be a faculty related to **clairvoyance**.

CONSULT: A. H. Bell (ed.), *Practical Dowsing: A Symposium*, Bell (1965); H. de France, *The Elements of Dowsing*, Bell (1948).

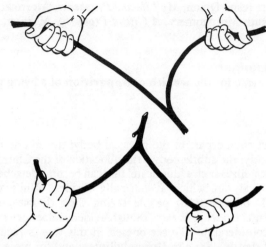

*Two methods of holding a dowsing or divining twig*

## Doyle, Sir Arthur Conan (1859-1930)

Novelist and creator of Sherlock Holmes; renowned advocate of **spiritualism**; a keen student of psychic and **paranormal** phenomena for over forty years.

After qualifying as a doctor at Edinburgh University, Doyle practised at Southsea from 1882 to 1890. Also in 1882 he published *A Study in Scarlet,* the story that introduced the most famous of all literary detectives. Among his longer Holmes novels the best known, *The Hound of the Baskervilles,* is based on the legend of the 'Black Dog of Dartmoor', a phantom hound with flaming eyes sometimes reported by late travellers on the moor. He also wrote historical romances, a history of the South African War (in which he served as a doctor), scientific romances (of which *The Lost World* is perhaps the most well known), a book of poems, a volume of reminiscences and a *History of Spiritualism* (1926). He was introduced to psychic matters in 1887 by General Alfred Drayson, a member of the **Ghost Club.** He established to his own satisfaction that **telepathy** worked between living human beings and began to explore the possibility of messages being relayed in a similar way from the dead. He began to read works on **theosophy** and **Swedenborg,** and by **Crookes** and **Myers** as well as on spiritualism.

In 1902 he met Sir Oliver **Lodge** at Buckingham Palace when both men received their knighthoods. Doyle's interest in psychic subjects then advanced to the extent that, before many years had passed, he was devoting himself entirely to the cause of spiritualism. By now wealthy and world-famous, he travelled extensively, proclaiming his message of hope to the bereaved of the First World War. He became president of the old London Spiritual Alliance and College of Psychic Science (*see* **College of Psychic Studies**). He sat with many mediums, investigated haunted houses, witnessed **apports, telekinesis,** and **materialization**; he experienced prophetic **dreams** and also solved several real-life mysteries. His old home at Crowborough, Windlesham Manor, is reputed to be haunted by his ghost. A little-known reminder of Doyle survives at Hindhead where he lived for ten years in the shape of a pair of gates with his initials in the iron tracery.

CONSULT: John Dickson Carr, *The Life of Sir Arthur Conan Doyle,* John Murray (1949); Sir Arthur Conan Doyle, *Memories and Adventures,* Hodder & Stoughton (1924).

## Dracula

Famous fictional **vampire** created by Bram Stoker in his novel of that name published in 1897; the word is sometimes used to describe a walking corpse that preys on the living and sucks their **blood,** and also to describe human murderers with blood lust. There have been many horror films based on the character, and the Romanian government has restored a castle which it has named Castle Dracula to exploit the area as a holiday attraction. A Dracula Society, to promote the appreciation and enjoyment of Gothic and supernatural literature, was founded in London in 1973; and there is a Count Dracula Society in the United States.

## Drawing, automatic

*See* **automatism.**

## Dreams

Mysterious activity that accompanies sleep and may be a state of consciousness during sleep; or a **hallucination** or **illusion** associated with the conditions of sleep.

We all experience dreams and research suggests that if we did not dream we could become insane. Experimentation has shown that it is possible for people to control their dreams, having first overcome the dream-state by becoming aware that one is dreaming. Dr Patricia Garfield, who teaches 'creative dreaming' at the University of

California, says that it is possible to learn to control the content of your dreams. Her method has been formulated as (a) as you lie in bed, clearly decide the contents of your intended dream; (b) put that intention into a concise and clear and positive phrase and keep it in your mind ('Tonight I will travel to Egypt in my dream', for example); (c) try to be as calm, contented and relaxed as you can; (d) as you become more and more relaxed, repeat the dream phrase several times aloud and then concentrate completely on the subject you have chosen; (e) visualize your chosen dream as if it were happening and picture yourself having the dream.

The psychological process of talking during sleep is not far removed from the process involved in many cases of so-called demonic **possession**, and the subconscious mind, with its memories of past experiences and desires, may well give expression to repressed instincts as well as colour and shape to dreams that have been such a source of inspiration in literature and the arts.

Dreams were once thought to be some kind of contact with another world or another level of existence, an idea that was both frightening and exciting in view of the variety of dream experience. In dreams, beings of all kinds are to be encountered, including dead people and fabulous creatures; travel presents no difficulty, time ceases to exist, and superhuman strength, power and abilities are by no means uncommon. It was thus inevitable that dreams should become associated with the supernatural.

Then they were thought to be a source of information, especially of divine warnings, a method whereby the gods could reveal themselves and evil **spirits** parade their temptations. In Egypt, during the Graeco-Roman period, a practice known as incubation involved sleeping in a temple to obtain divine advice through a dream or healing through dream-contact with a god. The interpretation of dreams has occupied man since biblical times when Daniel is presented as understanding 'all visions and dreams'; Freud believed that many dreams revealed sexual repression; Jung that they represented our unconscious life and could be the means of seeing into the future (**precognition**); while present-day dream analysts can interpret almost any dream.

There have been dreams that have prevented disasters, dreams that resulted in criminals being arrested, dreams that enabled lost objects to be found, and, most common of all, dreams that release the worries of the day and rearrange our past and our present – and possibly our future – and present it in fantastic patterns of terror and delight during the two hours of dreaming that each of us experiences each night. *See also* **lucid dreams**.

CONSULT: R. de Becker, *The Meaning of Dreams,* Allen & Unwin (1968); Sigmund Freud, *The Interpretation of Dreams,* Allen & Unwin (1950 reprint).

## Druids and Druidism

A caste of Celtic priests whose religion embraced Gaul and Britain and whose history is interwoven with folklore and legend. The word Druid probably has its origin in the Greek, *druss* = 'oak tree', a tree (*see also under* **trees and plants**) sacred to the Druids who taught the immortality of the human soul, which, they believed, passed into other bodies after **death**. Their ceremonies included culling the mistletoe; **divination** by means of human **sacrifice** (burning alive in wicker baskets); prophesying in a **trance** induced by drinking bulls' blood; circular dancing; cremation of the dead; oral wisdom-teaching by means of long poems; **fire** festivals and rites devoted to healing and astronomy, subjects on which they undoubtedly had great knowledge. Their reverence for the sun, in particular, is evident from their important first summer solstice ceremony.

Modern revivals of Druidism are gentle societies that tend to be somewhat divided and composed of a mixture of theology and bardic lore, traditional knowledge and romantic ceremony. There is also the Ancient Order of Druids, a friendly society founded in the eighteenth century that has no mystical or symbolic side. The thousands of megalithic monuments with names like 'Druid's Temple', 'Druids' Grove' and 'Druids' Altar' that abound throughout Britain may or may not have been the scenes of ancient druidical practices.

CONSULT: T. D. Kendrick, *The Druids,* Methuen (1927); Stuart Piggott, *The Druids,* Thames & Hudson (1968).

## Drummer of Tedworth

**Poltergeist** disturbances at the Tedworth (now Tidworth), Wiltshire, home of the magistrate John **Mompesson** in 1661. A drummer, William Drury, was arrested for vagrancy, and in the absence of Mr Mompesson, his drum was confiscated and taken to the magistrate's house. On his return home, Mompesson learned that since the drum had been on the property loud thumping and drumming noises had been heard at night by all the occupants; at times the sounds seemed to come in answer to specific requests. After the itinerant drummer had been sentence to transportation, the disturbances ceased; but when he escaped and returned to England, the noises began again. In addition, objects were moved, strange lights seen, sulphurous smells reported; drops of **blood** were found, and the disturbance of beds and bedclothes was especially noticed at night-time when the noises were often worse, sometimes waking up the whole village (!); they seemed to occur particularly in the vicinity of children. After about two years the disturbances ceased.

CONSULT: Joseph Glanville, *Sadducismus Triumphatus*, Part II, J. Collins (1681); Harry Price, *Poltergeist Over England*, Country Life (1945).

## Duncan, Mrs Helen Victoria (1898-1956)
British **materialization** medium. *See under* **spiritualism**.

## Dunninger, Joseph
American conjurer and mentalist who issues challenges to mediums, claiming that he is able, by means of trickery, to duplicate any phenomena they can produce. For some years Dunninger held Hallowe'en **séances** with the apparent object of getting the **ghost** or **spirit** of Harry **Houdini** to manifest and reveal the code, contained in an envelope, which Houdini is said to have sealed before his **death**. The medium Frank Decker once produced part of the ten-word key but it was insufficient, according to Dunninger, to gain him the award.

CONSULT: Joseph Dunninger, *Dunninger's Complete Encyclopaedia of Magic*, Hamlyn (1971).

## Duppy
West Indian **ghost**; in **voodoo** belief, the part of man that lives on after the **death** of the physical body. A duppy can be awakened by relations of a dead person and will leave the grave at their command, but care must be taken to ensure that it is the right grave, for to wake the wrong duppy can be dangerous. There is evil within everyone, but so long as he is alive a man's heart and brain control his actions; yet after death the duppy is no longer controlled and is capable (so it is believed) of doing many evil things. West Indian natives therefore have methods of forcing the duppy to stay in his grave and not return to torment living people. To be breathed on by a duppy brings on vomiting; to be touched by one causes fits. Duppies are wicked and can be bribed to do wicked things: rum or money thrown on a grave that is then beaten with a stick will make a duppy go and harm someone if he is told to do so.

Others roam of their own accord, but all must return to their graves by first light. If a duppy can be held from his grave until after cock-crow, he will be a harmless duppy for ever. Tobacco seed over doorways and windows will keep the duppy away.

*See also* **zombies**.

CONSULT: Zora Hurston, *Voodoo Gods,* J. M. Dent (1939); Joseph J. Williams, *Voodoos and Obeahs,* Allen & Unwin (1933).

## Eagle
*See under* **animals and birds**.

## Easter
*See under* **festivals**.

## Eckankar
'The ancient science of soul-travel'; American church of **astral projection** founded by Paul **Twitchell** at Las Vegas; a system of spiritual healing, spiritual and physical conditioning said to lead to 'God realization' through experiencing the release of the soul from the body.

CONSULT: Paul Twitchell, *Introduction to Eckankar*; *The Tiger's Fang*; and *The Far Country*, Lancer Books, New York (1971).

## Ectoplasm
A mysterious substance allegedly exuded from the natural orifices of a medium's body while he or she is apparently in **trance**; a substance which builds up into partial or complete **materializations**. The word, originated by Professor Charles Richet, a well-known physician and psychical researcher, is derived from the Greek words, *ektos* and *plasma* = 'exteriorized substance'.

Considerable argument surrounds the properties of ectoplasm, its origin and the effect of its outflow and return on the medium. Sceptics maintain that no such substance exists and that all photographs and the occasional rare specimen have shown it to be constituted of known physical substances such as egg-white, cheesecloth, etc. Spiritualists regard ectoplasm as the tangible proof of a physical medium's materializing powers and maintain that the substance has been established beyond doubt as matter, invisible and intangible in its primary state but assuming vaporous, liquid or solid conditions in varying states of condensation; has a smell reminiscent of ozone: varies in colour between white (the commonest) and black; is usually moist and cold to the touch; is sensitive to light and temperature; often seems to have folds or rucks in it when it first appears; is usually slow and reptile-like in mobility but can be amazingly quick; and is usually semi-fluid in consistency but has been known to become as solid as a rod of iron.

Most commonly, ectoplasm is described as a gelatinous and viscous mass seen to ooze from the mouth and slowly pour downwards until completely enveloping the medium; it may then proceed to build up into a materialized form, a psychic rod or a partial materialization. Its appearance sometimes varies according to its origin. In the case of Madame d'Espérance, where ectoplasm originated from her breasts, it appeared first as a luminous vapour; reported ectoplasm produced by Eusapia Paladino was described as a mass of swirling vapour; while other witnesses have described ectoplasm as first being·observed as luminous white spots about the size of a pea. Other investigations have described a 'dim phosphorescent column', a drop of luminous liquid or a white or vaporous mass as the first glimpse of ectoplasm. Often, while the drop or column or mass grows and moves, it seems to be tossed and agitated in every way for some time until suddenly it stops, and then 'out of it is born a living thing'.

Sudden light on ectoplasm seems to cause considerable inconvenience to the medium, even pain, as does the sudden jerking back into the medium of the ectoplasm, as may happen if any sudden attempt is made to touch or grasp the curious material. Conan **Doyle** recounted a case where a medium had received a bruise from breast to shoulder after the sudden retreat of ectoplasm, which has been likened to the snapping of an elastic band. The medium Franck Kluski is reported to have suffered an open wound; Evan Powell a bad chest injury; George Valiantine a black bruise; while other mediums are said to have suffered haemorrhage, unconsciousness and severe pain.

The investigator Baron von **Schrenck-Notzing** apparently obtained fragments of ectoplasm for laboratory examination, and his results spoke of a 'sort of transitory matter which originates in the organism in a manner unknown to us, possesses unknown biological functions and formative possibilities. . .'. As regards the structure, he reported 'conglomerates of bodies resembling epitheluim, real plate epitheluim with nuclei, veil-like filmy structures, coherent lamellar bodies without structure, as well as flat globules and mucus'. A bacteriological report stated: 'The substance is albuminoid matter accompanied by fatty matter and cells found in the human organism. Starch and sugar discoverable by Fehling's test are absent.'

On the other hand, Harry **Price**, in his examination of the 'ectoplasm' obtained in the presence of Helen Duncan, found it to be composed of wood-pulp and white of egg; he also produced photographic evidence of rubber gloves and cheesecloth and alleged that an X-ray examination had revealed that the medium had swallowed the necessary paraphernalia before the **séance**, evidently producing it by regurgitation as required.

*See also* **mediumship**; **spiritualism**; and, for a particularly spectacular example of 'ectoplasmic' production, **Crandon, Mrs L. R. G.**

CONSULT: Harry Edwards, *The Mediumship of Jack Webber*, Rider (1940); C. Flammarion, *Mysterious Psychic Forces*, Unwin (1907).


### Edwards, Harry (1893-1976)

Outstanding British practioner in **spirit healing** who worked from his 'sanctuary', Burrows Lea, Shere, Surrey, and claimed a 30 per cent rate of success for complete cures and 80 per cent for alleviation or improvement. Edwards maintained as a spiritualist (*see* **spiritualism**) that certain spiritual and universal laws exist which even God will not upset, so he rejected the idea that healing comes directly from God or that miracles can occur. He maintained, however, that he had been instrumental in 'taming' a whole range of 'incurable' diseases, including many forms of cancer, by employing and harnessing power from the **spirits** of the dead; Edwards claimed that he received something like 10 000 letters each week, and treated about 5 000 persons a year, the majority through 'absent healing', when the person concerned may not be aware that such 'healing' is being conducted but which nevertheless can produce remarkable results. Articles by Harry Edwards appeared regularly in *The Spiritual Healer*, a leading magazine devoted to spiritual healing that continues to be published monthly from Burrows Lea, Shere; many of his articles on various aspects of healing have been reprinted as leaflets. A record is also available from Burrows Lea on which Edwards describes spiritual healing and how it functions.

CONSULT: Harry Edwards, *The Power of Spiritual Healing*, Herbert Jenkins (1963); P. Miller, *Born to Heal*, Spiritualist Press (1962).

## Egyptian magic

The Ancient Egyptians were fascinated by the mysteries of creation and life and **death**, and their religion, rites and practices have attracted students of occultism throughout the ages. They represented their ideas on the cosmos, morality, the **double** or **'Ka'**, and rebirth in the form of symbols which sometimes contained undisguised eroticism (*see also* **phallic worship; sex magic**).

The two essentials of Egyptian **magic** are the serpent (the 'uraeus') and the scarab; and among the most powerful and mysterious magical signs is the Ankl or ansate cross, which may represent a human being (with the eye of the loop portraying the head); or the vaginal orifice being penetrated by a phallus (represented by a straight line); or a dam holding back the life-giving waters of the Nile, the maternal river. Egyptian magic embraced various **amulets**, a favourite one being composed of two outstretched fingers, a magic or benediction gesture in China, India and world-wide in Roman Catholic ritual; the other popular hand amulet was a clenched hand with the thumb (symbolizing the phallus) inserted between the first two fingers as a sign of the potentially mysterious procreative act. The ever-watchful guardian, Superior of Mysteries, was represented as a jackal, the god Anubis, while the scarab, representing the all-powerful sun god, was placed on mummified bodies near the position of the heart to help the dead on their journeys beyond the tomb (*see also* **mummification**).

CONSULT: Margaret A. Murray, *The Splendour That Was Egypt*, Sidgwick & Jackson (1949); Colin Wilson, *The Occult*, Hodder & Stoughton (1971).

## Eidetic imagery

Scientific name for a state in which people recall things they have seen earlier; a possible explanation for some reports of **visions** and 'visual **hallucinations**'. *See also* **Serios, Ted**.

## Elberfeld horses

Apparent mathematical wonders of the animal world discovered by William von Osten in 1891.

After being taught to count skittles by striking his hoof as many times as there were skittles on view, one of the horses began to perform seemingly astonishing mathematical calculations. Following the death of Osten in 1909, his work with the 'wonder horse' was continued by Herr Krall, a jeweller from Elberfeld, and he apparently taught four horses (one of them blind) not only the fundamental mathematical rudiments of addition, subtraction, multiplication and division, but also extracted square and cube roots. All answers were given by the horses stamping their hoofs. To signal the number forty-eight, for example, the horse would stamp four times with the left hoof and eight times with the right.

The dramatist Maurice Maeterlinck reported after a visit that one horse phonetically spelt out his name, solved almost immediately problems of which Maeterlinck maintained he did not know the answer himself, refused to give the square-root answer of a chance number which was afterwards found to have none, and seemed to express thoughts and feelings by stamping out the spelling of words by choosing cards with letters marked on them. After six months of teaching, the horses made no further progress, however, and sometimes 'said' that they were tired and declined to perform; mostly they seemed to possesss the intelligence of an eight-year-old child, but far in advance of such a child mathematically. No satisfactory explanation was ever discovered; precautions were taken to exclude the possibility of mind-reading or **telepathy**, and upwards of a dozen scientists vouched for the actuality of the facts of the 'talking' horses.

CONSULT: Maurice Maeterlinck, *The Unknown Guest*, Methuen (1914).

## Elder
*See under* **trees and plants**.

## Elements and elementals
The idea that everything was composed of differing combinations of the four basic elements, **fire**, air, earth and water, was accepted from a time some five hundred years before Christ until well into the seventeenth century. Each one of the four elements is said to have an individual class of spirit or elemental: gnomes being associated with earth, undines with water, sylphs with air, and salamanders with fire. Modern occultists have reinterpreted the idea of four elements to mean the four conditions in which energy can exist: gas = air, electricity = fire, solid = earth, and liquid = water. The same four elements provided a basis for attempts in **alchemy** at the artificial manufacture of gold.

The perfect man was thought to have four liquids (connected with the elements) in perfect balance: fire = yellow bile and irascibility; air = blood and confidence; earth = black bile and melancholia; water = phlegm and calmness. Symbolically, fire and air are regarded as active, positive, creative and masculine, while earth and water represent the passive, negative, receptive and feminine. The four elements have always been a part of **witchcraft** ritual, and in modern initiation ceremonies the initiate lies on his or her back within the **magic circle**, with arms and legs outstretched to correspond, with the head, to the five-pointed star (or **pentagram**), representing the four elements and the power that rules them all.

CONSULT: Richard Cavendish, *The Black Arts*, Routledge & Kegan Paul (1967); Grillot De Givry, *Witchcraft, Magic and Alchemy*, University Books Inc., New York (1958).

## Elixir of Life

*Elixir viae*, the elusive substance that was sought, along with the means of effecting transmutation of base metals into gold, by students of **alchemy** to prolong life indefinitely.

Those who are supposed to have perfected and possessed the Elixir of Life include the Count St-Germain, who won Madame de Pompadour's favour in 1759 with his 'water of rejuvenation' and who claimed to have lived for 2000 years; Sir Francis Bacon, who was thought to have 1000 years on earth and who many believe had a mock burial; the seventeenth-century Madame de Sévigné, whose methods included drinking human **blood** and eating vipers; George Berkeley (1685-1753), the Irish bishop and philosopher whose 'tar-water' owed its origin to the American Indians; and the Dutch alchemist Jan Baptist van Helmont (1577-1644), who was convinced that **Paracelus**, the German physician, had known the Elixir of Life and that it was contained in a 'secret' stone which could be dipped into liquids and then given to chosen people to drink – a miraculous medicine, the secret of which could only be revealed by inspiration.

Since belief in the Elixir of Life is a reflection of the theory that man is potentially divine, it is perhaps understandable that adherents of the idea are today somewhat rare, though certain occult and magical practitioners still base some of their rituals on their faith in the Elixir of Life.

CONSULT: Maurice Bessy, *A Pictorial History of Magic and the Supernatural*, Spring Books (1963); Richard Cavendish, *The Black Arts*, Routledge & Kegan Paul (1967).

## Elongation

The lengthening of the human body, a reported phenomenon associated with a few mediums (*see* **mediumship**), in particular D.

D. Home, who was reported to elongate as much as nine and twelve inches on occasions. Observers present maintained that they had been able to feel the flesh stretch and shrink. Devout nuns have reported similar sensations, and mediums who claimed to have experienced a partial elongation of the arms or legs have included Katie Cook, Eusapia Paladino and Alfred Vout Peters. Elongation has also been reported at occult and **witchcraft** rituals, and occasionally during manifestations at haunted houses.

CONSULT: E. J. Dingwall, *Some Human Oddities*, Home & Van Thal (1947); Nander Fodor, *Encyclopaedia of Psychic Science*, Arthurs Press (1934).

## Effigies
*See* **black magic; sympathetic magic.**

## Encausse, Dr Gérard
*See* **'Papus'.**

## Epworth
Scene of classic eighteenth-century **poltergeist** infestation at the Lincolnshire home of the Rev. Samuel Wesley (1662–1735). The disturbances seem to have originated during December (or possibly November) 1716 and to have continued through January 1717. They included 'dismal groans', 'strange knocking in divers places', the sound of running footsteps, crashing sounds, a winding noise. A creature something like a badger, or large white rabbit, was seen three times, as was a figure resembling a man in a loose nightgown. A doorlatch was lifted many times.

All the occupants of Epworth Parsonage experienced the disturbances, and so did many visitors to the house. On one occasion a great noise was followed into almost every room in the house, and it may be significant that the entity, nicknamed 'Old Jeffrey', manifested in a house full of girls and young women. In fact several witnesses reported that Hetty (the eighth of Wesley's sixteen children), then aged about nineteen, trembled strangely in her sleep and seemed to be much disturbed just prior to and during a 'visitation'. The Epworth poltergeist is one of the best-documented cases in the history of **psychical research**.

CONSULT: Harry Price, *Poltergeist Over England*, Country Life (1945); Peter Underwood, *Hauntings*, Dent (1977).

## Esbat
The compulsory weekly meeting for members of witch **covens**, held either in the open air at night, or inside a suitable building, preferably a church.

CONSULT: Christina Hole, *Witchcraft in England*, Batsford (1945); Margaret A. Murray, *The God of the Witches*, Sampson Low, Marston (1931).

## ESP
*See* **extrasensory perception.**

## Eternal preservation
*See under* **ancestor worship.**

## Etheric body, or double
*See* **double.**

## Eva C (c. 1890-c. 1943)
French **materialization medium.** *See under* **spiritualism.**

## Evil eye
The belief that certain people (especially those with blue or green eyes, and people with a squint) possess the power of injuring, bewitching or killing by means of a mere glance. Ancient records, including the writings of Virgil and the Bible, indicate the universal fear of the evil eye, a fear that reached its height during the heyday of the **witchcraft** mania, but has continued to this day when many people believe that gipsies, fortune-tellers and certain others have the power of affecting health and happiness by a glance or a more prolonged gaze.

The once-popular glass 'witch balls' have their origin in the fear of the evil eye, for by hanging one in the window it was thought that it could catch and nullify the effect of any such glance. In the late 1930s, King Alfonso XIII of Spain while in exile in Rome, was commonly thought to have the evil eye. Children and animals were thought to be particularly vulnerable, and any unexpected misfortune or illness affecting a young person or livestock would be considered the result of its having been 'overlooked'. **Charms** and **incantations** were common protections against the evil eye. One such precaution, a knotted cord, is still often a part of the equipment of the present-day witch, occultist or magician; incantations and **names of power** are repeated as the knots are tied, and this is thought to protect the wearer.

CONSULT: Rollo Ahmed, *The Evil Eye*, John Long (1936); Edward S. Gifford, *The Evil Eye*, Macmillan, New York (1958).

## Evocation
*See* **invocation**.

## Exorcism
The act of persuading evil **spirits** to abandon a person, place or object by command, ritual or prayer. Exorcism is used by the Christian Church to expel **demons** from persons who have, or believe they have, become possessed.

At first the power to perform exorcisms was considered to be a special gift which might be bestowed on anyone; later a special class of clergy, called exorcists, was entrusted with the practice; today anyone may perform an exorcism ritual, though the religious type of exorcism is usually performed by an ordained priest who has previously obtained special authorization from his bishop. There are a number of priests in the Church of England and the Roman Catholic Church who specialize in exorcisms and, indeed, carry out such services regularly; lay exorcisms are not infrequently conducted by occult practitioners who are well versed in **occultism** and **magic**. The principle of exorcism presupposes that it is possible to transfer a spirit or force from place to place by ritual acts and words, and while belief in such principles has decreased, the incidence of apparent or believed **possession** has grown.

Perhaps the commonest exorcisms are conducted to help persons who steadfastly believe that they are possessed by an evil spirit which is seeking to kill them or encouraging them to do bad things until they are afraid of the consequences. Very often treatment by a trained psychiatrist or medical practitioner with knowledge of psychosomatic illness would be more beneficial, but there is no doubt that the spectacle and impressive ceremony of exorcism does have an effect on some poeple. The adjuration usually begins with loud exortation addressed to the unseen spirit: 'I rebuke thee! I rebuke thee! I rebuke thee! I abjure thee and summon thee forth form this man. . .' Exorcisms are also carried out to purify and clear houses subjected to **hauntings** or **poltergeist** phenomena, and these may vary from a priest saying a prayer in each room to ritual fumigation; the sprinkling of holy water and continued visitations with **bell, book and candle.** Exorcisms by adepts of magic and the occult usually involve a **magic circle,** the conjuring by **invocation** of a good spirit to combat the evil.

one, some element of **sympathetic magic** and a symbolic **sacrifice** or ritual of **sex magic**.

An exorcism by a Church of England priest at Barnsley, Yorkshire, in 1975 was followed by the 'possessed' man killing his wife a few hours later, tearing out her eyes and tongue and causing her to choke on her own blood. No such tragedy has ever followed an occult exorcism, though there is not likely to be any lasting result whichever type of exorcism is used. Exorcist priests often sought to dispel evil spirits who were thought to be guarding buried treasure, and many exorcisms involved a circle being sprinkled with the **blood** of a black lamb and a white pigeon (making the rite one of **black magic**), the wearing of a new surplice and tall pointed cap and the timing of the ceremony for midnight. Christian exorcisms for the protection of a person ended with the sealing of the nine openings of the body with Holy Water so that no evil influence could regain entrance.

CONSULT: Roger Baker, *Binding the Devil*, Sheldon Press (1974); Christopher Neil-Smith, *The Exorcist and the Possessed*, James Pike (1974); John Richards, *But Deliver Us From Evil*, Darton, Longman & Todd (1974).

## Extra

An apparently **paranormal** manifestation, usually a face, that appears on an otherwise normal photograph; most frequently in photographs taken of mediums with the express purpose of obtaining an extra, but also occasionally on photographs where nothing unusual is expected, as sometimes happens in photographs taken at haunted houses. *See also* **psychic photography**.

## Extrasensory perception (ESP)

The faculty of receiving or transmitting information through means other than the known senses; the **'psi'** of the psychical researcher. **Clairvoyance** and **clairaudiance** are the ESP of objects or events, **precognition** is the ESP of future events, and **telepathy** is the ESP of direct contact between one mind and another without the use of the senses or muscles: these are the recognized types of extrasensory perception.

Such common experiences as 'just knowing' something is about to happen before it comes to pass and inexplicably being aware of some danger or tragedy before it happens are probably forms of ESP; **dreams** are sometimes vehicles for extrasensory communication, as is **dowsing**. ESP in various forms often diminishes with age: children apparently possess the faculty more strongly than most adults. Animals also appear to possess these mysterious forces which function at an unconscious level.

*See also* **Rhine, Joseph Banks**.

CONSULT: D. H. Rawcliffe, *The Psychology of the Occult*, Derricke Ridgway (1952); Paul Tabori and Phyllis Raphael, *Beyond the Senses*, Souvenir Press (1971); G. N. M. Tyrrell, *Science and Psychical Phenomena*, Methuen (1938).

## Eyeless sight

Common name for **paroptic vision** or derma-optical perception, sometimes called 'skin vision'; the apparent ability to 'see' objects when denied the use of the eyes.

Certain 'psychics' specialize in the production of extraordinary 'stunts' which do not seem to be explicable by trickery and are probably to be explained in a hypersensitivity of the finger-tips. Frederick **Marion** was such a person, and his autobiography is a fascinating record of apparent 'eyeless sight'. He carried out experiments under the observance of such authorities as Sir Julian Huxley, Harry **Price**, Professor R. H. Thouless and Dr B. P. Wiesner. Experiments in the United States have convinced investigators that when colour is distinguished by finger-tip vision, a delicate temperature sense is indicated, black, for example, being slightly warmer than white; while Russian investigators have found that colours can feel distinctly different, some smooth, others sticky and still others rough. Yellow, in the Russian experiments, was described as 'very slippery', green as 'sticky', orange as 'very hard' and violet as 'rough'. Dr Adam Novomeisky pointed out that, starting at each side of the middle colour in the colour spectrum, the colours apparently become increasingly rough towards both ends of the spectrum. Investigation into the phenomenon of eyeless sight is of potential value to blind people, and is almost certainly one so-called **paranormal** faculty that has a completely scientific explanation.

CONSULT: Sheila Ostrander and Lynn Schroeder, *Psychic Discoveries Behind the Iron Curtain*, Prentice-Hall, N.J. (1970); Jules Romains, *Eyeless Sight*, Putnam (1924).

# F

## Faculty X

Term coined by the author Colin Wilson to cover the latent power that the human mind has to reach beyond the present to other realities of time and place. Faculty X covers that sense that can be experienced momentarily of being present at past or distant places; it is the power to grasp reality, and the power that unites the two halves of man's mind, the conscious and the subconscious.

CONSULT: Colin Wilson, *The Occult*, Hodder & Stoughton (1971).

## Fairies

The belief in the existence of the 'little people', not only fairies but also of other diminutive races, pixies, hobs, goblins and gnomes, is widespread, persistent and of constant interest to the folklorist. Medieval legends and romances speak of the realm of fairyland with its king and queen, royal court and lesser subjects, an idea that has enriched our literature, poetry and art. Many perfectly sensible people insist that they have encountered a fairy-like creature at least once in their lifetime, and there have been some remarkable fairy reports in the twentieth century, notably the **Cottingley** case, where two girls produced photographs that have never been satisfactorily explained.

Air Chief Marshall Lord Dowding, after investigating hundreds of reports, came to the conclusion that there was sufficient intelligent evidence for people to believe in fairies, yet the belief disappeared to a great extent, though the fairies of pantomime and the Christmas tree still capture the imaginations of children. Ireland is still rich in fairy and 'little folk' tales, fairy trees and wells, changelings, **lepracauns**, water fairies and **spells** and enchantment.

Apart from the common people of fairyland, tradition asserts that there are tutelary fairies, guardians of one particular family; heroic fairies of romantic legend; nature fairies associated with streams and lakes and woods; and mischievous boggarts who delight in misleading travellers and playing practical jokes. Fairies vary in size and appearance, but often wear green; the ordinary ones are often beautiful, but the brownies are grotesque and the boggarts have long and sharp noses. Whether fairies are fallen angels, the dead who have died before their time, or a pre-Celtic and nocturnal race that once inhabited these islands, the realm of fairyland is a world that many people would like to believe in, and a surprisingly large number quietly accept.

CONSULT: Katharine Briggs, *A Dictionary of Fairies*, Allen Lane (1976); Thomas Keightley, *The Fairy Mythology*, Bohn's Antiquarian Library (1850).

## Fairy rings
Popular names for dark green circles that occur on lawns and meadows. They are the result of mushroom fungi in the soil, circles that increase annually as the spawn radiates from the centre outwards at a more or less equal rate. In folklore, **fairies** are said to dance round the rings at midnight, and as places with potential occult power, the rings are sometimes used by followers of **witchcraft** and **occultism**.

## Faith healing
Another name for **spirit healing**, the term preferred by the spiritualists, though it is a simple psychological fact that any healing is at least two thirds a mental process.

Faith healers do not accept that there is such a thing as an incurable condition, and many of them claim high success rates with serious cases that have been given up as incurable by the medical profession. Some healers maintain that they are only able to do their work with the help and cooperation and 'active' assistance of dead physicians; others claim that they are a channel through whom God heals. Most healers (like for example, Harry **Edwards**) have a private 'sanctuary', 'sanctum' or 'surgery'. Here they meet their patients, talk to them, place their hands on or about the affected part and sometimes join in prayer with them.

Certain physical disabilities are occasionally cured or alleviated instantaneously, while other conditions apparently respond to extended treatment. 'Absent healing' is often practised by faith healers who add a patient's name to a list of those for whom the healer and his helpers regularly pray and concentrate; sometimes absent healing has proved beneficial without the patient being aware that the healer is working on his behalf. Most faith healers are spiritualists (*see under* **spiritualism**), and many believe that dead physicians continue their healing work after death, though healers on earth often have no medical training whatever. For this reason, and because they may raise the hopes of patients and encourage them to undertake tasks that may be dangerous to them, the medical profession as a whole tends to frown on faith and spirit healers, though a number of doctors and a few hospitals cooperate with some healers since they recognize the considerable psychological benefit that patients can derive from unorthodox healing methods. There certainly have been a number of remarkable cures that can be attributed to faith healers and for which orthodox medicine can claim no credit.

CONSULT: George Chapman, *Extraordinary Encounters*, Lang Publishing Company (1973); L. Rose, *Faith Healing*, Gollancz (1968).

## Fakir

From the Arabic, meaning a spiritually poor person, but commonly ascribed to a religious Hindu or Mohammedan begger who lived on alms. The term has come to be applied in particular to Hindus who perform a variety of allegedly miraculous acts, such as being buried alive, sleeping on a bed of nails, snake charming – even the legendary **Indian rope trick**; and to Islamics who, renouncing the world and putting their trust in Allah, continually rove the country. Some fakirs subject themselves to unbelievable torture and self-mutilation as a means of acquiring spiritual or magical power; some bath in as many sacred rivers as possible, and seem to require hardly any rest; still others remain stationary in water up to their waists, or are to be found lying, sitting or standing on one spot for years on end. Many cover parts of their bodies with ashes, and such an appearance, together with the characteristic possessions – staff, crutch, begging bowl and tongs – indicate these 'holy' men and draw attention to their need for alms.

CONSULT: Hereward Carrington,'Hindu Magic', *Annals of Psychical Science* (1909); Paul Henze, *Fakirs, Furristes et Cié*, Paris (1926).

## Familiar

An important element in **witchcraft**: the **spirit** or **demon** which appeared in various forms and apparently attended and accompanied the witch or warlock.

A seventeenth-century *Guide to Grand-Jurymen* states: 'witches have ordinarily a familiar or spirit in the shape of a Man, Woman, Boy, Dogge, Cat, Foale, Fowle, Hare, Rat, Toade etc. And to these their spirits they gave names, and they meet together to Christen them.' The 'domestic' familiar was common in all parts of England long before the upsurge of witchcraft, when, however, it became a felony to feed, suckle or reward them; such familiars were always small creatures – a little dog, a small cat, a rat, a mole, a toad or a mouse – and they were usually kept in a box or pot in the witch's house, fed from time to time and often talked to. Thus the creature became tame and would follow its mistress wherever she went and return to her after it had worked its **magic**. A drop of witch's **blood** was always added to the animal's food so that it would become a part of her. 'Divining familiars' were often large animals: a horse or stag, a large bird or dog, and they did not belong to a witch or any particular persons, and any creature of the required kind could be used for **augury**, or in **divination**, or to draw **omens** from. The domestic familiar came into prominence during the trials of Essex witches in 1645–6 when the sensational reports of the witchfinders Matthew **Hopkins** and John Stearne resulted in familiars being regarded, erroneously, as an important and even essential part of a witch's outfit.

CONSULT: Christina Hole, *Witchcraft in England*, Batsford (1945); Margaret Alice Murray, *The God of the Witches*, Sampson Low, Marston (1931).

## Fertility magic
*See* **ithyphallic; phallic worship; sex magic**.

## Festivals
Since the days of the first farmer, man has observed customs involving **sympathetic magic** and seasonal ritual. Relics of such ancient festivals still survive, even in Western Europe, with old chants becoming nursery rhymes, **fire** festivals becoming associated with Guy Fawkes, pumpkin-head lanterns being made at Hallowe'en, and kissing under the mistletoe at Christmas.

*Christmas* is still one of the two great festivals of the year, and is pagan in origin. Christmas was derived jointly from the great Yule-feast of the Norsemen and the Roman Saturnalia (later the date was adopted by the church as the conventional anniversary of the death of Christ). This mid-winter celebration has always been a time of feasting and revelry, or exchange of gifts, dressing-up and a certain amount of sexual activity. The Saturnalia, a Roman orgy of sowing and husbandry that lasted from 19 December to 25 December, included choosing by lots of King of the Saturnalia, the ancient Lord of Misrule, usually a handsome young man who would be clothed in elaborate attire and attended by soldiers and maid servants and encouraged to indulge his passions to the full and taste every pleasure, no matter how base or shameful, for his merry reign would be short and at the end of the festivities he would be publicly castrated and have his throat cut on the altar of the god he had impersonated.

Such debauchery was abhorrent to the Christian Church, which sought to replace the pagan deities with saints. Yet the festival was far too deeply entrenched in popular favour and eventually the Church recognized the festival, providing it was presented in honour of the Christian God; so Christmas became fully established with many of its pagan elements intact. In many lands the spirit of Christmas is accompanied by a forbidding black companion, a ghost-like or **demon**-like figure, indicative of the old tradition that Christmas is a time of the year when **ghosts** and bad **spirits** are abroad.

The other great festival that is still celebrated (also pagan in origin) is *Easter*, originally a fertility rite in praise of Ostera, the Anglo-Saxon goddess of spring, with the traditional Easter eggs surviving from those heathen days and an annual public holiday enabling girls to wear new Easter bonnets or hats at traditional fairs, parades and general merrymakings. It is a moveable feast in the Christian calendar, Easter Day being calculated to fall on the first Sunday following the full moon of the vernal equinox.

One of the two nights of the year (*see also* Hallowe'en *below*) when the forces of evil were reputed to hold sway over the earth was *Walpurgis Night* (May Eve), when witches always gathered; and still today students of the occult consider 30 April to be an important date for casting **spells**, making **incantations** and performing magic practices.

Once *Beltaine*, the first day of the Celtic summer, as well as the middle of the Roman festival Floralia (celebrating the goddess of Flora, vernal productiveness), *May Day* itself became a great public holiday in medieval and Tudor England, with festivities, processions and merry-making beginning at dawn and lasting all day. All centred around the traditional maypole, which has been seen as a relic of even earlier **phallic worship**. May Day was one of the magic days of the year when **divination** and **prediction** were likely to have reliable results, as were **sorcery** and **magic** and occult practices which all had greater significance on that one day in the year. The Druidic custom of dragging one another through the smoke of May Day bonfires may have been a preliminary to human **sacrifice**.

Among today's May Day celebrations there survives the remarkable Padstow hobby-horse festival when the two hobby horses of rival teams (the Old or Red Ribbon 'Oss and the Blue Ribbon 'Oss) dance through the streets of the picturesque Cornish harbour town, following their respective bands. Each 'oss is a man covered in an enormous circular and full-skirted costume. The circular frame, about five feet across, is covered with black tarpaulin and completed with a horse's head at the front and a horse's tail behind. Each man wearing an "oss' sports a tall and pointed hat and a fierce face-mask, usually with whiskers and a lolling red tongue. Throughout the performance a 'teaser' dances backwards directing the 'oss with a curious padded sceptre. Both dance a series of small rapid steps to a haunting and persistent song, the "oss' repeatedly turning aside to pursue girls and women, sometimes catching one of them under his 'cloak'. Undoubtedly the Padstow hobby-horse dance was originally a fertility festival and there is little doubt that in olden days unwary females found themselves the centre of a sympathetic fertility rite.

Another ancient Cornish custom is celebrated each 8 May (unless that date falls on a Sunday or a Monday) at Helston, where the Furry or Flora (not Floral) Dance, dating from pre-Christian times, recalls the garlands once worn on Flora's Day. Now the local people, the men in morning dress and the women in garden-party costumes, assemble in the market place and dance their way up and down the street, round and round the town, and in and out the houses to a particular tune, called a 'faddy'; the 'Furry Song' recalls such misty characters as Robin Hood and St George, and speaks of the 'merry green wood' and of 'fetching the summer home'.

*Midsummer*, one of the principle days in the cycle of the sun and therefore of life on earth, has always been a time for bonfires (to strengthen the weakening sun and keep away bad spirits), a time for wheels to be covered with burning corn and rolled downhill to imitate the sun's descending course and to chase away harmful influences, for as the mighty sun began to lose its power, malevolent entities became more active. Midsummer Eve has long been regarded as the night when a person who has fasted, sitting in a church porch at midnight, will see the **spectres** of those parishioners who will die during the coming year; a night when the witches attended their **sabbaths**; a night when spirits and demons held unholy revelry in the vicinity of walnut trees and the evil power of darkness caused children begotten on Midsummer Night to possess the gift of the dreaded **evil eye**.

**Harvest time** was the end of the farmer's year and one of the most important of all primitive festivals associated with **death**, for had not the corn and other crops been nurtured underground where the dead reside? So rituals marked the festival all over the world, ceremonies that survive in Britain with the religious Harvest Festival service, formerly the Harvest Home, and the traditional Harvest Supper. The essential power that was thought to exist in the corn was believed to be contained in the last sheaf, and when this was cut it was subjected to various rites, including the making of **corn dollies**. Other, less pleasant, activities formerly accompanied harvest time in other lands. In India, for example, it was the custom, until brought to an end by the British authorities, to sacrifice a human being, often the descendant of previous victims. After the removal of all **hair**, the wretched person would be taken in procession to a virgin forest, anointed with oil and later, after being drugged, roasted over a fire and cut into small pieces which were ceremoniously buried in fields throughout the district. North American Indians use grotesque **masks** to drive away evil influences and ensure a bountiful harvest.

But it is **Hallowe'en** (31 October) that has the most superstitions attached to it. This is the day, or night, most used by present-day practitioners of the magic arts; the night when witches and warlocks rode to the **sabbath**, either on **broomsticks** or tabby-cats that changed into coal-black steeds; the night that **fairies**, goblins and bogies were abroad; when horrible fiends blighted crops and killed livestock, and babies and wives disappeared – stolen by wicked fairies and carried off to fairyland for a year and a day. Hallowe'en was Christianized as the eve of the feast of All Hallows, or All Souls' Day, originally introduced to commemorate Christian saints or martyrs on 13 May, but later moved to 1 November to displace the pagan festival of the dead. Hallowe'en was originally a festival of fire, so celebrated among the Celts, for whom it was the end of the Celtic year (the eve of *Samhain*) when they annually kindled a new fire to signal the new year and make sacrifices to the gods. This was the time of year when the sun was seen to reach the lowest part of its course, and was then thought to enter the dark gates of the underworld for a period: with the gates opening to admit the sun, the dead could return to the land of the living and the mysterious powers of the world beyond **death** could be surmounted and used. Now children with their pumpkin masks and fancy-dress dances keep alive the idea of Hallowe'en and recall the

night of terror that was the old festival observed by their forefathers.
CONSULT: C. A. Burland, *Echoes of Magic*, Peter Davies (1972); E. O.
James, *Seasonal Feasts and Festivals*, Thames & Hudson (1961).

## Fetch
Irish **double** or 'co-walker' of a person yet alive but soon to be counted
among the dead.
CONSULT: Lewis Spence, *Second Sight*, Rider (1951).

## Fetish
A supposed magic **charm** or **amulet**; a material, inanimate object that
is worshipped or respected because of its inherent virtue, either
temporary or permanent, and not because a god or **spirit** is believed to
reside in it or communicate through it.

The word 'fetish' dates from the fifteenth century when Portuguese
explorers encountered the worship of wooden and stone figures by
African tribesmen; Europe at the time was full of reputedly holy relics,
regarded as possessing magical virtue, and these were termed by the
Portuguese *feiticos* = 'charms'. In modern psychology (which
uses the term 'fetishism'), the wild enthusiasm about and adoration of
separate parts of the body (or even articles of clothing) to stimulate
sexual urges is reminiscent of the abandoned glorification of relics and
objects in religious cults. Common natural objects, such as a four-leaf
clover or a **horseshoe**, represent surviving beliefs in magical fetishism
for civilized mankind, while similar natural objects, impregnated by
medicine-men with 'magical' concoctions, extend the power of the
fetish to heal as well as protect. Native fetishism considers the fetish
either to contain **magic** powers or to act as a representative for a
particular spirit, and accordingly fetish figures vary considerably, as
do the fetish-like objects used in modern **witchcraft** and **occultism**.
CONSULT: Sir James George Frazer, *The Golden Bough*, Macmillan
(1913 edition); Alfred C. Haddon, *Magic and Fetishism*, Constable
(1906).

## Fire
One of the four elementary forces (the others being earth, air and
water), fire represented the seed of life, the agent of purification and
renewal. Since it was believed that the fire came originally from the
gods, it has been used in rites and **sacrifices** and **festivals** throughout
the ages in one way or another by every civilization. The **Druids** were

Masters of Fire, as were the alchemists (see **alchemy**), whose philosophy included the idea that physical substances, after being submitted to fire, left a residue of ash and smoke, representing respectively the body and the soul. Fire was, and still is, an essential element in magical practices, and the idea of fire **magic** persists in many hearth **superstitions**, including the notion that a poker placed upright against the bars of a fire (forming a cross) helps to make the fire burn brighter; and also the belief that the future can be read in the ashes of a fire.

CONSULT: Mircea Eliade, *The Forge and the Crucible*, Rider (1962); A. A. Krappe, *The Science of Folk-lore*, Methuen (1962).

## Fire immunity
*See* **fire-walking**.

## Fire-walking
A very ancient religious **festival** rite common to many races throughout all ages and still surviving in some parts of the world; it was originally performed in spring to ensure a plentiful harvest.

Details vary, but, in substance, priests, **fakirs,** holy men or devotees walk barefoot over scorching-hot stones, red-hot embers or glowing ashes with complete and utter immunity from burns. The phenomena was thought to be associated with a form of **possession** that induced anaesthesia; fire-walking was long thought to have a 'mental' explanation, and, indeed, Virgil (70–19 B.C.) in his *Aeneid* suggests that Europeans have followed the fire-walkers on to the fire without harm. This is explained by the professional fire-walker claiming to have extended his immunity to those that follow him.

Many reports of fire-walking are distorted and exaggerated. In 1935, Harry **Price** conducted a series of fire-walking experiments in England and reached the conclusion that the secret lies in the fact that each foot of the fire-walker comes into contact with the white-hot embers (surface temperature, 800 °C) for less than half a second, and that is for the entire foot; any one part of the foot was thus in contact only for a tiny fraction of a second. Price also established beyond any doubt that absolute confidence is essential in fire-walking, any hesitation resulting in burning.

CONSULT: Ernest de Martino, *Magic, Primitive and Modern*, Tom Stacey (1972); Harry Price, 'A Report on Two Experimental Fire-walks', University of London Council for Psychical Investigation, *Bulletin*, 1936.

# Firth, Violet Mary
*See* **Fortune, Dion**.

# Flagellation

Beating, whipping or scouging. Many of the **festivals** connected with fertility rites (*see also* **phallic worship; sex magic**) presented opportunities for the gods to be propitiated in various ways that would express the lengths to which men and women would go to secure their approval, shown by the gift of fertility. The Roman festival of Lupercolia, celebrated each 15 February, consisted of near-naked men armed with whips striking everyone within reach, but especially the equally near-naked women who invariably sought to place themselves so as to receive as many blows as possible; for it was considered that flagellation of this nature, and at this time, ensured the fruitfulness of both the women and the men.

Participants in **black magic** rites most frequently achieve ecstasy through some sensual activity, such as perverse sexual practices, homosexuality, flagellation, even cannibalism. Early sects (of **Satanism**), including the Brethren of the Cross in 1453, practised flagellation to provide power for Satan to expel Christ from heaven. Flagellation has always been an essential part of the practice of **witchcraft**, and is still so today, either in actuality or symbolically. It seems that flagellation is a mixture of pleasure and pain; witches have told of displeasing their leader at the **sabbath** so that they would be whipped; Isobel **Gowdie** said she teased the **Devil** so that he beat her with cords. Yet, to most witches, the sabbath was the source of ecstatic pleasure, and it seems possible that the flagellation and other activities represented a pandering to the sadistic and masochistic elements inherent in men and women.

Flagellation and self-flagellation for religious motives was a custom of the Church from its earliest years, and today is still a feature of some religious creeds. Flagellation has been regarded as an aphrodisiac since the thirteenth century when one abbot wrote: 'It is necessary for those who bewitch the brain and mind by their appearances of loveliness and charms, and who reduce virtue by chastity to extreme narrowness; it is necessary for their genital muscles to be cleaned with rods and whips so that vital spirits be torn away, and indeed that lustful movements be excited to obtain the required results.' Many of today's occultists agree with this principle: that in awakening erotic desires for magical purposes, the harder one works the more merit one receives.

CONSULT: Rollo Ahmed, *The Black Art*, John Long (1936); Richard

Cavendish, *The Black Arts*, Routledge & Kegan Paul (1967).

## Flying ointment

Essential feature of a witch's ingredients for flying, and reportedly a part of every witch's repertoire. It would appear that a witch had to cover her whole body with the ointment before she could fly naked to the **sabbath**, either seated astride a hayfork, a shovel, a cleft stick, a **broomstick**, or unaided. Some authorities maintain that the ointment need only be applied to certain parts of the body: the breasts, armpits and genitals. The ointment appears to have been either black or dark green and to have been manufactured from noxious substances which included the **blood** of bats, fat of babies, hellebore root, hemlock, soot, aconite and belladonna; the aconite would be likely to cause feelings of excessive excitement, and the belladonna delirum. Nevertheless it is difficult to dismiss all accounts of flying witches in terms of imagination, dreams or **hallucination**.

CONSULT: Richard Cavendish, *The Black Arts*, Routledge & Kegan Paul (1969); Margaret A. Murray, *The Witch-Cult in Western Europe*, Clarendon Press, Oxford (1921).

## Flying saucers

*See* **unidentified flying objects**.

## Fort, Charles Hoy (1874-1932)

American writer who collected some 100 000 press-cuttings about strange 'natural' occurrences and wrote four books, *The Book of the Damned* (1919), *New Lands* (1923), *Lo!* (1931) and *Wild Talents* (1932) – later published in one volume under the title *The Books of Charles Fort* (1941). These books are full of extraordinary happenings: green rain, blue moons, exploding hailstones, showers of fish or frogs or nails, strange appearances and disappearances, **poltergeist** disturbances, strange lights and luminous bodies, all fully documented with references. He also recounted (again with references) the most astounding coincidences. With tongue in cheek, he presented outrageous theories and hypotheses, conceiving a sort of cosmic poltergeist and inventing terms, such as **teleportation**, for strange flights of articles. The books are a mine of information on weird happenings which appear to have no explanation, and Charles Fort has become something of a cult figure in the United States. A Fortean Society was founded in New York City in 1931.

CONSULT: *The Books of Charles Fort*, Henry Holt, New York (1941);

D. Knight, *Charles Fort, Prophet of the Unexplained*, Gollancz (1971); Louis Pauwels and Jacques Bergier, *The Dawn of Magic*, Anthony Gibbs & Phillips (1963).

## Fortune, Dion (1891-1946)

Pseudonym of Violet Mary Firth who, brought up on the writings and religion of the founder of Christian Science, Mary Baker Eddy, became one of the great modern occultists, a 'priestess' and a practising magician. She joined the Order of the **Golden Dawn** and became a disciple of Aleister **Crowley**. Her books are some of the most important for students of the occult, and those published as novels often contain true case-histories and self-revealing observations to a remarkable degree. She regarded her enlightenment and inner wisdom as being the result of contact with elemental forces; was convinced that most people have magical power but are without knowledge of how to use it; and believed that, during the course of major initiation, she received direct teachings from other planes of consciousness: a process she described in her book *The Cosmic Doctrine* (1966).

CONSULT: Dion Fortune, *Moon Magic*, Aquarian Press (1958 reprint); *Psychic Self-Defence*, Aquarian Press (1959 reprint).

## Fortune-telling
*See* **divination**.

## Fourth dimension

A theoretical extra form of space that could have an important place in the explanation of some psychic phenomena. The fourth dimension is conceived as an additional direction: a line has one dimension, length; a surface two dimensions, length and breadth; a solid three dimensions, length, breadth and thickness; a fourth dimensional space-time continuum would specify the time of an event in addition to the accepted three spatial coordinates. Thus we have the supposed or assumed fourth dimension of space whose relation to the recognized dimensions of length, breadth and thickness is analogous to that borne out by any one of these to the other two. According to such a theory, postulated by the German physicist and astronomer, Professor Johann Zöllner, mediumistic and other psychic phenomena would lose their mystic or mysterious character and pass into the domain of accepted physics and physiology. In fact the conception has already been used by some investigators of **paranormal** and occult phenomena to explain certain superphysical manifestations which otherwise seem inexplicable.

### Fox sisters, Kate (1841-92) and Margaret (1838-93)
Pioneer mediums. *See under* **spiritualism.**

### Furry or Flora dance
*See under* **festivals.**

### Future, foretelling the
*See* **prediction.**

# G

## Gardner, Gerald Brosseau (1884-1964)

Eccentric British dabbler in occult practices, and **witchcraft** revivalist. After many years in the Far East connected with rubber plantations and customs work, he returned to England in 1936 and encountered by accident a group of witches in the New Forest who maintained that witchcraft was in fact the old pagan religion of Europe, still surviving underground. Gardner, who had long been interested in strange practices and **occultism** in general, became a willing convert, and before long he had founded a museum of magic and witchcraft on the Isle of Man; joined the Council of the Folklore Society; acquired, somewhat mysteriously, the degrees of M.A., Ph.D. and D.Litt; revived the still surviving interest in modern witchcraft; and written books on the age-old practices and beliefs of the **white magic** witch cult – according to Gardner, a pre-classical Greek and pre-Christian religion that had its roots in the Stone Age. His first and most influential book on the subject, *Witchcraft To-day*, carried an introduction by Dr Margaret **Murray**.

CONSULT: Gerald Gardner, *Witchcraft To-day*, Rider (1954); Francis King, *Sexuality, Magic and Perversion*, Neville Spearman (1971).

## Garlic
*See under* **trees and plants**.

## Garratt, Eileen J. (1893-1970)
British **trance** medium who founded the Parapsychology Foundation in New York. *See also* **R101 case**; **spiritualism**.

## Geller, Uri (b. 1946)
Controversial Israeli whose startling feats, especially of metal bending and breaking, have aroused considerable interest in the scientific

world and among the general public in the 1970s. His claim of detailed 'voice communication' with beings from outer space was received with scepticism, but the so-called 'Geller effect' has been found to exist in many other people, especially children, who can also bend spoons seemingly by mind-power alone.

Geller had a **vision** as a child, and was originally a stage performer who specialized in 'telepathic' demonstrations and blindfolded reading. Later he submitted himself to five weeks of controlled laboratory experiment at the Stanford Research Institute in the United States, but 'postponed indefinitely' a long-projected meeting with a panel of experts organized by the *New Scientist* magazine and side-stepped invitations to investigation by the British **Society for Psychical Research**. He has also submitted to a few tests at London's Birkbeck College, but there is controversy surrounding all the tests, and some doubts have been cast on the quality of the investigators. Geller always seems to be accompanied by an entourage, and almost invariably by an atmosphere of confusion in which it is very difficult to establish satisfactorily that **paranormal** activity has actually taken place. Nevertheless Geller has impressed people like Professor Fredbert Karger of Germany's Max Planck Institute for Plasma Physics, Dr Wernher von Braun, rocket designer for the United States, the Apollo astronaut Edgar Mitchell and Professor Gerald Feinberg of the Department of Physics, Columbia University.

Geller's mentor, associate and biographer, Andrija Puharich, is something of an electronic genius and has a number of radionic patents to his credit. It has been suggested that Geller (who says he has never read a book in his life) uses a minute and delicate radio *inside* a tooth, but there are technical difficulties to any known device of this character. Geller has refused to undergo tests in laboratory conditions under strict control, and only submits to examination of his powers when it suits him. On the other hand, he apparently converted Professor John Taylor during a television demonstration, and also Bryan Silcock, science correspondent of the *Sunday Times*, who maintains that he saw Geller bend a key without touching it in a taxi. And, as the result of a test organized by the *Sunday People* newspaper while Geller was in France, when he shouted 'Bend!' at a prearranged time, hundreds of people claimed that their cutlery had reacted or their broken watches started. Dr Hugh Pincott and members of the ESP Investigation Committee of the Society for Psychical Research are carefully examining all these reports.

Professional conjurers and members of the Magic Circle have

insisted that they can reproduce anything that Geller has done, and that there is nothing in any of his feats that need be of paranormal origin; on the specific subject of metal bending, they point out that mercury nitrode rubbed into most metals will erode the metal structure and cause it to be bent easily. The American magician Harold Braunhut has suggested that the secret lies in a device known to magicians as a 'twister' that Geller wears in his belt. During an exhibition in front of television cameras in November 1973, Geller performed apparent miracles which prompted Professor John Taylor to say that science had no explanation; later, however, it transpired that the forks bent during the programme had been in Geller's dressing room, unguarded, before the show.

CONSULT: Uri Geller, *My Story*, Robson Books (1975); John Wade, *The Trade of the Tricks*, Elm Tree Books (1974).

## Gemini
*See* **zodiac**.

## Geomancy
The art of **divination** where pebbles, sand, seeds, sticks, arrows, small bones, marbles, jewels or even earth itself is cast to the ground and divination drawn from the configurations made by the scattered objects. The term is also used for divination practised by observing the forms taken by **fire** ash in a hearth; by leaves that have fallen into a pool; or by ink blots, or pencil dots and marks made at random on paper. A certain amount of imagination is usually required for the seer to interpret any kind of pattern, and so practioners of this type of divination often 'magnetize' or 'bless' the materials used and thereby claim a special faculty for observing important signs.

CONSULT: Richard Cavendish (ed.), *Man, Myth and Magic*, 112-part work, Purnell (1970–72).

## Ghost Club
The oldest organization associated with psychic matters, the Ghost Club was founded (*c.* 1862) with the idea of unmasking fake mediums and investigating the psychic phenomena of the day by a select group of London gentlemen. In fact the club became so select that only eighty-two members were elected in the fifty-four years before the club wound up. Harry **Price**, however, revived the club in 1938; it was an immediate success and membership quickly had to be limited. Price ran the club on lines more in accord with the times: women were

admitted to membership and he emphasized that the club was not and never had been a spiritualist organization; in fact Price aptly described it as 'a body of extremely sceptical men and women who get together every few weeks to hear the latest news of the psychic world and to discuss every facet of the **paranormal** . . .'. Members at this time included people like Professor C. E. M. Joad, Sir Julian Huxley, Algernon Blackwood, Sir Ernest Jelf (Master of the Supreme Court), Sir Osbert Sitwell and Lord Amwell. The club continued to be successful until the war curtailed its activities and meetings ceased soon after the sudden death of Harry Price in 1948.

The present club was revived a few years later, and the present Council includes Peter Underwood (President) and Tom Perrott (Chairman). Special guests at annual dinners in recent years have included Air Chief Marshall Lord Dowding, Donald Campbell, Beverley Nichols, Henry Williamson, Colin Wilson, Dennis Wheatley and Sheila Scott. The Ghost Club is a place where people who are interested in unusual subjects can meet from time to time to discuss topics of interest and hear leading experts on a wide variety of subjects reveal to the club the latest developments in all branches of psychic investigation. The *New York Times* once described the club as 'the place where sceptics and spiritualists, mediums and materialists, meet on neutral ground'. Details of membership can be obtained from Peter Underwood, The Savage Club, Fitzmaurice Place, Berkeley Square, London W1X 6JD.

CONSULT: Harry Price, *Search for Truth*, Collins (1942); Peter Underwood, *A Host of Hauntings*, Leslie Frewin (1973).

## Ghost Dance

An emotional religious movement that spread like wildfire through the Sioux Indians at the end of the nineteenth century when their tribe and culture were disintegrating.

During an eclipse of the sun, and while he was suffering a high fever, the son of a Red Indian prophet had an experience which inspired the Ghost Dance. He believed that he went up to heaven and saw God and all the people who had died, and God told him to return to earth and instruct his people to be good and love one another, and he gave the Ghost Dance to the Indian people. The prophet told the Red Indians what they wanted to hear: that the white man would vanish from the earth and the Indian tribes emerge renewed; that the buffalo would return to the plains; that the Indians killed in battles with the white man would return from the dead; and that the old ways of life would continue for ever. It was only necessary for the Indians to abandon alcohol, farming and traditional mourning rites, since the day of resurrection was at hand, and they were to perform the Ghost Dance: a slow and shuffling movement unlike any other Indian dance.

The dancers formed circles with intertwined fingers and slowly followed the movement of the sun, both men and women taking part, with singing but no musical accompaniment; it was a dance that had to be performed for five consecutive days. **Hypnosis** was also used to induce **trances** and apparent communication with the dead, and the participants wore the cloth or buckskin 'ghost shirt' reputed to render the wearer immune to the white man's bullets. But the shirts proved ineffective in the decisive battle at Wounded Knee, and there, for all practical purposes, the Ghost Dance ended. And with it the last hopes of the Indian tribes.

CONSULT: William Howells, *The Heathens: Primitive Man and his Religions*, Gollancz (1949).

## Ghosts

Generally accepted term for appearances, images or **apparitions** of the dead.

Evidence for the appearance of spontaneous ghosts is as old as recorded history and sightings have been reported from every part of the world. There are similarities and differences in the descriptions of ghosts and their behaviour, and it seems likely that there are a number of different types of ghosts. Most witnesses agree that the spontaneous ghost of fact is not the wispy, transparent, ethereal figure of fiction but apparently substantial and three-dimensional, though it does often suddenly disappear and material walls and locked doors are no bar to its movements. There is good evidence for 'ghosts with a purpose', apparitions that seem to materialize for a specific reason – to draw attention to lost papers, to put to rights a wrong or to show the circumstances of their death, for example – and once this particular matter has been resolved, the ghost is seen no more. There is good evidence also for 'death-bed visions', appearances of a dying or recently dead person to a relative or a friend, often many miles distant, who is not aware of the death until later when it may often be established that the death took place about the time the ghost was seen.

There are many convincing reports of 'animal ghosts', apparitions of domestic and wild animals; and of 'haunted inanimate objects', particularly furniture. And there are certainly specific areas of ground that are repeatedly the scene of curious reports of apparent ghosts or ghostly manifestations. The traditional ghosts (and there are more ghostly nuns and monks than any other category) are those that walk in one particular place and are always doing one particular thing, such as the shrieking ghost of Catherine Howard at Hampton Court Palace and the phantom nun at **Borley**. It seems likely that such ghosts (if they exist outside the minds of those who see them) are a kind of atmospheric photograph and the idea that this type of ghost is basically a kind of 'tape recording' on the atmosphere (a view first put forward by Sir Oliver **Lodge** in 1900) is now accepted by many experts in this field. Indeed, there is considerable evidence to suggest that tragic and violent happenings can leave some kind of impression on the atmosphere which, under certain conditions and perhaps in the presence of certain people, can reappear.

Children often apparently see ghosts (*see* **invisible playmates**), and there are many credible accounts of ghost children. Some ghosts appear to be cyclic and reappear at regular intervals – be it a few hours or a few years – others seem to run down, almost like a battery, and come to be seen less distinctly and less often as years pass until finally they are seen no more. The ghost of oneself (a really frightening experience) is called a **Doppelgänger**. The **poltergeist**, another special type of ghost, usually manifests in the vicinity of an adolescent, moving objects, starting fires, causing articles to break and making various noises but not showing itself. The induced ghost of the **séance** room relies on the presence of a medium to enable it to materialize, (*see* **spiritualism**), but when one speaks of a ghost the reference is generally to a spontaneous appearance of the apparition of a dead person. Many of the thousands of newspaper reports of ghosts have no 'substance' in proof, but examination of the available evidence leaves no doubt that men and women with sound minds in sound bodies do sometimes see ghosts of dead persons in circumstances that rule out **illusion** or deception.

CONSULT: Dennis Bardens, *Ghosts and Hauntings*, Zeus Press (1965); Peter Underwood, *A Gazetteer of British Ghosts*, Souvenir Press (1971).

## Ghoul

A **demon** that feeds on human flesh, either alive or dead; it is the subject of many Oriental and Eastern legends, and certain members of a secret society in Haiti are said to turn into ghouls (or *baka*) and to feed on human flesh. Ghouls usually inhabit lonely places, deserts and mountainous regions – or graveyards. One writer and researcher, the late T. C. Lethbridge, considered ghouls to be the result of a kind of 'tape recording' of some unpleasant event which can be sensed by someone entering, for example, a house where a tragedy has taken place. The word ghoul is sometimes used to refer to **werewolves**, **vampires** and cannibal **spirits**.

## Gilles de Rais
*See* **Rais, Gilles de**.

## Glanville, Rev. Joseph (1636-80)
Philosopher, chaplain to King Charles II, prebendary of Worcester, an early Fellow of the Royal Society, but best-known for his third book, *Saducismus Triumphatus*, published posthumously in 1681. This contains detailed and personal investigations of the **Drummer of Tedworth** and other **poltergeist** cases, and contemporary evidence of **witchcraft**, **apparitions** and similar phenomena.

CONSULT: Harry Price, *Poltergeist Over England*, Country Life (1945).

## Glastonbury
Somerset town famous for its ruined abbey; for being the traditional site of the founding of Christianity in Britain; the enchanted Isle of Avalon and last resting place of King Arthur; and for such legends as the holy thorn, the 'Glastonbury Scripts' and the Glastonbury **zodiac**.

Christianity is said to have come originally to these islands during the first century A.D. when Joseph of Arimathea, the wealthy citizen who buried Christ, brought the Holy Grail to Avalon and, in response to a vision, built the first church at Glastonbury. Joseph is supposed to have planted his staff in the ground, and from it grew the Holy Thorn that blooms on the old Christmas Day (6 January); a story that is first recorded in 1716.

The 'Glastonbury Scripts' is the name given to a series of booklets containing communications obtained by **automatism** concerning the abbey and its history, edited by Frederick Bligh **Bond**, who told the story of the scripts, subsequent excavations and discoveries in *The Gate of Remembrance* (1918), *The Hill of Vision* (1919) and *The Company of Avalon* (1924). The Glastonbury Zodiac was discovered by Mrs K. E. Maltwood, a practising occultist, who, using an Ordnance Survey map of the area, found, by utilizing ancient natural features, roads, field tracts, earthworks, banks, rivers and pools, that she had a zodiac very similar to that of modern astrology. She presented her case and her theories in the book which she wrote

about the subject, *Guide to Glastonbury's Temple of the Stars* (1964).
CONSULT: Roy Christian, *Ghosts and Legends*, David & Charles (1972); R. F. Treharne, *The Glastonbury Legends*, Cresset Press (1967).

### Glossolalia
**Psychical research** term for speaking in unknown tongues, especially in the case of mediums using a pseudo-language. This is a form of **xenoglossy**.

### Glacial cosmology
*See* **Cosmic Ice**.

### Golden Dawn
The Hermetic Order of the Golden Dawn was a magical secret society, one of the very few 'repositories of magical knowledge' in the West in modern times. It is generally thought to have been founded in England in 1887 by a group of three **Rosicrucians**, and it had eleven degrees divided into three groups.

The original members were Dr William Woodman, a Supreme Magus of the Rosicrucian Society, his friend Dr Wynn Westcott, a London coroner and Secretary-General of the Rosicrucian Society; and Samuel Liddell **Mathers**, a learned occultist and former Rosicrucian who prepared and published a translation of the **Key of Solomon**. W. B. **Yeats** became a prominent member, as did A. E. **Waite**, while other members included Arthur **Machen**, Allan Bennett, Algernon Blackwood, Aleister **Crowley**, Gerald Yorke, Dion **Fortune**, Charles Williams, Evelyn Underhill and Dr Israel Regardie (who published the secret rituals of the society in America). Lodges were also started in Edinburgh, Paris, Bradford and Weston-super-Mare.

Mathers (later he called himself MacGregor Mathers, and later still, le Comte de Glenstrae) moved to Paris, where he proceeded to perform **Egyptian magic** rites based on ideas of **Cagliostro**; while Westcott perpetrated an elaborate hoax whereby he received apparent evidence that the Golden Dawn was the English branch of a long-established Continental occult order. In 1891 Woodman died, and in 1897 Westcott withdrew. Mathers then reigned as Supreme until 1900, when he appointed Crowley to take over the London lodge, which Crowley did in typical barbaric and cavalier fashion. The following year Yeats, who had written some of the society's rituals, published a pamphlet questioning the continuance of the Golden

Dawn as a magical order, and gradually the order sank into abeyance after Crowley broke away in 1905 to found his own magic order. However, it was in a way superseded by a new society, the Stella Matutina, and while that society is itself now dormant, it is arguable whether it is entirely defunct.

CONSULT: Ellic Howe, *The Magicians of the Golden Dawn*, Routledge & Kegan Paul (1972); Israel Regardie, *The Golden Dawn*, Llewellyn, St Paul, Minn. (1970 edition).

## Golem

An artificially created human being; the Jewish forerunner of the Frankenstein monster; a being created by magical means that threatens to destroy its master; a body without a soul, according to tradition fashioned from clay by a sixteenth-century rabbi called Judah Loew or Jodah Low Ben Bezalel or, possibly, Elijah of Chelm. At all events, he was a Talmudic scholar who had the idea of defending the Hebrew community of Prague against massacre and plunder following false charges of ritual child murders.

In the Talmud, the word *golem* is used to describe Adam's body during the first hours of its existence before it was fully endowed with life and consciousness. The golem of Prague was credited with enormous strength, uncanny instincts and gigantic size, but it could be reduced to dust in certain conditions. One way to bring a golem to life was to walk round it, uttering the appropriate combination of letters and mystical names of God; and then by walking in the opposite direction and reciting the magic formula in reverse, the golem would again be rendered lifeless (a ritual used in occult circles to this day). The golem legend has been the subject of four early continental films, the best-known being the German *Der Golem*, directed by Paul Wegener for UFA in 1920.

CONSULT: Richard Cavendish (ed.), *Man, Myth and Magic*, 112-part work, Purnell (1970–72); G. Meyer-Meyrink, *The Golem* (trans. Madge Pemberton), Ungas, New York (1964).

## Goligher Circle

*See under* spiritualism.

## Gould, Commander Rupert Thomas (1890-1948)

A writer well-known for his researches into unexplained 'facts'. He joined the Royal Navy in 1906 and was invalided out in 1915; he cleaned and reconstructed four eighteenth-century time-keepers now on exhibition at the National Maritime Museum, Greenwich; but he is best known as the author of *Oddities* (1928), a book of unexplained facts that includes chapters on the **Devil's hoof-marks**, the moving coffins of Barbados and the Berbalangs (**vampire**-like creatures) of Cagayan Sulu. A second volume of unexplained facts, *Enigmas*, was published in 1929. Commander Gould was a member of the **Ghost Club**, and he lectured there on sea-serpents and the Loch Ness Monster (*see under* **animals and birds**). He also wrote *A Book of Marvels* (1937) and several monographs on horological and geographical research.

## Gowdie, Isobel

Pretty, young, red-haired and loquacious seventeenth-century Scottish farmer's wife who made a remarkable and completely spontaneous confession concerning **witchcraft** in 1662. She said that her baptism into witchcraft had taken place one night in 1647 on the downs of Drumdewin, where she met the **Devil** and there made a compact, denying her Christian **baptism**; and putting one of her hands on the top of her head and the other to the soles of her feet, she swore to the Devil all between her hands. The man in black then baptized her and marked her on the shoulder, sucking out **blood** at that point and sprinkling it over her head.

It was Isobel Gowdie who declared that a witches' **coven** consists of thirteen people. She described the method that witches use to take the shape of a hare, a cat, a crow and other creatures, and the method of coming out of the shapes. She also described the rites in which she took part: the digging up of an unchristened child from its grave; the ritual cutting of corn in the name of 'Our Lord the Devil'; the taking away of a cow's milk; the modelling in clay of the Laird of Park's children to destroy them; the raising of wind; the sexual intercourse with **demons** and **fairies** and with the Devil himself – whose member was bigger than any man's and whose semen was ice-cold.

The odd thing about Isobel Gowdie is that no one seems to have had any idea that she was a witch until she confessed of her own accord; even her husband seems to have been ignorant of the fact – if fact it was. Certainly her evidence was given clearly, and without alteration or confusion or contradiction, during the course of four separate examinations. Indeed, she expressed repentance for the crimes she had committed, and seems to have been fully aware of the certain consequences of her confession, the most detailed and interesting ever recorded in a British witchcraft trial. After she was hanged, her body was burnt to ashes in accordance with the traditional belief that only **fire** can destroy a witch.

CONSULT: Christina Hole, *Witchcraft in England*, Batsford (1945); and *A Mirror for Witchcraft*, Chatto & Windus (1957).

## Grandier, Urbain (1590-1634)

A priest of **Loudun** who was convicted of bewitching the Mother Superior and other nuns at the Ursuline convent and enslaving them to Satan. At his trial in 1634 the pact he had made with Lucifer, written and signed in his own **blood**, was produced.

Grandier was already a handsome and cultivated parish priest whose fondness for young women and lack of discretion in his affairs had caused him to be the subject of discussion among his superiors, matters having come to a head in 1630 when he was accused of fathering an illegitimate child on the daughter of a local dignitary. He was arrested and found guilty, but managed to persuade the Archbishop of Bordeaux to set him free and restore him to his clerical duties. By the time he had returned to Loudun, however, his enemies had hatched a conspiracy to finally discredit him.

The plot involved some of the sisters at the Ursuline convent, who were ready to allege that they were possessed by **demons** and to confess under **exorcism** that Father Grandier had bewitched them. The Mother Superior, Sister Joan of the Angels, eagerly cooperated, and she and several other nuns soon began to show bizarre signs of demonic **possession**, with faked convulsions, alarming breath-holding, erotic posturing and frightening distortions of their faces, voices and bodies. At the crucial moment Grandier's name was mentioned as the cause of the possession; the Mother Superior also named Grandier as well as two devils, Asmodeus and Zabulon, whom, she said, had been sent by the bewildered priest to possess the nuns. The story was enlarged and exaggerated with each telling, and as it spread like wildfire, the Archbishop of Bordeaux came to Grandier's rescue, sending his own doctor to Loudun (who pronounced that the nuns were not possessed). The archbishop also instructed the convent confessor, one of Grandier's enemies and a party to the plot, to cease his exorcisms, forbad anyone . else to carry out any such services without his permission and confined the nuns to their cells. Like magic, the convulsions and all semblances of possession ceased immediately.

Peace at the convent was short-lived, however, for Cardinal Richelieu (spurred on by political motives) ordered a hand-picked commission to investigate the matter. It was arranged that a Crown agent would appoint three priests to exorcize the nuns in public. When the frightened sisters repeated their accusations of possession caused by Grandier and displayed even more grotesque and frantic symptoms, Grandier himself was coerced into taking part in the services of exorcism, whereupon the nuns accused the perplexed priest of incest, fornication, debauchery and gross immodesty while the Mother Superior added fuel to the flames by asserting that the bewitchment had been achieved by Father Grandier tossing over the convent walls bouquets of flowers which were picked up by the nuns and novices. Grandier was arrested and imprisoned in the castle at Angers. There he was searched for signs of the **devil's mark**, and four insensitive areas were duly found.

At his trial Grandier had no chance: an investigating committee, appointed by Richelieu, took the place of secular court proceedure; evidence on behalf of the priest was ignored and would-be witnessess were persuaded not to give evidence in case they should find themselves being accused of **witchcraft** sympathies; the retraction of previous statements was disallowed; even Sister Joan herself was forbidden to address the court when it became known that she wanted to alter some of her earlier evidence; and finally the prisoner was denied any right to appeal. Damning evidence of Grandier's guilt was produced in the form of an alleged pact signed by the **Devil** himself and Beelzebub, Leviathan and Astoreth – a document which the prosecution asserted in all seriousness had been stolen from the Devil's files. Words in the document were found to be written from right to left – so-called mirror writing – and since it was believed that the Devil and his followers performed many actions in reverse, to show their hostility to Christianity, this was a devastating culmination to a trial where the outcome was never in doubt.

Grandier was found guilty of practising **magic**, using magic to harm others, and causing several nuns to be possessed by demons; he was sentenced to be tortured to the 'first and last degrees' (so that he would reveal the names of his confederates) and then to be burned alive. So extreme was the torture that, a contemporary writer tells us, the marrow oozed from his broken bones, though Grandier steadfastly refused to name anyone else and was eventually burned alive; not that his death made any difference to the apparent possessions at Loudun, which affected Sister Joan of the Angels in particular and lasted for another four years.

CONSULT: Aldous Huxley, *The Devils of Loudun*, Chatto & Windus

(1952); Kurt Seligmann, *Magic, Supernaturalism and Religion*, Allen Lane The Penguin Press (1971).

## Graphology

The systematic attempt to read character from the handwriting. No two people produce handwritting that is identical in every respect, and graphologists take into account not only the formation of words and the handwritting itself, but also such aspects as the speed at which the writing is executed, the angle and slope, size, space between letters and words, general layout and arrangement, position of punctuation and the use the writer has made of the three zones: upper, middle and lower, representing respectively the spiritual, immaterial and abstract; the emotions, habits, character and everyday life; the material, the physical and the sexual.

CONSULT: H. J. Jacoby, *Analysis of Handwriting*, Allen & Unwin (1929); H. A. Rand, *Graphology*, Peter Owen (1962).

Upper zone

Middle zone

Lower zone

*Graphology: the three zones in handwriting*

## Great Amherst mystery, the
*See* **Amherst mystery, the great**.

## Great Beast, the
A mythical creature described in the Apocalypse as 'a beast rising out of the sea, with ten horns and seven heads . . . and a blasphemous name upon its heads' to which the **Devil** gave his power and great authority on earth; the Antichrist, and the name by which the magician Aleister **Crowley** called himself. A 'great beast' has been said to have been conjured up by magicians and occultists throughout the centuries and to have appeared within **magic circles**.

## Gremlins
Mythical air **spirits** or **imps** that rode in aeroplanes and made

aviators' lives a misery, moving or removing objects, making odd noises, interfering with the controls and generally annoying airmen of the Second World War. The origin of the word 'gremlin' is said to be the amalgamation of the name Grimm (of fairy tale fame) and Fremlin, producer of the popular Elephant Ales, by the men of a British bomber squadron in India in the 1930s; and it was probably coined as a frivolous explanation for the strange anti-gravitational phenomenon that takes place when an aircraft makes sudden and violent changes of direction, causing loose articles to be temporarily suspended in mid-air.

## Grenier, Jean

French thirteen-year-old boy who, in the seventeenth century, reportedly turned into a wolf-like beast and attacked, killed and ate animals and human beings.

The matter came to light following an account by some teenage girls who had noticed a disturbance among the sheep on a hillside. Going to investigate, they had come upon a youth seated on a log – a lad whose appearance surprised and somewhat frightened them. His unruly and long hair was tawny red, covering his narrow brow and almost hiding his dark olive face and his small, deep-set and cruel eyes. His teeth were strong and canine in appearance, and protruded over his lower lip even when his mouth was closed. His hands were large and powerful, the nails black and pointed like talons. His clothing was nothing but rags, revealing lean and powerful limbs. The youth had told the startled girls that sometimes he wore a wolf-skin, and that when he did he became a **werewolf**. As he described killing and eating dogs, sheep and little girls, his listeners turned and fled from the frightful creature.

The wolf-boy, Jean Grenier, for that was his name, often told another village girl how he had sold himself to the **Devil** in return for the power of being able to turn himself into a wolf. When this girl returned home one day, torn and bleeding and tearfully relating how she had been attacked by the wolf-like creature with red hair and a small head, her parents and the rest of the villagers were reminded of several little girls who had disappeared and went to the authorities. Jean was apprehended, and in court related that three years or so earlier he had met a black man in the depths of the forest; a man who had later 'signed' him with his nail on each thigh, given him a salve and a wolf's pelt. Thereafter, whenever he used the unguent and the wolf-skin, he seemed to be transformed into a wolf, and in this shape had attacked and eaten animals and children.

The fact that the lad had attacked and killed was proved beyond doubt. On 6 September 1603 judgement was pronounced by President Dassis, who pointed to the age and intelligence of the boy, asserted that **lycanthropy** was a **hallucination**, and ordered Jean Grenier to be imprisoned perpetually in the strict Franciscan friary of St Michael Archangel at Bordeaux. No sooner had the boy been admitted there than he dropped on all fours and ran frantically about the cloisters and gardens until, finding a heap of bloody, raw offal, he quickly consumed it. Notwithstanding all the difficulties, the good friars did their best to look after the wolf-boy. He continued to act like a wolf from time to time, and at length died after seven years in confinement; during which time he was visited and independent accounts of his case placed on record.

CONSULT: Sabine Baring-Gould, *The Book of Werewolves*, Causeway Books, New York (1973); Montague Summers, *The Werewolf*, Kegan Paul (1933).

## Grimoire

Textbooks of the European tradition of ceremonial or ritual **magic** that reveal how to use **invocations** to summon infernal powers (**spirits** or **demons**) and how to use them when they appear: how to cause people to die; how to gain power over another person; and how to force women to submit.

Many old grimoires, full of prayers to God and the angels, instructions for fasting, self-mortification and elaborate preparation, still exist, including the celebrated **Key of Solomon**, of which a sixteenth-century copy is preserved in the British Museum. The earliest ('gramarye' is an old term for magic and enchantment) probably dates from the fourteenth century, and places great emphasis on **names of power**, as did all grimoires, where Jewish, Egyptian, Christian, Greek and Latin names abound. The *Lemegeton*, or *Lesser Key of Solomon*, contains powerful names which God revealed to Adam; the name that Shadrach, Meshach and Abednego cried out in the fiery furnace and were preserved; the name Moses used to bring down the plague of frogs upon the Egyptians and that which turned to blood the rivers of Egypt. The *Black Pullet* grimoire reveals the names that can discover hidden treasures, open locks and call up all the powers of heaven and hell.

The grimoires not only reveal the names of power, the individual spirits who should be conjured up for specific purposes and the preliminaries and preparation ritual; they also detail the necessary equipment, the special vestments, hat and shoes, the **pentagrams**, silk cloth, pen and ink, baton, parchment, **salt**, **fire**, water, sword, **bell** and trident, and give detailed descriptions of various **magic circles**.

CONSULT: Idries Shar, *The Secret Lore of Magic*, Muller (1957); A. E. Waite, *The Book of Ceremonial Magic*, University Books, New York (1961).

## Gris-gris
Protective **amulets** of African tribesmen; also the witchdoctors and magicians who wear them and control their use.

## Group-soul
Philosophical concept of a number of souls, bound together by one spirit, acting and reacting one with the other in the progression of psychic evolution. The possibility that individual minds can become integrated, completely, partially or temporarily, is regarded in **psychical research** as the theory of group minds, and Whately Carington explored and examined this idea in some depth.

CONSULT: Geraldine Cummins, *The Road to Immortality*, Nicholson & Watson (1932); Whately Carington, *Telepathy*, Methuen (1945).

## Guardian spirits
The belief that we all have individual guardian **spirits** who watch over our welfare is very old and widespread. In primitive societies, the belief is evident from symbolic acts and ritual appeals, while many civilized men and women retain an inexplicable conviction that 'something' warns them of impending danger, advises them on a certain course of action, and responds to their need for occasional special protection. Guardian spirits, many people believe, are responsible for this feeling, and it is interesting to note that modern man has turned what was originally a guardian spirit into intellectual or artistic talent, for *genius* was the Latin word for the spirit protector of a man or a place.

*See also* **lares**.

## Guide
Spiritualists believe that a helpful, benevolent and guiding influence protects everyone individually; and that when **mediumship** is developed, the guide acts as operator on the 'other side' and takes

charge of **séance** proceedings. Thus a guide (who is always in attendance) used the entranced medium's body to deliver direct or relayed messages to sitters. Such a guide also keeps away 'undeveloped' or evil **spirits** who might cause danger or confusion at sittings. *See also* **spiritualism**.

CONSULT: D. H. Rawcliffe, *The Psychology of the Occult*, Ridgway (1952).

## Guppy, Mrs Samuel (c. 1860–1917)

Physical medium. *See under* **spiritualism**.

## Guru

Hindu spiritual or religious instructor; a venerable person or teacher.

# H

## Hair
A magical link is said to be evident according to the law of **magic**
which asserts that anything that once formed part of a man's body (and
especially the head – the abode of forces of great power) retains its
connection even when physically detached from the parent body.
Hair, in common with nail clippings, blood and sweat, was often used
in **black magic** to create a link with the victim in rites of imitative and
**sympathetic magic**. Believing that such parts of the body retain, for
a while, the vital power of the body from which they originate, makes it
possible to affect that body, it was thought; perhaps even to draw
energy from the body by using a component of the body as a magnet.
Ritual burning of a lock of hair was said to project the pains of fire into
the body of the victim. The shaving of all body hair was thought to
render witches helpless and to neutralize their magic powers;
accordingly, witches and sorcerers were often depilated before
execution.

Clippings of a person's hair were a much-sought ingredient in the
preparation of a wax image fashioned in the likeness of the person to be
harmed: when the wax figure was scorched above a lamp and words
repeated over and over to the effect that it was not wax that was being
scorched but the heart, liver and spleen of 'so-and-so' (naming the
unfortunate individual), it was thought that the victim named would
feel the pangs of burning and, if the **charm** was continued, would
ultimately die. The effect was enhanced if other ingredients could be
obtained, such as soil from the centre of the footprint of the person
concerned, nail-parings, saliva, sweat, tears, **blood** and sexual fluids.
Many magicians, including Aleister **Crowley**, were careful to ensure
that none of their hair, nail-parings and so on fell into the hands of rival
magicians.

Hair was also one of the parts of the body that would be given up or sacrificed to preserve the whole; thus hair – or even, part of a finger – would be cut off to placate the evil influence or as an offering to the gods, to avert evil; hair has also been used for curing sickness as well as, more frequently, harming people. It used to be thought that a child's whooping-cough could be cured by putting hair from a child's head into a sandwich and giving it to a dog; if the dog coughed while eating it, the whooping-cough was transferred to the animal and the child was cured.

Less extreme uses for hair, with its magical powers and association with virility, include using it in **love potions and philtres**: a custom that lived on with the exchange of locks of hair between lovers, an 'act of surrender and faith' since, according to the laws of magic, such a gift gave the recipient complete and absolute power over the life and existence of the giver. Hair has long been regarded as an indication of character: fair hair indicating timidity; red hair a sign of bad temper; brown and black hair bodily strength, with jet-black in particular being very lucky; straight and lank hair was said to be the sign of cunning while curly hair indicated good temper.

CONSULT: Ernest Crawley, *The Mystic Rose*, Macmillan (1902); Sir James George Frazer, *The Golden Bough*, Macmillan (1913 edition).

## Hallowe'en
*See under* festivals.

## Hallucination
An experience or perception of something that does not correspond with any physical fact but is experienced in a way entirely consistent with normal perception; definite and apparently very real impression that occurs when no external objective stimulus is discernable that could have caused it. Visual, auditory, tactile and olfactory hallucinations have been defined and examined by investigators. Veridical hallucinations are those that correspond with external events in an indirect manner; there is some degree of accuracy to an external object, person or event, but the hallucination is not caused by that object, person or event. Possible physical explanations for hallucinations include the chronic irritation of a sense-organ.

CONSULT: William McDougall, *An Outline of Abnormal Psychology*, Methuen (1926); Werner Wolff, *The Threshold of the Abnormal*, Medical Publications (1952).

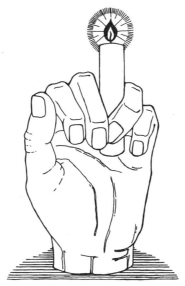

*The Hand of Glory*

## Hand of Glory

A lighted candle in, or made from, a dead man's hand: a popular element in **witchcraft** and **spells**, often included in contemporary pictures of witches, sometimes standing on the mantel of a chimney up which initiates are preparing to fly. The hand had to be severed from the body of a hanged felon still on the gibbet; it had to be wrapped in part of a funeral pall and then well squeezed. The pulp thus obtained was placed in an earthenware vessel with 'zimit', nitre, salt and long peppers (according to a French recipe published in 1722). The ingredients were then well powdered and left for a fortnight. After that period they were exposed to full daylight during the dog-days until the mixture became dry. If the sun was not strong enough, the compound was put into an oven and heated with fern and vervain. The hand was then stuffed with the mixture. A kind of candle was next fashioned, comprised of the fat of a gibbeted felon, virgin wax, sesame and 'ponie', and the Hand of Glory was used as a candlestick to hold this candle. It was believed that such a Hand of Glory had the power to stupefy those to whom it was displayed so that they were totally unable to move. 'Zimit' and 'ponie' present difficulties as we no longer know what these ingredients were. It is possible that zimit could have been

zimar-verdigris; while ponie still means horse-dung in the dialect of
Lower Normandy.

An alternative Hand of Glory was made from the dried and pickled
hand of a hanged man; the five fingers then being lit like candles. This
hand was also reputed to have the power to cause a deep and stupefying
sleep.

## Hardy, Sir Alister (b. 1896)

Marine biologist and psychical researcher; Hon. Fellow of Exeter
College, Oxford; Hon. Fellow of Merton College, Oxford (Fellow,
1946–63); Professor Emeritus, University of Oxford; Director,
Religious Experience Research Unit, Manchester College, Oxford.
Chief Zoologist to the *Discovery* Expedition, 1924–8; President of the
**Society for Psychical Research**, 1965–9; and permanent Vice-
President and Hon. Life Member of the Unitarian Society for
Psychical Studies. He has collected a mass of evidence for children's
**invisible playmates** and apparently inexplicable religious experiences. His book *The Divine Flame* was an examination of religious
phenomena from the scientific point of view, and a plea for science to
take seriously **psi** phenomena.

## Hare Krishna

One of the many religious off-shoots founded on **Hinduism**, the Hare
Krishna Fellowship leapt to fame after being patronized by members
of several popular music groups. The members of this vast
organization, with their shaved heads and saffron-coloured robes, are
dedicated to chanting the words, 'Hare Krishna', 'Krishna Krishna',
'Hare Hare', 'Hare Rama' and 'Rama Rama' in sequence for hours on
end as they walk the streets of European and American cities. This
chanting is said to bring them to the realization of God and a state of
spiritual joy. The International Society for Krishna Consciousness has
scores of temples where, at the end of the Hare Krishna year,
celebration parties are held called 'The Holy Rathayatra Festival of
Lord Jagganath'. Followers of the Hare Krishna movement forsake
sex except for the purpose of procreation within marriage.

CONSULT: N. Freedland, *The Occult Explosion*, Michael Joseph
(1972).

## Harris, Alec (d. 1972)

Welsh **materialization** medium. *See under* **spiritualism**.

# Harvest
*See under* **festivals**.


# Hatha yoga
The most popular of all **yoga** exercises; the yoga that is said to enable the determined yogi to 'get whatever he desires'. The initiate, after practical preparation and precautions against possible obstacles, has to proceed through eight stages: *yama* and *niyama*, which develop the moral fibre; *a sana*, or posture, which is believed to develop and concentrate occult power; *pranayama*, a control of breathing, itself divided into four stages (inhaling, retaining, exhaling and holding), that opens many paths to supernormal faculties; *pratyahara*, the technique of withdrawing the senses from objects to which they are drawn by habit; *dharana*, the development of concentration; *dhyana*, **meditation** proper; and finally, *samadhi*, the **trance** state.

CONSULT: T. Bernard, *Hatha Yoga*, Rider (1950); Sir Paul Dukes, *The Yoga of Health, Joy and Love*, Cassell (1960).


# Hauntings
Visitations of spontaneous **ghosts**; disturbances of a supernatural nature. Houses that have habitual ghostly manifestations are regarded as haunted houses, and there are thousands of such places throughout the world, from the White House, Washington, D.C., and stately homes and castles, to isolated humble cottages and miscellaneous buildings of every description – rectories and vicarages, farms and fire stations, theatres, public houses and hotels, churches and shops. There are also records of haunted open spaces, haunted trees and haunted ships, cars, trains and mountains. The manifestations vary greatly, from strange noises to objects displaced, lights seen, sensations of coldness, draughts, inexplicable smells and an indefinable atmosphere of terror as well as **apparitions** and ghosts of people and animals, and **poltergeist** phenomena. Certain people also appear to be haunted. Hauntings have been reported from every part of the world since the beginning of recorded history, and such organizations as the **Society for Psychical Research** have mountains of evidence from every possible type of witness while the **Ghost Club** is among organizations that carry out investigations into hauntings.

CONSULT: William Oliver Stevens, *Unbidden Guests*, Allen & Unwin (1949); Peter Underwood, *Haunted London*, Harrap (1973).

## Hawthorn
*See under* **trees and plants.**

## Hazel
*See under* **trees and plants.**

## Healing
*See* **faith healing; spirit healing.**

## Hell
Thought to be the place of eternal punishment; the final resting-place of the damned; the home of Hades, the god of **death**; the place in which the wicked are condemned for all eternity. Hell was also thought to be the supreme deterrent to atheism. It was said to lie either far away to the west where the sun goes down, or deep underground, and the Styx, a stream that disappeared into the ground, was said to be the principal river of hell across which the dead had to be ferried by Charon. As early as the third century A.D. it was suggested that the torments of hell did not last for ever and that the wickedest, even the **Devil** himself, would eventually be redeemed; it was also suggested that the fire of hell might not be a real fire but rather the terrible pangs of guilt and bad conscience. The word 'hell' is derived from the Anglo-Saxon, 'to cover' or 'to conceal', and obviously applies to a grave. Theologians, scholars and various religions all have had different ideas of hell, some peopling it with fallen angels while others maintain that it is entirely populated by human beings; still others assert that hell is a state of mind.

CONSULT: H. B. Bonner, *The Christian Hell*, Watts (1913); Edward Langton, *Supernatural*, Rider (1934).

## Hell-Fire Club
Notorious eighteenth-century society, also known as the Monks of Medmenham, formed by Sir Francis Dashwood at the Medmenham Abbey and High Wycombe caves in Buckinghamshire; the leading members of the brotherhood were rakes, aesthetes and politicians (among them John Wilkes), and they practised a kind of **satanism** in elegant surroundings and amid personal delights. Pornographic pictures adorned the walls of the chapel at Medmenham, and parodies of conventional church furniture and fitments formed the background for **initiation** ceremonies that were travesties of religious worship. Obscene parodies of the Mass were enacted involving naked female

participants, **flagellation** and bondage, a mockery of the missal, lewd use of rosaries and chalice followed by a general **orgy**. There were other Hell-Fire Clubs in London and throughout Britain at this time, but they all seem to have died out as the 'Orders', usually with twelve members, themselves grew weary and died. The caves at High Wycombe, modernized and commercialized, are now open to the public.

CONSULT: R. Fuller, *Hell-Fire Francis*, Chatto & Windus (1939); Burgo Partridge, *A History of Orgies*, Blond (1958).

## Helston Furry Dance
*See under* **festivals**.

## Herbs
*See* **trees and plants**.

## Heresy
Opinion contrary to accepted doctrine, especially to that of the Christian Church, where it was considered to be a grave evil punishable by death. The **Inquisition** was set up with the express purpose of dealing with heresy, and caused thousands of heretics to be burned alive. It also dealt with **witchcraft** where this was connected with heresy. During the Middle Ages heretical sects sprang up throughout Europe; some were soon extinguished by persecution, but others, such as the Waldenses, the Petrobusians and the Catharists, gained popular support and persisted for many years as a serious challenge to the established church, eventually going underground as Devil-worshippers, satanists (*see* **satanism**) and secret societies of witches; so witches and magicians and dabblers in the black arts have long been branded as heretics.

CONSULT: G. Leff, *Heresy in the Later Middle Ages*, Manchester University Press (1967); Robert S. Lopez, *The Birth of Europe*, Dent (1966).

## Hermetic Order of the Golden Dawn
*See* **Golden Dawn, Hermetic Order of the.**

## Herne the Hunter
Reputed to have been a keeper of Windsor Forest in the days of Henry VIII who dabbled in the black arts and who was hanged in the forest on an oak tree that was known thereafter as Herne's Oak. Tradition

asserts that after Herne's death his **ghost** haunted the vicinity of the tree, where it was seen by Henry VIII, and sometimes other parts of the forest, but his was no harmless **spectre** for he wore frightening stag horns on his head and sometimes was mounted on a fast horse and accompanied by a band of spectral hounds like the members of the **wild hunt**. Furthermore, his appearance boded ill for any who saw him, and for centuries local misfortunes were attributed to this malignant and **demon**-like ghost.

Another version of the origin of Herne's ghost takes the story back to the days of Richard II and relates that Herne saved the king's life by

*Herne the Hunter dressed in deer-skin clothes and wearing*
*stag's antlers, astride a horse that breathes fire*

killing a wounded stag that attacked the king in the forest, but in so doing was severely injured himself. A mysterious stranger then appeared who said he could save the royal forest keeper; he cut off the stag's head and bound the antlers to Herne's brow. The keeper duly recovered, helped perhaps by the king's promise that, on his return to health, he would be made head keeper; a promise that so annoyed the rest of the keepers that, once out of the king's hearing, they threatened to kill the meddling stranger unless he ensured that Herne never attained the promised office. This the stranger agreed to do, providing they were prepared to accept Herne's **curse** for the rest of their lives. Although he recovered his health, Herne's knowledge of hunting had mysteriously left him and the king had no option but to dismiss him from office altogether. The same night Herne went into the forest and hanged himself, and thereafter the ghost was seen with antlers on his head, and one by one the other keepers were executed as the curse worked.

Shakespeare refers to Herne three times in *The Merry Wives of Windsor*, and Harrison Ainsworth powerfully describes the **apparition** in his novel, *Windsor Castle* (1843). Margaret **Murray** associates the 'foul fiend' with the **horned god** of **witchcraft** and takes the representation back to palaeolithic days. The original tree, shown on Collier's map of 1742, was destroyed in either 1796 or 1863, and Edward VII planted a new oak on the site in the Little Park. This is not open to the public, but reports of Herne's ghost, in the vicinity of the original site and elsewhere in the park, continue to this day. The figure is said to have been seen in 1931, 1936 and 1939, while in 1926 Mrs Walter Legge, J.P., twice heard the baying of hounds which she was totally unable to account for; she described the sound as 'like Herne the Hunter's hounds'; and as recently as 1964 a young couple in the park after nightfall reported glimpsing in the moonlight the figure of a shaggy man, mounted on a fast horse, and wearing antlers.

CONSULT: Margaret A. Murray, *The God of the Witches*, Sampson Low, Marston (1931); Peter Underwood, *A Gazetteer of British Ghosts*, Souvenir Press (1971).

## Hex

A **spell** or **curse** that seeks to injure a person or damage his property; also a counter-**charm** against the power of **witchcraft** and the **evil eye**. There are hexters today in Pennsylvania: 'hex doctors' who claim to remove the malediction or counter the **magic** formula or protect their clients or their property from being hexed; this they do by indicating certain signs and **symbols** that can be worn as **amulets** on the person or drawn over the doorways of their dwellings to provide protection.

CONSULT: Edward S. Gifford, *The Evil Eye*, Macmillan, New York (1958); William Howells, *The Heathens: Primitive Man and His Religions*, Gollancz (1949).

## Hexagram

Two triangles superimposed, one pointing upwards and the other downwards, symbolizing occult power: the male and the female, the 'above' and 'below', **fire** and water. The Star of David ('David's

Shield') is a hexagram and appears on the national flag of Israel. Hexagrams are used in ceremonial and **ritual magic** along with the **magic circle** and the **pentagram**; often within a magic circle, where the 'Seal of Solomon' (Solomon is said to have owned a seal-ring so engraved as to give him power over all **spirits** and **demons**) adds great power by uniting control of spirits with protection for the magician. A double hexagram, combining a circle, a hexagram and a **name of power**, was often embroidered on a magician's robe. In **black magic** ritual, **sacrifice** is usually made in the centre of a hexagram.

CONSULT: Richard Cavendish, *The Black Arts*, Routledge & Kegan Paul (1967).

## Hinduism

A comprehensive term to cover the social customs and religious beliefs of the majority of Indians. To most Hindus some form of either the god Vishnu or the goddess Shiva is the highest object of their worship: Vishnu representing the conservative principle; Shiva the destroying, but also generative, principle. Hinduism teaches the doctrine of **Karma** and accepts the inevitability of transmigration of the soul after **death** to some other body and ultimate absorption by 'the Infinite' (*see also* **reincarnation**). Certain Hindus worship the sun god Surya, and all respect animal life, and cows in particular. The mystical core of Hinduism, with its **Yoga** techniques, enables mankind to realize the eternal and divine within himself, although eroticism has always had an accepted place in Hindu religion and many temples and carvings feature a refreshingly frank sexuality.

CONSULT: A. C. Bouquet, *Hinduism*, Hutchinson (1966 reprint); S. Radhakrishnan, *The Hindu View of Life*, Allen & Unwin (1963 reprint).

## Holly
*See under* **trees and plants**.

## Holy seal

The scar left after complete castration, often by cauterization, for religious reasons as practised by the Russian Skopzies; also in extreme cases of **initiation** or rites of **sex magic**. In the later instances, the Holy Seal becomes the centre of veneration.

CONSULT: Charles Humana, *The Keeper of the Bed*, Arlington Books (1973).

## Home, Daniel Dunglas (1833–86)
*See under* **spiritualism**.

## Home circles
*See under* **spiritualism**.

## Homunculus
A tiny man, produced artificially and endowed with **magic** powers. The possibility of such a creation occupied the students of **alchemy**, and their sealed vase, 'the philosopher's egg', was filled with raw material that would produce the seven vital components that in turn would produce a homunculus. Such a being is variously depicted as a tiny winged Mercury; a manikin urinating; and a miniature bisexual. The latter was believed to belong to a supernatural race which could reproduce itself without sexual intercourse through the power of love.

**Paracelsus**, the sixteenth-century German physician who asserted that it was possible to produce an artificial man (and, indeed, said he had done so), also maintained that 'nothing exists without semen', so one ingredient was established. His process consisted of enclosing some semen and the necessary chemicals in a glass phial and

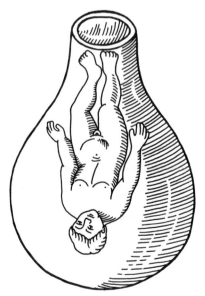

*The homunculus of the alchemists*

incubating for forty days in horse manure, the result being then 'magnetized'. A transparent and indefinite dwarf would now be found to have developed, and if this was then fed with human **blood** for forty weeks, it would evolve into a tiny reproduction of a human being. Paracelsus claimed to have manufactured many homunculi which never grew or showed much intelligence. It is significant that semen and blood, both regarded as soul-substances, should be essential ingredients. Other physicians who claimed to have produced homunculi included Borel, physician to Louis XIV (he apparently used distilled blood), and the Englishman Robert Fludd, physician, philosopher and paymaster to the first Queen Elizabeth.

CONSULT: J. B. Craven, *Doctor Robert Fludd, the English Rosicrucian*, William Peace (1902); Kurt Seligmann, *Magic, Supernaturalism and Religion*, Allen Lane The Penguin Press (1971).

## Hoodoo
Form of cult magic practised by Negroes of the southern United States that is virtually identical with **voodoo**, the native **magic** of Haiti; both originated from Africa. 'Hoodoo hands' are magic **charms** that bring good **luck** to the wearer and bad luck to his enemies when directed against them.

## Hope, William (1863-1933)
'Spirit' photographer. *See under* **spiritualism**. *See also* **psychic photography**.

## Hope diamond
Famous for the misfortune said to plague its owners, this enormous blue-black diamond is said to have been stolen from an Indian temple by a Frenchman in 1638 and sold to Louis XIV in 1668, when it became part of the French Crown Jewels but disappeared during the French Revolution. It eventually turned up in London in the 1820s and was bought by the Hope banking family, so acquiring the name by which it has since been known.

The man who originally stole the diamond was apparently torn to pieces by a pack of dogs; the stone was then picked up by another Frenchman who took it to France and ultimately sold it to the king. As soon as the transaction was completed, this man suffered many misfortunes and eventually lost all his money. He set sail for India once more with plans to make a second fortune, but died in somewhat mysterious circumstances during the voyage and was buried at sea.

Before the diamond became part of the French Crown Jewels, Louis XIV had presented it to his current mistress, the ambitious Marquise de Montespan, whose popularity and success waned from the moment she wore the jewel at a court ball. In desperation that she was fast falling into disfavour with the king, she decided to resort to **black magic** in an effort to achieve complete power, and a circle of magicians led by the Abbé Guibourg performed a **black mass**, cutting an infant's throat over the naked body of the marquise, who wore only the sparkling diamond between her breasts. (It has been suggested that, over the years, the jewel became 'charged' and 're-charged' by similar repeated blasphemies, murders and profanities.) In spite of all her efforts, the marquise continued to fall from favour and soon disappeared from the scene.

The diamond reappears when it is given to Marie Antoinette by Louis XVI, only to be the centre of disaster in the Affair of the Diamond Necklace, an incident that contributed to the events leading up to the French Revolution. Marie Antoinette apparently loaned the diamond to the Princess de Lamballe, who was soon afterwards butchered by the mob. Following the executions of Louis XVI and Marie Antoinette in 1793, the fateful diamond vanished with the rest of the French Crown Jewels.

Thirty years later a beautiful blue-black diamond appeared in Holland, and although it was smaller than the original, there is little doubt in the minds of experts that this was the larger part of the missing stone, with the Duke of Brunswick's 'Blue Drop' – which appeared about the same time – one of the missing fragments. The new owner was an Amsterdam cutter of precious stones, but his son stole the jewel, causing disgrace and ruin to the old man; and having passed the diamond to a Frenchman named Beaulieu to take to England, himself committed suicide. Beaulieu, having parted with the jewel to a dealer named Eliason, promptly met his death in mysterious circumstances. In 1830 the diamond was still in London, and was bought by Henry Thomas Hope for a reported £18 000. The prosperous Hope banking family then experienced misfortune and ill-luck for seventy years until the stone passed to the possession of Lord Francis Hope, who married, survived a divorce but lost all his money. Again the diamond disappeared for a time until a second-hand dealer bought it among other effects after the death of a woman thought to have been the former wife of Lord Frances Hope.

It continued to pass from owner to owner, always leaving misfortune in its wake, and eventually turned up in the possession of

Sultan Abdul Hamid of Turkey. When he was dethroned (and probably assassinated) it was found among the possessions of one of his mistressess after she had been murdered. Later it was owned by a certain Jacques Colet, who committed suicide; by Prince Ivan Kanitovitsky, who was murdered by a man named Simon Montharides, whose coach, containing himself, his wife and their son, hurtled over a cliff, killing them all. Habib Bey seems to have been the next owner, having paid a reported £80 000 for the jewel, only to sell it quickly to a firm of New York jewellers who in turn sold it to an Englishman who was drowned in the *Titanic* on his way to collect his purchase. The jewel was then sold to a millionaire named McLean, whose wife had the jewel blessed. Nevertheless the McLeans lost most of their fortune; their eldest son was killed in a motor accident when only eleven years old; a daughter died from an overdose of sleeping tablets; and McLean himself died in an asylum. His widow died in 1947, leaving the diamond jointly to her six grandchildren, who were, however, never allowed to touch it. In 1967 one of these grandchildren, Miss Evalyn McLean, a former Dallas débutante, was found dead at her home: she was just twenty-five. A dealer had meanwhile bought it from the estate in 1949, and presented it to the Smithsonian Institution in Washington, where it resides at the present day.

In 1965 it was disclosed that when the famous – or infamous – diamond had been loaned to the De Beers laboratory in Johannesburg for study, it had glowed like a red-hot coal after exposure to ultra-violet light; something unknown in any other diamond.

CONSULT: Elliott O'Donnell, *Famous Curses*, Skeffington (1929); Peter Underwood, *Deeper Into the Occult*, Harrap (1975).

## Hopkins, Matthew (d. 1647)
The seventeenth-century self-styled 'Witch-Finder General', the date of whose birth is unknown.

The son of a Puritan minister, Hopkins had studied law and practised for a time without marked success before moving to Manningtree in Essex. It was here in 1645 that he 'became aware' that seven or eight witches lived near him, and thereafter spent a year, and earned himself a considerable fortune, in 'discovering' and 'denouncing' witches in Essex, Suffolk, Huntingdonshire, Cambridgeshire, Northamptonshire and Bedfordshire, often with the willing cooperation of the communities he visited. But growing hostility to his methods (and possibly symptoms of the illness that was to cause his death the following year) led him to give up his work in May 1646,

*Matthew Hopkins, self-styled 'Witch Finder General', two witches and examples of familiars. After the frontispiece to Hopkins's* Discovery of Witches *(1647)*

though he was determined to publish a defence of his methods, which he did in 1647 under the title *The Discovery of Witches*. He was probably responsible for the deaths of more than two hundred people whom he and his associates were convinced were witches. At least one authority suggests that Hopkins was himself accused of being a witch (or warlock), and that he suffered the fate he had brought upon so many others; but it seems beyond doubt that he actually died in bed, and there is an entry in the parish register of Mistley-cum-Manningtree of his burial on 12 August 1647.

CONSULT: Eric Maple, *The Dark World of Witches*, Robert Hale (1962); Philip W. Sergeant, *Witches and Warlocks*, Hutchinson (1936).

## Hörbiger, Hans (1860-1931)
*See* cosmic ice.

## Horned god
The god of the witches in the 'Old Religion'; Margaret **Murray**'s **Devil** in the form of a goat; the pagan god of Western Europe; a god of fertility and ruler of the underworld who accepted homage from his followers at the **sabbath** when the worshippers dressed in **masks** of animal heads and skins, but otherwise went naked, and attained something resembling divinity by sexual union with the horned god. A similar god is worshipped by modern witches at the great pagan **festivals**. Some people refer to the Devil of Christianity as the 'horned god'.

CONSULT: Richard Cavendish, *The Black Arts*, Routledge & Kegan Paul (1967); Margaret A. Murray, *The God of the Witches*, Sampson Low, Marston (1931).

## Horoscope
Astrological birth chart or diagram based on the position of the planets at the moment of birth of an individual, or of a country, animal or organization; in effect, a simple statement of certain astronomical facts, and as such an objective scientific document.

From this basic information, the astologer proceeds to chart the sun, **moon** and planets in their respective positions; but then the student of **astrology** descends to unscientific conclusions by attempting to deduce what influence the planets would be likely to have on the person, animal, country or organization born at that particular time at that particular place.

A horoscope is a circular diagram divided into twelve segments: the twelve signs of the **zodiac**. The horizontal line represents the horizon, and the vertical line the middle of the heavens, with the points below exactly opposite. These twelve segments, or divisions, are known as the twelve houses of the horoscope. The four 'angles', or quarters, have special astronomical significance. The aim of the astrologer is to know the degree of the zodiac rising in the east at the time of birth (called the 'ascendant'), the degree on the 'midheaven' (often called the M.C.), and the degrees on the other house 'cusps' (the division between one house and the next). In addition, astronomical significance is placed on the relationship between the position of the twelve 'planets' (the ten planets plus the sun and the moon); and the four 'elements', (**fire**, earth, air and water), each of which has three signs attributed to it; and the three 'qualities' ('cardinal', 'fixed' and 'mutable'), each of which has four signs attributed. Then, with the help of an appropriate **'Raphael's Ephemeris'**, which details the aspects and positions of the planets at all times for each day, the adept can produce a horoscope.

CONSULT: Rupert Gleadow, *Your Character in the Zodiac*, Phoenix House (1968); Joan Quigley, *Astrology for Adults*, Blond (1970).

## Horseshoe

A lucky **charm** wherever the horse is found. It is possibly a remnant of pagan horse worship, or sex worship (the horseshoe resembling the **Yoni**); or its crescent shape recalls **moon** worship and the sign of Diana, the moon goddess; or it is a possessor of supernatural powers since it is composed of **iron**, a **magic** metal, worked with **fire**, a mysterious element.

At all events, for centuries the horseshoe, especially one that is found, has been thought to bring good **luck** when nailed over the doorway; generally with the prongs upward 'to hold in the luck', but sometimes downwards 'to protect that which travels under it'. Either way it is widely held to be a powerful protective against bad luck and the **evil eye**, and the horseshoe is perhaps today the most popular modern emblem of good luck. The horseshoe cult has widened to the stage where water in which horseshoes have been boiled is said to cure impotence; where whooping cough is cured by feeding from a plate branded with a horseshoe. And the fact of the horseshoe's long association with marriage has led to the German saying that when a girl loses her virginity 'she has lost a horseshoe'. Admiral Lord Nelson, a great believer in the protective power of the horseshoe, had one nailed to the mast of the *Victory*; indeed, it was a common habit to do so in the Navy of his time.

CONSULT: Sir James George Frazer, *The Golden Bough*, Macmillan (1913 edition); M. Oldfield Howey, *The Horse in Magic and Myth*, Rider (1923).

## Houdini, Harry (1874-1926)

The pseudonym of Ehrick Weiss, an American magician who specialized in escapes from handcuffs, mailbags, straight jackets, locked trunks and sealed boxes. Some of his escapes were carried out under water, and several times he narrowly escaped death. His tricks depended on specially prepared apparatus, but much of his fame and success as an escapologist was the result of his dexterity and daring and the frequent challenges he made to police and other authorities whom he successfully defied to confine him. So mysterious were some of his escapades that several people, among them his friend Sir Arthur Conan **Doyle**, believed that the only explanation could be that Houdini was a genuine natural medium and that he 'dematerialized' and 'rematerialized' (*see* **dematerialization** and **materialization**) to effect his spectacular escapes. Houdini became deeply interested in **spiritualism** and psychic phenomena and 'exposed' many mediums to his own satisfaction, including 'Margery' (*see* **Crandon**, Mrs L. R. G.). When he died – as the result of an unexpected punch to the stomach by a reporter – he left a sealed message that he said would prove life after death if it was ever solved; reports of the success or otherwise of the exercise are conflicting.

CONSULT: Milbourne Christopher, *Houdini: The Untold Story*, Cassell (1969); Harry Houdini, *A Magician among the Spirits*, Harper, New York (1924).

## Hurkos, Peter (b. 1911)

Dutch clairvoyant who has given valuable assistance to the police forces of several countries. After falling more than thirty feet from a ladder during the Second World War and fracturing his skull, Hurkos, recovering in hospital, discovered that he had the gift of **second sight**, for he somehow *knew* facts and details about his fellow patients, and in particular about the fate in store for a British agent, who was assassinated two days later. Since then he has been associated with many spectacular cases from the stolen Stone of Scone to the mysterious Boston strangler, and he has reportedly used **clairvoyance** to help to solve nearly fifty murders in a score of countries.

CONSULT: Peter Hurkos, *Psychic*, Arthur Barker (1961); Psychic Magazine editors, *Psychics*, Turnstone Press (1973).

## Hydesville
Small hamlet of New York State, twenty miles from Rochester, where modern **spiritualism** was born at the home of the Fox sisters.

## Hypnagogic state
That state which is neither sleeping nor waking, but somewhere between the two; the borderland of drowsiness, when **hallucinations** and **visions** are frequently reported.

## Hypnotism
An artificially induced state of heightened suggestibility, though its exact state and status has been debated for two hundred years.

Hypnotism is a fact, and with training most people can learn to practise it to some extent. But since the suggestibility of the person hypnotized is sometimes heightened to a considerable degree, and the effect on a person by an inexperienced or unqualified hypnotist cannot be reliably forecast, public demonstrations of hypnotism are banned in Britain and the practice of this little-understood phenomenon discouraged.

Hypnotism is the inducing of a sleep-like **trance** state by repeated commands and mental concentration in which the mind of the subject becomes passive, acting readily upon suggestion or the direction of the hypnotist. On regaining normal consciousness, little or no recollection of the actions carried out or instructions received during hypnosis are retained. Friedrich Anton **Mesmer** (hence the alternative term 'mesmerism') was an early pioneer in hypnotism, which he called 'animal magnetism' believing it to be an occult force; he caused something of a sensation by apparently curing a number of prominent Parisians with his new force.

Hypnotists can make a subject perform crimes (contrary to popular belief); hypnotism has been used with outstanding success by medical men and by the military for extracting secrets when physical torture has been unsuccessful. Under hypnotic influence, certain subjects can recall long-forgotten events and experiences, and there have been occasional instances of regression to very early years, and even to apparent previous incarnations (*see* **reincarnation**). Hypnotism can be self-induced and occultists have produced several sets of exercises based on auto-hypnotic procedure.

CONSULT: Simeon Edmunds, *Hypnotism and the Supernormal*, Aquarian Press (1961); Peter Underwood and Leonard Wilder, *Lives to Remember*, Robert Hale (1975).

# I

## I Ching

Ancient Chinese *Book of Change*, arguably the oldest complete book in the world, which has been used as a system of philosophy and for **divination** for thousands of years, certainly since before Confucius 551–479 B.C.). The basis of *I Ching* (sometimes spelt 'Yi King' and pronounced ee'jing) is that the whole of the universe and everything therein is a combination of the negative, Yin, and the positive, Yang (*see* **Yin and Yang**). The main part of the book is comprised of sixty-four **hexagrams** or sections or oracles made up of six lines, some broken in the middle (Yin lines), and the others unbroken (Yang lines). Each combination of lines has meaning, and the pattern is decided either by using yarrow stalks (a lengthy process) or by tossing three coins. If the coins fall with more 'heads' than 'tails', a Yang line is indicated; and if there are more 'tails' than 'heads', a Yin line is formed. By this means, six lines are created forming a hexagram whose meaning can then be looked up.

The remarkable aptness and helpfulness obtained from the serious use of *I Ching* has been repeatedly remarked upon by those who perservere with the system, and it seems likely that the act of asking questions and interpreting the replies prepares the mind to enter a state similar to that reached in accepted forms of **meditation**. The great psychologist C. G. Jung believed that the symbols and words contained in *I Ching* conveyed messages direct to the unconscious mind.

CONSULT: J. Blofeld, *The Book of Change*, Allen & Unwin (1968); R. Wilhelm, *The I Ching*, Routledge & Kegan Paul (1951).

## Illusion

The result of misinterpretation in the perception of a real object or objects that may be seen, heard or touched. An illusion is the sensory perception that originates from an actual stimulus but which is misinterpreted as something else. Familiar natural illusions include the apparently increased size of the setting sun or the **moon** when they are near the horizon, and the fact that apparent distance is distorted by the speed of travel so that a distance seems longer when walked than when one is a passenger in a car; the same distance will also seem longer the first time the route is covered. During war time, anticipatory fears frequently transformed the noise of a car changing gear into the first notes of an air-raid warning; the echo of one's own footsteps are often taken to be those of a pursuer; one's own shadow assumes the shape of an assailant. Mirages are also illusory.

A number of reported **ghosts** are illusions – as distinct from **hallucinations** – and there are many examples in the literature of **psychical research** where an apparently perfectly distinct image, say of a man with a sallow complexion, grey eyes, greyish moustache, attired in a dressing-gown tied with a dark cord, is in fact the result of a shadow cast by a street lamp through a partly curtained window

*An example of an illusion. Look steadily at the three dots in the centre of the drawing for ninety seconds, then look into space or at a large plain surface. The drawing will appear in reverse*

combined with reflection from a polished wooden surface. Such illusions are most usually the result of poor light and/or defects of the eyes, such as astigmatism or short-sightedness, on the part of the person observing the illusion. Auditory illusions can be the explanation for apparently inexplicable sounds and are often reported during any disturbance in health, either in mind or body. Both auditory and visual illusions occur frequently in the semi-dreaming so-called **hypnagogic state** between sleep and full consciousness.

CONSULT: Adrian Parker, *States of Mind: ESP and Altered States of Consciousness*, Malaby Press (1975); Helen E. Ross, *Behaviour and Perception in Strange Environments*, Allen & Unwin (1974).

## Image magic
*See* **black magic; sympathetic magic.**

## Imitative magic
*See* **sympathetic magic.**

## Imp
A small **demon**; a witch's **familiar.** An eighteenth-century Frenchman, Alexis Vincent Charles Berbiguier, who was known as the 'Bottler of Spirits', seems to have been persecuted for years by demons, and it is reported that his room was full of pins, each transfixing the body of a wriggling imp.

CONSULT: Eric Maple, *The Dark World of Witches*, Robert Hale (1962); Philip W. Sergeant, *Witches and Warlocks*, Hutchinson (1936).

## Incantation
The use of magic words or **names of power** for enchantment, influence, help or **exorcism**; magic formula or ceremony. Incantations and the chanting of prayers for purposes of **magic** were used by the Ancient Egyptians (*see also* **Egyptian magic**), by the pilgrims and holy men of the East, as they repeatedly turned their prayer wheels or shook their prayer bells, by native witch doctors and by adepts of magic for centuries, as is evident from the incantations in the **grimoires** right up to the present day. Incantations are usually chanted, steadily rising in intensity as the ritual proceeds. Although the magical use of words can be found in prayers as well as in incantations, the essence of incantation is command, with the magician ordering supernatural forces to do his bidding. Some magicians maintain that incantations are most effective when they are expressed

silently, acting through the power of thought alone. *See also* **ritual magic**.

CONSULT: Idries Shar, *The Secret Lore of Magic*, Frederick Muller (1957); A. E. Waite, *The Book of Ceremonial Magic*, University Books, New York (1961 reprint).

## Incubus

Male **demons** who as a rule assumed human form before venting their lust on women. With their power over sleep – nightmares of horror and eroticism were considered to originate from incubi or **succubi** – the incubus could cause a heavy sleep to overcome a whole household, even affecting the husband to the extent that the demon lover could enjoy his wife in the same bed. An interchange of gender was thought to be possible between these male and female demons, and it was believed that the incubus ejaculated semen which it had previously collected when in the guise of a succubus.

CONSULT: William J. Fielding, *Strange Superstitions and Magical Practices*, Blakiston Co., Philadelphia (1945).

## Independent voice
*See* **direct voice**.

## Independent writing
*See under* **automatism**.

## Indian rope trick

The best-known and most mystifying of all tricks and magical feats. Remarkably vague yet oddly persistent tales of the strange performance continue to come out of India, though it is incredibly difficult to locate any person who can honestly claim to have himself seen the legendary trick.

Although there are several variations, the commonest version consists of a **fakir**, 'juggler' or some travelling showman, dressed only in a loin-cloth, who carries a large basket into an open space in the centre of a village. He is accompanied by a boy of about ten years old. The showman, having collected a crowd of onlookers, will ensure that they are all close to one another and that they form an unbroken circle. He will then talk incessantly and rapidly, fascinating his audience and ensuring that everyone is paying close attention; and he never ceases his elaborate and detailed explanations until the whole show is over. Against the background of this continual chatter the alert showman produces an old sheet from his basket and a thick rope, about fifteen feet long, and both are passed round among the onlookers for inspection. When he receives the rope back in his hands, the showman gives it a sudden flick and miraculously it stiffens and remains upright, as rigid as a pole. It seems to reach far higher than one would expect and its top is hidden by what appears to be a small cloud. Still talking monotonously, seated beside the rigid rope, the showman tells the boy to climb; the lad does so with adroitness and disappears from sight into the apparent cloud still hiding the top of the rope.

The man now produces a knife, and placing it between his teeth (and *still* talking!), himself climbs the rope and disappears from view although his voice still reaches the expectant watchers on the ground. After a few seconds what appear to be the severed limbs of the boy, bleeding profusely, thud down on to the ground, one at a time, followed by the mutilated trunk. The showman then reappears at the top of the rope and climbs down, using one hand, the bloody head of the boy grasped in the other and the bloodstained knife between his teeth. Talking rapidly and continuously, he throws the head, the trunk and the limbs into the basket, covers them with the sheet and, to pile horror upon horror, plunges his knife deep into the heap in the basket. Before the spectators have time to recover the showman takes a grip on the rope, shakes it and it falls in a heap on the ground. Then the cloth in the basket begins to move of its own accord and the boy steps out, unharmed and smiling broadly. The man then calmly packs up his equipment while the boy makes a collection from the crowd.

It seems likely that the secret (as with so much conjuring) is in the continual talking, and that the answer lies in mass suggestion or hypnotic influence (*see* **hypnotism**) – at all events it is a remarkable feat, and if there is such a deception as the Indian rope trick, the solution is almost certainly in the realm of **hallucination** or a subconscious impression of some kind. Harry **Price** tried unsuccessfully to arrange an exhibition of the Indian rope trick in England in 1935.

CONSULT: John Keel, *Jadoo*, W. H. Allen (1957); Harry Price, *Confessions of a Ghost-Hunter*, Putnam (1936).

## Inductor

Article handled by psychometrists (*see* **psychometry**) that apparently enables them to obtain detailed information about the person with whom the object is connected.

## Inedia

Name given to the apparent ability of saints, mystics, **fakirs** and other 'wonder men' to survive without food.

## Initiation

Ceremonial admission into a select society, organization, fraternity, community or association which represents a new birth (*see also* **baptism**) and is an accepted ordeal to acquire a new status in both tribal cultures and civilized societies throughout the world and throughout the ages. Many native initiations are performed as puberty rites and involve circumcision and clitoridectomy. Secret societies have initiation ceremonies that often humiliate and symbolically try the strength and endurance of the candidate. In **magic** and **witchcraft** the initiation ceremony often includes symbolic or actual sexual intercourse, while other initiation ceremonies, including those of some North American Indians, include torture and revolting ingredients.

CONSULT: M. R. Allen, *Male Cults and Secret Initiation in Melanesia*, Melbourne University Press (1967); M. Eliade, *Rites and Symbols of Initiation*, Harper, New York (1958).

## Inquisition

Roman Catholic tribunal, originally instituted in 1233 to suppress **heresy** and (later) **witchcraft**; also the notorious Spanish Inquisition established in 1479. Inquisitors were allowed to accept anonymous denunciation and to employ solitary confinements, secret trial and torture to break resistance, and so 'cruelty' became synonymous with the word 'inquisition'. The Inquisition began the destruction of the **Knights Templar** and the word is sometimes used in present-day occult circles to denote a particular inquiry or search stimulated by hidden motives. The infamous **Malleus Maleficarum**, the *Hammer of Witches*, was written by two Dominican inquisitors. During the course of about 150 years, the Inquisition was probably responsible for the burning of 30 000 so-called witches.

CONSULT: G. G. Coulton, *Inquisition and Liberty*, Heinemann (1938).

## Institut Métapsychique International

Founded by Jean Meyer in 1918 at 89 avenue Niel, Paris, the institute's first director was Dr Gustave Geley, later members including Dr Charles Richet; Camille Flammarion; Sir Oliver **Lodge**; Ernesto Bozzano; and Dr Eugene Osty. With its official publication,

*La Révue metapsychique*, and scientific instruments of considerable capability, the leading French organization for investigating **paranormal** phenomena and **psychical research**, continues to do excellent work that began with experimentation with such mediums as Eva C. (*see under* **spiritualism**) and Rudi Schneider (*see* **Schneider brothers**). Present address: 1 Place Wagran, Paris 750 17.

## Invisible playmates
The common companions of children, though they have apparently, no objective reality. Many children, most often but not always lonely children, have such playmates (or, more usually, one such friend) whom they name and with whom they talk and play without any self-conscious embarrassment. In recent years such experiences have been the subject of study by bodies like the Religious Experience Research Unit, Manchester College, Oxford, where the researches of Sir Alister **Hardy** and his assistants have shown that 'mystical' but vivid experiences like these are comparatively common. Children often have an innate moral sense based on logic and an unbiased and reasonable view; perhaps, even, a wisdom which their parents have lost. Further work in this field is likely to be revealing and rewarding.

## Invocation
The calling, seeking or summoning of a saint or god or devil or evil **spirit**; evocation is the act of calling out an evil spirit, as in **exorcism**.

## Iron
A metal long credited with supernatural powers. Thirteen hundred years before Christ, **amulets** of meteoric iron (since it came from the sky, it must be 'heavenly') were placed in the tomb of Tutankhamun as protection against evil forces. Iron pyrites kept dragons at bay in China; throughout Europe iron was a guard against lightning; in India it was an integral part of funeral rites; and it is still thought to be a powerful repellent of evil spirits that escape from corpses, and a potent force against the **evil eye**. Magicians sometimes use a chain of magnetized iron around a **magic circle**, as a barrier against evil forces, and invariably they include iron nails in **ritual magic**. The **horseshoe** may be considered 'lucky' because it is made of iron.

## Ithyphallic
'With an erect phallus'; exhibiting or characterized by such an object; religious symbolism in antiquity (*see* **phallic worship**). Male gods

were so depicted in many parts of the ancient world to emphasize their virile fertilizing and creative power. Ithyphallic figures are to be found in prehistoric cave paintings and as hill figures, in many Egyptian and Greek carvings, and in pictorial and sculptural representations of religious and magical rites in India, Africa, South America and Italy, including at Pompeii. Ithyphallus is a common feature of **sex magic** rites and ceremonies of the twentieth century.

CONSULT: Hargrave Jennings, *Phallicism, Celestial and Terrestrial,* Redway (1884); Francis King, *Sexuality, Magic and Perversion,* Neville Spearman (1971).

## Ivy
*See under* **trees and plants.**

# J

## Joan of Arc (1412–31)

French patriot, and one of the most remarkable women who ever lived. Little is known of her childhood except that she was a pious child who heard, without believing, a story of **fairies** that might be encountered around a tree near a local spring. In her thirteenth year she first heard voices. She believed it to be the voice of God and vowed, under the 'fairy tree', to remain a virgin and lead a pure and godly life. For the next five years she heard voices two or three times a week and saw **visions** of Saint Catherine and Saint Margaret and Saint Michael.

The seige of Orleans began in October 1428, and the voices told Joan to go there to raise the seige. She approached the commandant of the nearest fortified town, but was told to return home. She was then in her sixteenth year. Two months later Joan spent a fortnight with a woman who kept an inn, and this visit has been the cause of suggestions that Joan, by now well-built, handsome and with a bright face, was a sensual woman who enjoyed the company of men; at all events, shortly afterwards she was summoned for breach of promise of marriage.

Six months later, in January 1429, Joan again left her village determined to respond to the voices and raise the seige of Orleans. After many difficulties and submitting to **exorcism**, she reached the presence of the Dauphin, with whom she talked for two hours, saying she was God's messenger sent to tell him he was the king's son and the true heir to France. At length she obtained the necessary approval, and at Tours, famous for its armourers, she was fitted with a suit of 'white armour'. She marched on Orleans with 4 000 men and raised the seige, Joan herself planting the first scaling-ladder and receiving a shoulder wound. On 8 May a thanksgiving procession originated the great festival of Orleans. Two months later the king was crowned with Joan standing beside him.

Less than a year later Joan was captured by John of Luxembourg, the Burgundian commander sympathetic to the English, and after a long consultation with her 'voices' made an attempt to escape by jumping from the tower in which she was imprisoned; she injured herself but not seriously. She then passed into (most probably being sold) the hands of the English and was imprisoned at Rouen. The authentic records of the trial, in 1431, still exist. Joan was charged among other things, with **sorcery**, the worthlessness of her visions, her 'signs' given to the King and her alleged gift of prophecy. She was eventually burned at the stake in the Old Market Square at Rouen. Some of the watchers thought that her **magic** had caused her to disappear and escape death, and the executioner dug out the remains, cut open the body, burnt what was left of the entrails, and the ashes were thrown into the Seine. Margaret **Murray** has suggested grounds for believing that the 'holy maid of France' was in reality a witch.

CONSULT: Hereward Carrington, *The Invisible World*, Rider (1948); W. S. Scott, *Jeanne d'Arc*, Harrap (1974).

# K

## Ka

The **double** or vital power of the Ancient Egyptians; a kind of second, less dense, copy of the dead king which lived in the tomb; an exact reproduction. The purpose of **mummification** and the elaborate burial provisions were all to prolong the life of the Ka. Should insufficient attention be paid to the well-being of the Ka, it was thought to be able to leave the tomb and haunt those responsible. Occultists have reported encountering the Ka or 'vital force', an integral part of gods and human beings, during rituals of Ancient **Egyptian magic**. A lotus-shaped alabaster cup in the tomb of Tutankhamun bore round its rim the formal titles of the king followed by: 'May thy Ka live! Mayest thou spend millions of years, O thou who lovest Thebes. . .' This Ka is not to be confused with the Ba, or soul, which was thought to have left the material body, and the Ka (or double) at the moment of **death**.

CONSULT: E. A. Wallis Budge, *A Short History of the Egyptian People*, J. M. Dent (1914); Margaret A. Murray, *The Splendour that was Egypt*, Sidgwick & Jackson (1949).

## Kabala
*See* **Cabala**.

## Kardec, Allan, or Alan, or Alain (1804-69)
*See under* **spiritualism**.

## Karma
From the Sanskrit noun for a deed or action; the idea that every activity receives its punishment or reward; a theory that could be plausible if several lives are allowed for retribution or recompense to take place, as is believed by the adherents of **reincarnation**,

**Hinduism** and **Buddhism**. Reward for the virtuous, punishment for the wicked and not only virtuous or wicked deeds but also thoughts, conscious and unconscious, harmless fantasies, pleasurable dreams – the law of karma excludes nothing; everything counts and every shred of man's hidden personality is measured; as long as he is on earth, he is subject to the inexorable shackles of karma, say the Buddhists, the Hindus, the reincarnationists and many others.

CONSULT: S. Radhakrishnan, *Indian Philosophy*, Allen & Unwin (1948); K. M. Sen, *Hinduism*, Penguin (1961).

## 'Katie King'

Alleged **materialization** through the mediumship of Florence Cook (*see under* **spiritualism**).

## Kelley, Edward (1555-95)

Alchemist, necromancer, forger, dabbler in **magic** and associate of John **Dee**, the Elizabethan astrologer and scientist. With a friend named Waring, Kelley is said to have dug up a corpse in a Lancashire churchyard and by magic **incantations** to have forced it to speak; an event that forms the subject of a well-known print.

Kelley worked himself into Dee's confidence and described marvellous **visions** and angelic messages which Dee faithfully recorded. When a rich Pole, the Count Adalbert Laski, was introduced to Dee while on a visit to England, Kelley said that the **spirits** foretold that Count Laski was a man with a wonderful destiny. Swallowing the bait, the wealthy nobleman entertained Kelley and Dee in lavish style in Poland where, it was planned, they would by **alchemy** transmute **iron** into gold. As the experiments continued and the count's money dwindled, so the 'communicating spirits' were less encouraging and sympathetic to Laski, and finally Dee received an 'angelic' invitation from the Emperor Rudolph II in Prague. There the two men lived well for a few months, but were eventually expelled from the country.

Kelley had long lusted after Dee's second wife, who was young and pretty, and now the 'angelic communications' decreed that the Dees and the Kelleys should share everything, including their wives. After some argument such an agreement was drawn up and signed by all the four persons involved, and although we are not told how successfully this Elizabethan wife-swapping turned out, we do know that before long there was a final separation between Kelley and Dee. Kelley went back to Prague (where he had been knighted), and found himself immediately flung into prison. A few months later he was released,

*John Dee and Edward Kelley summoning the dead.*
*After a seventeenth-century engraving*

wandered as a vagabond through Germany and was arrested as a
sorcerer. In jumping a wall in an effort to escape in 1593, he injured
himself internally and died two years afterwards. Although a
charlatan, Kelley was a man of considerable abilities – usually misused
– and he had a well-developed imagination. He is credited with some
poems, and his other writings include a treatise in Latin on the
**philosopher's stone**.

CONSULT: John Dee, *Life of John Dee*, T. H. Munday (1842); Colin
Wilson, *The Occult*, Hodder & Stoughton (1971).

## 'Key of Solomon'

Celebrated and famous **grimoire**, of medieval European **ritual
magic**. Many later grimoires are based on the *Key of Solomon*. Mainly
in terms of cabalistic and astrological **magic** (*see also* **Cabala** and
**astrology**), elaborate preliminaries are described, together with the
importance of the selection of a suitable time and place, weapons and
articles, robes, **pentagrams** and diagrams, the drawing of the

magic circle and the incantations necessary to summon spirits and control them. The grimoire is named after the biblical king, who certainly had the reputation of being a powerful magician and a worshipper of strange gods; as far back as the first century A.D. King Solomon is credited with having been the author of a book that revealed the secrets of conjuring up demons. A translation by MacGregor Mathers has been published in the United States (Weiser, New York, 1970) and in Britain (Routledge & Kegan Paul, 1970).

CONSULT: Émile Grillot de Givry, *Witchcraft, Magic and Alchemy*, University Books, New York (1958); Sirdar Ikbal Ali Shah, *Occultism: Its Theory and Practice*, Rider (1952).

## Kilner, Dr Walter J. (1847-1920)

A doctor at St Thomas's Hospital, London, whose experiments, involving a solution of coal-tar dye hermetically sealed between two pieces of glass, convinced him that it was possible to make the aura visible to normal sight. 'Kilner screens' for this purpose are still available from suppliers of psychic apparatus.

CONSULT: Harry Boddington, *The University of Spiritualism*, Spiritualist Press (1947); W. J. Kilner, *The Human Atmosphere or the Aura Made Visible by the Aid of Chemical Screens*, Redman (1911); University Books, New York (1965).

## King's evil, or scrofula

The belief that scrofula could be healed by the touch of a king, or queen, caused this disease to be known as the 'king's evil'. The superstition that the touch of a monarch can heal has been recorded throughout history from Christ, 'the King of Kings', through the emperors of Rome, who were thought to possess this quasi-divine power, down to anointed kings and queens. In England, the earliest monarch to have performed the ceremony is said to have been Edward the Confessor (1004-66), and the last, Queen Anne (1665-1714).

The power to heal by touching was thought to be a special gift from God, given to kings and queens, and the words, as they touched the person to be healed, were always the same: 'I touch, but God healeth'. Afterwards, the monarch would hang a small piece of gold or silver about the person's neck, which he, or she, was required to wear for the rest of their life; this was known as a 'touch-piece' and often had a ship on one side and the Archangel Michael defeating the dragon on the other. It is recorded that during his reign Charles II touched nearly

100 000 persons for scrofula, and that on one occasion the pressure to get near him was so great that several people were trampled to death; perhaps it was as much the anticipation of receiving a gold or silver coin as actually having a disease to be cured.

CONSULT: Sir James George Frazer, *The Golden Bough*, Macmillan (1913 edition); W. Carew Hazlett, *Faiths and Folklore*, Reeves & Turner (1905).

## Kirlian photography

A system of photography using high-frequency electric currents, named after its discoverers, Semyon and Velentina Kirlian, a Russian electrician and his journalist wife, who discovered – or invented – an entirely new method of 'photography' that encompassed some fourteen patents.

To produce results, a specially constructed high-frequency spark generator is connected to a camera plate, and the object to be 'photographed' (be it the finger of a human being, a leaf, insect or any living thing) is placed directly on to the photographic plate. The generator creates a high-frequency field which apparently causes the object under investigation to radiate a kind of bioluminescence in the darkness which is recorded on the photographic plate (without a camera being used) as an uneven halo of coloured light radiating from the object under study. For some reason not yet discovered, the result varies each time the experiment is carried out. This may be because of varying pressure on the photographic plate, emotional change in the individual concerned or some entirely different reason.

The fact remains that Kirlian photography, interesting as it is, cannot be considered of scientific interest since it is not repeatable under investigation; or, rather, the results of repeated experiments do not correspond. Could the 'halo' be the **aura** that psychics and clairvoyants have long claimed to be able to see surrounding the human body; or an **astral body** that reflects the mental and physical state of the individual?

Kirlian photography, one of the most fascinating, puzzling, remarkable and baffling discoveries in **psychical research** could well be electromagnetic in nature: a kind of gathering together of electrical particles; it could equally be the result of the many thousand volts of electrical discharge. Its advocates point to its possible use in such fields as dentistry, criminology, geology, agriculture and medicine.

CONSULT: Sheila Ostrander and Lynn Schroeder, *Psychic Discoveries*

*Behind the Iron Curtain,* Prentice-Hall (1970); Lyall Watson, *Supernature,* Hodder & Stoughton (1973).

## Knights Templar

In 1118, nine knights, inspired by idealism, chivalry and religious fervour, and concerned for the safety of pilgrims to the Holy Land, founded the Order of the Temple. Two hundred years later the organization had become the most powerful single entity in Europe, and less than fifty years later it was charged with **heresy**, unnatural vice and devil worship, put to trial and utterly destroyed.

The Templars cut their hair, accepted chastity (they were even forbidden to kiss their mothers), and took vows of poverty. Usually they owned only their clothes and weapons and articles granted to them at their initiation; yet so popular did the simple cross on the white mantle become that the noblest of the lands sought to join, or endowed the Order with riches, lands and produce. So poor were the Templars in their early days that two knights had to share one horse, a state of affairs commemorated by their Great Seal decades after they had become one of the richest communities of all time.

Their laudable aims (in spite of their devotion to fighting and the total secrecy that surrounded their chapters, ceremonies and **initiations**) won the Templars religious privilege and immunity. But as time passed, and the power and wealth of the Order grew and spread, the reputation of the knights became tarnished and King Philip IV ('the Fair') of France (who tried unsuccessfully to join the Order) set about collecting damaging evidence so that he might ultimately lay his hands on the enormous wealth the Templars had acquired. In collusion with Pope Clement V, he began with a charge of heresy, arrested the Grand Master in the Paris Temple and seized other members all over France. Torture extracted confessions that damned the Order for ever: neophytes had been required to spit or urinate on the cross and renounce Christ; indecent kisses and unnatural sexual acts had been practised and encouraged; Baphomet (*see under* **demonology**) had been worshipped. How much of this extorted material was true will never be known since the lives of all those who confessed were spared (and there were some very strange confessions) and none of the charges was proved conclusively. When it was nearly all over the Grand Master was brought out of prison to make a public confession; instead he maintained that he was only guilty of one offence: that of allowing torture to cause him to lie and he declared that the Order was pure and innocent and always had been.

He was slowly burned to death on 18 March 1314, still protesting his innocence, and there were those among the watching crowd who maintained that with his last breath he summoned Pope Clement and Philip the Fair to meet him at God's judgement seat within a year. By strange coincidence both died within twelve months of the death of the Grand Master of the Temple.

CONSULT: E. Simon, *The Piebald Standard*, Cassell (1959); E. J. Martin, *The Trial of the Templars*, Allen & Unwin (1928).

*The original Great Seal of the Knights Templar*

## Kyteler, Alice or Agnes

The first recorded witch to have been accused for her faith and the subject of the best-known **witchcraft** case in Ireland. In 1324 Dame Alice Kyteler was a wealthy and influential aristocrat, but she was suddenly accused of denial of God, **sacrifice** to a devil, seeking knowledge of the future with the help of **demons**, conducting mock religious services, illicit love, injuring men and beasts with a concoction which included unbaptized children's brains and, surely the last straw, of having caused the deaths of her first three husbands. Her fourth husband, Sir John le Poer, it seems, once his suspicions were aroused by the sickness he was himself suffering, discovered in her possession a 'wafer of sacramental bread, having the Divel's name stamped thereon instead of Jesus Christ' and 'a pipe of ointment wherewith she greased a staffe upon which she ambled and galloped through thicke and thin, when and in what manner she listed'. Sir John le Poer denounced his wife to the authorities, but although she was excommunicated, Alice Kyteler dodged all warrants and summons and escaped.

CONSULT: Margaret A. Murray, *The God of the Witches*, Sampson Low, Marston (1931); Philip W. Sergent, *Witches and Warlocks*, Hutchinson (1936).

# L

## Lamias

Legendary desert **demons** in the shape of women who haunt cemeteries and (like **ghouls**) disinter corpses and eat the flesh. They are also said to tempt and devour living persons by exhibiting themselves as attractive females, but they can always be distinguished by their inability to speak; they hiss like serpents. Lamias were said to favour beautiful youths with whom they made love before devouring them. Lamias were the objects of **sacrifice**, and their goddess was Hecate, the goddess of the dead. Ancient Rome established a lyceum of clairvoyant priests who were trained in the skill of combating lamias, apparently conjured up by sorcerers in desert regions.

CONSULT: Ornella Valta, *The Vampire*, Tandem Books (1965).

## Lancashire witches

The sensational trial and execution of ten alleged witches from Pendle Forest achieved great notoriety in 1612, with wild accusations and confessions from two rival families, beggars and poachers in the main, who were believed to have sold their souls to the **Devil**. The charges included the murder of children and other people, and the damning testimony included that of a nine-year-old girl who incriminated, among others, her own mother. In 1634 a second great witch trial involved more Lancashire witches. Today it is possible to tour the Pendle witch country, visiting the homes of some of the principal characters concerned and even meeting local people who claim the dubious distinction of being descended from Lancashire witches.

CONSULT: E. Peel and P. Southern, *The Trial of the Lancashire Witches*, David & Charles (1969).

## Lang, Andrew (1844-1912)

Scholar, folklorist, poet and philosopher, born in Selkirk, Scotland, the son of the county sherrif-clerk. He was educated at Edinburgh, St Andrews, Glasgow and Balliol College, Oxford, later becoming a Fellow of Merton. He married in 1875 and settled in London to make a living by writing, which he did successfully, since he had great versatility and could write at any time and in almost any circumstances. Apart from his delightful series of *Fairy Books* for young readers, he published volumes of verse, literary essays, historical works, translations of the classics, books on Homeric problems and ambitious anthropological volumes on *Custom and Myth* (1884), *Myth, Ritual and Religion* (1887) and *The Making of Religion* (1898). His *Cock Lane and Common-Sense* (1894) contained chapters on **spiritualism, psychical research,** haunted houses, the **Cock Lane ghost, hallucinations, crystal-gazing, second sight** and **table turning;** while his *Book of Dreams and Ghosts* (1897) contained a wealth of well-known and little-known cases of **hauntings, dreams, visions** and **ghosts.** He also wrote a consideration of **Joan of Arc** in the light of psychical research (*The Maid of France,* 1908), and several articles on psychical research for the *Encyclopaedia Britannica.* A member of the **Society for Psychical Research** for the last six years of his life, he was its President in 1911.

## Lares
Usually accompanists of **guardian spirits,** lares were commonly venerated by the Ancient Romans, shrines to them being found in almost every Roman household as well as at **crossroads.** Sometimes they were a family's particular guardian, and protected the occupants and the house itself. There were also public Lares who guarded the city, and some occultists maintained that they would contact a Lare (or Lar) to obtain through them an introduction to more powerful entities.

CONSULT: Sir James George Frazer, *The Golden Bough,* Macmillan (1913 edition); Edith Hamilton, *Mythology,* Little, Brown, Boston (1940).

## Laurel
*See under* **trees and plants.**

## Levater, Johann Kaspar (1741-1801)
Mystic, poet, theologian and physignomist born at Zürich; and lived there all his life as deacon or pastor at one or other of the Protestant churches. A friend of Goethe, and a stout defender of **Cagliostro,** he produced some popular mystical writings, but is chiefly remembered

198 LEE, ROBERT JAMES

for his monumental work on **physiognomy**– the judging of a person's character from his physical features, or, as he put it, 'the knowledge and realization of the link between the exterior and the interior, the visible surface to the invisibility it covers'; and he collected a mass of case-histories of apparently miraculous happenings, a remarkably forward-looking idea for two centuries ago.

CONSULT: J. C. Lavater, *Physiognomy,* W. Simmonds (n.d.).

## Lee, Robert James (1844-1931)

English medium to Queen Victoria. *See under* **spiritualism**.

## Left hand

Traditionally associated with the side of evil; the 'Left-hand Path' is **black magic**, and 'moving to the left' or anti-clockwise (*see* **withershins**) is in **magic** working on that which is intended to be harmful and to attract evil influences. Sorcerers place great emphasis on left-hand movements and the use of the left hand in working **spells** and **incantations**. Babylonian soothsayers considered that the left-hand side revealed bad **omens** and the right-hand side favourable ones. One of the rules of **augury** involved the direction in which the birds flew, and while those flying to the right emphasized the favourable aspect of the omens, birds flying to the left were invariably unfavourable. Some magicians, in particular a defrocked priest, the Abbé Boullan, had significant signs tattooed near the left eye. In **witchcraft**, too, the left-hand side plays a definite and evil part in the rites, and those witches who told of the **Devil** drawing **blood** for writing pacts often said that the blood was taken from their left hand. In **palmistry**, the left hand is said to reveal the qualities one is born with while the right hand indicates what one makes of oneself.

CONSULT: Michael Barsley, *The Left-Handed Book,* Souvenir Press (1966).

## Lemuria

Reputed lost continent, now submerged in the Indian Ocean but once the birthplace of the human race. Often associated with **Mu**, Lemuria was more extensive than **Atlantis**, or so said those nineteenth-century scientists whose enthusiasm for new biological discoveries and analysis did reveal some very odd coincidences, including animal, plant and geological similarities in lands now separated by thousands of miles of ocean; similarities that we now know can be explained in terms of continental drift. The name Lemuria was invented by a zoologist and

Fellow of the Royal Society, P. L. Schater, and his case for the submerged continent was summed up in his assertion that so invariable was the law of adjoining countries producing similar animals and plants that the converse must be true; if the animals and plants of two countries are alike, they must once have been geographically connected. Men like the scientist Thomas Huxley (1825–95), the naturalist Alfred Russel Wallace (1823–1913) and the biologist Ernest Heinrich Haeckel (1834–1919) regarded Lemuria as a highly probable suggestion. The idea was received enthusiastically by students of **occultism**, and in particular by Madame **Blavatsky**, who included her 'esoteric ethnology' in her book *The Secret Doctrine* (1888) and pointed out that it agreed with the conclusions of Schater and his fellow scientists.

CONSULT: Robert Charroux, *Lost Worlds*, Souvenir Press (1973); W. Scott-Elliot, *The Story of Atlantis and the Lost Lemuria*, Anthroposophical Publications (1923).

## Leo
*See* **zodiac**.

## Lepracaun
Fairy or dwarf or gnome in Irish-Celtic folklore that is supposed to know the whereabouts of buried treasure and hidden wealth which, if captured by a mortal, he will reveal in exchange for his liberty, though he will vanish in a trice if you take your eyes off him for a moment. When a mortal discovers the hiding-place of the treasure or 'crock of gold', however, it disappears. The lepracaun is usually described as a little old man with a wrinkled face; they live alone and vary in height from a few inches to about two feet. *See also* **fairies**.

CONSULT: W. B. Yeats (ed.), *Fairy and Folk Tales of Ireland*, Colin Smythe (1973).

## Levi, Eliphas (1810-75)
His real name was Alphonse Louis Constant, and he was the leading French occultist of the nineteenth century. Born in Paris, he married a girl half his age who left him after a few years; the former theological student and political agitator then turning to **magic** and **occultism**. After years of study, Levi achieved such remarkable results from his high or 'transcendental' magic that, notwithstanding his great knowledge and experience, he collapsed in terror. Levi visited England twice and became friendly with Edward Bulwer-Lytton (later

Lord Lytton, and for years the most popular author in England) who was deeply interested in the occult and who produced a fanciful portrait of Levi as the magician in his story 'The Haunted and the Haunters'. Eliphas Levi's monumental *History of Magic*, perhaps the best of all studies of magic, contains information on such diverse occult aspects as magic in India, the **Cabala**, **mysticism**, virginity, **superstition**, magical monuments, the **Devil** and **black magic**, **alchemy**, freemasonry and **hallucinations**.

CONSULT: Richard Cavendish, *The Black Arts*, Routledge & Kegan Paul (1967); Eliphas Levi, *The History of Magic*, Rider (1913).

## Levitation

The rising and hovering in the air of physical objects or persons contrary to the laws of gravitation, by **paranormal** means; often the term is used to refer only to levitation of the body. Levitation is recorded in the Bible and is an ability attributed to many saints, holy men, spiritualist physical mediums, ecstatics and victims of demonic and other types of **possession**. A classic instance of apparent levitation by a saint is the remarkable case of St Joseph of Copertino, whose story is fully documented in Eric J. Dingwall's *Some Human Oddities*. Among the mediums who claimed levitation among their powers, perhaps the best known is D. D. Home (*see under* **spiritualism**). Levitation (real or imagined) was an essential part of **witchcraft**, with the witches using **flying ointment** and riding forth on **broomsticks**, and is often encountered in haunted houses and during **poltergeist** infestations, where the commonest reported incidents are movement and levitation of objects, particularly associated with bedsteads and sometimes persons themselves.

CONSULT: Eric John Dingwall, *Some Human Oddities*, Home & Van Thal (1947); Raynor C. Johnson, *The Imprisoned Splendour*, Hodder & Stoughton (1953).

## Leys

The name given to patterns of alignments between ancient stone circles, standing stones, dolmens, mounds, and megalithic remains generally throughout Britain and other areas of the globe, that are believed to be significant lines of power. In 1921 Alfred Watkins, an amateur archaeologist, observed from maps and field work that prehistoric remains, together with most pre-Reformation churches, fell into alignments, and these he called leys. He believed that the frequency with which straight lines joined these remains and supposedly 'Roman' roads revealed a network of neolithic trade routes. Subsequent investigation has suggested the possibility of the alignments carrying flows of a subtle energy, and **dowsing** has verified that megalithic sites do contain centres of energy and that certain stones are at times charged with a power akin to electromagnetism. In recent years a growing number of investigators and 'ley-hunters', including John Michell, the major exponent of a theory of leys, have tested the hypothesis that stone circles were formed as planetary observatories and have discovered scores of paths of power that could be of value to the archaeologist, the psychical researcher and the occultist. A bi-monthly magazine *The Ley Hunter,* founded in 1969, is now published by Paul Devereux, P.O. Box 152, London N10 1EP.

CONSULT: Alfred Watkins, *The Old Straight Way,* Garnstone Press (1971 edition); Paul Screeton, *Quicksilver Heritage,* Thorsons (1974).

## Libra
*See* **zodiac**.

## 'Light'
The oldest English spiritualist periodical, founded in 1881 by Dawson Rogers and Stainton Moses as a weekly representing the official organ of the London Spiritualist Alliance. This 'review of psychic and spiritual knowledge and research' is now issued quarterly by the **College of Psychic Studies** from their address, 16 Queensberry Place, London SW7.

CONSULT: Harry Price, *Fifty Years of Psychical Research,* Longmans, Green (1939).

## Lilith
*See under* **demonology**.

## 'Lines of power'
*See* **leys**.

## Lingham
The phallus, emblem of male generative and creative power; an object of reverence in **phallic worship**, and from earliest times, as is evident from ancient Indian art where it is often combined with the **yoni**.

*See also* **sex magic**.

CONSULT: H. Cutner, *A Short History of Sex Worship,* Watts (1940).

## Lobsang Rampa

In 1956 an Englishman, Cyril Henry Hoskin, published a book entitled *The Third Eye*, under the name of Lobsang Rampa, a Tibetan high priest. After publication the real author was found to be living in Dublin, having previously lived in a cottage at Thames Ditton. In the commotion that followed, Lobsang Rampa asserted that he was a genuine Tibetan priest or lama inhabiting the body of Hoskin. The apparent exposure had no effect on sales of *The Third Eye*, which has continued to sell steadily since its publication; and there is no doubt that, whatever the explanation, the man now legally known as Lobsang Rampa and resident in Montreal is a fascinating, unique and impressive personality. *See also* **third eye**.

CONSULT: Lobsang Rampa, *The Third Eye*, Secker & Warburg (1956); *The Rampa Story*, Souvenir Press (1960).

## Loch Ness Monster

*See under* **animals and birds**.

## Lodge, Sir Oliver (1851-1940)

Distinguished physicist and champion of survival after **death**. Born at Penkhull, Staffordshire, and educated at Newport Grammar School and University College, London, he became Professor of Physics, Liverpool (1881-1900), and Principal of Birmingham University (1900-19), a position he followed with an extensive American tour. He was awarded the Rumford Medal by the Royal Society in 1898, and the Albert Medal of the Royal Society of Arts in 1919; he was elected a Fellow of the Royal Society in 1902 and knighted in 1902. A pioneer in radio telegraphy, he studied electrolysis, electromagnetic radiation and invented several scientific instruments. He explored thought-transference (*see* **telepathy**) and took part in other experimental work and sat with many mediums (*see also* **mediumship** and **spiritualism**), particularly Eusapia Paladino, Mrs Leonore Piper, William Hope, Mrs Helen **Duncan**, and Mrs Gladys Osborne Leonard, through whom he was convinced he communicated with his son Raymond, who had been killed during the First World War. Lodge published the story of Raymond's 'spirit return' through various mediums (including Mrs Piper, Mrs Leonard, Vout Peters) in a volume entitled *Raymond, or Life and Death* (1916). The book was an enormous success, and at that time of emotional stress there is no doubt that it was responsible for convincing thousands that death was not the end.

Lodge was President of the British Association, the Physical Society, the Radio Society and the Röntgen Society; and of the **Society for Psychical Research** from 1901 to 1903. He is likely to be remembered as a dedicated propagandist for survival.

## London Spiritualist Alliance
*See* **College of Psychic Studies**.

## Lord of the Flies, or Beelzebub
*See under* **demonology**.

## Lorelei, or Lurlei
Tall, steep rock in the Rhine near St Goar, 427 feet high and possessing a remarkable echo. Among the many legends associated with the Lorelei Rock is the story of a beautiful maiden who sits on the rock, combing her flowing hair and tempting passing boatmen with her lovely and fatal singing until they venture too close and meet their deaths on the treacherous rocks; a variation tells of a beautiful maiden who was seen on the rock by many passing boatmen until some sad and unknown tragedy drove her away for ever. Other legends associate the rock with a scaly monster and identify it as the hiding-place of the Nibelung's treasure. The legends have been immortalized in poetry, song and music.

CONSULT: Wilhelm Ruland, *Legends of the Rhine,* Hoursch & Bechstedt, Cologne (14th edition, 1937).

## Loudun
Scene of a famous French case of apparent demonic **possession** in the seventeenth century when a priest, Urbain **Grandier**, was accused of bewitching the nuns at an Ursuline convent.

One of the nuns in the convent had been a young woman called Sister Joan of the Angels, and although certain dubious activities on her part did not pass unnoticed, the convent was poor and she was the daughter of the rich Baron Louis Bécier. In due course, and when she was only twenty-five, Sister Joan became Mother Superior, and since there was no longer the necessity to veil her habits and inclinations, she openly instructed the nuns to whip her. For several years, Grandier, as a young and attractive parish priest, had attracted criticism for his amorous reputation with young ladies. He had made enemies in high places, and in 1630 narrowly escaped being suspended from his parish duties by his archbishop. He seemed to the young and hysterical Mother Superior (there had been bitter opposition to her appointment, and she was unpopular with the nuns and novices) the epitomization of the forbidden pleasure of the flesh.

When Grandier's opponents spoke to Mother Joan of a conspiracy that would bring Grandier in close and constant attention, she wholeheartedly cooperated. In accordance with a preconceived plan, she and several other nuns began to show signs of demonic possession, speaking gibberish, twitching and making convulsive movements that included overt erotic gestures and postures and strange distortions of their faces, bodies and voices. At the height of the bizarre disturbances, one of the nuns mentioned the name of Father Grandier as the cause of the 'possessions', whereupon the Mother Superior, not to be outdone named not only the priest as being responsible but also two of the devils who did his bidding, Asmodeus and Zabulon (*see* **demonology**).

Grandier, as the alleged cause of the trouble, was sent to the convent to conduct **exorcisms**, and there, in the presence of witnesses, the frenzied nuns accused him of crimes that included fornication and unbridled lust. The Mother Superior then sealed his fate by asserting that she had witnessed the bewitchment of both nuns and novices, which he had accomplished by throwing bouquets of flowers over the convent walls. When Grandier was arrested, four **devil's marks** were found on his body, and he was tortured before being burnt alive in 1634. But by this time, Mother Joan and many of the occupants really did seem to be possessed, and Grandier's death had no affect on their behaviour. The situation got out of hand, news and exaggerations of the affair spread far and wide and the authorities decided to exorcize the Mother Superior herself. She began to have mystical **visions**, and only recovered from the possession after a visit to the tomb of St Francis de Sales in Italy four years later.

Her autobiography suggests that she had a strong exhibitionist streak in her make-up, and obtained excessive pleasure from the gyrations 'and other peculiar things' which 'the devil' did with her body. There is still confusion as to whether Mother Joan was a fraud, a hysteric, a schizophrenic or possibly an epileptic. Later she claimed visions, prophetic utterances and healing powers, and **stigmata** which took the form of the names of Jesus, Mary, Joseph and Francis de Sales appearing on her left hand.

CONSULT: Aldous Huxley, *The Devils of Loudun*, Chatto & Windus (1952); Kurt Seligmann, *Magic, Supernaturalism and Religion*, Allen Lane The Penguin Press (1971).

## Loup-garou

French name for **werewolf**, a person who turns into a wolf at night. They so appear only between sunset and dawn, and are particularly active in the vicinity of death; they can kill and devour human beings, but singing will keep them at bay. However, only a consecrated bullet or succeeding in making them bleed while in wolf form can kill or cure a loup-garou. Some authorities maintained that three drops of **blood** taken from the monster while it was in human form could be used to cure the loup-garou, in a ritual similar to that used by sorcerers who believe that, by drinking a man's blood you absorb his qualities.

*See also* **lycanthropy**.

CONSULT: Sabine Baring-Gould, *The Book of Werewolves*, Causeway, New York (1973); Montague Summers, *The Werewolf*, Kegan Paul, Trench, Trubner (1933).

## Lourdes

French watering resort at the foot of the Central Pyrenees, famous for its grotto where the young peasant girl known as **Bernadette** is said to have seen the Virgin Mary eighteen times between 11 February and 16 July 1858. The **apparition**, which was seen only by Bernadette, revealed the whereabouts of a spring which apparently made its appearance at this time and which has subsequently become the greatest centre of pilgrimage for healing in the Roman Catholic world.

Pilgrims by the thousand pay devotion to 'Our Lady of Lourdes', and there have been numerous reported cures of bodily ailments, some instantaneous and some announced to be miraculous after inquiry by ecclesiastical authorities. A medical bureau examines persons who claim to have been cured, and a church, an underground basilica accommodating 20 000 pilgrims, and many hotels and souvenir shops cater for an annual influx of two million visitors. Most of the cures seem to come within the general pattern of so-called **faith healing**, and there is little to suggest that they are any more numerous or more or less miraculous than the general run of such cures.

CONSULT: Alan Neame, *The Happening at Lourdes*, Hodder & Stoughton (1968); D. J. West, *Eleven Lourdes Miracles*, Duckworth (1951).

## Love potions and philtres

Magical aphrodiciacs which were supposed to cause the consumer to fall in love with the next person he or she saw; usually a concoction of narcotic perfumes, the testes of bulls or other animals, ginger and cinnamon, human hearts, urine, semen and mandrake pounded and mixed to a liquid with **salt** in it, to arouse passion, while a magical **incantation** was spoken. Love potions could be directed towards one particular person, and then the ingredients, to be really effective, would have to include something of a personal nature from the person concerned: a snippet of **hair** from the head or body, nail cuttings, a spot of **blood** or sexual secretions.

Lust-killing potions or anaphrodisiac philtres were also available, ranging from the relatively innocent 'rings of oblivion' (for women who wished to be able to forget their old loves and turn to new ones) to such drastic endeavours at dampening the fires of lust as ingredients that included lizards soused in urine and mouse dung. Some of these materials are used to this day by practitioners of **black magic**.

CONSULT: Richard Cavendish, *The Black Arts,* Routledge & Kegan Paul (1967).

## Lucid dreams
Term coined by Celia Green of the Institute of Psychophysical Research for dreams in which the dreamer has learned to be aware that he, or she, is dreaming; such dreams can be used to prevent nightmares, but they raise questions about states of consciousness, **telepathy** and **extrasensory perception**.

CONSULT: Celia Green, *Lucid Dreams,* Hamish Hamilton (1968); and, with Charles McCreery, *Apparitions,* Hamish Hamilton (1975).

## Lucifer
*See under* **demonology**.

## Luck
Good fortune; a vague, indefinite quality that certain objects are said to possess and can confer on their owners; luck exists, it would seem, all about us, sometimes working for us and at other times avoiding us. Luck, according to magicians, can be summoned; and it would appear to be a quality possessed by certain individuals. There are lucky signs or **omens** (finding a pin or money or a four-leafed clover); but also **taboos** which, if broken, will bring bad fortune (walking under a ladder). The speaking of certain words or following certain actions (such as touching wood) and other rituals can bring good luck (crossing the fingers, making a wish on birthday-cake candles). The innumerable lucky objects, **amulets** and **talismans** that ward off evil, range from a **horseshoe** or a rabbit's foot to a stone with a hole in it

and phallic symbols. There are said to be lucky numbers, lucky days, lucky colours, lucky stones and lucky faces. The principal of a lucky **charm** is that the wearer concentrates his thoughts on the object and so creates an effective psychic barrier against bad luck or produces a focus of psychic influence that promotes good luck.

*See also* **superstition**.

## Lull, Ramón, or Raymond Lully (c. 1235-1315)

Spanish mystic, philosopher and poet. Known as the 'enlightened doctor', and describing himself as 'God's own madman', he was inspired by a **vision** of Christ; and turning from a life of dissolution he dedicated himself to solitude and **meditation**, followed by mystical philosophy and preaching Christianity to the heathens. Miracles are said to have taken place at the site of his burial beneath a mausoleum in the cathedral at Palma. Lull was thought to practise **alchemy** and to possess the **elixir of life** and the **philosopher's stone** because of his familiarity with signs, words and letters that were unintelligible to most people. He met his end by being stoned to death by Moslems whom he was attempting to convert.

CONSULT: E. A. Peers, *Ramón Lull,* Franklin, Chicago (1969).

## Lycanthropy

Scientific term for the magical **metamorphosis** of man into beast, or the belief that such a transformation takes place. Derived from the Greek meaning 'wolf' and 'man', it is particularly applied to the **werewolf**, the changing of men into wolves, said to have been a common occurrence among the North American Indians. There are also reports from various parts of the world of lycanthropy involving tigers (the 'tiger-men' of Bengal), leopards (the 'leopard-men' of Africa), bears (the 'bear-men' of Russia) and jackals (the 'jackal-men' of the Congo). The metamorphosis apparently took place either through enchantment or by donning the actual skin of the animal; and the idea has also been used by secret societies to terrorize and control people, as was evident during the Mau Mau disturbances in Kenya in the 1950s. Some writers, including Pliny, considered lycanthropy to be a form of punishment, and believed that lycanthropes were doomed to suffer in this way for a specific number of years. The idea of donning a wolf's skin may be a survival of wolf-worship or a form of **sympathetic magic**. The term lycanthropy is also used to denote a form of insanity in which the sufferer believes that he, or she, is a particular animal and behaves accordingly.

*See also* **Grenier, Jean; loup-garou; totems and totemism.**
Consult: Robert Eisler, *Man Into Wolf*, Routledge & Kegan Paul
(1951); William Seabrook, *Witchcraft: Its Power in the World Today*,
Harrap (1941).

# M

## 'Mabinogion, The'

A collection of eleven medieval Welsh stories written down between the eleventh and thirteenth centuries but based on earlier oral traditions that originated in mythology, folklore and heroic tradition. They belong to a forgotten Celtic Britain, express a pagan past of lore and legend and have had a profound effect on European literature. *The Mabinogion* contains some of the earliest surviving material pertaining to King Arthur.

CONSULT: *The Mabinogion*, J. M. Dent, Everyman's Library (1948 edition).

## Machen, Arthur (1863-1947)

Scholar, literary man, actor, journalist, sometime member of the Order of the **Golden Dawn**, raconteur and good companion; best known for his short story, 'The Bowmen', which originated the legend of the **Angels of Mons**.

## Magi

Originally a learned and priestly tribe of Medians and ancient Persians (singular 'magus'), and later Zoroastrians, who preserved traditional lore and practised sacred rites; the keepers and custodians of the secret things; tutors of kings, philosophers, augurs and astrologers. Magi were the wise men, adepts of the occult arts, magicians, and the three wise men who came from the East to salute and worship the infant Jesus are referred to as Magi. Greek and Roman writers assert that the Magi were also dissolute and licentious, and immoral under the guise of austerity. At all events, the Magi gradually lost their high class and exclusiveness and, from a position where no transaction of importance took place without or against their advice, they became strolling jugglers, fortune-tellers and diviners. 'Magi' is derived from the same Persian word as our word '**magic**'.

## Magic

The means whereby can be discovered unknown forces of nature, and the harnessing and employment of those forces. The ultimate aim of magic is said to be the total domination of the universe, and magicians believe that they invoke intelligences that enable them to control natural laws, and thus they can, it is maintained, influence people at a distance, be in two places at one time, read the minds of others, know the future, affect the elements, and, in fact, 'do all things'. A magician's aim is hence power, its acquisition and use: supreme power over all things; although he accepts that a lifetime is insufficient and many **reincarnations** may be necessary.

A magician loves secrecy and preserves his secrets at all costs: it is the obscure, the mysterious, the cryptic, the strange and the concealed that appeal to him, and he closely guards his knowledge and his discoveries. With **magic circles** – full of mystic symbols – and rites that incorporate the hidden mysteries of the ages, he and his assistants seek to conjure up all-powerful forces and at the same time protect themselves. In magic there is no good and no evil, for ultimately these do not exist, and therefore the magician feels free to exercise his practices in any way and using any person he feels to be advantageous to his purpose.

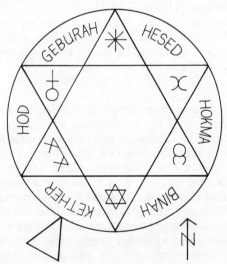

*'Magical circle' found in a deserted cottage at Layer-de-la-Haye, Essex, in 1972*

It is said that the history of man is the history of magic, and certainly magic can be found to have been practised from earliest times through **Druidism**, the **Magi**, the Egyptians (*see* **Egyptian magic**), Greeks, Romans, Jews (*see* **Cabala**), **Knights Templar**, the Church, the orient and in **witchcraft** right up to the present day with Aleister **Crowley**, Gerald **Gardner** and their followers attempting to harness the ancient powers and, by means of either **white magic** or **black magic** (or both), to reach the acme of perfection in the magical arts.

CONSULT: C. A. Burland, *The Magical Arts,* Arthur Barker (1966); Eliphas Levi, *Transcendental Magic,* Rider (1968 reprint).

## Magic circle

Area of ground prepared in a special way by a sorcerer or magician as a place of refuge against evil **spirits**. The essential quality in magical practice is for everything that is used to be virginal, new, unused, full of original force with nothing dissipated by previous use or a previous owner which could prove dangerous to the magician. Often the implements of a magician's trade are made entirely by himself, and this invariably applies to the magic circle, which is often drawn by the magician's **wand** (or phallic symbol), a switch of hazel, nineteen and a half inches long, cut at sunrise with the magician's knife or **athame**, stained with **blood** to 'capture' energy. Magic circles are usually drawn clockwise, but in **black magic** are drawn **withershins**.

Students of **magic** have always considered the circle to be a strong source of power in itself: stone, tree and mound circles abound; groups of people linked by a common interest or aim call themselves a circle; the **zodiac** is a circular plan of the sun's apparent progression through the stars in a twelve-month cycle; clocks, depicting time's relentless passing, are usually circular, and indeed the circle, because it is composed of an endless line, has been used as a symbol for eternity. The magic circle keeps away or outside the circle evil spirits, retaining within its confines the magical energy summoned up and guarding those who remain inside its protective bounds. A magic circle can be drawn on the ground or floor, preferably with a sword or knife but also with charcoal or chalk, and the outer limits must be nine feet in diameter. Within this circle another is drawn, eight feet in diameter, and between the two circles are placed items and substances that reinforce the strength of the barrier between the magician and malign forces: bowls of water, crosses and crucifixes; **names of power** and plants such as vervain (the 'holy herb') and dill (the 'herbe better known than desired') and other articles disliked by **demons**.

*Sixteenth-century magic circle for all conjurations*

Once the magician and his associates have entered the safety of the circle, carefully 'closing' it behind them to ensure that there is no break or gap to allow entrance to any harmful spirit, they must on no account step out of the circle until the proceedings are completed. Within the protective circle will be four medallions or **pentagrams** with, between them, the 'terrible' names of the creator of the universe: between the east and south, Tetragrammaton; between south and west Eheyt; between west and north, Elijon; and between north and east, Eloha.

A magic circle reproduced in *Le Dragon rouge* (Avignon, 'dated' 1522, but actually 1822) is in fact a Triangle of Pacts, and to be effective it had to be made with the skin of a kid and nailed with four nails. The triangle within the circle would be traced with an 'enamelled 'stone', and the 'kersi' or magician stood or sat within the larger circle (see page 314) while his associates occupied the remaining two circles. To each side lighted candles would burn, surrounded by wreaths of vervain, while in front of the magician a fire burned in a new brazier, consuming willow-wood charcoal, brandy, incense and camphor. With appropriate **incantations** and magical passes with the wand, the magician gradually progressed along the 'Path of the T' which leads to Satanic treasure. Behind them the three practitioners of the secret arts were protected with crosses and the inscription JHS – meaning 'Jesus'. Other magic circles, of varying complexity and originality, can be found in sources devoted to the study of magic.

CONSULT: Richard Cavendish, *The Black Arts,* Routledge & Kegan Paul (1967); Émile Grillot de Givry, *Witchcraft, Magic and Alchemy,* University Books, New York (1958).

## Magic squares

Since, in **magic**, numbers and letters are containers of power, the arrangement of numbers and letters in a certain way may be still more powerful and act as **talismans,** have curative properties, put out fires

| S | A | T | O | R |
|---|---|---|---|---|
| A | R | E | P | O |
| T | E | N | E | T |
| O | P | E | R | A |
| R | O | T | A | S |

| S | A | L | O | M |
|---|---|---|---|---|
| A | R | E | P | O |
| L | E | M | E | L |
| O | P | E | R | A |
| M | O | L | A | S |

| M | I | L | O | N |
|---|---|---|---|---|
| I | R | A | G | O |
| L | A | M | A | L |
| O | G | A | R | I |
| N | O | L | I | M |

| C | A | S | E | D |
|---|---|---|---|---|
| A | Z | O | T | E |
| B | O | R | O | S |
| E | T | O | S | A |
| D | E | B | A | C |

*Magic letter-squares: those with words that read the same from any direction are usually used to promote good luck and as protection from evil; the Milon square enables the future to be seen (if written on parchment and placed on the top of the head) and the Cased square is so sinister that it should never be used; it is said to 'overflow with unrestrained lust'*

| 4 | 9 | 2 |
|---|---|---|
| 3 | 5 | 7 |
| 8 | 1 | 6 |

| 4 | 14 | 15 | 1 |
|---|----|----|---|
| 9 | 7 | 6 | 12 |
| 5 | 11 | 10 | 8 |
| 16 | 2 | 3 | 13 |

*Magic number-squares: each number must appear once
only and the vertical and horizontal rows and the two
diagonals must each add up to the same total. The smaller
Square of Saturn (the oldest known number square) is
generally regarded as protective and helpful but can also
be destructive and cause discord. The large Square of
Jupiter is said to have curative properties*

and cause **spirits** to be conjured up and reveal secrets. In a magic-number square, each and every number must appear once, and the addition of the numbers, vertically, horizontally and diagonally, must achieve the same total (see diagram); while magic-letter squares must read the same from left to right, from right to left, and downwards and upwards (see diagram). It is because of the difficulties and complications involved that the squares are thought to have magical power. Dion **Fortune** tells of a man who was unable to control the force he unleashed using a magic square from **Mathers**'s *Sacred Magic*.

CONSULT: Richard Cavendish, *The Black Arts*, Routledge & Kegan Paul (1967); S. L. Mathers, *The Book of the Sacred Magic of Abramelin the Mage*, De Laurence, Chicago (1932).

## Magpie
*See under* **animals and birds**.

## Maithuna
Tantric term for sexual intercourse. *See also* **tantrism**.

## 'Malleus Maleficarum'
Famous *Hammer of Witches*, written by two Dominican inquisitors,

Heinrich Kramer and Jakob Sprenger, first published in 1486. It is a text-book covering every aspect of **witchcraft**, and generally accepted as the most authoritative work on the apparent activities of witches and **demons**, and the methods of interrogation, torturing, conviction and execution of witches. There is an excellent English translation by Montague **Summers**, for which he also wrote an introduction and supplied a bibliography and notes (Pushkin Press, 1948).

## Mandala
Sanskrit word meaning 'circle', and used in Eastern cultures to denote a mystical diagram; one of the most widespread of all **symbols**, often denoting eternity or wholeness, found in religious and profane art throughout the world. Occultists maintain that the mandala becomes charged with the presence of the **spirits**, deities or gods that are represented within the mystic circle. Mandalas can also be used as an aid to **meditation**, and there are temple walls in Tibet covered with elaborate mandalas, each different in design, that are said to be full of occult significance.

CONSULT: C. G. Jung, *Archetypes and the Collective Unconscious*, Routledge & Kegan Paul (1959); G. Tucci, *The Theory and Practice of the Mandala*, Rider (1961).

## Mandrake
*See under* **trees and plants**.

## Manning, Matthew (b. 1956)
Contemporary psychic with apparent diagnostic and healing powers, automatic writing and drawing ability (*see* **automatism**), and metal-bending and influencing powers. He was also a centre of **poltergeist** activity when he was younger. Manning is not a spiritualist, and in fact has no religious views, but he does believe that he is able to communicate with something that survives **death**, and the interesting thing is that he seems to be able to turn on his psychic powers at will. This means that it is possible to undertake scientific experimentation in laboratory conditions, and after three weeks at the Toronto Society for Psychical Research in 1973 a consensus of twenty scientists decided that his powers look more like a part of nature, like electricity and magnetism, than anything else. They discovered, for example, that when he 'switched on' for the purpose of bending a piece of metal or moving a compass needle, his brainwaves changed completely and seemed to be of the very low frequency that we usually associate with

deep sleep. They also believed that the source of the electrical energy being produced was in the central part of the brain, the oldest part known as the 'animal brain', about which very little is known. They concluded that the psychic power demonstrated by Manning was an innate function and ability probably lost in most of mankind during thousands of years of evolution. Dr George Owen has studied the Matthew Manning case closely, including the poltergeist activity that used to take place in his vicinity; the psycho-kinetic powers that developed later; his ability to see **auras**; his automatic writing and drawing, some of which Manning freely admits may originate in his own subconscious mind; and his healing abilities. In 1975 three emissaries of the Pope are reported to have sought the aid of Matthew Manning.

CONSULT: Matthew Manning, *The Link*, Colin Smythe (1974).

## Mantra

Sanskrit word for '**spell**'; words or sounds spoken in a certain order and manner which are said to have magical effect; a formula whose repetition drives away disease and bodes well for the person to whom it is directed. A mantra consists of words or sounds of power, the foundation of all **magic**; and supreme among the most potent mantras is the monosyllable 'Om', which is said to contain the ultimate formula for universal knowledge and ultimate power.

CONSULT: Richard Cavendish, *The Black Arts*, Routledge & Kegan Paul (1967); Sirdar Ikbal Ali Shah, *Occultism: Its Theory and Practice*, Rider (1952).

## 'Margery'

Pseudonym of American physical medium, Mrs L. R. G. **Crandon**.

## Marion, Frederick

Czech telepathist, hypernesthetric (ultra-sensitive) and psycho-metrist, real name Josef Kraus, who became well known for his many lecture-demonstrations in **telepathy** and **psychometry** and for his willing cooperation with investigators. Part of the skill of 'Marion' (as he was known professionally) lay in his ability to obtain unconscious hints from his audience and those who were present. Generally, the more he was obscured, the less successful he was in finding hidden objects. Experiments with Marion were conducted by Harry **Price** at the National Laboratory of Psychical Research.

CONSULT: Frederick Marion, *In My Mind's Eye,* Rider (1949); Harry Price, *Fifty Years of Psychical Research,* Longmans, Green (1939).

## Mark, witch's
*See* **devil's mark.**

## Marryat, Florence (1837-99)
English daughter of the celebrated author Captain Marryat; she knew and sat with practically all the important mediums of Britain and the United States in the 1870s and 1880s, experiencing many remarkable happenings, which she recorded in her books, *There is No Death* (1891) and *The Spirit World* (1894). Florence also claimed to possess certain psychic powers, including the ability to summon the living by other than normal means.

## Mars
The fourth planet from the sun, known for its antiquity and its apparent red colour which suggested its identification with the gods of war. Mars was originally an agricultural deity, and the Salian priests chanted and pounded the ground as they prayed to him to promote fertility; later magicians believed (and believe) that they could use the current of destructive energy associated with the planet against their enemies. The colour for Mars is scarlet; the metal, **iron**; number, five; the animals, horse, bear and wolf; the plants, the absinthe and rue; the letters, 'p' and 'e'. Sorcerers invoked Mars with a mixture that included saffron and the **blood** of a black cat. The ruby represented Mars, and while this jewel was worn for its beneficial virtues, increased purity and power of excluding sorrow, it also had a darker side with its ability to stir up strife and cause disharmony. In **astrology**, Mars, as the planet of aggressiveness, activity and determination, indicates from its position on the birth chart how active and energetic the subject is likely to be.

## Masks
Coverings for the face used for protection, disguise or concealment; a death mask is a plaster cast of a face taken soon after **death.**

Masks have been used in many cultures for ceremonial and religious purposes, and their use for entertainment and festivity is of comparatively minor importance. Early man, as evidenced in cave drawings, made gods in his own image, and facial masks played a big part; another ancient use of masks was by the Egyptians, who believed that a mask resembling the living person and buried with the mummy (*see* **mummification**) aided return to life. In the Eastern cultures of Burma, Ceylon, China, Japan, Java, Siam and Tibet, masks have always played an important part in dramatic performances, dances and religious rites, while such different aspects of culture as the Greek theatre and the medieval European mumming and miracle plays have also played their part in the popularity and wide use of masks.

In New Guinea, natives were in the habit of carving masks of dead relatives and concocting masks with the skin of their ancestors in an effort to preserve for themselves and their descendants the virtues of their predecessors. Mystery plays and the devil-dancing cult of Tibet, ostensibly used in the **exorcism** of malignant **demons**, saw the emergence of terrifying masks that were thought to frighten bad **spirits** – an idea paralleled by African and other native witchdoctors; and the horned and grotesque mask with stag horns familiar at mid-European festivals (also used in **witchcraft** rites) is reminiscent of an earlier, heathen period connected with the summer and winter solstices (*see also* **festivals**).

Masks have been used for such varying purposes as **initiation** rites and by fraudulent mediums to aid the production of fake **materializations**. They have also been used by modern followers of witchcraft cults in their rites and practices when, in the past, witch **sabbaths** saw the worshippers as well as the 'gods' dressed in masks, often animal heads and skins, but otherwise naked to facilitate sexual union with the **horned god** with his enormous (usually artificial) phallus; where no artifice was used, the face and body mask of the horned god enabled the occupant to be changed. Masks are commonly used in secret and occult societies where they are thought to endow the wearer with magical powers as he takes on the appearance of someone more powerful, mystical and stronger than himself.

CONSULT: Ken Baynes, *Art and Society,* Lund Humphries (1975); Ernest Crawley, *The Mystic Rose,* Watts (1902).

## Materialization

The production in darkness by an unknown agency of temporary **spirits** or entities, in varying degrees of solidification, in the form, likeness and appearance of human beings, in whole or in part, and said to be composed of **ectoplasm**. Materialization is the pinnacle of a physical medium's ability, and there exists convincing evidence for recognized materializations both full-size and minute at **séances**; and although photographic evidence (captured by infra-red apparatus) is abundant, it is less satisfactory. Outstanding physical mediums reported to have produced convincing materializations include Florence Cook, Eva C, the **Schneider brothers**, Helen Duncan, Jack Webber and Alec Harris (*see also under* **spiritualism**). In recent years, physical mediums of all kinds, and particularly materialization mediums, have become exceedingly rare.

See also **mediumship**.

CONSULT: Dr Gustave Geley, *Clairvoyance and Materialisation,* T. Fisher Unwin (1927); Baron von Schrenck-Notzing, *The Phenomena of Materialisation,* Kegan Paul (1920).

## Mathers, Samuel Liddell (MacGregor) (1854-1918)

British magician closely connected with the Order of the **Golden Dawn** after he apparently deciphered (with the help of his clairvoyant wife, sister of the philosopher Henri Bergson) a mysterious manuscript in code picked up by a clergyman (Dr Woodman) on a street bookstall in 1884. Mathers's solution revealed that the manuscript was concerned with the **Cabala** and the **Tarot**. He was invited to join the Order of the Golden Dawn, and before long had succeeded in forcing out the founders and putting himself in command.

Mathers, whose house in Paris was decorated in the style of an Egyptian temple, officiated at 'Egyptian Masses' in a white robe embroidered with mystic and zodiacal bracelets on his wrists and ankles and a leopard skin over one shoulder. W. B. **Yeats**, another member of the Order, often visited the Mathers, and it is recorded that they used to play a form of chess for four players, Mrs Mathers and Yeats pitting their skill against Mathers and a **spirit** he apparently conjured up for the purpose. For a time, Mathers acted as a kind of magical patron to Aleister **Crowley**, but the two soon quarrelled and became bitter enemies, each vying with the other to harm his opponent by magical means; indeed, when Mathers eventually died many of his friends believed that Crowley was responsible. Mathers's most notable contribution to **magic** was his English translation of the **Key of Solomon**, the famous **grimoire** of **ritual magic**. He also translated and edited *The Book of Sacred Magic of Abramelin the Mage, The Grimoire of Armadel* and *The Kabbalah Unveiled.*

CONSULT: Ellic Howe, *The Magicians of the Golden Dawn,* Routledge & Kegan Paul (1972); Francis King, *Ritual Magic in England,* Neville Spearman (1970).

# May Day
*See under* **festivals**.


# Meditation
A part of every culture and religion of man; the fourth state of consciousness (distinguished from waking, sleeping and dreaming). Meditation is said to allow the mind to turn in on itself, and is often achieved by the constant repetition of a word or phrase, usually a single-syllable word or **mantra**, producing 'more clarity of mind' and a growth of consciousness, awareness, inner peace and apparent knowledge. Transcendental Meditation (known as TM) has become widely popular, and teaching colleges exist in nearly every country in the world; while such groups as the Hindu **Hare Krishna** movement, actually the International Society for Krishna Consciousness (ISKON), with its chanting, dancing, incense, sitar recitals and lavish drama presentations, proceeds from strength to strength in an age of unbelief.

CONSULT: J. H. M. Whiteman, *The Mystical Life,* Faber & Faber (1961); L. K. Yu, *The Secrets of Chinese Meditation,* Rider (1969).


# Mediumship
The apparent ability to act as intermediary between the spirit world and the normal and everyday world. A medium, usually either a 'physical medium', producing physical phenomena, or a 'mental medium', producing mental phenomena, is a person by or through whom **paranormal** phenomena are produced. Spiritualists maintain that mediumship is as natural as the operation of the five senses and that mediums (sometimes called '**sensitives**'), unlike most people, discover these latent faculties and learn to utilize them.

To develop mediumship, the potential medium will spend many hours sitting with sympathetic and like-minded persons at regular times; such sittings are known as 'home circles', and spiritualists claim that this natural, uncritical and undisturbed form of development is the bedrock of the spiritualist movement (*see* **spiritualism**) and a method that has produced most of the best mediums. There are also rare, 'born mediums' who have apparently been aware of their 'gift' before realizing that it was mediumship, but even these remarkable people benefit from **meditation** and 'sittings' to develop their psychic awareness.

Prominent among the products of physical mediumship is **ectoplasm**, a strange substance which is exuded from the bodily orifices of the medium while in the **trance** state, and apparently capable of forming itself into rod-like appendages that make possible the movement of physical objects; into a 'voice-box' that makes **direct voice** speaking possible; into hand-like appendages that can touch other sitters and produce writing and drawings; into cloud-like formations that incorporate likenesses of dead people; and, the ultimate achievement, can build itself into a human form (minute or full-size) that is recognizable as a deceased person. Such ectoplasm (which is usually produced in darkness) is said to be composed of material partly supplied by the physical body of the medium, and any light or sudden shock causes it to retreat into the medium's body, resulting in discomfort, pain and distress.

During the several stages of mediumship, each seemingly making 'communication' easier, there seems to be an increasing degree of dissociation until the medium reaches a degree of trance in which his or her normal personality is replaced by a totally different identity which spiritualists accept as a discarnate human being who has taken over the medium's body and become the **control**. There is no doubt that some communications received during **séances** and some physical phenomena produced in conjunction with mediumship have no scientific explanation and, indeed, suggest contact in an unknown way with intelligent but deceased personalities; hence the subject of mediumship merits the serious consideration that it receives from dedicated psychical researchers.

Prominent mental mediums have included the American Mrs Leonora Piper, who was most thoroughly investigated by competent researchers; Mrs Osborne Leonard, who convinced Sir Oliver **Lodge** of survival after **death**; Mrs Eileen Garrett, who was the medium at the remarkable **R101** séances, and Douglas Johnson, who has taken part in many scientific experiments. Well-known physical mediums have included D. D. Home, who demonstrated **levitation** and was never caught cheating; Eusapia Palladino, who could also produce puzzling phenomena but who certainly cheated on occasions, and the **Schneider brothers**, Rudi and Willi, who were thoroughly and scientifically investigated by Harry **Price** and other investigators.

CONSULT: Rosalind Heywood, *The Sixth Sense,* Pan Books (1966); Muriel A. Hillier, *The Development of Mediumship,* Psychic Press (1964); Harry Price, *Fifty Years of Psychical Research,* Longmans, Green (1939).

## Medmenham Abbey, and monks of
*See* **Hell-Fire Club**.

## Mephistopheles
The name, in the Faust legend, of the **demon** or evil **spirit** to whom, in return for his assistance, Faust sold his soul; possibly derived from the Greek, meaning 'he who loves not light', a development of ancient Mespotamian religion where the direct opposite was Marduk, 'the lord of light'; both have been called on by latter-day occultists for purposes of **sorcery**. In Marlowe's *Dr Faustus*, Mephistopheles is a mischievous spirit, but also the **Devil**, a fallen angel who eventually drags Faust down to **Hell**. In Goethe's *Faust*, he appears in animal and human form, but also as the Devil: at the witches' **sabbath** on the Brocken he is hailed as 'the knight with the horse's hoof'.

## Mermaids
Legendary creatures that were beautiful maidens above the waist, but otherwise had the shape and form of a fish; they were seductive and dangerous enchantresses whose ancestors were the sirens who lured sailors to destruction with their plaintive cries. Mermaids, and their male counterparts, mermen, were said to haunt the rocks and sandbanks of coastlines, often holding a **mirror**, symbolic of association with the **moon**.

Sailors have always regarded it as bad luck to glimpse a mermaid, for merpeople were thought to lure sailors to the underwater world and imprison their souls for ever. Many stories of sailors and the sea relate that the sighting of a mermaid preceded misfortune: a storm, an accident, a death on board, shipwreck. The only way mortals could exert power over a mermaid was to obtain one of her possessions: her mirror or her cap or belt. There are many stories of marriages between mer-creatures and human beings, and of mermaids taking human shape to gain for themselves an immortal soul. At Zennor, in Cornwall, a legend, perpetuated by a carved mermaid in the little parish church, tells of a visit by a mermaid 'many years ago' who was lured ashore by the beautiful singing of Matthew Trewhella in Zennor Church; Matthew became bewitched by the beauty of the mermaid and was himself lured into the sea and his singing was heard during many years afterwards from deep beneath the waves.

CONSULT: S. Baring-Gould, *Curious Myths of the Middle Ages*, Longmans, Green (1897); David Thomson, *The People of the Sea*, Turnstile Press (1954).

## Mesmer, Friedrich (or Franz) Anton (1733-1815)

Austrian doctor who believed in **astrology** and conceived the idea that the stars and planets could affect human beings; and having identified the supposed force with magnetism, he began to stroke patients with magnets. Ten years later he abandoned the use of magnets and decided that the mysterious curative influence or occult force resided within himself and could be transmitted through the nervous system and hands of the operator. He began to hold **séances** in Vienna, but was moved on by the police. He then went to Paris, and it soon became fashionable to attend Mesmer's consultations. He devised a *baquet*, or large wooden tub, which was filled with water and iron filings and bottles of 'magnetized' water. Iron rods which protruded from it were then applied to diseased patients, while the originator of 'animal magnetism' (as Mesmer called the influence) moved among his patients, dressed like a magician, to a background of soft music and dim lighting. The medical faculty denounced him as a charlatan and the 'magnetic fluid' as a myth, but grateful patients proclaimed cures, and Mesmer, undoubtedly honest in his beliefs, remained popular for years. Mesmer left France in 1789 and moved to Switzerland, where he died in obscurity thirty-six years later. Mesmer's name lived on in the word 'Mesmerism', later to become **hypnotism**.

CONSULT: A. Weitzenhoffer, *Hypnotism*, Wiley, New York (1953); E. J. Dingwall (ed.), *Abnormal Hypnotic Phenomena: a Survey of Nineteenth-Century Cases*, Churchill (1967-8).

## Mesmerism

*See* **Mesmer**.

## Metagnomy

Name given to knowledge that has been acquired other than through the five senses, i.e. through **cryptesthesia**.

## Metamorphosis

Change of shape in zoology, and a common phenomenon in myths, legends and the folklore of many countries. The gods took on human or animal form; witches changed into black cats; magicians into loathsome and hissing forms. **Werewolves** are a form of metamorphosis, as are **vampires**, and some sorcerers are said to have achieved the ability to change shape.

*See also* **lycanthropy**.

## Metaphysics

The philosophy and science of being, thought or reality; abstract speculation. Originally the name applied to the books of Aristotle which followed his *Physics*; now a philosophical term, with ontology, for immaterial concepts of essence, existence, natural theology, etc.; a science that looks at the fundamental problems of knowledge and reality.

CONSULT: J. S. Mackenzie, *Outline of Metaphysics*, Macmillan (1902); W. H. Walsh, *Metaphysics*, Hutchinson (1963).

## Metapsychics

A term coined by Professor Charles Richet in 1905 for the phenomena of, and experimentation in, **psychical research**. He described metapsychics as 'a science dealing with mechanical or psychological phenomena due to forces which seem to be intelligent, or to unknown powers, latent in human intelligence'.

## Midsummer

*See under* **festivals**.

## Mind reading

*See* **telepathy**.

## Miracle

From the Latin *miraculum*, denoting an occurrence that excited wonder; a supernatural event; a visible marvel. Reported 'miracles' often involve a religious statue or picture that is said to move or exhibit such human attributes as bleeding or crying: in such 'miracles' the belief probably produces the **hallucination** and the hallucination confirms the belief. The expression 'miracle cures' is sometimes used in describing **faith healing** or **spirit healing**, and in respect of **stigmata** and even such events as the **Indian rope trick**. Most of the biblical miracles can be explained within the framework of what we now know of man and his environment.

CONSULT: C. F. D. Moule (ed.), *Miracles*, Mowbray (1965); Robert D. Smith, *Comparative Miracles*, Herder, St Louis (1965).

## Mirror

Ever since the first man or woman looked into a woodland pool and saw their reflection, imagination was stimulated and mirrors have been associated with **divination**, although there was always the fear that the reflection was the soul and that it might be stolen by water **spirits** and dragged into the unknown depths below, leaving its owner to languish and perish without one. If the reflection remained clear and unruffled, the future was equally calm and free of danger, but if the reflection was broken or disturbed, trouble, misfortune or possibly **death** were thought to lie ahead. As man progressed, manufactured mirrors inherited the qualities formerly to be found in pools and still water, and **catoptromancy**, the art of mirror divination, was developed and practised by seers and 'scryers' who, for many years, held an important social position and were consulted by the highest in the land as much as by the lowliest.

**Scrying** reached its peak in England in the reign of Elizabeth I, when the witch-hunters employed it as an infallible means of rooting out a witch. Mirrors were also used by sorcerers, alchemists, diviners and magicians, with Dr John **Dee** perhaps the best known. Mirrors were thought to repel the **evil eye**, a belief that gave rise to the fashion for wearing an ornamental mirror in the hat (popular in the seventeenth century) and the so-called 'witch balls', originally composed of reflecting glass. Mirror magic included the ability to deter evil spirits and to strike fear into the hearts of **vampires**, who had no reflection.

Even today the breaking of a mirror is regarded as portending ill-fortune, bad luck and all sorts of disasters for a period of seven years: the period the body was believed to take to undergo physical renewal. However, the bad luck from breaking a mirror could be averted by burying the pieces in hallowed ground or casting them in a stream or river so that the harmful influences would be carried away in the running waters. The danger of seeing one's own reflection is expressed in the Greek story of Narcissus, the youth who was so entranced with his own beauty reflected in a pool that he reached out for it and was embraced by death; while the mirror as a door through which the soul can find freedom finds expression in many **superstitions** and in the continued use of mirrors in **witchcraft** and **sorcery**.

CONSULT: Sir George James Frazer, *The Golden Bough*, Macmillan (1913 edition); Edith Hamilton, *Mythology*, Little, Brown, Boston (1940).

# Mistletoe
*See under* **trees and plants**.

## Moleosophy

Character **divination** by studying the location of moles on the body. The possession of moles is considered to be lucky on the whole, and lighter-coloured ones are said to be luckier than those that are dark in colour.

A brief survey of this art shows distinction between a round mole: a good character; an angular mole: a bad character; and an oblong or irregular-shaped mole: wealth. And the position of the mole on the body is regarded as follows: a mole on the ankle denotes a quick person with ambition; on the arm, an industrious and happy person; on the back, a cautious, inquiring, possibly timid person; on the breast, a lazy, quarrelsome and unpleasant person; on the buttocks, a person without ambition; on the calf, a resourceful and bright person; on the cheek, a quiet and studious person; on the chest (centre), a friendly and helpful person; on the chin, a generous, trustworthy person; on the elbow, a talented person who loves travel; on the feet, a thoughtful and moody person; on the finger, a person who worries; on the genitals, a lustful person; on the hand, a happy person; on the hip, a contented and intelligent person; on the knee, an extravagant person; on the neck, a generous, lucky and loving person; on the stomach, a fun-loving and happy-go-lucky person; on the thigh, an unhealthy person; on the toe, an artistic person who appreciates beauty; and on the wrist, a dependable and solid person.

## Mompesson, John

Magistrate and owner of Tedworth (now Tidworth) Manor House, Wiltshire, in 1661 during classic **poltergeist** disturbances that became known as the **'Drummer of Tedworth'**.

## Monition

In **psychical research**, a supernormal revelation or **precognition** of some past or future event by other than the normal senses. The event may be trifling or momentous, but monitions always occur accidentally and are invariably truthful. In simultaneous and collective monitions, the warning or revelation is received or perceived by several people at the same time. 'Monitions of approach' are inexplicable foreknowledge of an imminent meeting with someone.

## Mood stone

Small oval ring set on a **silver** band that is said to provide biofeedback – subtle information from within the body concerning the mind and emotions. While one may not normally be aware of these inner feelings, the possession and wearing of a mood ring apparently provides the owner with this information and expands his, or her, self-knowledge. With each ring, marketed by Bonwit Teller, the New York store, a colour key gives the meaning for each colour, which extends from black ('tense, inhibited, harassed . . .'), through blue (relaxed . . . emotions flowing . . .') and amber ('strained with anxieties . . .') to bright yellow ('unsettled scattered thoughts . . .').

## Moon

The moon has always been full of mystery to mankind, and although man has now walked on its surface, the lure and mystery surrounding it still linger on; indeed, the only successful experiments in **extrasensory perception** from space were conducted by the moon astronaut Edgar Mitchell.

While the sun is universally regarded as beneficial and possessing life-giving properties, the moon is widely considered to be mysterious, to emit occult power, to draw to itself hidden forces of the stars and constellations and to rule over growth and the unknown processes of nature. It is also said to be the cause of men becoming sex maniacs (hence 'lunacy'), of affecting the menstrual cycles of women, of making animals bay and act in strange ways and causing plants to wax or wane; and to have provided a trigger for the Jack the Ripper murders.

Babylonians worshipped the moon as Queen of the Night, while a Mesopotamian cult, the Sabians, was equally preoccuped with the moon deity in its Temple of Sin. In 1949 a carved stone pillar was discovered near the ancient city of Harran which bore the insignia of the god Sin, and the geographical location corresponded with Latin writers' description of the moon-shrine to which the Emperor Caracella made a pilgrimage on the day of his assassination in the spring of the year 217.

Early calendars marked the passage of time by the moon's phases, and lunar reckoning still exists among the Mohammedans. **Superstitions** connected with the moon abound, and include bad luck following the first glimpse of a new moon through glass, turning money in the pocket and wishing, bowing to the new moon for **luck**, never pointing to the new moon or ill luck will follow, as it will if the new moon is first seen on your **left hand** or behind, although good luck will follow if you first see the new moon ahead of you or to the right. The magnetic quality of the moon, with its effect on the tides of the sea, can also affect the semi-liquid human brain, say the occultists, who believe the moon to be associated with the male phallus since both increase and diminish. So the moon was, and is, an important element in magical operations of love and reconciliation; in reviving the dead to life; in forging the magician's knife or **athame**; in preparing magical transactions; in conjuring up **ghosts** and **spirits**; and in the worship of Selene, Hecate and Diana - all moon goddesses.

Robert Graves discovered that the idea of the moon goddess - or white goddess - permeats many ancient religions and pre-Christian mythologies, and he maintains that a 'knowledge system' familiar to the ancients resulted in the building of Stonehenge and other 'lunar observatories'. Hecate, incidentally, was the three-fold goddess who ruled the night and darkness, tombs and terror, ghosts, dogs, **blood** and **crossroads** (where offerings of food were left for her), and she is the goddess most often invoked by witches and magicians.

In **astrology**, the moon, secondary to the sun, represents the exterior behaviour of a person, and only if the sun and moon are in conjunction will a person appear to others as he considers himself to be; otherwise the many aspects of the moon affect his behaviour as evident to other people. With the moon strongly placed on the meridian, a man will show many feminine characteristics; and a woman will be essentially and totally feminine, and very aware of the fact.

CONSULT: Aileen Adair, *The Moon is Full*, Allan Wingate (1957); H. S. Bellamy, *Moons, Myths and Man*, Faber & Faber (1949 reprint).

## 'Most haunted house in England, the'
*See* **Borley Rectory**.

## Movement of objects
*See* **apports**; **asports**; **levitation**; **parakinesis**; **poltergeists**; **telekinesis**.

## Mu
Reputed lost continent (like **Atlantic** or **Lemuria**), now submerged in the Pacific Ocean, according to Colonel James Churchward, who claimed that a Hindu priest and **guru** taught him 'Naacal', the original tongue of mankind, and showed him ancient stone tablets bearing strange inscriptions. The deciphering of these fragmentary tablets, a task of investigation and research that extended over fifty years, Churchward published in books with such titles as *The Lost Continent of Mu*, the result perhaps of the late nineteenth-century preoccupation

with unsolved mysteries, occult symbolism and mystical experience, for although his last book, *The Cosmic Forces of Mu*, was not published until 1934, it was, apparently, begun in 1870.

CONSULT: James Churchward, *The Lost Continent of Mu*, Neville Spearman (1963 reprint); L. Sprague De Camp, *Lost Continents*, Dover, New York (1971).

## Mummification

Embalming of dead persons and animals that became a religious ritual with the Ancient Egyptians before 2000 B.C. They believed that the physical body was an essential requisite for life after **death**. Mummified bodies, 'mummies', have become objects of curiosity and awe, and not a few have reportedly been the centre of superphysical manifestations or the fulfilment of a **curse**.

Excellent mummification was achieved by the Egyptians, and the process involved removing the brain through the nostrils with an iron hook and emptying the rest of the skull by rinsing with drugs. The flank was then slit, and the whole of the abdomen removed and the inside washed thoroughly with palm wine and an infusion of pounded aromatics. The cavity was filled with bruised **myrrh**, cassia and other spices (though never frankincense) and the opening sewn up. The body was then soaked in natron for seventy days and entirely covered. At the end of this period it was washed, wrapped from head to toes with bandages of fine linen cloth, smeared with gum, and enclosed in a wooden case prepared in the size, shape and likeness of the dead person. Two less costly methods of mummification were also employed, one involving the injection of cedar-oil, which dissolved the stomach and intestines and was drained out through the anus, after which the body was steeped in natron to dissolve the flesh but retain the skin and bones; the other involved the removal of the intestines by liquid injected through the anus and again soaking the body in natron.

Mummification can also be achieved by natural processes, as in the vaults of St Michan's Church, Dublin, where bodies have laid for centuries without any sign of decomposition; and by a drying process as formerly practised in a monastery at Palermo. Some mediums profess to be able to 'mummify' organic matter, but investigation has proved to be inconclusive. Hebrew necromancers used to use mummified bodies for **divination**, while Egyptian sorcerers (*see also* **Egyptian magic**) are said to have practised the same art several hundred years earlier. Mummified bodies were also kept as household gods, fulfilling the roles of **oracles** and questioned whenever the

house or its inhabitants were troubled or experiencing difficulties.
CONSULT: Rollo Ahmed, *The Black Art,* John Long (1936); E. A. W.
Budge, *The Mummy,* Cambridge University Press (1925).

## Murray, Margaret Alice (1862-1963)

English Egyptologist, archaeologist, anthropologist and writer on
**witchcraft** who propounded the theory that the witch-cult was the
survival of a pagan religion that worshipped the great mother goddess
and the **horned god**. Starting with the usual idea that witches were
old women who suffered from illusions about the **Devil** and his world,
her research among medieval records convinced her that witches were
members of an old and primitive form of religion and that their
slaughter was an act of religious persecution. It was an explanation that
appealed to many readers, and it has certainly influenced and affected
modern witchcraft, though it is rejected by some scholars.

CONSULT: Margaret A. Murray, *The Witch-Cult in Western Europe,*
Clarendon Press, Oxford (1921); *My First Hundred Years,* William
Kimber (1963).

## Murrell, James (known as 'Cunning Murrell') (1780-1860)

Essex 'witchdoctor'; the seventh son of a seventh son who set up as a
professional herbalist, cattle-doctor and seer. He also claimed to be
'the Devil's Master' and to be able to exorcize evil **spirits** from
haunted houses (*see also* **exorcism**) and overcome the power of
**witchcraft**. He practised the art of **scrying** to discover lost or stolen
property with the use of a small **mirror** or by spreading a black liquid
on the surface of a bowl of water; and there were those who claimed to
have seen, in the black liquid, events and happenings many miles
distant. His astrological predictions are said to have been remarkably
accurate. For combating witchcraft, Murrell used his 'witch bottle'
into which he inserted a specimen of the **blood** of the witchcraft
victim, together with head and body **hair**, nail parings, genital
discharge and nails from a **horseshoe** that either belonged to the
sufferer or Murrell had specially made for his use. Murrell also
claimed to be able to evoke **elementals**; and by **astrology** he foretold
his own death 'to the minute'. His death certificate gave his profession
as 'quack doctor'.

CONSULT: Arthur Morrison, *Cunning Murrell,* Methuen (1900).

## Muscle reading

The interpretation by the operator of unconscious muscular movements on the part of the subject, and while no **paranormal** faculties
are involved, muscle reading has been used (sometimes unconsciously)
by people who believe they achieve the result by psychic means.

CONSULT: George Miller Beard, *The Study of Trance, Muscle Reading
and Allied Nervous Phenomena*, New York (1882); Max Dessoir,
'Experiments in Muscle Reading and Thought Transference',
*Proceedings of the Society for Psychical Research*, vol. IV, Part 10,
(1886–7).

## Music

Music plays a part in most religions. Its emotive element is easily
exploitable; it is a part of ritual and cult expression; and with dance, it
is probably the earliest form of symbolic action. Certain types of
music, however, are regarded as the opposite of religious, and have the
effect of arousing anything but religious feelings; indeed, the Greeks
once condemned the *aulos*, a kind of oboe, because of its links with
mystic **trance** and undisguised ecstasy. And music as a prescription
for depression – and perhaps for dismissing evil **spirits** – has a history
dating from biblical times: 'When the evil spirit from God was upon
Saul, David took a harp and played with his hand. So Saul was
refreshed and well.'

Unexplained music is a common experience in haunted houses, as is
the chiming of **bells** or '**paranormal**' organ-playing in churches;
while, on the credit side, it now seems to be proved that music is
conducive to better growth in plants and to have a beneficial and
possibly a healing power on human beings. Yet certain musical
instruments and musicians and musical compositions are associated
with ill-fortune and the **Devil**: the violin, bagpipes, drum; Paganini
and Tartini; 'I Dreamt I Dwelt in Marble Halls', Tchaikovsky's
*Pathétique* Symphony and Jacques Halévy's opera *Charles VI*, to
mention a few.

Dead musicians are said to have 'influenced' living persons: Florizel
von Reuter, Yelly d'Aranyi, Victor Kolar, Eileen Joyce, Anna Pavlova,
Cyril Scott, Dennis Gray Stoll, and, of course, Rosemary **Brown**, who
appears to be the channel through whom various well-known
composers, including Liszt, Chopin, Schubert, Beethoven, Schu-
mann, Debussy and Rachmaninov, continue to produce music. In
**sorcery**, **black magic** and fringe occult organizations, music, if not
the food of love, is certainly used to produce a background conducive

to ritual and ceremony that, in turn, contributes to the production of the magicians' desires.

CONSULT: Peter Underwood, *Deeper Into the Occult*, Harrap (1975); Lyall Watson, *Supernature*, Hodder & Stoughton (1973).

## Myers, Frederic William Henry (1843-1901)

A pioneer of organized **psychical research**; author of the monumental and posthumously published *Human Personality and its Survival of Bodily Death* (1903); a classical scholar of outstanding ability; and one of the principal founders of the **Society for Psychical Research**.

Myers, the son of a Yorkshire-born rector, was himself born at Keswick; after an education that included Cheltenham College and Trinity College, Cambridge, he travelled in Italy and Greece, toured Canada and parts of the United States, visited Scandinavia, married a wealthy and fashionable young woman and settling at Cambridge where they had three children. Revisiting Rome in 1900 for unorthodox medical treatment, he died there the following year and his body was brought back to England and buried in Keswick churchyard. Myers, one of the great names in psychical research, knew both Henry Sidgwick and Edmund Gurney at Trinity College, Cambridge, and these three, at the instigation of Sir William **Barrett**, founded the Society for Psychical Research in 1882. Myers became joint Honorary Secretary after the death in 1888 of Gurney, with whom he had worked on the enormous undertaking, *Phantasms of the Living* (1886), and President of the society in 1900. In those early days of scientific psychical research, the main subjects for investigation were **hypnotism**, hysteria, multiple personality and abnormal psychology, and he coined the words '**telepathy**', 'supernormal' and 'veridical' (coinciding with reality). Myers became convinced of the survival after **death** of human personality, and believed that all human beings were composed of two interconnected substances: the purely physical body and the completely immaterial psyche. He took seriously evidence for such **paranormal** phenomena as **out-of-the-body experiences**, veridical and collective **hallucinations** and secondary personalities.

CONSULT: Alan Gould, *The Founders of Psychical Research*, Routledge & Kegan Paul (1968); Harry Price, *Fifty Years of Psychical Research*, Longmans, Green (1939).

## Myrrh

A gum resin, highly esteemed as an ointment and perfume and used for incense and embalming (*see* **mummification**). Myrrh, the product of a small tree that grows in Africa and Arabia, was one of the three gifts (the others being gold and frankincense) that the **Magi** took as gifts to the infant Jesus. In **magic**, where the smoke from burning myrrh mixed with incense, camphor and cloves will keep evil influences at bay, myrrh is associated with Saturn (in common with other sinister and evil-smelling substances: civet, henbane, musk, mandrake, opium, sulphur and the powdered brains of a black cat), and is ruled by the sun, myrrh being offered to Ra, the sun-god, when he reached his zenith at midday. Myrrh is an ingredient of the 'Incense of Abramelin', used by Aleister **Crowley** in conjunction with a **magic circle** for conjuring up **spirits**.

## 'Mystery of Edwin Drood, The'

Charles Dickens's last novel, uncompleted at the time of his death in July 1870. Then, between December 1872 and July 1873, an American mechanic from Vermont, T. P. James, produced a series of automatic writings (*see* **automatism**) purporting to originate from Dickens and to be the continuation and completion of *The Mystery of Edwin Drood*.

When the original and posthumous sections were published together in 1874, it was evident that the new matter, longer than the original, did present a surprising continuity of the author's manner of thought, style, artistic expression and peculiarities of spelling. However Dickens's friend and biographer, John Forster, pointed out that after Dickens's death he had discovered a whole scene in *Edwin Drood*, written in advance and intended to figure later in the volume; yet no such scene existed in the automatic scripts, and Forster rightly argued that it was incredible that the author (who seemingly remembered the first part of the book so vividly that it was necessary to introduce only three new characters in the whole of the rest of the work) should have totally forgotten the chapter he had written and left in manuscript.

Although the spiritualists hailed the book as convincing proof of spirit return, Sir Arthur Conan **Doyle** felt that the actual inspiration of Dickens was 'far from established', and that the second, 'automatic', part read 'like Dickens gone flat'. Professor Théodor Flournoy demonstrated to his own satisfaction that Dickens had in fact had nothing to do with the matter, and that all could be easily explained by 'processes of latent incubation and subconscious imagination' within the medium, T. P. James. The general consensus of opinion seems to be unfavourable from a psychic point of view, and while there are certainly very successful 'Dickens-like' passages, there are others quite out of tune with anything Dickens ever wrote.

CONSULT: Professor Theodor Flournoy, *Spiritism and Psychology*, Harper, New York (1911); Nandor Fodor, *Between Two Worlds*, Parker, New York (1964).

## Mysticism

A phase of thought, or possibly feeling; a religio-philosophical system of introspection; the art of unity with reality. Mysticism is reached through endeavouring to enable the human mind to grasp the divine essence or ultimate reality, and in so doing to enter and enjoy communion with supreme goodness. Mystical experiences usually refer to what are believed to be direct experiences of the love of God, or some religious experiences which appears to come from God. **Buddhism**'s ultimate goal, Nirvana, could be a description of mysticism for it has been described as a deathless state of perfect peace, wisdom and enlightenment. Mysticism has also been described as a state in which the bonds of the personal nature of life seem to fall away, revealing an undivided unity.

CONSULT: Evelyn Underhill, *Practical Mysticism for Normal People*, J. M. Dent (1914); R. C. Zachner, *Mysticism: Sacred and Profane*, Oxford University Press (1957).

# N

## Names of power

The names of gods and others that have been handed down through generations – some Hebrew, some Greek and others of unknown origin – that are considered to be significant and effective in **magic** because they contain and transmit the power of the god or **demon**. The various **grimoires** and the **Cabala** contain names of power which are used during **incantation** in the construction of a **magic circle** when the relevant names are chanted over and over again, in the course of invoking '**spirits**' and making them obey the magician's wishes. The pronouncing of a name of power automatically brings the power of the god or demon into operation, and the repeated chanting of the name not only 'taps' the power of the entity being summoned, but also works the magician up into a state of frenzy in which supernatural forces and his own inner energy become united and reach a pitch where he is satisfied that he is able to compel the 'spirit' to appear and obey commands.

Such names include Abac, Achides, Achilia, Adam, Adonai (ADNY), Agios, Agla, Agnon, Aldal, Alpha, Asmoedeas, Aumgn, Beroth, Buseeognation, Cados, Craton, Delgaliel, Derisor, Destatur, Diaton, Ehyeh, El, El Oristan, Eloa, Elohim, Emmanuel, Gabriel, Gomeh, Guthae, Guthor, Hain, Havayoth, Helim, Hilay, Hudac, Iat, Ischyros, Isis, Jehovah, Laaval, Ledieha, Lendiction, Lon, Mach, Maton, Melekh, Messias, Metatron, Michael, Milia, Monachiel, Muriton, Noth, Ob, Omega, Panthon, Pentessaron, Radisha, Raphael, Ruach, Sabaoth, Sadai, Sechiel, Shaddai, Sibylla, Sifton, Sorthie, Sorthios, Sorthis, Tegra, Tetragrammaton, Tistator, Uriel, Venibbeth, Yah and Yod He Vau He (YHVH).

CONSULT: Richard Cavendish, *The Black Arts*, Routledge & Kegan Paul (1967); Sirdar Ikbal Ali Shah, *Occultism: Its Theory and Practice*, Rider (1952).

# Necromancy

The art of raising the dead and controlling their **spirits** that takes its name from Greek words meaning 'dead' and '**divination**'. A universal practice of great antiquity, only the profoundly initiated, brave and single-minded magician had any chance of success in such a venture, always considered to be extremely dangerous, for not only was a pact with the **Devil** necessary, but it was thought that the 'astral corpse' had an intense desire to live again and could, by absorbing life-energy from living creatures, prolong its life idenfinitely; thus, unless he had taken adequate precautions, the magician might be in great danger.

Scent and odours, always important in dealing with the unseen world, would be carefully produced from burning substances for their powerful influences – often extremely revolting odours designed to drive away evil spirits. Elaborate preparations would include careful study of the positions of the planets, and especially of the **moon** and the influence of Saturn. The magician would then concoct a **magic circle**, use **names of power**, wear special robes embroidered with mystic symbols, light sacred fires and candles, chant long and mysterious **incantations** and, with the help of various herbs, wines and secret rites, prepare for the body to come to life. Sometimes certain creatures or articles were used in the practice of necromancy, notably the necromantic bell of Giradius which, it was claimed, summoned up the dead without difficulty if buried in the appropriate grave for seven days. Necromancy, almost certainly practised by John **Dee** and Edward **Kelley**, and by Dr Simon Forman who has involved in the murder of Sir John Overbury, and frequently by the North American Indians, is as a practice by no means a thing of the past, as the many churchyard desecrations and corpse stealings that still take place bear witness.

CONSULT: Richard Cavendish, *The Black Arts*, Routledge & Kegan Paul (1967); Emile Grillot de Givry, *Witchcraft, Magic and Alchemy*, University Books, New York (1958).

# Necrophilia

Sexual intercourse with the dead; often the culmination of lust murders. Such psychopaths and sado-masochists may still regard the body of their victims as living, and there remains in their minds an after-image of the sensation produced by physical torture and mutilation that extends beyond time and space and reason, even beyond the grave. Necrophilia has been the aim of digging up newly buried bodies, and it seems to have been a part of **black magic** ritual.

CONSULT: J. Paul De River, *Crime and the Sexual Psychopath*, Charles C. Thomas, Illinois (1958).

## Neumann, Teresa, or Therese (1898-1962)

Celebrated bearer of **stigmata** who was born and lived all her life at Konnersreuth, Germany. Her first employment was at a local inn, and then, during the First World War, she worked on a farm, and on 10 March 1918, while helping to put out a fire at a neighbouring farm, she slipped and injured her back. It was the beginning of a complicated medical history. After unsuccessful treatment in hospital, her health deteriorated at home and she became bedridden and suffered temporary blindness and deafness, paralysis of the legs, appendicitis, convulsions and purulent sores on her back and feet. Although medical diagnosis suggested that the afflictions were largely hysterical in origin, it was not until 1923 that she regained her sight (after praying to St Teresa of Lisieux on the day of saint's beatification), and in 1925 she renewed her prayers (to St Teresa on the day of the saint's canonization), shortly afterwards recovering from the rest of her ailments and enjoying some semblance of health.

During Lent in 1926 Teresa Neumann began to exhibit signs of stigmata, the wounds suffered by Christ on the Cross appearing particularly, but not exclusively, on her hands, feet and side. The disturbance was accompanied by visions of the Passion and spasmodic **precognition**; and during this period she is said to have abstained completely from food. From then on for some years, each week, in bed in her home, she appeared to witness and partly re-enact the scenes of the suffering of Christ. Usually the manifestations began on the Tuesday night, when her stigmata would bleed, she would relapse into a **trance**-like state and utter cries as though she was suffering or witnessing painful scenes. The bleeding seemed to be profuse and to issue from her hands, feet and side as well as from her forehead, as if from a crown of thorns. She is said to have survived solely on a spoonful of water each day, and even gave this up in September 1927, thereafter existing on the daily Holy Communion.

By this time Konnersreuth had become a place of pilgrimage, and crowds flocked to the Bavarian village, especially at Easter time, so long as Teresa Neumann lived, despite reservations on the part of the Roman Catholic Church, who 'disowned' her in 1938. Towards the end of her life the phenomena seemed to diminish, and from 1957, until her death five years later, little was heard of the stigmatization, the visions or the precognition. The alleged fasting had been insufficiently controlled to satisfy either the Church authorities or the medical profession; the actual bleeding had never been seen to flow by an expert witness, and blood (which one analysis showed to be of menstrual origin) only appeared on the wounds after Teresa Neumann had either been completely covered by the bedclothes or during the absence from the bedroom of the expert.

CONSULT: Hilda Graef, *The Case of Therese Neumann,* Mercier Press, Cork (1952); Paul Siwek, *The Riddle of Konnersreuth,* Brown & Nolan, Dublin (1954).

## Nictalopes

Human beings who can see in the dark. These are extremely rare individuals, but a French doctor apparently discovered an eighteen-year-old girl, Marie Verdun, who possessed this ability in 1874; and Auguste Müller, a somnambulist from Stuttgart, also reportedly saw perfectly well in total darkness.

## Nostradamus (1503-66)

French astrologer, whose real name was Michel de Notre-Dame. He studied humanity and philosophy at Avignon, took the degree of doctor of medicine at Montpellier in 1529, lived for a time at Agen, travelled widely and finally settled at Salon, near Aix-en-Provence. He practised as a doctor for many years and gained distinction for his professional skill during outbreaks of the plague. He published a book of rhymed prophecies, or quatrains, under the title of *Prophèties,* in 1555, followed by an enlarged edition in 1558. Earlier he had published annual predictions of local events. The apparent fulfilment of some of these predictions brought Nostradamus to the attention of Catherine de' Medici, who introduced him to court, where he became physician to Charles IX.

Nostradamus' prophecies were divided into ten, each containing a hundred quatrains, but they were in no apparent order of sequence and the style is awkward, the language a mixture of derivatives from French, Greek and Latin and so deliberately obscure that the texts are difficult to understand even by those who have studied them for years: various interpretations have been made on almost every rhyme. There is, however, a hard core of prediction – especially perhaps the quatrains pertaining to the flight of Louis XVI to Varennes, the French Revolution, the accession of Napoloron (*sic*) and those referring to Hister (translated as Hitler) – which makes it difficult to dismiss the writings of Nostrodamus lightly.

CONSULT: Erika Cheetham, *The Prophecies of Nostradamus*, Corgi (1975); James Laver, *Nostradamus, or the Future Foretold*, Penguin Books (1952).

## Numerology

The study of numbers which may be regarded as a simple method of analysing character or perhaps of **prediction**; but since it is also claimed to be a major guide to understanding the true nature of the universe, it occupies an important place in any study of **magic** and **occultism**.

Ever since Pythagoras said, 'The world is built upon the power of numbers,' men have sought to fathom the secrets of numbers. Numerologists turn everything into numbers, beginning with the name by which you commonly think of yourself. Each letter of the alphabet is given a numerical value, and there are two systems for doing this: one is to run straight through the alphabet, giving each letter a number, one to nine, and then one to nine again (see figure A); but the other, based on the Hebrew alphabet, is the one generally used

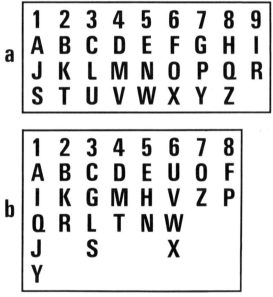

*The English (A) and Hebrew (B) methods of using the letters of the alphabet in numerology*

by the serious student of numerology (see figure B). Numerologists reduce all figures to one of the nine primal ones, and to do this you simply add the numbers together until you reach a single digit. Thus to find the number for a name, using the Hebrew system, Peter Underwood would become 85452654526774, and these numbers added together make 70, and 7 and 0 added together make 7, which is the number for this name. Each of the primal numbers are said to have distinct attributes which can be summarized as follows.

*One*: suggests powerful and dominating personalities, single-minded, positive, obstinate, ambitious and self-reliant. Often highly individualistic, their great powers of concentration, organization and origination make them inspiring leaders. They are the inventors, the pioneers, the designers and planners who often push ahead with their plans and schemes without thought or care for some of the people involved. They are loners and place little value on friendship or closer relationships; they often have few close friends since they tend to try to dominate everyone with whom they come into contact. They are the type of people who 'look after number one'.

*Two*: often the number of kind and gentle people, those with even tempers, sweet natures, the quiet and tactful ones, possessing perhaps the more feminine qualities. These people, essentially followers rather than leaders, are always happy to play second fiddle; they fill subordinate roles perfectly, being conscientious, thoughtful, tidy and inclined to be unambitious although they often seem to end up getting their own way, not by asserting themselves but by gentle persuasion and quiet charm. The double-quality in the make-up of these people is evident by their tendency to change their minds, to put off until another time things which they could easily do, and hesitation about almost everything; this duality can also show itself in aspects of cruelty and deception, quite foreign to the general nature of these people.

*Three*: usually the extra-bright ones, the intelligent, lucky, witty, versatile, imaginative, hearty and energetic. The ones who sparkle with life, seem to have the power to charm everyone, and invariably enjoy success in everything they set their hand to. Often possessing considerable artistic talent as well as personal attrraction, these are the artists, the sculptors, the great fiction writers, the actors and the fine musicians. Ambitious, talkative, proud and sometimes overbearing, their weakness lies in their love of pleasure and in their unrelenting attempts to be popular whatever the cost. They also have to contend with an inherent tendency to take nothing seriously.

*Four*: the solid, dependable, practical, salt-of-the-earth who make up for their lack of ideas and originality by their calm, steady and efficient organization and administrative abilities. Although these pillars of society may appear to be stern, grim, unresponsive and cold, they are hard workers who pay attention to detail, and you can be sure of fair treatment in any dealings with those whose lives are ruled by the number four. On the other hand, numerologists do tend to consider these people the unlucky ones; there is often an odd side to their characters, they are sometimes subject to fits of depression and unwarranted outbursts – and any success they achieve in life usually seems to the outsider to have been paid for dearly, a fact that appears to be reflected in the characteristically grim faces of these individuals.

*Five*: much brighter people altogether; they are the clever, impatient, eager people, always on the move. 'Fives' live on their nerves, love travel and movement of all kinds, enjoy meeting people and taking part in new experiences. These are the people who know a little about everything and a lot about nothing, and characteristically they are attracted to everyone and everything but never consider themselves tied to anyone or anything. They are the adventurous, sporting, responsibility avoiding and hasty, quick-talking individuals often typified by the bright and breezy salesman. Often physically attractive, they are inclined to be inconsiderate towards others, and sometimes are self-indulgent too; but they are also resourceful, resilient, many-sided and quite irresistible. Five is the number associated with sex (which itself adds up to five), and 'five people' usually have a varied and interesting sex life – though their love lives rarely run smoothly, and sometimes this side of their nature shows itself in sexual excesses or perversions.

*Six*: the number associated with harmony and peace and happiness, those kindly, tranquil, well-balanced people who really value their friends, their home and family life. These are the loyal ones, the conscientious, the sincere, affectionate, contented and happy. They may not occupy the centre of the stage or stand out in a crowd or have a very well-developed business sense, and some of them may be fussy, conceited and self-satisfied, but in general the happiness they radiate is the facet of their characters that is most evident.

*Seven*: said to be the number of the introspective scholar, the bookworm, the philosopher, the thinker, the mystic, occultist, magician, recluse and dedicated investigator. These are the people who prefer to be apart from the main bustle of humanity and enjoy being alone with their books and their thoughts. Reserved in the company of strangers, their dignity is a precious possession; self-controlled and serious in their outlook, they have no time for whimsy or frivolity in any shape or form. They place money and personal comfort low in their list of priorities, and while they often appear to be unhappy or disappointed, aloof from the world and their associates, in fact they have powerful and penetrating intellects, are highly imaginative and the most loyal of friends. On occasions they are a little strange – there is something 'not of this world' about them – and they are often extraordinarily bad at expressing themselves and putting their ideas across, and invariably they dislike questions and avoid arguments whenever they can.

*Eight*: the number for power, wealth and achievement, representing the strong, determined, practical, business-minded, politician types whose successful careers are built on hard work, constant effort and considerable strain. Often they are regarded as hard and materialistic, even selfish and unscrupulous, and while they are rarely attractive individuals, at least they are aware of the fact and beneath the harsh exterior often show a pleasing and surprising dash of eccentricity.

*Nine*: regarded as the number of high achievement, either mental or spiritual. These are the visionaries, the romantics, the idealists. Their breadth of mind makes them inspiring people, always endeavouring to help and serve humanity in general rather than any particular individuals, and from their ranks come many of the brilliant scientists, the teachers, the missionaries, the dedicated healers and religious instructors. Strength of mind, determination and unselfishness stand out in the make-up of 'nines', and although they tend to be easily hoodwinked, are often overfond of the limelight and tend to be fickle in affairs of the heart, they have genuine horror of ugliness, bad taste, poverty, laziness, old age and unnecessary unhappiness, both for themselves and for others; and so they will go to extreme lengths to ensure that their surroundings, their associates and their lives are as tastful and beautiful as they can be. Because their whole outlook is coloured by this desire for good taste in all things, they are sometimes uncharitable and intolerant and their very genuine desire to be good can make them appear to be conceited and egocentric to a degree that is repellent. Nine to the numerologist is an attractive and inspiring number, and he will point out that two of the finest U.S. presidents, Abraham Lincoln and John Kennedy, were 'nines'.

Although, as a general rule, numbers above nine are added together and reduced to a single digit the numerologist is always on the lookout for significant repetitions and important combinations, and in this respect eleven and twenty-two are considered especially notable; eleven being the number associated with visionaries and martyrs, and twenty-two being regarded as the 'master number', the number of truly great men and women, the powerful, influential, successful, brilliant personality whom everyone admires; it is also the number of the master black magician.

Besides ascertaining the number obtained from the name by which you think of yourself, the numerologist also looks at the name you are most commonly known by – a nickname, a changed name; he will also look at the number obtained by the vowels alone (representing the inner self); the consonants alone (the outer personality); the birth date; the number of times each number appears (repeated numbers can mean an unbalanced personality); and which numbers are missing (showing the qualities lacking). Numerology can also be used to discover a subject's birth number and as an aid to improving one's life and fortunes: discovering suitable partners, suitable dates for important events and transactions, 'lucky' numbers for gambling and so forth. The 'art' is also used to indicate the best food for a particular person and thereby improve health; the best place to live; the most important year of one's life; and a great deal besides.

CONSULT: E. T. Bell, *The Magic of Numbers*, McGraw-Hill, New York (1946); C. Butler, *Number Symbolism*, Routledge & Kegan Paul (1970).

# O

## Oak
*See under* **trees and plants**.

## Obeah
The **magic** (equivalent to the **voodoo** of Haiti) of Jamaica and other West Indian islands: a supernatural power, originally evil magic used to harm others. Obeahmen and their **spells**, often involving the use of parts of human bodies, birds and animals, **blood** and graveyard soil, have, however, given the poverty-stricken and oppressed natives an apparent means of 'getting back' at a hostile world; and the Obeahman, who uses familiar objects to contain occult force, has come to be regarded as a person of repute whose prestige is high in the community in which he lives.

CONSULT: Joseph J. Williams, *Voodoos and Obeahs*, Allen & Unwin (1933).

## Object reading
*See* **psychometry**.

## Objective phenomena
Observed events that are distinguished from subjective phenomena and considered to be factual and outside and distinct from the minds of those witnessing such happenings.

## Occultism
Term used to cover **mysticism, theosophy** and **spiritualism**, but more specifically the study of theories and practices leading to the attainment of higher powers of the mind and the spirit; the practical implementation of these ideas sometimes produces **objective phenomena** that are of considerable interest.

## Odic force

An allegedly all-penetrating force, discovered in the nineteenth century by Baron Karl von **Reichenbach**, who, having observed that persons in a nervous condition sometimes saw luminous emanations from magnets in total darkness, confirmed these observations with perfectly healthy persons. Reichenbach claimed that odic force existed also in the rays of the sun and **moon**, crystals, plants, metals and in animal and human bodies; that it could be conducted by all solid objects and liquid substances; that bodies could be charged with the force and that it could be transferred from one body to another by direct contact, although close proximity, without actual contact, was sufficient to produce a charge of odic force of lesser degree. He believed that the mouth, hands, forehead and back of the head represent the main centres of odic force in the human body, and claimed that 'odic tension' varied throughout the day and night, diminishing with hunger (and increasing after taking food) and at sunset. Reichenbach maintained that 'odic flames' were material radiations that are affected by breath or currents of air. He believed that this force was observed by mediums and **sensitives** as the **aura**, and that it was the basis of mediumistic ability to speak, write, move objects and produce raps, and that the human body was the meeting-place of odic force and psychic phenomena. His books include *Psysico-Physiological Researches on the Dynamics of Magnetism* (1850) and *The Odic Force: Letters on Od and Magnetism* (1852).

CONSULT: Alan Gould, *The Founders of Psychical Research*, Routledge & Kegan Paul (1968); Karl von Reichenbach, *The Odic Force*, Humphrey (1968 edition).

## Ointment, witch's

*See* **flying ointment**.

## Olive

*See under* **trees and plants**.

## Omens

Signs that indicate good or bad fortune; some phenomenon or unusual event that is seen as foretelling either good or evil in the immediate future; also warnings which men have heeded and so avoided misfortune and achieved success. Such omens vary from the sight of a shooting star (bad luck ahead); the appearance of a spotted dog (good luck); a shark following a ship at sea (ominous); the falling of a picture (a death in the family); a spluttering fire (a family quarrel); a black bird alighting on the roof of a house (forthcoming sorrow), and stumbling (poor prospects for the matter currently in hand); to the sight of a phantom coach, the **ghost** of oneself (*see* **Doppelgänger**; **double**) or the sound of a **banshee**, which are all said to be omens of **death**, as are mysterious and unaccountable knockings in a household. *See also* **augury**.

CONSULT: William J. Fielding, *Strange Superstitions and Magical Practices*, Blakiston, Philadelphia (1945); Lewis Spence, *Second Sight*, Rider (1951).

## Oneiromancy

The practice of **divination** from dream interpretation. The belief that **dreams**, with their unconscious origin, have hidden meaning is ancient and widespread. Every possible item and activity to be encountered in dreaming is said to be the symbolic representation of some future event, and there are countless dream books giving a variety of meanings to dreams. Some people choose the **Tarot** card (*see also* **cartomancy**) mostly closely connected with a dream, and interpreation of the symbolism of that card is said to interpret the dream.

CONSULT: R. de Becker, *The Meaning of Dreams*, Allen & Unwin (1968); Stern Robinson and Tom Corbett, *The Dreamer's Dictionary*, Souvenir Press (1975).

## Ophiolatry

Snake or serpent worship. *See under* **animals and birds**.

## Oracle

Revelation from a divine source; the place where the ancient Greeks consulted a deity and obtained guidance; the, usually ambiguous, advice given; and the priest who gives the supposedly infallible counsel.

The inhabitants of Ancient Greece, who possessed no sacred writings to which they could turn, expressed their deep need for guidance in all aspects of life by consulting the oracle; the most influential being that of Apollo at Dephi. Answers were given by a priest or priestess in **trance**, the implication being that the gods, and in particular Apollo, used the subconscious of the priests to make known their responses to questions. A parallel is to be found in present-day trance mediums, who allegedly pass on messages from the beyond to their sitters.

Usually the visitor to the oracle would put his question to a priest and hear it relayed, and another priest would convey the answer, often in verse and rarely with any degree of frankness; rather the reply would be enigmatic in the extreme, allowing the questioner to form his own opinion of the wishes of the gods. Consultation days were somewhat infrequent, about one a month (often the seventh day of the month), and expensive. Present-day occultists have sometimes used the seventh day of the month as especially receptive for contacting **spirits**.

CONSULT: H. W. Parke, *Greek Oracles*, Hutchinson (1967); H. J. Rose, *A Handbook of Greek Mythology*, E. P. Dutton, New York (1959).

## Orgy

Sexual revel that results in conventional restraints being thrown aside and the release of primitive impulses – often assisted by unbridled dancing, unrestrained drinking and the help of drugs. It is thought that by such activity man can rise to the level of previously unknown realms of consciousness. Such magical orgies date from the worshipping rites of the Greek god Dionysus, and can serve a useful purpose in as much as they relieve tension. Magicians and occultists have always maintained that powerful sexual energy can contribute to their practices and achieve results not otherwise obtainable, and sexual orgies, by releasing a wealth of such energy, are thought to enable previously impossible mental and physical phenomena to occur.

*See also* **phallic worship**; **sex magic**.

CONSULT: Francis King, *Sexuality, Magic and Perversion*, Neville Spearman (1971); Burgo Partridge, *A History of Orgies*, Blond (1958).

## Ouija board, or planchette

Device for alleged automatic writing (*see* **automatism**). Commonly a piece of heart-shaped polished wood mounted on two wheels or castors with a pencil providing the remaining support.

The operator (sometimes blindfolded or working in darkness) lays the hand or finger-tips lightly on the board which has been placed over blank paper, whereupon the board moves, seemingly of its own volition, and writes messages and answers questions. Variations of the device include a board mounted to move in a fixed track with a pointer to select letters of the alphabet arranged at the head of the board. Simple forms include the letters of the alphabet arranged in a circle with an inverted wine-glass in the centre; those taking part are situated around the circle and place their forefingers lightly on the wine-glass,

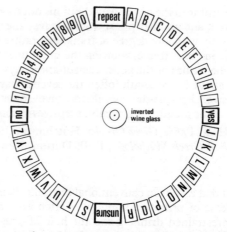

*Simple layout for 'planchette' séance with inverted wine-glass*

which proceeds to move in circles and spell out messages and answers to questions by touching the appropriate letters.

Although much of the material obtained through the use of ouija boards or planchettes is gibberish, there are occasions when something comes through that seems unlikely to have originated in the subconscious of the sitter or sitters, or to be the result of unconscious muscular exertion – the kind of explanations commonly put forward these days, whereas formerly the messages were thought to originate from the dead. In recent years there has been agitation from church and lay dignitaries to ban the sale of ouija boards, sold purely for amusement purposes in Britain, on the grounds that evil forces might be contacted and the operators influenced in some harmful way; but while the messages can certainly be frightening, obscene or embarrassing, there is little evidence that the practice is in any way harmful to well-balanced individuals, and ouija boards have been openly on sale as toys for many years in the United States without any appreciable ill-effects.

Experiments have shown that **telepathy** plays a part in ouija board 'messages', but there is also evidence, especially when used in haunted houses and when operated by or in the presence of mediums or psychically sensitive persons, that some agency can be at work which does not fit into the pattern of the physical world as we know it.

CONSULT: Sir William Barrett, *On the Threshold of the Unseen*, Kegan

Paul (1918); D. H. Rawcliffe, *The Psychology of the Occult*, Derricke Ridgway (1952).

## Out-of-the-body experiences

The impression of leaving the physical body and viewing the external world from a position completely divorced from the material body. Such experiences have been divided by psychical researchers into two kinds: (a) parasomatic, where the subject appears to be inside another body that is a replica of his actual body; and (b) asomatic, in which the subject has no sensation of being associated with any body, simply feeling that he is a disembodied consciousness.

Many out-of-the-body experiences seem to take place at moments of crisis, as when the subject is involved in an accident, undergoing surgery or very ill. But there are plenty of examples from people who are fit and well and occupied with everyday matters: perhaps they are walking downstairs, or in the street or a shop, or walking through woods when they suddenly experience the sensation of being outside their physical bodies. Often they feel that they are floating about fifteen feet above ground level and can see their physical bodies below them continuing to act in a completely normal way. Such experiences seem to last only a few seconds.

Some individuals appear to be able to leave their physical bodies at will, and methods of inducing or encouraging such practices include physical-relaxation exercises, **meditation** and concentration, and the cultivation of **lucid dreams**, in which the subject is aware that he is dreaming. Out-of-the-body experiences raise considerable problems for philosophers and psychologists. Research, including exploration of the electrical activity of the brain during out-of-the-body experiences, is being conducted at the Institute of Psychophysical Research at Oxford.

*See also* **astral projection; astral travel**.

CONSULT: Celia Green, *Out-of-the-Body Experiences*; and *Lucid Dreams*, Hamish Hamilton (1968); Oliver Fox, *Astral Projection*, University Books, New York (1962).

## 'Overlooking'

*See* **evil eye**.

# P

### Padstow hobby-horse, or old 'oss
*See under* **festivals** (May Day).

### Painting, automatic
*See* **automatism**.

### Palladino, Eusapia (1854–1918)
Italian physical medium. *See under* **spiritualism**.

### Palindrome
A word (or a verse or sentence) that reads the same whether it is read in direct or reverse order; 'eye', 'noon', 'pap', 'did', 'tit' or 'toot', for example. The answer attributed to Napoleon when asked whether he could have successfully invaded England is a palindrome: 'Able was I ere I saw Elba.' Some palindromes are words of power, and their use in **magic squares** is thought to increase the power of the square.

### Palmistry
The foretelling of the future from the lines, marks, valleys, mounts and, in fact, every feature of the hand. It is an age-old belief that, because every man's palm is different, his individual destiny is imprinted on his hands.

When reading palms it is essential to consider every line and feature of the hand separately, and then to interrelate all the features, corresponding them with balancing or emphasizing aspects. First the student of palmistry or cheiromancy will look at the general shape of the hand, noting the overall impression of the whole hand, the thumb and fingers and nails; he will carefully consider the form and colour, look at any projections and depressions, and will then study the lines and how they are affected by crosses and other marks. He looks at both hands, because it is his belief that the left hand will reveal the inherited tendencies, weaknesses and advantages, while the right hand will depict the traits of character that the subject has himself acquired.

A long hand indicates a gift for detail, a person who reflects and considers a course of action before taking it; a small hand suggests the intuitive type, usually inclined to be impetuous and to walk into situations without giving much consideration to the outcome. Large hands, when in contrast to the general build of the person, usually denote the type of individual who never goes ahead with his ideas before making elaborate plans and going into quite unnecessary detail. The possessor of small hands in relation to their overall size, however, is a person who likes to do things on a big scale and who will often make plans and go ahead with grand schemes without going into sufficient detail; often impulsive and hasty people, these have alert and quick minds and usually reach the right decision instinctively.

The shape of the palm is next looked at, and in general this will be either narrow or wide, indicating opposite types of character: those who possess narrow palms (where the palm is longer than it is broad) are likely to be selfish, inclined to be introspective, self-centred, inward-looking and not very good mixers, although they are often hard and loyal workers and possess great powers of concentration. Those with broad palms (where the palm is wider than it is long) are inclined to be sympathetic and kindly, adaptable and sociable, good mixers and talkers, people who thrive on companionship and cooperation and do their best work when they are part of a team.

Next the fingers are examined, first in general and then individually. There are considered to be two main types of fingers: those that grow more or less evenly out of the palm and those that are unevenly set; and the student of the hand will regard the former as possessing an innate common sense, self-control and the ability and willingness to adapt readily to new situations and different people; while those with unevenly set fingers will be considered to be less adaptable, to show less common sense, to be less ready to adjust to a fresh situation, and people who sometimes lack self-control. It is said that the negative or defective aspects of the character are governed by the position of the different fingers, but even more important is the significance apparently evident from the varying shapes of each finger, and in particular the thumb, but first the hand-reader will look at the fingers in general.

Straight fingers show aptitude for development, a natural faculty for expression (often in one of the arts) and good expectations; while crooked fingers, sometimes called 'symbols of defect', suggest that they belong to people who prefer fiction to fact, who are suspicious and unnecessarily cautious, who find life difficult because they lack the ability to take it as it comes and, somehow or other, always seem to do things the difficult way. Smooth fingers with no exaggerated bulges at the joints are said to belong to quick thinkers whose alert minds take in and assess a situation, and who act promptly and effectively in any given circumstance. But those who possess uneven fingers with bulges at the joints are considered to be slower in thought, word and deed; they are the hesitant and careful ones who think a lot before taking action, who love order, method and punctuality and hate disorder of any kind. The owners of tapering fingers which are broad at the base and become narrower at tips, sometimes almost coming to a point, are thought to be very fond of food: they invariably have good appetites and are often sensual individuals. Those who possess thin fingers are more interested in matters of the mind than matters pertaining to the physical body, and are the artistic ones, the intellectuals, and those members of the human race who prefer quality to quantity in all things.

Finger-tips are also scrutinized, for they are regarded as being a guide to the general character and composition of the person concerned. *Conic tips* – those fingers that taper gently and gracefully – are thought to belong to people who appreciate beauty in art and nature, people who prefer to discuss, talk, even argue, rather than *do* something; the thinkers as opposed to the doers of this world, emotional people: often unconventional and sometimes lacking in powers of concentration and persistence, they prefer creative and individual work that is often profound and thought-provoking. The owners of fingers that are broader at the tips than at the first joint (known as *spatulate tips*) are enterprising and busy people who find it difficult to relax and are happiest in the midst of activity. They also love travel and are invariably fascinated by gadgets and mechanical matters. Another type of flat-topped finger, known as *square tips*, are those where the tips are not wider than the first joint, but are 'normally' shaped and often particularly smooth – flat as opposed to being rounded or pointed at the tip; and such people are realistic and law-abiding, often religious and content to conform, lacking in originality or any kind of pioneering spirit but prepared to work hard and long to achieve security – the 'salt of the earth', in fact. Finally on the question of finger-tips, there are people who possess fingers with different tips and these, known as *mixed tips*, predictably denote adaptability, versatility, the 'jack of all trades', the open-minded, fair person who may have no aptitude for routine work but who gets on well with most people and sorts out most problems without too much difficulty.

The thumb is said to reveal much. Its size, length, constitution, position and general appearance are all said to be pointers to the character of its owner. The thumb, unlike the four fingers, has only two segments, and the lower section is considered to denote the reasoning ability of its owner and the upper half his will-power. The length and size of the thumb are considered in relation to the hand as a whole, and if the thumb is short and appears to be stunted and out of proportion, it is said to belong to a person whose will-power and sense of volition are undeveloped; such are usually inhibited and lack individuality, and are likely to remain obscure and uncelebrated throughout their lives. A large and long thumb, on the other hand, suggests a personality that is well developed, a person who knows where he is going and how to get  there, a person with excellent powers of reasoning and judgement, someone to be reckoned with and the type who usually makes a success of their life. Should the thumb curve away from the palm to any great degree, the owner is likely to be impulsive, adaptable, generous and easily influenced by others, while those who possess a straight thumb are strong, physically and intellectually, with unlimited will-power, drive and initiative, and are completely self-sufficient. Such people, having confidence in themselves, stick to their beliefs and opinions through thick and thin, are reliable, logical and sincere, and make friends for life. Should the thumb be set comparatively high on the palm (that is, close to the first finger), the owner is likely to be somewhat narrow in his outlook, a mean, selfish person with no independence; while the owner of a thumb that is set low (towards the wrist) is independent in outlook, loves freedom and liberty in everything, has the courage of his convictions and is usually open-minded, candid, straightforward, uncomplicated and generous in all his dealings. Depending upon the position of the thumb, so the space between the root of the thumb and the first finger will vary, and since this side of the hand denotes strength of character, it is considered that, the greater the distance, the stronger the character. A thumb that is thick and bulging at its tip is known as a *clubbed thumb*, and while such a thumb suggests a lack of culture and an obstinate and excitable disposition, the shape of the tip – pointed or square – is said to reveal the owner's powers of determination and persistence.

It is the lines of the hand, however, which reveal most. The main lines of the hand are the Heart Line, the Line of Fate or Destiny, the Sun Line or Line of Fortune, the Line of Head, the Line of Life, the Lines of Marriage and the Line of Health (see illustration).

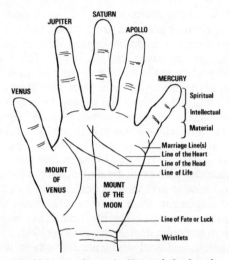

*Palmistry: the main lines of the hand*

**Line of Life**: possibly the most significant line on the hand from the view of character divination – the line that circles the base of the thumb, a line said to reveal the general health and constitution, sexual potency and length of life of its owner. Should the line sweep round the fleshy part of the palm at the base of the thumb (the Mound of Venus) in a pronounced curve, a strong constitution is indicated: physical fitness, vitality, energy, staying power and the necessity and capability for, and love of, a full and uninhibited sex life. Such a line, the sure sign of a creative and active person, is never to be found on the hands of inhibited bachelors or narrow-minded spinsters. Should the line appear to be straight rather than generously curved, with comparatively little space between the root of the thumb and the apex of the 'curve', a restrictive attitude is indicated to those qualities attributed to the line: a weak constitution, poor physical condition, a low sex drive; the cold and unfriendly person often has such a line.

A long Life Line is said to foretell a long life for its owner, although a short Life Line does not necessarily mean a short life but does suggest ill-health, often in later life. It must be remembered that students of palmistry maintain that the lines of the hand alter and change with the personality, activity, circumstances and outlook of the person concerned, and there are cases on record of a person with a short Life Line who has a health defect remedied, and then finds that the Life Line has grown or extended, indicating a longer span of life than originally indicated. The approximate length of life is said to be ascertained by drawing a straight line from the upper base of the thumb to the lower root of the thumb and dividing the area enclosed between this line and the Line of Life in three equal parts diagonally; and the length of life is judged by the Life Line in relation to these sections.

A Line of Life that ends near the wrist by turning towards the thumb indicates the home-lover; one that turns towards the outside part of the hand reveals a desire to travel and possibly live abroad; while a definite division of the line at the wrist end suggests a person who has a strong desire to enjoy foreign travel but who will always return home in the end and will never live abroad. A Life Line that is alternately thick and thin or deep and shallow reveals an uncertain state of health and often an uncertain temper too! A light and thin Line of Life suggests a poor constitution and lack of vitality; such a person always seems to have something wrong with them. A Life Line that is composed of chain-like loops is also suggestive of a persistently poor health and possibly internal trouble, while light lines that twist about the Life Line indicate a tendency to nervous and digestive troubles; it is important however to take in other relevant aspects and, in the case of the Line of Life, a sweeping and curved line always shows ability to overcome health hazards while a straighter line tends to exaggerate the bad indications.

Next in importance is perhaps the *Head Line, or Line of Mentality*; revealing the intellectual capacities. It will either slope, which usually suggests an artistic outlook, or be more or less straight, a line that usually belongs to the materialistic practical person, a realist who bases his life on reason and logic. He who possesses a straight Head Line that slopes as it approaches the outer part of the hand is regarded as having the best of both worlds; he is practical and realistic, but also creative and imaginative, and such people succeed in incorporating into their methodical lives an artistic and intellectual quality. It is said to be possible to judge the mental and intellectual powers of a person by drawing three imaginary lines down the hand from between the four fingers, and, according to how far the line extends from the inner side to the outer side of the hand, so is the individual's power of reasoning and intelligence measured. Where the Head Line and the Life Line begin together it is regarded as a sign of sensitiveness, lack of self-confidence, and such people, although easy to offend, usually readily respond to a sympathetic approach and thrive on encouragement; while clear and distinct Head Lines suggest the self-reliant, impatient and energetic person. A Head Line that ends in a fork is said to reveal an aptitude for expression and description, and such a mark is often found on the palms of writers, lecturers, lawyers and actors; but where the fork is very wide, occupying perhaps a third of the whole line, indecisiveness, uncertainty and over-cautiousness are indicated.

The **Heart Line** is said to reveal the emotional attitude and the condition of the heart of the individual concerned, and while a straight line suggests a certain restriction of the emotions, a coldness and lack of response intellectually, sexually and socially, a curved line reveals a warm-hearted, sexually active and friendly individual. A short Heart Line is regarded as showing a lack of the power to love, a heartless kind of person, while a long line reveals a 'big-hearted' person who loves his fellow men and women. Upward sweeping branches from the Heart Line indicate an ability to appreciate the attractive attributes of others and a friendly and helpful approval to everyone, while downward branches reveal bitterness, disappointments and unhappiness in love.

*Line of Fate or Destiny*, in consultation with the subject's Line of Life, reveals his pattern of life and his likely material benefits. The person who possesses a long and unbroken Fate Line, extending from the wrist to the base of the middle finger without twisting or turning or becoming mixed with other lines, is rare, but such people are extremely fortunate, possessing a fine sense of direction and timing and excellent financial prospects. More often the Fate Line begins in the area of the Mount of the Moon (the fleshy area at the base of the outer part of the palm), and while this can suggest a person who tends to gain money from devious and sometimes unrealiable sources, it also denotes a strong personality and is frequently seen on the self-employed. A Fate Line that ends below the middle finger is said to indicate a person who constantly strives for material security, a routine and determined individual who builds for himself a career worthy of acknowledgement; a person who takes no chances but works hard and sees virtue in economy and savings.

The owner of a Fate Line that sweeps towards the root of the first finger is the person who desires power, is ambitious to the point of being thoughtless of others but has organizing and managing powers which cannot be disputed. A Fate Line ending below the third finger reveals a craving for fame and recognition in one of the arts, for this fleshy part of the palm is known as the Mount of the Sun or Apollo, representing artistry, exhibitionism, success and fantasy. A break in the Line of Fate, where the ends overlap, indicates a big change in the life of the individual with some anxiety before the new life becomes established. Islands (where the line divides and then joins up again) are said to suggest periods of disappointment or financial loss, times of uncertainty; while a double line across the Fate Line is thought to indicate an obstruction or delay in a career, and an obvious break in the line reveals the possibility of a complete break in the career. When the Fate Line ceases at the Heart Line, a defect in the psychology of the individual is said to be indicated. Lines that ascend from the Fate Line are thought to reveal creative improvements and progress, and a branch that extends towards the base of the fourth finger is suggestive of material success, progress and expansion.

The *Line of Success, or Sun or Apollo Line* is often short and runs down the palm from the base of the third finger, but when it is long, straight and unbroken it is said to belong to a person of outstanding talents who is destined to be showered with honour and riches. A Line of Success that begins near the Life Line is thought to reveal a person who possesses a capacity for hard work perfectly executed, and this also often brings rewards in the shape of personal success and honour. A Success Line beginning near the Heart Line reveals an inbred appreciation of the arts, and although such a person often works hard and long in his early life, he invariably reaps the benefit in later life. A Success Line begining at the Head Line is usually indicative of a good brain, and such a person, who uses foresight and planning and seizes his opportunities often achieves considerable success. Many short Lines of Success, when considered in relation to other factors, indicate a versatile and adaptable individual with a talented nature who can bring much happiness to those around him, but if the Success Line is wavy or looped, the owner is said to be frustrated and unsuccessful.

The *Line of Health, or Mercury* (sometimes called the Line of Liver) is regarded as indicating the health and physical well-being of its owner, and a good clear line, free from distortion, apparently signifies excellent health; yet, when no Health Line at all is visible, there is no need for the person concerned to be anxious about his health, it is simply taken as indicating that such a person can take any amount of hard work and use all his energy but still have no health problems. A Health Line stemming from the Life Line is thought to indicate a highly strung person who often suffers from digestive troubles, and while such people are advised to take care in matters of diet and overworking, and to rest and build up of their health when they can, such people are said to possess sound hearts. A loop at the beginning of the Health Line is often found on the palms of habitual sleepwalkers, and loops elsewhere in this line are said to indicate internal disorders; it is an interesting fact that when such troubles are treated and disappear, the 'islands' also disappear from the palm.

The *Marriage Lines, or Lines of Union* are the short lines that begin on the outer edge of the hand and run towards the palm above the Heart Line and below the base of the little finger. Often several lines can be distinguished, but the palm-reader will only take into account the more distinct ones, although a number of lines, indistinct and thin, are believed to suggest a light-hearted individual who enjoys little affairs of the heart and is in fact unlikely to marry. Distinct and straight marriage lines are usually found on people who are capable of sincere love and deep and loyal emotional involvement, and such people invariably marry; the nearer such a line is to the Heart Line, the earlier can that person be expected to marry. Marriage Lines that end in a fork are thought to be indicative of broken marriages, while a second deep Marriage Line suggests the involvement of a third person in the marriage and the indefinite continuation of such a situation. A Marriage Line that curves downwards and touches or crosses the Heart Line is said to suggest that such a person will outlive his partner, while an upward-curving Marriage Line reveals the person who never settles down. Tiny upright lines on the Marriage Line are said to indicate the number of children of the marriage, the heavier ones being boys and the lighter one girls; when one of the child lines touches the Heart Line, it is said to suggest that the owner loves the child more than his partner.

Other lines looked for by the reader of palms include the *Line of Intuition* (a short curved line that circles the fleshy outer part of the palm beneath the little finger), which is said to reveal the intuitive powers and insight of the individual; the *Girdle of Venus* (another short line running across the base of the second and third fingers), regarded as indicating the passion of the owner; the *Cross Line* (running diagonally across the base of the first finger), considered to denote the power to govern and control others; the *Martian Lines* (short lines running from half-way down the outer side of the palm, below the Marriage Line) thought to indicate military or professional glory and personal triumph; the *Travel Lines* (short lines running from the lower outer part of the palm below the Martian Lines), said to show the journeys, discoveries and revelations to be undertaken and borne by the owner; and the *Bracelets of Health, Wealth and Happiness* (parallel lines that run across the wrist), considered, from the palm downwards, to indicate respectively the health, wealth and happiness of the individual. When the lines are clear and distinct and not distorted or broken, the owner is thought to be fortunate in all three fields; when poorly formed, broken or indistinct, the opposite is thought to be indicated, but it is the first or top line that is often considered to be the most important, and some palm-readers look at this line first of all as an infallible sign of health and destiny. When formed like a chain, a life of hard work is said to be indicated, with some anxiety which will lead to success and final achievement.

Other lines and marks that are looked for include the crossing of several lines over a single line (called the Medical Stigmata), such people being believed to possess considerable healing powers; a cross often indicates an interest in occult matters. Straight lines, curved lines, stars, islands, squares, bars and grilles are all considered, some being good signs, some bad, but always the position and proximity to other marks and lines has to be taken into account, as does the hand in general, its overall shape, size, texture, colouring. The same applies to the nails and the way the person uses his hands, not only how he shakes hands (although that is also important) but the use of the hands in gesticulating – clenching hands, relaxing hands, hiding hands – all have a message for the student of hands.

Palmistry has always fascinated mankind, and today there seems to be scientific basis for the study since some doctors assert they can diagnose certain physical diseases from the hands before they are apparent from other symptoms, and criminals and mental defectives are usually apparent from the lines on the hand.

CONSULT: N. Jaquin, *Practical Palmistry*, Skilton (1965); L. Lehman, *The Key to Palmistry*, Bell (1969).

# Pan
Pagan god and pastoral **spirit** of hills and woods, flocks and herds; son

of Hermes and Callisto. Represented (e.g. in the Homeric Hymn in his honour) as a horned and goat-footed deity, playing on his pipes and wandering through woodland glades accompanied by nymphs, though he was also capable of exciting sudden and irrational fear (hence the word 'panic'). Pan was worshipped on the Acropolis, and associated by the Greeks with satyrs, Dionysus, the god of orgiastic release, and Aphrodite; and by the Romans with Faunus. The cult of Pan, half-man and half-goat, lustful, energetic and merry, reached its peak when it spread throughout the Greek empire and was honoured by yearly **sacrifices** and torch races. Many magicians and dabblers in the occult have found themselves drawn to Pan, Prince of the **Succubi**. Aleister **Crowley** composed a *Hymn to Pan* which was recited at his funeral at Brighton in 1947, and both before that and since the Great God Pan has been invoked by many lesser and some wiser men than Crowley.

CONSULT: Richard Cavendish, *The Black Arts*, Routledge & Kegan Paul (1967); John Symonds, *The Great Beast*, Rider (1951).

## Pan's pipes

One of the earliest forms of wind instruments, invented, according to Greek fable, by the god **Pan**. It consists of short hollow tubes of varying lengths fastened together so as to form a musical scale. The pipes of Pan and their **music** were reputed to possess a magical quality which certain magicians and students of the occult have sought to utilize, and there have been a number of reports from people who claim to have heard the haunting sound of Pan's pipes in conditions which appear to obviate a natural or rational explanation.

## 'Papus'

Pseudonym of Dr Gérard Encausse (1865–1916), a French physician and prolific author, lecturer and popularizer of such subjects as the **Cabala**, the **Tarot** and **astrology**. He has been regarded as the chief instigator of the widespread interest in **occultism** in France during the late 1880s; perhaps his best-known book was *The Tarot of the Bohemians* (1889), a volume that has influenced many subsequent writers on the subject.

CONSULT: Ellic Howe, *Urania's Children*, William Kimber (1967); Kurt Seligmann, *Magic, Supernaturalism and Religion*, Allen Lane The Penguin Press (1971).

## Paracelsus (1493-1541)

Physician, philosopher and mystic whose enigmatic, egotistical, peevish and unorthodox personality caused him to be an outsider and who was detested or ignored by the medical establishment, but whose preoccupation with **alchemy, astrology,** the **astral body** and the **'elixir of life'** has made him a commanding figure of attention for students of **occultism.** This controversial character of the sixteenth century is today considered to be the first modern medical scientist, a man who foresaw microchemistry, antisepsis, present-day methods of wound surgery, homoeopathy and other modern medical achievements. His writings, often involved and obscure, contain an enormous amount of original information; works like *De Occulta Philosophia* and *Archidoxis Magica* – hermetic writings which, unfortunately, we can no longer comprehend.

CONSULT: Paracelsus, *Selected Writings,* Routledge & Kegan Paul (1951); Kurt Seligmann, *Magic, Supernaturalism and Religion,* Allen Lane The Penguin Press (1971).

### 'Paragnost'
*See* **Croiset, Gerard.**

### Parakinesis
The movement of objects by human physical contact which is, however, insufficient to explain the movement. *See also* **psychokinesis.**

### Paranormal
Term used in **psychical research** to describe phenomena outside accepted experience of cause and effect; the parapsychologist's term for what the scientist would call the supernatural; that which is beyond or outside the normal: the supernormal.

### Parapsychology
**Psychical research,** especially experimental work in **extrasensory perception** and **psychokinesis**; the scientific study of apparent abilities to contact the world about us without the use of known senses or muscles.

The ability to receive knowledge by unknown means is called extrasensory perception (ESP), while the ability to transmit such powers – 'mind over matter' – is known as psychokinesis (PK). These are the subjects primarily concerned in parapsychology (from the German *Parapsychologie*), although the term is increasingly used when referring to the serious and scientific study of the subjects covered by psychical research: **clairvoyance, precognition, tele-**

**pathy,** spontaneous and induced psychic phenomena, **dowsing or divining, faith healing** and, in fact, all apparently **paranormal** phenomena beyond consciousness.

CONSULT: Richard Cavendish (ed.), *Encyclopaedia of the Unexplained,* Routledge & Kegan Paul (1974); J. Beloff, *New Directions in Parapsychology,* Elek (1974).

## Paroptic vision

**Eyeless sight;** skin vision; derma-optical or cutaneous perception; names given to the idea that some people can see – or perceive – through the skin, usually the finger-tips but sometimes above the cheek-bones. There are certainly people whose sense of touch is so highly developed that it is possible for them to differentiate between colours; darker colours, they say, feel warmer.

CONSULT: Jules Romains, *Eyeless Sight,* Putnam (1924).

## 'Patience Worth'

An alleged **spirit** entity that manifested through the American medium Mrs John H. Curran of St Louis, first through the **ouija board** and then through **direct voice,** dictating, in medieval English and with great rapidity, literary works of varying merit. The case was investigated by Dr Walter F. Prince, whose book *The Case of Patience Worth* details the reputed life of 'Patience Worth' who claimed to have lived in Dorset in the seventeenth century before going to America where she was killed by Red Indians. Some of the information was verified and a professor from Manitoba University asserted that the case 'must be regarded as the outstanding phenomenon of the age'. For ten months, in 1918, a monthly magazine was published to provide an outlet for the prolific literary activity.

CONSULT: Walter Franklin Prince, *The Riddle of Patience Worth,* New York (1926); Casper S. Yost, *Patience Worth: A Psychic Mystery,* Holt, New York (1916).

## Pendulum

Weighted line that is held lightly in the hand and is said to swing backwards and forwards or in circles to indicate the presence of mineral or other material during **dowsing or divining.**

## Pentagram, or pentacle

Five-pointed star-like figure, composed of five straight lines, that includes a pentagon (a figure with fire angles and five sides). The form of a pentagram is to be found on ancient Greek coins; it was used by the Pythagoreans as a symbol of perfection and by medieval astrologers (and some modern occultists) at the beginning of their letters as a symbol of health; and its popularity as ornamentation on houses (especially doors and doorways) can be traced to its efficacy in repelling witches.

The pentagram holds an important place in **ritual magic**, where it is regarded as a kind of fluidic transmitter, and the compilation of the pentagram takes many rules and aspects of **magic** into account. It is usually engraved either on a metal belonging to a planet (**iron** for Mars, gold for the sun, **silver** for the **moon, quicksilver** for Mercury, copper for Venus, tin for Jupiter and lead for Saturn), or depicted in a colour representing such metal. Symbolic and magical figures, letters and words are inscribed on the pentagram, the symbolic and magical value of its form and the form of the designs being regarded as very important, as well as the time when the pentagram was to be used, the purpose of its use and the identity of those present at its use. The pentagram had to be consecrated whatever its purpose, and this was done by the magician breathing on it, sprinkling it with holy water, oil or sexual secretions, excretions or **blood**, according to the purpose for which the pentagram had been made; then it would be dried with incense, finely chopped pubic hair or ash from human bones, and finally had to be sealed with holy or diabolic **names of power**; and then the room was draped with crimson material and the pentagram left for twenty-four hours in darkness before it could be used.

When using the pentagram the magician wore a scarlet robe and an iron ring bearing a ruby, and he lit five candles, black or white according to the purpose of the pentagram. Various other preparations included fasting – or consuming unholy liquid and matter; abstinence from contact with women – or sexual excess; and the introduction of other articles (**a mirror**, an altar, a tripod); and, if required, the presence of other participants, suitably prepared, was said to guarantee the success of the operation.

CONSULT: Richard Cavendish, *The Black Arts*, Routledge & Kegan Paul (1967); Émile Grillot de Givry, *Witchcraft, Magic and Alchemy*, University Books, New York (1958).

## Phallic worship

Ancient form of worship in which adoration was paid to the generative function symbolized by the phallus, the male organ. (*See also*

**ithyphallic.**) There are grounds for accepting that the study of phallicism is the study of religion, for there is no doubt that the origin of organized religion lies in the intermixture of **magic** and religion which is evident from the early fertility cults, essentially sexual, that existed in all primitive communities; a principle underlying nature worship, with its emphasis on the Great Mother, that prospered in Asia Minor, the cradle of civilization. Similar worship was formerly widespread in India (where the phallus is called the linga or **lingam**, and the female counterpart the **yoni**); and in Ancient Egypt where many of the lesser-known sculptures show explicit phallic attributes in the worship of Seti, the creator, and Osiris, and by symbolism in many other art representations.

In early Greece, Italy, Britain, indeed throughout the whole of Europe and the ancient world, there is considerable evidence of phallic worship from sculpture, coins, **amulets** and ornaments, monuments, temples and writings. These all proclaimed the wide belief that a magical power resided in the male (and female) organs of sex (*see also* **sex magic**). Phallic worship (in particular of Priapus, the Roman god of fruitfulness and procreative power), its ancient ceremonies often including an enormous representation of the male phallus being carried in procession and talismanic figures popularly supposed to bring good **luck** or offspring and to ward off evil **spirits**, bad luck and disease, went underground with the emergence of Mohammedanism and Christianity. But it remained in the subconscious to await Freudian psychology, which seemed to confirm the sexual symbolism of articles stylized as elongations or points, or in ovals and circles, throughout the succeeding generations. Many such representations can be dismissed as fanciful, but the underlying motivation is quite clear.

Since phallic worship, the root of all religion, was a feature of the earliest religions, it became a part of magic and the accepted opponent of evil and darkness; but, as time passed, the sexual aspects became degraded and sexual rites became a part of **black magic** with religious sodomy again being practised, as it had been in Hebrew temple groves. Naked female participation also became an essential part of the **spells**, enchantments and performances of rites of **satanism**, demonism, **witchcraft**, the **black mass** and secret societies; an ingredient that is today used and encouraged by the less reputable practitioners of the black arts.

CONSULT: Richard Payne Knight, *Two Essays on the Worship of Priapus*, printed privately, London (1865); O. A. Wall, *Sex and Sex Worship*, C. V. Mosby Company, St Louis (1922).

*Osiris taking the phallic oath*

## Phantasms of the living

**Apparitions** of people who are alive at the time that their spectral form or figure or phantasm is seen by others, as opposed to the more usual apparitions of the dead. Phantasms of living people have frequently been reported by close friends or near relatives at a time of crisis for the agent (the original of the apparition): when that person is dangerously ill, just before his or her **death**, or immediately before or at the time of an accident, tragedy or disaster.

CONSULT: Edmund Gurney and F. W. H. Myers, *Phantasms of the Living*, Trübner (1886); G. N. M. Tyrrell, *Apparitions*, Duckworth (1943).

## Phelps, Rev. Dr Eliakim

Presbyterian minister of Stratford, Conn., whose house was the scene of **poltergeist** disturbances between 10 March 1850 and 1 October 1851; an infestation that became known as the 'Phelps case'.

The whole family, which included girls of six and sixteen, experienced manifestations, the most striking of these being the strange construction of eleven figures in tableau, composed of clothing and depicting a scene of devout worship; a figure consisting of a blanket formed to look like a figure sitting by the fire; and other figures which were constructed and arranged, from clothing collected all over

the house, in conditions which seemed to exclude human participation. Other phenomena included pinching experienced by the
children; paper inexplicably found alight; raps and taps which spelt
out obscene messages; the movement of small objects such as keys,
nails and cutlery, some of which were bent almost double during their
transportation (*see* **teleportation**), **levitation** of a table and the
upsetting of crockery and knives and forks laid out for a meal; the
slashing to ribbons of one of the boy's suits; and the transportation of
the older boy, who seems to have been lifted, carried across a room and
then gently lowered to the floor in the presence of a witness. A score of
windows in the house were broken, thirty figures were 'constructed',
fifty-six articles were picked up after having been thrown about the
house, and some of the papers whereon Mr Phelps had recorded
something of the strange happenings were found torn to pieces or
destroyed by fire in locked drawers.

CONSULT: Harry Price, *Poltergeist Over England*, Country Life (1945);
Sacheverell Sitwell, *Poltergeists*, Faber & Faber (1940).

## Philosopher's stone

The ultimate aim and purpose of the operations of the alchemist, who,
thinking that all substances were ultimately derived from one primary
material (their *prima materia*), sought to separate and remove the
various different attributes and, by complicated treatment and
manipulation, eventually to reach the 'first matter', which would be
one of the two varieties of the philosopher's stone: either red, for the
production of gold; or white, for the making of **silver**. The term
'philosopher's stone' was thus used in **alchemy** for any element,
mixture or solid substance thought to possess the property of
converting base metals into gold or silver; and also for any matter that
was thought to be a cure for many illnesses and afflictions. The latter
was also known as the Elixir, another name used by the alchemists for
the elusive philosopher's stone. The **hexagram** is the symbol of the
philosopher's stone, since it unites the triangular symbol of **fire** and
the inverted triangle of water.

CONSULT: Sidar Ikbal Ali Shah, *Occultism: Its Theory and Practice*,
Rider (1952); A. E. Waite, *The Secret Tradition in Alchemy*, Stuart M
Watkins (1972 reprint).

## Photography, psychic or spirit

*See* **psychic photography**.

# Phrenology

The art of reading character and potential ability from the general shape of the head and from the location, size and distribution of bumps on the skull. Phrenologists maintain that a man's character is determined or revealed by the interaction of various organs of the brain located in specific positions of the head; the size of these organs can be ascertained by a phrenologist from the shape of the head, and by feeling certain areas he can tell how well or how poorly the subject's intellectual and other faculties are developed.

Phrenology, one of the more modern occult arts, owes its origin in part to the Rev. Johann Kaspar **Lavater**, a nineteenth-century Swiss mystic and author who saw the human body, and particularly the head, as a reflection of the soul or inner man and produced a detailed work on the character of a person according to the shape of his head, his features and the lines on his face (**physiognomy**). As a pseudo-science, phrenology was devised and constructed entirely on the basis of trial and error by Franz Joseph Gall (1758–1828) and his disciples, J. K. Spurheim and G. Combe. Hundreds of heads were examined before some thirty-five different areas, each concerned with specific character or intellectual ability, were located and defined for future phrenologists.

The areas extended from the area above the neck (revealing the amorous nature) to the central area above and at the back of the head (generative properties) bordered by qualities of combativeness. Towards the top of the head at the back was thought to be the area concerned with self-esteem, flanked by centres revealing love of approbation; while almost at the top of the head was the area dealing with conscience and belief, with each side locality denoting solidarity and firmness. The centre of the top of the head was said to reveal reverence, with, on each side of it, areas concerned with optimism and anticipation. The centre of the front of the skull was said to be concerned with charity and kindness, bordered by areas pertaining to imitation and extending to areas devoted to wonder and excitment, adjoining the part of the skull devoted to idealism (said to be the part of the head touched by poets while working on compositions).

The front of the head, according to the phrenologist, revealed indications of causality, comparison, and reaction to unexpected eventualities; that area immediately above the nose denoted individuality, adjoined by areas concerned with the faculties of finding one's way, recognition, size and demension, and weight and valuation. Immediately over the eyes were said to be the areas concerned with colour, and outside those areas the places devoted to order and method; between the eyes, the abilities of numbering, counting and collecting were said to be revealed, while high over the eyes were situated the areas denoting musical appreciation and concord and, above again, the area concerned with wit and humour. Other areas were thought to be concerned with time and occasion; constructiveness, destructive tendencies, secretiveness, acquisition, cautiousness, and language and speech.

Phrenology probably reached its greatest popularity during the nineteenth century, although there are still flourishing societies devoted to the art as well as a number of contemporary phrenologists. Like many other systems of divination of character, including physiognomy, phrenology has had its convinced supporters (among them Walt Whitman, Edgar Allan Poe, Alfred Russel Wallace and Charles Darwin), and it can certainly be startlingly right at times, though the general verdict of informed opinion is a mixture of acclaim and criticism.

CONSULT: J. Coates, *Phrenology: How to Read Heads*, Foulsham (1920); Frances Hedderly, *Phrenology*, Fowler (1970).

## Physiognomy
Character analysis from the face and features.

The student of physiognomy selects the round, square or triangular face as depicting respectively the happy, outward-looking person; the active and reliable person; and the intelligent, scholarly and less physical person. From the modification of the initial selection, he then decides on one of the seven basic planetary forms: the *solar*: the round and jovial face, usually topped with fair hair; the *venus*: classical features and fair hair; the *martian*: square face with heavy and coarse features (the rugged look); the *mercurial*: fine classical features but dark colouring and dark hair; the *lunar*: cold, pale and melancholy; the *jovian*: noble and strong features; and the *saturnine*: mournful-looking and dark-haired.

Then the physiognomist examines each and every feature, the mouth, teeth, nose, eyes, cheek bones, ears, forehead, lips and chin; even the lines and wrinkles of the face are, it is claimed, evidence of deep inner meanings and significance for those learned in the subject. Furthermore, the face, it is said, is divided into three parts: the forehead represents the divine world; the centre of the face, the nose and eyes forming a triangle with the mouth, represents the physical world; and the inverted triangle formed by the jaw and chin represents the material world. When Johann Kaspar **Lavater** produced his best-seller on the reading of character from the face in the eighteenth century, he was convinced that physiognomy could become as exact a science as any. His monumental work is copiously illustrated.

CONSULT: Rev. Johann Kaspar Lavater, *The Whole Works of Lavater on Physiognomy*, trans. by George Grenville from the last Paris edition, in 3 vols., London (n.d.); original publication: *Physiognomical Fragments*: 1775-8.

## Pigs
*See under* **animals and birds**.

## Pike, James Albert (1913-69)
Episcopal Bishop of California who, almost single-handedly it has been said, turned the thoughts of Americans to the possibility of life after **death** as a reality.

During his early years Pike was a Roman Catholic, and while attending St John's Military Academy in Los Angeles exhibited distinct academic and leadership qualities. Later, at Hollywood High School, he was assistant editor of the yearbook and won the school's scholastic debating contest and the Los Angeles city-wide competition. After high school, Pike entered the Jesuit University in Santa Clara, California, but two years later transferred to the University of California at Los Angeles to study law. He graduated in 1936 with degrees in law and the arts and went on to Yale, where he was awarded a degree of doctor of science of law.

In the Second World War Pike served first as an attorney with the Security and Exchange Commission in Washington, then became a member of the bar of the U.S. Supreme Court and taught law at the George Washington University; later he served as a naval intelligence officer and attorney at the Maritime Commission and War Shipping Administration. At this time he joined the Episcopal Church, and in 1944 was ordained as a deacon; later he was made a curate, and, having taken religious studies at the Virginia Theological Seminary and the Union Theological Seminary in New York, he was awarded a bachelor of divinity degree, ordained to the priesthood in 1946 and appointed Fifth Episcopal Bishop of California in 1958, having already been dean of St John the Divine in New York City, the largest Protestant church and cathedral in the world.

Pike now became well-known for his liberal views on leading social issues; he wrote books, including *You and the New Morality, A Time for*

*Christian Candour, What is this Treasure?*, and the controversial *If This Be Heresy* and *The Other Side*, the latter appearing in 1968, two years after his son had killed himself after experimenting with drugs. When Pike began to experience **poltergeist**-like phenomena, he thought his son might be trying to communicate, and during the course of **séances** with mediums in the United States (including Arthur Ford and George Daisley) and in Britain (with Ena Twigg), he received messages that, he was satisfied, originated from his dead son. Pike died in the Israeli desert in 1969 after being lost, and three days before his body was found he apparently communicated with Ena Twigg and related the circumstances of his death and the whereabouts of his body. His widow was satisfied that the communication had come from her husband.

CONSULT: Psychic Magazine editors, *Psychics*, Turnstone Press (1973); Ena Twigg, *Ena Twigg Medium*, W. H. Allen (1973).

## Piper, Mrs Leonora E. (1857-1950)
American mental medium. *See under* **spiritualism**.

## Pisces
*See* **zodiac**.

## PK
*See* **psychokinesis**.

## Planchette
*See* **ouija board**.

## Plants
*See* **trees and plants**.

## Poltergeist
Mischievous **ghost**, entity, intelligence, elemental or secondary personality whose unpleasant characteristics include noises of every kind, the breaking of crockery and other articles, movement of objects, the starting of small fires, the appearance and disappearance of objects, the throwing of stones, coal or other fragments which are sometimes warm to the touch; and occasionally imitations of the human voice: whistling, singing, talking or whispering. In short, poltergeists make an unmitigated nuisance of themselves in a dozen ways, using the minimum of energy.

The word poltergeist is derived from a German folklore term incorporating *polter*, meaning a noise or racket, and *geist*, a spirit or ghost. Poltergeist infestations or visitations begin quite inexplicably, run their course and then cease as mysteriously as they began. An adolescent (more often a girl than a boy) is almost invariably present in the affected household, and this young person appears to be the nexus and attraction of the occurrences. Should he or she be moved at the height of the strange happenings, the disturbances will often move with the adolescent and reappear wherever he or she goes.

Apparent poltergeist phenomena have been reported from all parts of the world and in all civilizations, but they are commonest in the British Isles. Poltergeists have been variously attributed to evil **spirits** – 'Satan's imps' – undeveloped elementals or nature spirits, shrinking timbers and underground water, an 'offshoot' of the adolescent mind, a secondary and unconscious personality, a working off of emotional tension, or just plain fraud, deception or faulty observation. But none of these explanations adequately covers all the hundreds of poltergeist cases that have been witnessed, investigated and recorded by hundreds of observers. It seems likely that there is a psychological basis, but physical objects have undoubtedly moved under conditions which preclude fraud, and it may be that an unusual combination of psychological tension, sexual awakening, physical energy and intense (but possibly unconscious) concentration and single-mindedness may produce a poltergeist. The one comforting thought is that poltergeist disturbances do not usually last long: sometimes only a few hours, and rarely more than a few weeks.

Certain observations have been made: poltergeist-projected objects invariably finish up at a lower level than the one they were at originally, thereby using the minimum amount of energy; such objects are never seen to commence movement, and the human eye seems to be a deterrent, objects flying through the air often dropping to the ground as soon as they are observed; many of the young people involved are above average in intelligence, and usually healthy, although some are subject to hysterical outbursts; poltergeist disturbances do not occur when the young person in the case is enjoying a normal sleep, and so it would appear that the higher centres of the brain are in some way involved. **Apparitions** are not usually encountered in poltergeist cases, but there are exceptions, including the **Borley Rectory** haunting.

For other examples of poltergeist manifestations, *see* **Amherst mystery; Cock Lane ghost; Drummer of Tedworth; Epworth; Phelps; Zugun.**

CONSULT: Hereward Carrington and Nandor Fodor, *The Story of the Poltergeist Down the Centuries*, Rider (1953); Alan R. G. Owen, *Can We Explain the Poltergeist?*, Helix Press, New York (1964).

## Poppy
*See under* **trees and plants**.

## Possession

A state in which gods, **spirits**, devils or a personality other than that of the individual concerned take charge of his body and mind: he is then considered to be possessed. Possession, and in particular demonic possession, is a phenomenon as old as man himself, and there is an enormous amount of literature on the subjects of gods, **demons** and various discarnate entities believed to be able to enter the human body and take control of the personality.

While possession by a god or holy spirit may be regarded as a high and valuable experience, it would seem that, conversely, possession by an evil spirit or a bad personality can be damaging and highly dangerous. Possession has been variously described as ecstasy, hysteria, enthusiasm and mania; and perhaps partly explained by the fact that a characteristic of possession is always a feeling of giddiness – a word derived from *gidig*, which meant to be possessed by a god. States of possession have been induced from earliest times, during Dionysian celebrations, through medieval Europe to the present-day preoccupation with **music**, dancing, physical exercise, alcohol, drugs and sex. Some states of possession, both induced and spontaneous, include physical changes: the person becomes changed facially and witnesses see evil features appear; the body may become wasted, the stomach distended; the complexion pales and there may be vomiting and foul breath. Internal discomforts have also been experienced, described by the victims as like an animal eating away at the entrails. Often the subject will experience sudden body blows which leave marks; there may be convulsions, fainting fits and catatonic withdrawal and posturing; the voice may become gruff and the language obscene or blasphemous; and, very often, there is a feeling of extreme coldness in the vicinity of the affected person.

Psychologists believe that cases of possession have nothing to do with spirits of any kind, but that the answer lies in greatly increased brain activity, often the result of emotional excitment or upheaval; while the student of the **paranormal** points to the relative ease with which apparent possession is achieved, the spontaneous appearance of possession in many diverse individuals, and the evidence of anthropologists whose researches show that states of possession are achieved in primitive societies in ways that vary from rhythmic drumming to excessive sexual excitation. Ninety-nine per cent of cases of possession have an emotional basis.

CONSULT: Brian Branston, *Beyond Belief*, Weidenfeld & Nicolson (1974); T. K. Oesterreich, *Possession*, Routledge & Kegan Paul (1930).

## Potions

A draft or large dose of liquid with alleged magical properties; **love potions and philtres** were commonly used by medieval magicians; potions have also been employed by present-day sorcerers and occultists. Indeed, in 1975, many strange potions with reputedly odd properties were seen to be openly on sale in Istanbul: 'Donkey's Tongue' changed a talkative person into a silent one; 'Soil of the Dead', spread on the carpets of one's enemies, brought about a quick and painful death; 'Devil's Excrement' cured hoarseness and made voices beautiful; 'Satan's Potency Paste' increased the sex drive; 'Flower Flour' was for slimming, 'Pomegranate Power' for ulcers, 'Trout Oil' for paralysis and 'Brother's Blood' cured bad **dreams**.

## Precognition

The knowledge of future happenings that cannot be inferred from present knowledge; a type of **extrasensory perception**. There are many striking examples of spontaneous precognition, including the wholesale **premonitions** of tragedies such as the Aberfan disaster and individual precognition by people like the clairvoyant Gerard **Croiset**, who foretold the occupant of a certain seat at a studio performance six weeks in advance; and Irene Hughes, who foresaw the assassinations of John F. Kennedy and Robert Kennedy. Prophetic **dreams** are a common occurrence and valuable work in experimental precognition was pioneered by J. B. **Rhine** at America's Duke University. Various ways of apparently harnessing the faculty, include the employment of **astrology** and **palmistry**.

*See also* **retrocognition**.

CONSULT: D. H. Rawcliffe, *The Psychology of the Occult*, Derricke Ridgway (1952); S. G. Soal and F. Bateman, *Modern Experiments in Telepathy*, Faber & Faber (1954): G. N. M. Tyrrell, *Science and Psychical Phenomena*, Methuen (1938).

## Prediction
A prophecy, presentiment or forecast regarding some future event; the act of foretelling something; the thing foretold. There is considerable evidence for the prediction of future events, more properly called **precognition** or **premonition** – a type of **extrasensory perception**. Psychical researchers who have investigated the evidence and been convinced that some human beings can predict the eventual life of another have included Dr Eugéne Osty, Professor Cesare Lombroso, Professor Charles Richet and Camille Flammarion; while among leading present-day prophets is Jeane **Dixon**, the so-called 'Seeress of Washington', who has correctly forecast many national events.

CONSULT: 'Cheiro', *Mysteries and Romances of the World's Greatest Occultists*, Herbert Jenkins (1935); Psychic Magazine editors, *Psychics*, Turnstone Press (1973).

## 'Prediction'
British monthly, founded 1936, that seeks to cover all aspects of an occult or **paranormal** nature in an open and impartial manner. The magazine's original policy stated: 'If there be truth here, let its champions disclose it; if there be chicanery, let it be unmasked – whatever facts we discover, let us seek to find their implications for ourselves as individuals. . . The function of *Prediction* is to explore these subjects that have too long been exploited, in the belief that if there be any truth in them, it will yield to patient and reasonable enquiry.' Issues include articles on such subjects as **ghosts** and **hauntings**, **dreams**, **superstitions**, the **Tarot**, **sorcery**, auto-suggestion and astrological profiles of well-known people; while there are regular contributions on **palmistry**, **graphology**, **spiritualism**, dream interpretation, astrological forecasts, a reader's service on occult and allied subjects and book reviews and current news.

*Prediction*'s editor (1976) is Jo Logan; the address: Link House, Dingwall Avenue, Croydon, Surrey.

## Premonition
Awareness of a future event, often some impending tragedy: a **death**, accident, misfortune or danger. Premonitions may vary from a distinct cameo of an event that happens in the future to a vague feeling of foreboding, a presentiment of some impending disaster, unspecified evil or overpowering adversity. They often occur during the borderland time between sleeping and waking. Providing the

premonition is not inferred from conscious knowledge, it is a type of **precognition**.

CONSULT: J. C. Barker, 'Premonitions of the Aberfan Disaster', *Journal of the Society for Psychical Research* (December 1967); Alan Vaughan, *Patterns of Prophecy*, Turnstone Press (1974).

## Priapus, worship of
*See* **phallic worship**.

## Price, Harry (1881-1948)
Enigmatic psychical researcher and ghost-hunter who aroused world-wide and enthusiastic support for his untiring battle to obtain official recognition for scientific **psychical research**. He probably did more than any man before or since to awaken the man-in-the-street to the mysteries and fascination of psychic phenomena.

Price became interested in the subject through conjuring – a life-long interest – and he employed his considerable knowledge of sleight-of-hand in his inquiries into spiritualistic phenomena and frequent exposures of fraudulent **mediumship**, though he did not hesitate to endorse with equal enthusiasm such mediums as he believed to be genuine. His investigations and activities covered the **Indian rope trick, fire-walking**, ancient experiments in **ritual magic, stigmata**, a 'talking mongoose', **psychic photography**, founding the first laboratory for psychic investigation, reviving the **Ghost Club**, collating a unique library and presenting it to the University of London; and over some twenty years a more or less continuous investigation of the **Borley Rectory** haunting: an investigation which came in for considerable publicity and criticism after Price's death when three members of the **Society for Psychical Research** (where Price never held any official position, although he was at one time Honorary Research Officer of the **American Society for Psychical Research**), published a devastating critique. Price was, however, essentially a 'loner', and never had any intimate collaborator or close contact with the various societies and organizations that he belonged to, apart from the Ghost Club, which seems to have been very close to his heart.

An informed but impartial estimate of the character of Harry Price suggests that he was neither a totally dedicated, saintly, much-wronged scientific researcher, nor an out-and-out fraud on whose views or whose word no reasonable person could ever rely. He was a mixture of the two, and he possessed a genuine and very knowledgeable enthusiasm for all facets of psychic research, mysteries and the unknown, and devoted much of his time, energy, money, gifts and ingenuity to these interests. On the other hand, there is evidence that, where his personal self-esteem was involved, he was capable of the most extraordinary double-dealing, spite and intrigue. His books, apart from valuable monographs on such subjects as the mediumships of Rudi Schneider (*see* **Schneider brothers**) and Helen Duncan, published as *Bulletins* of the National Laboratory of Psychical Research, include *Revelations of a Spirit Medium* (with Eric J. Dingwall) (1922), *Stella C. An Account of Some Original Experiments in Psychical Research* (1925), *Rudi Schneider: A Scientific Examination of His Mediumship* (1930), *Leaves from a Psychist's Case-Book* (1933), *Confessions of a Ghost Hunter* (1936), *The Haunting of Cashen's Gap: A Modern 'Miracle' Investigated* (1936), *Fifty Years of Psychical Research* (1939), *'The Most Haunted House in England': Ten Years Investigation of Borley Rectory* (1940), *Search for Truth: My Life for Psychical Research* (1942), *Poltergeist Over England* (1945) and *The End of Borley Rectory* (1946). Literary agent for the Harry Price Estate since 1974 has been Peter Underwood.

CONSULT: David Cohen, *Price and his Spirit Child Rosalie*, Regency Press (1965); Paul Tabori, *Harry Price – the Biography of a Ghost Hunter*, Athenaeum Press (1950).

## Proxy sitting
Term used in **psychical research** and **spiritualism** when the place of a sitter visiting a medium is represented by someone else – a proxy – who knows nothing about the dead person from whom a communication is expected. Thereby it is sought to rule out the possibility of telepathetic communication between the inquirer and the medium, and to obviate the possibility of the medium obtaining any information from the sitter, by **telepathy** or other means.

## Psi
Term used in **parapsychology** and **psychical research** for 'psychic' ability or phenomena: **clairvoyance**, **precognition**, **telepathy**, **psychokinesis** – abilities which apparently enable contact to be made between the subject and the world around him without the involvement of the five senses or normal muscles. It was coined by J. B. **Rhine**. Some people have been noticed to possess a distinct lack of psi ability. 'Psi – missing' is the involvement of psi ability in such a way that, while the target may be missed, the psi faculty is still evident.

## Psychic museums

Collections of **apports**, automatic scripts (*see* **automatism**) and artistic representations, photographs, musical instruments, relics from haunted houses and other miscellaneous objects concerned with psychic happenings. A number of such collections have been gathered together at different periods: Sir Arthur Conan **Doyle** founded one at 2 Victoria Street, London, in 1925; the Psychical Research Department at Leland, Stanford University, California, possesses a collection of apports; Dr Chengery Pap established a museum of objects apported during the mediumship of Lajos Pap in Budapest in the 1930s; Father V. Jouet founded the Other World Museum in Rome, which contained many rare objects and documents concerned with apparent manifestations of life after **death**; the Harry Price Library at the University of London includes several items of psychic interest; the **Society for Psychical Research** in London has a number of interesting **séance**-room objects; and Peter Underwood (President of the **Ghost Club**) has amassed a collection of exhibits concerning the **Borley Rectory** haunting, other haunted houses, **mediumship** and psychic curiosities. Unfortunately none of these collections is suitably arranged for display or open to the general public.

## 'Psychic News'

Spiritualist weekly newspaper, founded 1932, which claims a readership of over 100 000. The present editor, Maurice Barbanell, is also the founder. The periodical produces each Thursday all the news of the week in the realm of **spiritualism, psychical research, ghosts** and **hauntings**. Address: Psychic Press Ltd, 23 Great Queen Street, London WC2B 5BB.

## Psychic photography

Photographs that show recognizable 'spirit extras' or inexplicable shapes and forms, whether taken in the **séance** room ('spirit photography'), at a haunted house, or anywhere else, which depict an image impossible to account for on an otherwise normal print or negative, are deemed to be examples of psychic photography. The history of spirit photographers (who specialize in the production of 'spirit extras') is full of conflicting evidence and even fraud, though there are undoubtedly many instances of such extras being produced in the séance room under controlled conditions and which defy normal explanation, given the stated circumstances. Thought pictures ('thoughtographs') obtained by Ted **Serios** have received considerable attention from scientists and spiritualists alike since 1963, but there have also been critics. Photographs of forms at haunted houses and elsewhere are rare, though in recent years a few puzzling examples have come to light, in particular a curious veiled form apparently mounting the tulip staircase at the Queen's House, Greenwich. This photograph was taken by the Rev. and Mrs R. W. Hardy, who state that nothing was visible on the staircase when they took it; and photographic experts all agree that the photograph has not been tampered with in any way and that there was no double exposure.

CONSULT: Sir Arthur Conan Doyle, *The Case for Spirit Photography*, Hutchinson (1922); Peter Haining, *Ghosts: the Illustrated History*, Sidgwick & Jackson (1974).

## Psychic rod
*See* **ectoplasm**.

## Psychical research
The scientific study of the facts and causes of alleged **paranormal** phenomena beyond consciousness, phenomena that include **telepathy, clairvoyance, extrasensory perception, psychokinesis, precognition, dowsing, spirit healing, hauntings**, spiritualistic phenomena, **dreams** and **automatism**. Organized psychical research began with the founding of the **Society for Psychical Research** in London in 1882, followed by the **American Society for Psychical Research**, and such organizations as the **Institut Métapsychique** in Paris, the Toronto Society for Psychical Research, the Rhodesian Society for Parapsychology, the Israel Parapsychology Society, the Psychological Institute of Bucharest and the Dutch Society for Psychical Research. The International Congress for Parapsychological Studies and the International Parapsychology Seminar are examples of the wider associations that meet periodically in various parts of the world.

*See also* **metapsychics; parapsychology**.

CONSULT: J. Beloff, *New Directions in Parapsychology*, Elek (1974); Harry Price, *Fifty Years of Psychical Research*, Longmans, Green (1939).

## Psychokinesis (PK)
The power of mind over matter; the apparent ability to influence objects other than by physical or any other discernable contact, as in **parakinesis**. Extensive experimentation in **parapsychology** has

established that the human mind plays a part in card-guessing, dice-throwing and similar activities to a degree hitherto undreamed of; for example, it has been suggested that significant correct 'hits' in card guessing experiments may be the result, not of **precognition**, but of an ability on the part of the person who shuffles the cards so to influence the shuffle that the fall of the cards matches the 'predictions' made by the subject being tested. It is considered by psychical researchers that **extrasensory perception** and psychokinesis are effects of a single ability which they term **'psi'**. Considerable research into such subjects has been conducted at Duke University, North Carolina, and at the American and British societies for psychical research, and while the exercise of such abilities is at present too slight and uncertain for them to be of serious practical use, it is likely that they will eventually become reliable – with far-reaching consequences.

CONSULT: Louisa E. Rhine, *Mind Over Matter*, Macmillan, New York (1970); J. B. Rhine and J. G. Pratt, *Parapsychology, Frontier Science of the Mind*, Blackwell (1958).

## Psychometry

Object reading; the apparent 'reading' of the history of an article associated with people, either living or dead. The ability to 'read' the history of an object by holding it in the hands. The word was invented by an American scientist, Professor Buchanan, in the Eclectic Medical Institute in Covington, Kentucky, in 1842. Buchanan was intrigued when Bishop Polk mentioned to him that if he touched brass in the dark he knew it by a metallic taste in his mouth. Buchanan tested Polk, and discovered that he was able to identify many substances merely by touching them. Many of his students showed the same curious ability, being able to identify various chemicals and other substances even when wrapped up in brown-paper parcels. Extremely sensitive 'psychometrists' were even able to identify geological specimens, and give an accurate account of their history. The article – or **inductor** – apparently enables the psychometrist to receive detailed information concerning the person with whom the object is connected. Psychometry, since its operation often appears to include **telepathy** and **clairvoyance**, is considered to be a part of the broad concept covered by the term **extrasensory perception**.

The psychometrist, a medium or **sensitive**, usually takes the object, which they like to be a personal object that has had a long association with its owner, a watch or ring or something of the sort, holds it quietly in his hands and seeks to absorb something of the person to whom the object belongs or once belonged. Then a few scraps of information are likely to be related, followed by more and more detailed information, much as a medium often seems to 'tune in' to a sitter before being able to impart detailed information. Research suggests that, in certain cases (as in some cases of **mediumship**), the explanation lies in telepathic communication between the mind of the psychometrist and that of the person present who knows the history or associations of the object; but there have been many curious examples of apparent psychometry where telepathy has clearly played no part. It is also evident that a lowered state of consciousness on the part of the psychometrist is favourable to results, and again one is reminded of other forms of mediumship.

The distance between the psychometrist and his subject seems to present no difficulty, and even **time** seems to be surmountable, for extensive experiments appear to have established that some pschometrists can not only pick up associations from the past history of the object, but also predict ones in its future history. Psychometry has been used in crime detection, but it is by no means infallible and, in common with other forms of mediumship, is treated with reserve by most police forces of the world.

CONSULT: Simeon Edmunds, *Hypnotism and the Supernormal*, Aquarian Press (1961); Paul Tabori, *Crime and the Occult*, David & Charles (1974).

## Pyramidology

The study of the Great Pyramid in relation to the belief that it was built with supernormal knowledge that included the measurement of the earth and astronomic understanding; and that, embodied in its measurements, were prophecies in cipher which concerned events recounted in the Bible and the future history of mankind. Pyramidologists also believe that the Great Pyramid (the only surviving 'wonder' of the ancient Seven Wonders of the World) was not built by the Ancient Egyptians, but by a race that invaded the country and built the edifice under divine inspiration and guidance; a race whose descendants included the Israelites and Anglo-Saxons.

The structure of the 'greatest single building ever erected by man' does, indeed, incorporate many problems – even mysteries – for orthodox scientists: its rigorous geometry; its positioning precisely in line with the cardinal points of the compass; the perfect joining and measuring and working of the huge blocks of stone; and the odd result (very close to the value of pi) that is obtained from doubling the height

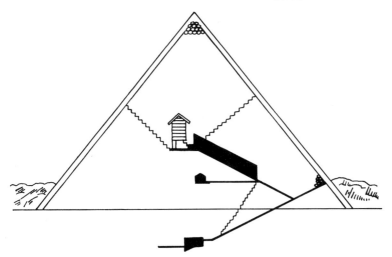

*The Great Pyramid, showing the position of the passages*

of the pyramid and dividing that figure into the perimeter. By taking measurements of many aspects of the Great Pyramid – sides, height and layers of stone; height, width and length of inner chambers, galleries and corridors – the students of pyramidology can arrive at dates of importance in the world's history and, it is claimed, events still to take place. One of the main prophecies was said to foretell the Second Coming of Christ, variously detailed as 1911 and 1936. One interpretation of the pyramid is that it represents in stone the sun's rays shining towards the earth through a gap in the clouds, and that by its possession the pharaoh could transport himself at will to the celestial kingdom of the sun god.

CONSULT: William Kingsland, *The Great Pyramid in Fact and Theory*, Rider (1932); C. Piazzi Smyth, *Our Inheritance in the Great Pyramid*, W. Isbister (1864).

# Q

## Qabalah
*See* **Cabala**.

## Quicksilver
Popular and common name for metallic mercury; 'live silver' – a reference to the mobility of the metal that is also a liquid, but a liquid that is not wet. Quicksilver has always played an important part in the experiments and beliefs of **alchemy**.

## Quintessence
Concentrated extract or embodiment of any substance which contains its virtues or essential principles; hence, figuratively, the purest form and most essential part of anything. In the Pythagorean doctrine and in **alchemy**, quintessence (the 'fifth essence') was the highest, last and celestial essence, beyond and above the four **elements** of earth, air, **fire** and water; it was thought to be the constituent of the heavenly bodies and to exist in latent form in all earthly things.

# R

## R101 case

On Sunday, 5 October 1930, the British airship R101, the largest dirigible in the world, crashed in flames near Beauvais, France, on her maiden voyage to India, with the loss of forty-six lives, including that of the airship's commander, Flight Lieutenant H. Carmichael Irwin. Three days before the disaster Harry **Price** had arranged for a **séance** to take place on 7 October at his National Laboratory of Psychical Research with Mrs Eileen **Garrett**. Mrs Garrett was already an established **trance** medium, and later became one of the world's leading **sensitives**, submitted to many scientific investigations both in England and the United States and was always considered to be of the highest integrity. Price wanted Mrs Garrett to try to communicate with Sir Arthur Conan **Doyle**, who had died three months earlier, at the request of an Australian newspaperman, Mr Ian Coster, who was present at the séance, as was Price's secretary, Miss Ethel Beenham.

As soon as the medium breathed heavily and relaxed into the trance state, her **control**, 'Uvani', said, 'I see for the moment Irving or Irwin. He says he *must* do something about it . . . apologizes for coming . . .' Then, speaking through Mrs Garrett, and in an agitated voice, the former commander of the crashed airship revealed in a long series of spasmodic sentences that the 'whole bulk of the dirigible was . . . too much for her engine capacity . . . useless lift too small . . . gross weight computed badly . . . elevator jammed . . . oil pipe plugged . . .'. As the strange voice droned on and on, Ethel Beenham laboriously noted everything that was said, all the technical and confidential details, the unfamiliar jargon, the detailed descriptions of how and why the airship crashed. (Afterwards Sir Arthur Conan Doyle is alleged to have communicated.) Later Mrs Garrett gave sittings to a Major Oliver Villiers, and during the course of them further apparent communications with Irwin were reported. An examination of the R101 tragedy reveals a story of bungling, pig-headedness and covering-up, while the story of the part played by Mrs Garrett and the apparent communications of Flight Lieutenant Irwin also reveals tensions and in-fighting; but, in addition, there was considerable evidence that some of the information obtained through the medium could not have been in her normal knowledge or, on certain points, in the normal knowledge of any living person.

CONSULT: Eileen Garrett, *Many Voices*, Allen & Unwin (1969); Harry Price, *Leaves from a Psychist's Case-Book*, Gollancz (1933).

## Rabbit
*See under* **animals and birds**.

## Radiesthesia
A 'fringe medicine' technique which employs a **Black Box** – an object of much antagonism and ridicule, but in fact as rational as **dowsing or divining**; it has been described as an attempt to apply to medicine the techniques used in dowsing or divining. By using a spot of the patient's **blood**, the radiesthetist professes to be able to diagnose the disease or illness from which the patient is suffering. It is emphasized that the spot of blood in itself means nothing, but is simply a method of 'tuning-in' to the patient and to make rapport with him. It is by no means impossible that some extra sense may be involved which certain sensitive people may be able to contact and use for the benefit of the person concerned, but the employment of a 'box' with an apparently nonsensical electrical layout and circuit has resulted in the system being scorned by doctors and scientists.

Radiesthesia involves the acceptance of two concepts: that all matter radiates on its own wavelengths, and that all living organisms emit electro-magnetic wave radiations whose intensity and frequency depends upon the general vitality, health and metabolism of the subject. Many interesting experiments have been conducted and some successes recorded, but the whole issue must remain in doubt until orthodox medicine investigates the claims made by radiesthetists.

CONSULT: Brian Inglis, *Fringe Medicine*, Faber & Faber (1964); T. T. B. Watson, *Radiesthesia and Some Associated Phenomena*, Markham House Press (1957).

## Rais (or Retz), Gilles de (c. 1396–1440)
Marshall of France whose possessions included the barony of Rais, south of Loire, on the marches of Brittany.

As a redoubtable soldier, Gilles de Rais raised seven companies of men-at-arms and conducted active warfare against the English, accompanying and watching over **Joan of Arc** at Orleans, where he fought by her side, as he did at Jargeau and Patay. In 1432 he seems to have suddenly retired from military service and, along with an abiding interest in **alchemy**, almost immediately commenced the grisly career of diabolical cruelty for which he is chiefly remembered. This outwardly cultured and honourable man of wealth and position, knowledgeable on **music** and drama and skilled in the ornamentation of illuminated manuscripts, was subsequently charged with murdering during the course of savage and obscene rituals 140 children (he was probably responsible in all for the deaths of over two hundred women and children); other charges including **heresy**, apostasy, conjuration of **demons**, sodomy, sacrilege and the possession of forbidden works on **magic**.

The evidence recorded at the trial, held before the Bishop of Nantes in 1440, describes monstrous sexual perversions on living and dead children. A Florentine priest and sorcerer, Francesco Prelati, had claimed that he could invoke a demon, named Baron, who would reveal the secret of manufacturing gold, provided the correct rites and sacrifices were carried out; and terrifying ceremonies followed, with de Rais supplying a child's heart, eyes, hands and **blood** for **sacrifice**. Under torture, de Rais admitted all the charges, and next day made a public confession, describing every horror in great detail, begging forgiveness of the bereaved parents of his victims and piously beseeching all present to love and honour God and the Church. The Bishop of Nantes embraced de Rais and prayed that he be purged and redeemed. Even so, de Rais (sometimes erroneously confused with the much older Breton legend of Bluebeard) was sentenced to death and duly hanged and burnt to the sounds of a procession of clergy singing prayers for his salvation.

CONSULT: Georges Bataille, *Procès de Gilles de Rais*, Paris (1959); Eliphas Levi, *The History of Magic*, Rider (1913).

## 'Raphael's Ephemeris'

Annual publication used in **astrology** which details the positions of the planets, the sun and the **moon** at noon or midnight for each day of the year, their declinations and other information including a Table of Houses showing the various platitudes of the planets and logarithms for determining the correct positions of the planets for the time and place of the birth required. 'Raphael' has been the pseudonym of a succession of astrologers from 1826 to the present day. Address: Foulsham, Yeovil Road, Slough, Berkshire.

CONSULT: Ellic Howe, *Urania's Children*, William Kimber (1967).

## Rasputin, Gregori Efimovich (1872-1916)

Russian mystic and charlatan who was born in the Tobolsk province of Siberia. He had no education, no occupation, and his reputation was that of a rowdy and ignorant peasant, a horse thief, a drunkard, seducer of young girls and generally a rogue and blackguard. Indeed, he remained largely illiterate all his life, and his only attributes were great physical strength and apparent attraction for the opposite sex. Coarse-featured and adorned with a heavy black beard, he possessed strange, deep-set and piercing eyes. He seems to have impressed many people with his alleged powers of **hypnotism** and **clairvoyance**, and there is no doubt that he had gifts of healing and prophecy. In 1901 he abandoned his wife and three children, claiming he had received religious enlightenment in the form of a **vision** of the Virgin Mary, and took to the road as a holy begger.

Intelligent, a schemer and a shrewd judge of character, Rasputin managed to survive and make his way to St Petersburg, where he became accepted in certain circles. By this time he was a member of the ancient and notorious Khlysty sect ('Men of God') which practised **flagellation** and sexual orgies, believing the world to be divided into spirit and flesh, the spirit being the good part of man, the flesh the evil. The Khlysty also thought that Christ kept returning to earth in the form of a man, and that the Holy Spirit had the power to inspire young virgins to become begetters of Christ. And they believed in healing through prayer, in prophecy and in the expelling of **demons**; which arts, it is claimed, were studied by Rasputin, who became proficient in all of them. He also accepted and extolled their dogma that to repent one first must sin.

In 1905 Rasputin was presented to the Tsar, and quickly became the friend, guide, father-confessor and advisor to the Romanov household. There is no doubt that after Rasputin stopped the bleeding of the three-year-old Tsarevich Alexis, who suffered from haemophelia, he could do no wrong, and that both the Tsar and the Tsaritsa followed whatever Rasputin said with blind faith; ministers were appointed or dismissed, state policy was decided on his wishes, and he became in truth the power behind the throne of Imperial Russia. Rasputin was also responsible for many acts of comforting and healing, and apparent miracles, but his formidable power and repressing influence with the

Tsar and Tsaritsa created many enemies, and nine attempts were made to murder him before the tenth succeeded.

CONSULT: René Fülöp-Miller, *Rasputin: the Holy Devil*, Putnam (1928); R. J. Minney, *Rasputin*, Cassell (1972).

## Raudive, Dr Konstantin (1909-74)

German psychologist who, while recording bird songs, met Frederick Jurgenson, a Swedish artist and writer, whose recordings of bird song also contained faint but unmistakable human voices, even though no human being had been anywhere near when the bird-song recordings were made. Intrigued, Raudive experimented, sitting at a table in his home with two tape recorders and inviting any **spirit** entities present to speak. He arranged for two observers to vouch for the authenticity of his experiments. Raudive claimed to record 72 000 different voices in three years of experimentation. The recordings were mostly of short jumbled sentences or phrases purporting to be spoken by discarnate beings and largely directed to Raudive himself, in several languages; the alleged communicators ranging from Raudive's mother to the late Dr Carl Jung. A full account of the 'electronically recorded spirit voices' was published in Raudive's book *Breakthrough – An Amazing Experiment in Electronic Communication with the Dead*, Colin Smythe (1971).

## Raven

*See under* **animals and birds**.

## Regardie, Dr Francis Israel (b. 1907)

An Englishman who has spent most of his life in the United States; he was at one time secretary, companion and disciple of Aleister **Crowley**. Regardie's exceptionally illuminating books on **magic**, and, in particular, four volumes detailing the rites of the Order of the **Golden Dawn**, are among the most important published works on the subject. Indeed, Israel Regardie is considered by those who should know as the foremost living authority on magic. His books include: *The Art of True Healing*, Helios Books, Toddington (1964); *Roll Away the Stone*, Llewellyn, Minnesota (1968); *The Golden Dawn*, Llewellyn, Minnesota (1969); *The Tree of Life*, Weiser, New York (1969); *The Philosopher's Stone*, Llewellyn, Minnesota (1970); *The Eye in the Triangle*, Llewellyn, Minnesota (1970); *The Enochian Dictionary*, Sangreal Foundation, Texas (1971); and *My Rosicrucian Adventure*, Llewellyn, Minnesota (1971).

## Regression
*See under* **hypnotism**.

## Regurgitation

Controversial theory to explain the presence of **materialization** phenomena at **séances** by fraudulent means: that some mediums are able to swallow cheesecloth or a similar material before a séance and disgorge it during the séance and present it as **ectoplasm**. The idea of regurgitation at will (which some people consider to be impossible) was first suggested during the investigation of the medium Eva C at the **Society for Psychical Research** in 1922 and revived by Harry **Price** during séances with Helen Duncan.

CONSULT: Harry Houdini, *Miracle Mongers and their Methods*, Dutton New York (1920); Harry Price, 'Regurgitation and the Duncan Mediumship', *Bulletin*, I (1931), National Laboratory of Psychical Research.

## Reichenbach, Baron Karl von (1788-1869)

German physicist who claimed to have discovered a radiation or force, which he termed the **odic force**, that was possessed by human beings – and animals, plants, magnets, metals and crystals – and that could be seen as a kind of light beam or **aura** type of luminosity by **sensitives** in darkness. Some early spiritualists thought that **spirits** of dead people used the odic force in a medium's body to communicate by means of speech, writing, knocking or moving objects, and occultists have attempted to harness and use the force during various occult practices.

CONSULT: Alan Gould, *The Founders of Psychical Research*, Routledge & Kegan Paul (1968); K. von Reichenbach, *The Odic Force*, University Books, New York (1968 reprint).

## Reincarnation

The idea that an essential element, independent of the physical body, is repeatedly reborn into different bodies; that this element – or soul – must pass through a number of cycles of birth and **death** and rebirth before achieving ultimate salvation. It is a belief that has formed an integral part of **Buddhism, Hinduism** and other Eastern religions for hundreds of years (the Tibetans believe that the Dalai Lama is perpetually reincarnated); and it has attracted increasing interest in the Western world during the last decade.

There exists convincing evidence for reincarnation, and especially for young children apparently remembering details of a former life for a few years; and there are many sane and sensible people alive today who are quite certain that they have lived before on this earth and that they will return in the future. Some reincarnationists believe that each person has at least three lives (one as a man, one as a woman and a third as the sex in which the 'soul' fared best), while others consider that the birth-death-rebirth cycle continues indefinitely; again, some people think that reincarnation occurs immediately, others only after many years. Dr Ian Stephenson, a Trustee of the **American Society for Psychical Research**, has made an extensive study of reincarnation, and his writings in the society's *Journal*, from 1966 to the present date, should be examined together with the Bridey Murphy case in the early 1950s when an American businessman hypnotized a young housewife who then supplied information about a previous life in Ireland in the nineteenth century.

Interesting experiments have been conducted by regression through **hypnotism** and suggest that if a person has been someone else on earth at an earlier period, they manifest as that person; and there are records of such previous incarnations being historically established with varying degrees of certainty. In March 1975, villagers in Central Ceylon refused to help Sri Lanka's Archaeological Department to drive away hornets that swarmed around an ancient rock fortress during excavations because they believed the creatures to be reincarnations of the soldiers of King Kassapa I who had occupied and guarded the fortress in the fifth century A.D. Reincarnation is an attractive hypothesis, one that eliminates all fear of death, explains the heartbreak of death in infancy, makes sense of the fact that some people have happy lives and others considerable unhappiness, is sympathetic to man's weaknesses and promises, by gradual progression, eventual peace and satisfaction in all things. Unfortunately reincarnation is not at present verifiable for it is impossible to eliminate totally ancestor memory, **telepathy**, **clairvoyance** and other means whereby the information imparted might be acquired.

CONSULT: Joan Grant and Denys Kelsey, *Many Lifetimes*, Gollancz (1969); Ian Stevenson, *Twenty Cases Suggestive of Reincarnation*, University of Virginia (1974 edition); Peter Underwood and Leonard Wilder, *Lives to Remember, A Case-Book on Reincarnation*, Robert Hale (1975).

## Rescue circles

Spiritualist system of informing the dead of their true state and freeing them from being earthbound **spirits**. The necessity for rescue circles is based on the idea in **spiritualism** that, in certain cases, and especially in instances of sudden **death**, the subject is unaware of what has happened and remains in a state of bewilderment and a certain attachment to the land of the living until released by prayers and the sympathetic understanding of a spiritualist circle of sitters.

CONSULT: Usborne Moore, *Glimpses of the Next State*, Watts (1911); Dr Carl Wickland, *Thirty Years Among the Dead*, Los Angeles (1924).

## Retrocognition

Knowledge of past events or states obtained by means other than through the known senses; **extrasensory perception** of the past as opposed to **precognition**, which is the knowledge of future events.

## Revenant

**Ghost, spectre**, one who returns from the dead. A revenant may return to right some wrong, exact some revenge, prove some crime or simply to comfort loved ones. Most often revenants are kindly and harmless, but occasionally, it is said, they are wicked and return for evil purposes. Sorcerers attempt to invoke and contact revenants since they are restless and usually amicable ghosts.

## Rhabdomancy

The science of **dowsing or divining**.

## Rhine, Professor Joseph Banks (b. 1895)

American psychical researcher and pioneer of experimental research in **parapsychology**; former Director of the Parapsychology Laboratory, Duke University, Durham, North Carolina; also Executive Director of the Foundation for Research on the Nature of Man. The publication in America in 1934 of his book on **extrasensory perception** (a term invented by Rhine) gave great impetus to experimentation in **telepathy** and other forms of ESP; and although the tests numbered nearly 100 000 and the results seemed to suggest something far in excess of chance expectation, later tests and tighter controls did not produce the same results. Rhine, together with his wife and fellow-researcher Louisa, is in no doubt that man has powers which seem to be beyond the five senses, and he has always looked forward to the day when parapsychology would be accepted as a 'respectable' science, though only a 'revolution in thinking' can lead to this taking place.

As the 'father' of parapsychology (another term he invented, together with **psi**, meaning psychic phenomena), Rhine has survived controversy, humiliation and scandal – so often a death-blow to workers in the field of psychic phenomena. When he retired from Duke University in 1965 after thirty-eight years of work, he had the humiliation of seeing his parapsychology laboratory closed down; and then, in 1974, he found that Walter Levy, the man he had appointed to run his parapsychological laboratory at North Carolina, had been faking results. This discovery, which Rhine immediately announced, nullified five years' work, and he set out to devise a new method of analysis which would indicate exactly the evidence for psychic research that is beyond dispute. He has done much to fight the prejudice that many scientists have against parapsychology, and he has certainly gained some acceptance of the subject as a science: Duke University still conducts experiments in many psychic matters, and there is a course in parapsychology at Yale University; while the summer schools run by Rhine and his wife continue to attract increasing numbers of young graduates, medical men, psychologists and physicists.

In recent years, Rhine has devoted much of his time to the problems of religion: having refuted the materialistic enemy of religion, for he is convinced that he has proved the existence of ESP over and over again, he feels that to discover the mysterious 'something' that man can draw on could be his greatest achievement. Rhine's books include *Extra-Sensory Perception*, Faber & Faber (1935); *New Frontiers of the Mind*, Farrar & Rinehart, New York (1937); *The Reach of the Mind*, Faber & Faber (1948); and *New World of the Mind*, William Sloane, New York (1953).

## Ritual magic

The principle of summoning a strong supernatural force, entity, power or **spirit** for the purpose of gaining material and spiritual power; contacting another world of spirits and **demons**, who can be harnessed to be the means of gaining love, wealth, influence – anything that is desired by ceremony, ritual, **names of power** and magical preparation and operation.

Old textbooks or **grimoires** detail various processes and practices said to subject such forces to the will of the magician, who can then obtain whatever information he wishes. The spirit, demon or force is usually commanded to appear by **incantation**, and with the use of **magic circle**, symbols, **talismans** and words of power, the entity is summoned, dominated and bent to the will of the magician. Preparations vary, but often include lengthy **meditation**, concentration, confession, deprivation of worldly distractions and pleasures, and abstinence to create a reservoir of sexual energy. Magical instruments, all constructed to strict specifications and conditions, include a sword, a staff, a **wand**, a lancet, a hook, a sickle, a poniard, a white-handled knife, a black-handled knife (**athame**); also a swastika, a crown, a spear, a scourge, a lamp, a tripod, cup, cross; and articles of special clothing that include a girdle, apron, sandals, robes and white paper crown: all these carry magic symbols, names and devices.

The magician is careful to act out the ritual magic (usually in some secluded place such as a graveyard, woodland or a specially furnished room hung with red curtains) from within the safety of his carefully constructed magic circle, at an appropriate time and on a significant day or night. The actual ritual will depend upon the spirit or demon that is to be called, and the purpose for which it is summoned, and here again the grimoires and other works describe the elaborate preparations and ceremonies necessary for success. Once the ritual is perfect in every respect, and provided the magician has followed every detail of preparation and execution, it is said that the spirit or power manifests and that the magician, in an ecstasy of passion, commands the spirit conjured to subject itself to him – and so, in effect, the entity and the magician become one.

CONSULT: E. M. Butler, *Ritual Magic*, Cambridge University Press (1949); Francis King, *Ritual Magic in England*, Neville Spearman (1971).

## Robin
*See under* **animals and birds**.

## Robin Goodfellow
Another name for Puck, a folk-character and friendly hobgoblin who was described in a seventeenth-century pamphlet, *The Life of Robin Goodfellow*, as half-human and half-fairy (*see* **fairies**). A popular figure in mummers' plays, Robin Goodfellow's origin probably lies in a minor fertility god, the goat's feet and horns, reminiscent of the **horned god**, accounting for his part in magical practices where his ability to change shape (exploited by Shakespeare in *A Midsummer Night's Dream*) has been a particular attraction.

CONSULT: K. M. Briggs, *The Anatomy of Puck*, Routledge & Kegan Paul (1959).

## Rosalie case

A remarkable and baffling case of apparent **materialization** experienced by Harry **Price** and published in detail in his *Fifty Years of Psychical Research* (1939). Under his own controlled conditions Price saw, touched from head to foot and conversed with an apparent materialization of a little girl of six, 'Rosalie', in a home circle that included the dead child's mother. Subsequent inquiries by many researchers have failed to locate the house where the events took place, the people concerned or any real confirmation of the story, though it must be remembered that Harry Price was sworn to secrecy. He certainly told a number of people about the incident at the time, including Mrs K. M. Goldney, R. S. Lambert (former editor of the *Listener*), his wife and his secretary.

CONSULT: David Cohen, *Price and His Spirit Child Rosalie*, Regency Press (1965); Paul Tabori and Phyllis Raphael, *Beyond the Senses*, Souvenir Press (1971).

## Rosemary

*See under* **trees and plants**.

## Rosicrucians

A name that has been used by many occult groups, but originally a fifteenth-century German mystical order whose power and influence reached its zenith in the seventeenth century. Today the word 'Rosicrucian' is often associated with any arcane, mystic or occult teaching, and the original Fraternity or Brotherhood of the Rosy Cross, with its strange rites and practices, has been forgotten and submerged into freemasonry and cults of esoteric and secret societies.

CONSULT: R. S. Clymer, *The Book of Rosicruciae*, Philosophical Publishing Company, Quakerstown, Penn. (1946–9); F. A. Yates, *The Rosicrucian Enlightenment*, Routledge & Kegan Paul (1972).

## Rowan

*See under* **trees and plants**.

## Runes

Ancient stone scripts dating from pre-Christian times until well into the sixteenth century, often considered to be **charms** and memorial inscriptions. The word *rune* means 'secret' or 'mystery', and it is thought that the Nordic peoples attributed **magic** powers to these mysterious symbols scattered throughout Northern Europe, particularly in Germany and Scandinavia. The god Odin is said to have waited nine days to win mastery over the magic runes; German nationalists and occultists at different periods have also credited runes with mysterious powers; and there have been occasional attempts at rune occultism, with emphasis on the magic names and symbols depicted on the stones.

CONSULT: Sven Jansson, *The Runes of Sweden*, Dent (1964); Guido von List, *The Secret of the Runes*, List Society, Vienna (1908).

# S

## Sabbath

Witches' meeting (sometimes written 'sabbat', the Latin and French spelling of sabbath); a gathering of **covens**, usually visualized as a huge assembly of young and old witches and warlocks, often masked, presided over by a black goat-like figure on a throne, while in the flickering light of huge black candles, smoking torches and a bonfire, wild and unbridled passions are given rein; human **sacrifice** is made, and, once obscene homage has been paid to the naked and sexually aroused 'god', a general orgy takes place.

Real sabbaths, if they existed outside the imagination or **dreams** of those who confessed (under torture) to flying to such meetings to be taught harmful **magic** in return for obedience and sacrifice, were almost certainly gatherings of small groups of **witchcraft** adherents for the purpose of renewing pacts with their deity, exchanging news and magical formulas and, possibly, ending the meetings with **sex magic**. Nevertheless there was widespread belief from the fourteenth to the seventeenth centuries, among bishops, judges and men in authority throughout much of Europe, that there existed a vast society of witches and adepts who trained others and themselves practised acts of witchcraft.

There is some evidence, in line with Margaret **Murray**'s theories, to suggest that the witch cult was a survival of pure paganism and that sabbaths were originally a religious ceremony, dating from prehistoric times, at which the **horned god** was worshipped and at which magical and fertility rites were practised. At all events, sabbaths were held at regular intervals, at night, and in remote and lonely places. Witches dedicated their children to the horned god, vows were taken and pacts renewed (for a period or for life). New members were given a new name and initiated with a sharp pinch on some part of their bodies which was said to leave an unfading and insensitive blue mark: the

**devil's mark** that interrogators searched for. In return for complete subjection and renunciation of the Christian faith, the converts received the spiritual, material and physical protection of the horned god, identified by Christians as the **Devil**, who gave them a **familiar** to help in their practice of witchcraft and the guarantee of the support and help of the rest of the community of witches in enjoying their exciting hidden knowledge and secret power. Feasting and drinking would follow the serious business, and then ritual and sexually exciting dancing, with the naked participants linking hands around the great fire, facing outwards and then pairing off and dancing with abandon back to back until finally the Grand Master of the sabbath led the way to sexual licence and orgiastic frenzy before dawn signalled the end of the proceedings.

CONSULT: Rollo Ahmed, *The Black Art*, John Long (1936); Peter Haining, *Anatomy of Witchcraft*, Souvenir Press (1972).

## Sacrifice
An offering to a deity, usually upon an altar; not infrequently a ritual killing, the **blood** symbolizing the offering of a life.

Anthropologists argue about the origin of the idea of sacrifice. Some lean towards a kind of parrallel with the Christian Eucharist, the worshippers eating a sanctified meal with their god and so becoming united with him. Others prefer to think that primitive man regarded human sacrifice as the finest gift man could make to appease and curry favour with the gods; or that animals were killed as scapegoats to carry away sin and evil as a form of **exorcism**. Others, again, feel the origin lies in a sort of recompense, to expiate a broken rule or **taboo**. Still others point to the close link between sacrifice and cannibalism, and believe the main object was the consumption of the sacrifice and that the gesture to the god was incidental.

Whatever its origin, sacrifice has been a part of history, myth and legend from remotest times. From the mortal battles for the 'sacred kingship' in the Grove of Nemi and the biblical sacrifices, and through the wholesale slaughter of the ancient Mexicans to **witchcraft** and the rites of present-day sorcerers, occultists and black magicians (and white witches), sacrifice has played an essential part in the history of religion and man's relationship with unseen powers. The Pawnee Indians used to select a young girl, give her everything she wanted for six months and then kill her, cut up her body and distribute it among the cornfields in spring in the belief that they were giving a new life to the earth; an idea that is practised symbolically to this day in the East, and is even reflected in the sacrificial slaughter of animals by some present-day religions.

CONSULT: Garry Hogg, *Cannibalism and Human Sacrifice*, Robert Hale (1958); E. O. James, *The Origins of Sacrifice*, John Murray (1933).

## Sagittarius
*See* **zodiac**.

## St John's wort
*See under* **trees and plants**.

## Salem witch-hunt
In 1692 the best-known and most notorious witch-hunt in America took place at Salem Village, a rural community in Massachusetts, New England, some distance from Salem proper (since renamed Danvers). In those early colonial days, most people believed implicity in the reality of **demons** and witches, and stories of **witchcraft** so frightened a group of eight girls that first two of them, and then the rest, began to act strangely, evidently afflicted with a hysterical contagion. Almost in a state of disassociation, they moaned and groaned and threw themselves about, shrieking for no apparent reason, crawling on all fours and seemingly the victims of **possession**. The symptoms spread to other children in the settlement, and parents, seeking spiritual advice, called in the village pastor. When he questioned some of the girls, they told him that certain aged persons in the community were witches and had cast **spells** upon them; and eventually two of the girls named three inhabitants.

When these three women were arrested, two of them denied everything, but the third seems to have produced some kind of confession in which several more people were named as servants of the **Devil**. The girls were noted to have hysterical outbursts whenever they were in the presence of any of those named as witches and the panic spread like wildfire. One after another people were named, arrested, charged with witchcraft and thrown into prison; two hundred in all were arrested. Everywhere the terrified villagers thought they saw evidence of the work of the servants of Satan, few dared to venture from their homes at night and every animal was suspected of being a witch in disguise. As the troubles increased, the governor of the colony appointed a special high court to try the accused, which found nineteen prisoners guilty of witchcraft; in all, thirty-four persons throughout New England (mostly women, but also some men) died on the gallows as witches before, at last, reason prevailed. The special commission was cancelled, and gradually the populace realized with horror what they had done in their panic. Colonial America never again carried out the death sentence for witchcraft.

One of the reasons for the persistent fascination that the Salem case has for many people lies in the fact that it arose among Puritans in a Puritan colony. Today the affair is regarded as a part of America's history and there is a Witch House at Salem Village where posters are sold detailing the story of the sad event, while Arthur Miller produced a dramatic treatment of the outbreak in his play *The Crucible*.

CONSULT: Chadwick Hansen, *Witchcraft at Salem*, Brazillier, New York (1969); Marion L. Starkey, *The Devil in Massachusetts*, Robert Hale (1952).

## Salt

Sodium chloride; formerly regarded as one of the elementary substances. Obtained by evaporating or freezing ocean water (3 per cent of the weight of the oceans is salt) or water from saline lakes and springs; or by mining a bed of rock-salt.

Salt's healing, restorative and antiseptic properties, and the fact that it is a necessary ingredient of food for most mammals, led to religious and social significances being attributed to it by early peoples. Salt was traded in Neolithic times, and the Roman armies and labourers were paid partly in salt, hence the word 'salary' from the Latin *salarium* or 'salt allowance'. Salt is the symbol of both sterility and perpetuity. Lot's wife was turned into a pillar of salt when she looked back at Sodom, one of the five biblical cities of the plain said to be buried under or near the Salt or Dead Sea in whose waters no living thing exists.

Salt was often used in **sacrifices** to propitiate the gods or the **spirits**; and as a preservative from corruption and dissolution. It was customary at the ratification of solemn treaties for both parties to eat a few grains of salt – 'taking salt together' bound two men in eternal friendship. As with other essentials, such as **iron**, salt was thought to have a supernatural origin, and its place in religion varies from the covenant of salt that symbolized the eternal bond between God and Israel to the bloodthirsty Aztecs with their goddess of salt. With its universal sanctity, salt has long been an element of holy water used in **exorcism, baptism** (a form of exorcism) or fighting the powers of evil. Salt by itself is said to keep away devils and witches; its qualities were and are recognized and used by sorcerers, alchemists, witches, black magicians and necromancers, who never use it, however, if they wish to attract devils or **demons**.

**Superstitions** involving salt are legion. They include neutralizing the ill-effects that can follow spilling salt (unlucky since it was once a very valuable commodity) by throwing a little over the left shoulder into the **Devil**'s face as he seeks to whisper in your ear, emboldened by the spilling of the salt; the use of salt by fishermen, who sprinkled their nets with the substance, and boat builders, who placed some between the planks of a new boat in an unconscious offering to the sea to ensure the safety of boat and crew; burning salt, seven mornings in succession, to force a straying lover to return. Salt in a bride's pocket during the wedding ceremony is lucky – sailors sometimes carry salt for the same reason; and salt clenched in the hands of a mother giving birth is considered helpful. New-born children used to be rubbed with salt, or would receive the gift of a little salt to counteract **witchcraft** (those who could afford it replaced the salt with **silver**, which had the same power); and even the dreaded gipsy's **curse** could be rendered harmless if some salt was thrown after him as he departed.

CONSULT: Richard Cavendish, *The Black Arts*, Routledge & Kegan Paul (1967); Douglas Hill, *Magic and Superstition*, Hamlyn (1968).

## Samadhi
The eighth and ultimate stage of **yoga**; the state of super-consciousness, unqualified blessedness and appreciation of the oneness of self and the infinite; the awareness of the bliss of the absolute.

## Sasquatch
'Wild man of the woods'; American Indian name for the Bigfoot. *See under* **animals and birds**.

## Satanic mass
*See* **black mass**.

## Satanism
The worship of Satan, the Master to Satanists, for whom he is the personification of good. Satan, his followers believe, will eventually triumph over the evil Christian God, and they look to him, temporarily vanquished by the God of Love, for power and pleasure in this world and in the life to come.

The essence of Satanism is to overthrow the order and worship of the Christian God and to reverse Christian values. Everything is therefore the opposite of the conventional, things are upside down or back to front, that which the majority regard as right is wrong; for the Prince of Darkness himself is really the Lord of Light or Lucifer, the giver of light. The Satanist replaces the Christian virtues of humility, purity, compassion and self-restraint with pride, uninhibited delight in sexual pleasures, domination by force, and a ruthless struggle for power and pleasure. Satanists maintain that the New Testament supports their view that Satan is all-powerful. They point to the story of the temptation in the wilderness where the Devil offers Jesus (Matthew 4:1–11) 'all the kingdoms of the world, and the glory of them', with the clear implication that such things were his to offer; to John 8:44 where Jesus tells the Jews that their father is not God but the **Devil**; to John 12:31, where the Devil is called 'the prince of this world'; and to where Paul calls him 'the god of this world' in 2 Corinthians 4:4. Even theologians admit that the evidence for the actual personality of Satan is comparable with that for the Holy Spirit and angelic spiritual beings.

Satanism was at the heart of the **witchcraft** persecutions and some **heresies**, and both earlier and later Satanism has been practised in many guises and under many names; Cathars were branded as worshippers of Satan, as were the Waldensians, the Luciferans, the **Knights Templar**, the **Hell-Fire Club** and other less-known cults and sects. Today there are such survivals of Satanism as the American organizations styling themselves 'Our Lady of Endor Covan', 'The Ophite Cultus Sathanas' and 'The Church of Satan', while continuing desecration of churches and churchyards points to the survival, underground, of Satanism and the Satanic or **black mass** with its black candles, human **sacrifice**, blasphemous ritual and sexual licence. It is a sacrament of matter and flesh, as opposed to the Christian ceremony of spirit, and of adoration of the power in opposition to Christianity, with manifestations of evil, glorification of sin and the welcoming of the powers of darkness; sometimes, it is said, using the naked body of a girl as an altar.

CONSULT: Edward Langton, *Satan, A Portrait*, Skeffington (1946); H. T. F. Rhodes *The Satanic Mass*, Rider (1954).

# Saturnalia
*See under* **festivals**.

# Schneider brothers, Willi (1903-71) and Rudi (1908-57)

Famous physical mediums born at Braunau, Austria, two of the twelve sons of a printer. Baron von **Schrenck-Notzing** made a study of both brothers, as did Harry **Price**.

Willi, from the age of sixteen, impressed many investigators with partial **materialization**, the movement of objects without contact (**parakinesis**), causing matter to pass through matter and similar phenomena. In common with his younger brother Rudi, he was a bright, intelligent youth, fond of sports, and with a happy disposition. Yet there is no doubt that, under the strictest supervision and control, he produced, or was responsible for, while in a state of self-induced **trance**, movement of objects, raps, a materialized hand-like form, and many other happenings; but after an initial flourish of impressive phenomena, Willi's power of **mediumship** seemed to decrease and eventually to disappear, though not before it had been witnessed by such organizations as the Psychological Institute of the University of Munich and the **Society for Psychical Research** besides numerous independent scientists, doctors and psychic investigators, including Dr Eric Dingwall and Dr E. Holub, a Viennese psychiatrist, most of whom became convinced that the phenomena were genuine.

Willi apparently discovered his mediumistic ability while his family were playing at holding a **séance**. An entity calling itself 'Olga' (and sometimes claiming to be Lola Montez, the colourful mistress of King Ludwig of Bavaria) manifested. Then, at a later séance, when Willi's mediumistic powers seemed to be dwindling, 'Olga' requested the presence of Rudi, and while the boys' mother protested and Olga insisted, in walked the eleven-year-old Rudi, apparently sleep-walking. He sat himself down next to his brother and proceeded to speak as 'Olga'. Thereafter Willi developed another trance personality called 'Mina', and 'Olga' remained with Rudi for the rest of his mediumship. Rudi was totally unaware of 'Olga', except when he was in trance, a state marked by incredibly rapid breathing and extreme muscular tension; on occasions he reached a sexual climax.

Rudi was probably the most exhaustively investigated and carefully controlled physical medium of all time. From the onset of his phenomena at the age of eleven (probably the start of his adolescence) he was under the watchful eyes of experienced scientists and medical men; he never refused any condition suggested or imposed by researchers, and the detailed, signed and dated records of hundreds of séances which exist suggest that his is the best-authenticated case of mediumship in the history of **psychical research**. Furthermore, Rudi never made any money out of his mediumship, for the various investigators (Schrenck-Notzing, Osty, Schwaiger, Price and others) only contributed travelling expenses and reimbursed no more than Rudi would have earned as an apprentice mechanic; nor did he ever earn any money through publicity or any other method as far as his mediumship was concerned.

Perhaps the most important investigations were carried out by Dr Eugene Osty in Paris in 1930–31 when it was established scientifically that 'an invisible substance' was shown to interfere with infra-red beams and to set off alarm bells and photographic flash-lights, although nothing was ever discovered to account for the triggering off of the experimental and observed systems: such demonstrations took place on demand and were repeated later in London.

Very few charges of fraud were ever made against the Schneider brothers, and Mrs Anita Gregory (principal lecturer in the Department of Teaching Studies at the North London Polytechnic, who carried out research on Rudi Schneider as Perrot-Warwick student at Trinity College, Cambridge, and probably knows more about the Schneider mediumship than any other living person) maintains that a careful study reveals that not a single charge would be acceptable as evidence in any context other than psychical research. The photographic evidence for a celebrated 'exposure' by Harry Price is revealed to be highly unsatisfactory and ambiguous, and the available documentary evidence leaves little doubt that Price acted with lack of scruple towards Rudi and his fellow investigators. At the time of his death from a stroke, Rudi, happily married for many years, was the owner of a small driving school.

CONSULT: Harry Price, *Rudi Schneider*, Methuen (1930); and 'Further Experiments with Rudi Schneider', National Laboratory of Psychical Research, *Bulletin*, IV (1933).

## Schrenck-Notzing, Baron Freiherr Albert von (1862–1929)

Important German pioneer in **psychical research** and medical doctor of considerable standing who sat with and investigated many physical mediums, including Eva C., **Stanislava P.**, Eusapia Paladino and Willi Schneider of the **Schneider brothers**. He also studied somnambulism, **hypnotism**, **telepathy**, sexual anomalies and criminal psychopathology, and has been described as having done more than anyone to establish the physical phenomena of psychical research, largely with his monumental work, *Phenomena of Materialization* (1920).

CONSULT: Nandor Fodor, *Encyclopaedia of Psychic Science*, Arthurs Press (1934); Paul Tabori, *Pioneers of the Unseen*, Souvenir Press (1972).

## Scorpio
*See* **zodiac**.

## Screaming skulls
Skulls that are said to have emitted sounds or caused strange happenings when they have been moved from their accustomed places. A number of reputedly haunted houses in Britain possess, or once possessed, skulls associated with such legends, among the best-known being Bettiscombe Manor, Dorset; Burton Agnes Hall, Yorkshire; Higher Farm, Chilton Cantelo, Somerset; Tunstead Milton, Derbyshire; Warbleton Priory, Sussex; and Wardley Hall, Lancashire.

CONSULT: R. Thurston Hopkins, *Ghosts Over England*, Meridian Books (1953); Elliott O'Donnell, *The Screaming Skulls and Other Stories*, Foulsham (1964).

## Scrofula
*See* **king's evil**.

## Scrying
Ancient method of **divination**, also known as **crystal-gazing**. The seer may see **visions** or symbolic images of the past, the present or, more usually, the future in any polished surface – a **mirror**, bowl of water, brass, glass or even a pool of water – and there is no doubt that whatever is used is merely a focal point for concentration.

While some advocates of modern scrying maintain that mystic names in gold must be engraved around the crystal ball, it has been established that one person in twenty will 'see' something after concentrating for ten minutes, although several sittings are often necessary before any results are obtained. Before attempting to scry (the term derives from the old English word 'descry', to see) a number of precautions are advisable. The crystal ball should never be handled by anyone except the owner (though anyone can look into it), since handling by various people is said to 'mix the magnetism' and 'destroy the sensitiveness'; it should be 'magnetized' frequently by passing the right hand over it, for five minutes at a time, which gives the ball strength and power; and similar passes with the left hand are said to increase the sensitiveness of the crystal. One side of the ball should always be distinguished as the back, and this part can face the light, although the opposite side, the 'front', should never face the light.

To achieve results in scrying, it has been suggested, a beginner should select a quiet room uncluttered by mirrors, pictures or ornaments. After selecting a comfortable position for both himself and the crystal ball, with his face about a foot away from the ball and looking downwards at an angle, the aspirant scryer should attempt to look into the depths of the crystal with a steady and calm gaze for no more than ten minutes at a time, although the periods can later be extended. After a while the crystal will be seen to look dull or cloudy with pin-points of light. Soon these tiny stars will glitter and move to form patterns, images and pictures. Cloud-like appearances often precede or intermingle with pictures, and the significance of the colour and movement of these visions have been distinguished as follows: white clouds: goodness, affirmation, agreement; black clouds: badness, misfortune, disagreement; green or blue clouds: anticipation of good fortune, happiness, excellent prospects; red, orange or yellow clouds: a warning of danger, trouble, illness, deception, loss and unpleasantness. Ascending clouds indicate affirmative replies to questions; and descending clouds denote negative answers.

CONSULT: Theodore Besterman, *Crystal-Gazing: a Study in the History, Distribution, Theory and Practise of Scrying*, Rider (1927); J. Melville, *Crystal-Gazing and the Wonders of Clairvoyance*, Weiser, New York (1970 reprint).

## Séance

French word for 'a sitting'; usually used to describe a spiritualist gathering or group of people who sit for the purpose of obtaining supernormal manifestations or in an attempt to establish communication with the dead; similar practices have been reported from Haiti, the North American Indian tribes and the Maoris. Best results are obtained when an experienced medium is present, and luminous **trumpets**, simple musical instruments and **bells** are often said to have been used by spirit **controls** at séances.

Four, six or eight people are considered to provide an ideal 'circle', although more are often equally successful and the sitters do not need to be psychic although the manifestations will be stronger if some of them have psychic powers. It has often been found that an equal mixing of the sexes helps, and that regular sittings with the same people, preferably young and fit, provide the best conditions. After a few moments in quiet contemplation, the sitters should link hands to form a chain or place their hands on a table with finger-tips touching. They can then engage in general conversation, or sing quietly, 'to help the vibrations'; artificial music is sometimes used at this stage of the proceedings. A natural, easy and relaxed atmosphere has been shown to be the most conducive to psychic phenomena, and once the medium is 'in **trance**' or 'contact' has been established, some mediums prefer the chain contact of the hands to be abandoned while others prefer it to be retained; in any case, it has been found helpful for the legs not to be crossed; and if the chain is dropped, the hands should be held limply in the lap, separated and with the palms uppermost. A plainly furnished room is best, with few carpets, cushions or heavy hangings (which all absorb psychic force), but with plain wooden chairs and table (which appear to store up the force); and the same room should be used each 'time for the séance and should, between meetings, be disturbed as little as possible. A cold draught is usually the signal for some kind of manifestation. After the séance it is usual for all the sitters to feel somewhat fatigued and weak, though they soon regain their former vitality.

A local spiritualist church will often put serious inquirers in touch with a circle. **Rescue circles** are séances held at haunted houses in an attempt to give peace to earthbound **spirits**.

*See also* **mediumship; ouija board; spiritualism; table turning**.

CONSULT: Maurice Barbanell, *They Shall Be Comforted*, Psychic Press (1936); Harry Boddington, *The University of Spiritualism*, Spiritualist Press (1947).

## Second sight
Pre-vision; the ability to foretell future events and to discern occurrences at distant places; to perceive things not visible to ordinary sight by unknown means. Evidence suggests that while some people have this ability to a marked extent (frequently among them twins and seventh children of seventh children), nearly everyone may have it to some degree as a latent faculty that can come to the fore in times of crisis. Second sight differs in form and may be observed in **dreams**, 'hunches', **divination** or prophecy (*see* **premonition**).

CONSULT: Norman Macrae (ed.), *Highland Second Sight*, George Souter, Dingwall (1909); Lewis Spence, *Second Sight*, Rider (1951).

## Sensitive

A person who possesses psychic powers, but who, unlike a medium, is apparently unable to establish contact with the dead. Sensitives are often very good at **psychometry, telepathy, clairvoyance** and most forms of **extrasensory perception**. Whereas a medium may be merely an instrument for alleged communication, a sensitive claims no external source for his or her gift; they have no **'guides'** and produce no **ectoplasm** or other physical phenomena.

## Seraph

A type of angel; one of the order of heavenly beings that ranked immediately above the cherubim in the celestial hierarchy. Seraphs have six wings but otherwise human forms; and, according to the Bible, they were seen by Isaiah beside the throne of God. As some of the highest among the angels, excelling in wisdom, swiftness and zeal, they have frequently been extolled in poetry and portrayed in art, where they are often depicted in clothing of red since the word seraph was thought to be derived from the word meaning 'to burn' and seraphs were said to be consumed with the ardour of love. Occultists have occasionally claimed to have used or contacted seraphs, and they not infrequently figure in **visions** and **dreams** of a heaven-like existence.

*A seraph, after a ninth-century design*

# Serios, Ted (b. 1918)

American medium whose **psychic photography** consists of apparently causing images – 'thoughtographs' – to appear on photographic film; the images include recognizable pictures of the White House, the Pentagon, the Taj Mahal, cathedrals, statues and historical and architectural landmarks, all produced in a windowless room.

Serios is a Roman Catholic who says he does not understand his 'gift' and is reported to suffer from poor health as a result of the strain and tension caused by the production of these 'thought pictures'. At one time he used a cardboard tube around the lens to prevent his hand inadvertently covering the aperture, and he also held a rosary; soon both were discarded. Most of the time Serios uses a Polaroid hand camera which develops and prints the results in a matter of seconds. Although the camera is set to take pictures at infinity (making anything close to the lens an indistinguishable blur), Serios himself has been carefully examined to establish, for example, that he does not have tiny images concealed in his contact lenses; his clothing has also been minutely inspected since he usually points the camera at himself when taking the photographs. Dr Jule Eisenbud, Professor of Psychiatry at the University of Colorado, has conducted a number of elaborate experiments, his precautions to eliminate fraud including both placing Serios in a lead-lined chamber and in a bath of mercury; yet the camera outside still recorded images. Many other scientists have witnessed Serios in action and have signed statements vouching for the authenticity of what they have seen.

Serios himself is a casual man who enjoys his beer. He sometimes works stripped to the waist, but the aspect of the procedure that has particularly interested a number of researchers is the use of a 'gismo', a small, make-shift tube which Serios holds in front of the lens of the camera; it is when the gismo is shifted that an image appears. The curious gismo does not appear to fulfil any useful function, although Serios regards it as vital and refers to it as a 'lucky **charm**'. On a number of occasions Serios has produced apparently supernormal results while investigators have held both camera and gismo.

Suggestions have been made that Serios may have a unique faculty to influence light; certainly magnetic fields seem to have no effect on him. Physically during the operation he builds up intense concentration, his eyes open, lips compressed and a noticeable tension of the muscular system: mounting into a kind of rage, his face becomes suffused and blotchy, the veins on his forehead stand out and his eyes become bloodshot. Psychoanalysis of Serios has indicated some measure of immaturity, and it seems likely that there is a link between **psychokinesis** and childlike behaviour; many children have the ability to retain a vivid visual image of what they have seen after looking briefly at a picture and then shutting their eyes; an ability known as **eidetic imagery**.

CONSULT: Jule Eisenbud, *The World of Ted Serios*, Jonathan Cape (1968); E. Jaensch, *Eidetic Imagery*, Kegan Paul (1930).

## Serpents and serpent worship
*See under* **animals and birds**.

## Sex magic
The overwhelming and all-consuming aspect of sexual desire, experience and activity long ago led man to believe that there was a supernatural element in sexuality; usually he regarded sex forces as protective and beneficent **and sought** to invoke them to operate against evil, for they symbolized life as opposed to **death**, fertility against sterility, and an expression of joy and thanksgiving. The many carvings and representations throughout the world of sexual acts, especially those on Hindu temples, suggest that the primitive concept of the generative act was one of awe and worship before a force which was incomprehensible as well as being boundless and infinitely wonderful.

The sex organs themselves have been regarded with reverence (*see* **phallic worship**), and while the phallus was thought to have the power of conquering **demons** and the **evil eye**, the exposure of the female organs was thought to be able to quell storms and control elemental forces. Since magical power was thought to reside in the sex organs, **amulets**, **talismans** and **charms** of a sexual character were evolved, either in actual form or symbolized; as were sex rites with sacred male and female prostitution and religious sodomy; and even castration and the disfigurement of the sex organs.

The passive worship of the nude body degenerated in time into sensual depravity, and the use of sex magic was diverted to **Satanism** and demonism and exploited during ceremonies that involved **witchcraft**, secret societies and religious cults. Sexual substances, semen and female fluids were used not only to manufacture **love potions and philtres** and objects to promote sexual potency, but also in efforts to induce supernatural powers to manifest and act in accordance with the wishes of the sorcerer. In **necromancy** the operator performed intercourse with a corpse before attempting to revitalize it.

Sex magic, both ancient and modern, has involved the use of everything sexual, not only the fluids but also pubic hair and partial circumcision (sacrificial amputation), such articles being mixed with **blood** and then either burnt, buried or consumed. Repeated sexual excitement induces orgasmic collapse and, sometimes, a state corresponding to deep hysterical **trance**; it is then that sorcerers believe a supernatural power to be present which can be harnessed, and Aleister **Crowley** was only one of many performers of ancient **magic** who used such techniques as abstinence followed by excessive masturbation and other activity in his experiments in sexual magic.

A study of Indian **mysticism** shows that the tantric cults practised long and complicated proceedures that produced a hypnotic effect which, combined with ritual sexual intercourse and breath control, apparently enabled worshippers to reach a sexual cl:max comparable with a religious experience. Sexual magic can be traced from earliest times to Hindu, Jaina and Buddhist **Tantrism**, to the Chinese sexual alchemists, the **Knights Templar**, the German Illuminati, the French occultists, such English societies as the **Golden Dawn** and **Hell-Fire Club** and right up to the present day in the United States and Britain. The strange belief that there is a hidden side to sex, a secret knowledge that enables orgasm to become a supernatural rite for the ardent believer and practitioner, who can thereby attain a union with forces of unknown power, will probably always linger.

CONSULT: Francis King, *Sexuality, Magic and Perversion,* Neville Spearman (1971); E. Laurent and P. Nagour, *Magica Sexualis,* Falstaff, New York (1934).

## Shamanism

The belief that all good and all evil in life has been brought about by **spirits** and gods who can be influenced by priests called shamans: types of medicine man. This religious belief is to be found in particular throughout tribes in the Arctic regions, from Lapland to Siberia, and in the American Indians.

The shaman not only cures sickness and directs communal **sacrifices**, he also escorts the souls of the dead to the other world, for he has the power to leave his body at will. In some tribes a man becomes a shaman through hereditary procedure, in others he is singled out because of his strange behaviour (solitary, visionary, hysterical), or following an unusual accident or event, such as being struck by lightning or suffering a fall with little or no injury: such happenings are accepted as indications by the gods. Sometimes an elaborate initiatory ordeal is conducted. Homosexuals and sufferers from nervous disorders are frequently found among the shamans, their defects being regarded as flaws through which unseen powers are able to manifest. The shaman is thought to be able to die and return to life many times, and his extraordinary powers include the ability to turn himself into various animals (**lycanthropy**), to kill at a distance and to foretell the future (**precognition**).

CONSULT: Ernest De Martino, *Magic: Primitive and Modern*, Tom Stacey (1972); M. Eliade, *Shamanism: Archaic Techniques of Ecstasy*, Routledge & Kegan Paul (1967).

*A shaman (after a nineteenth-century drawing) with crutches that assist him in alleged psychic journeys*

## Sibyls

Prophetesses, commonly regarded as priestesses of Apollo, who were thought to live a thousand years; variously numbered from one by Plato to twelve by later writers, including classical Egyptian, Babylonian and Delphic scribes. The Sibyls' prophecies often seem to have referred to wars and plagues and other disasters, and it was sometimes said they could make their voices heard after their death. They are among the subjects included by Michelangelo in his series of paintings in the Sistine Chapel at Rome.

The best-known Sibyl came from Erythrae on the coast of Asia Minor, and Plutarch quotes Heraclitus in describing her as uttering prophecies 'without smiles', 'with raving mouth' and 'without graces'. There is a legend of nine Sibylline books being offered by the Sibyl of Cumae to King Tarquin of Rome, who considered the price that was asked too high; whereupon the Sibyl destroyed three and offered the remaining six at the same price; again they were refused and another three were destroyed. The augurs (*see* **augury**) then insisted that the final three be purchased, and they were bought for the original price asked for the nine books and preserved for centuries by the Roman Senate, who kept them from public view but consulted them during crises or alarming occurrences; they are said to have been used in the Latin wars and during the threats to Rome by the Gauls and Hannibal. **Sacrifices** were necessary after such consultation, and in 226 B.C. there are reports of sacrifice by the burial alive of several persons. The original Sibylline Books are thought to have been destroyed in a fire in 83 B.C., but a new collection that was assembled was preserved until A.D. 405. The *Oracula Sibyllina* is a collection of prophetic poetry in Greek hexameters.

CONSULT: M. S. Terry (trans.), *The Sibylline Oracles*, Hunt & Eaton, New York (1890).

## Sidereal zodiac

Ancient and original zodiac, as distinct from the traditional, tropical or popular **zodiac**, which is, some astrologers assert, inaccurate with the constellations as a result of the progression of the equinoxes; but since the sidereal zodiac places many people in a different zodiacal sign from that to which they have long been accustomed, the sidereal system, though arguably correct, has never gained much popularity in Western **astrology**.

CONSULT: Rupert Gleadow, *Your Character in the Zodiac*, Phoenix House (1968).

## Silver

The metal of the **moon** and an important ingredient in **alchemy**, where much attention was paid to creating the 'White Stone' which would turn any metal to silver. Its brightness – like the moon at night, seeming to turn objects to silver – resulted in the widespread use of silver articles in **witchcraft**, **sorcery**, **necromancy** and other occult practices. A silver bullet was thought to be the only object powerful enough to stop an evil **spirit** or kill a **werewolf** or **vampire**.

CONSULT: Richard Cavendish, *The Black Arts,* Routledge & Kegan Paul (1967); F. Sherwood Taylor, *The Alchemists,* Heinemann (1951).

## Skull

Symbol of mortality and the vanity of earthly life, but also the centre of psychic energy and the dwelling place of the soul. Skulls were frequently used in **alchemy** as receptacles of transmutation or psychic alteration; in **witchcraft, black magic, sorcery, necromancy** and native ritual as the seat of soul power; and in ancient medicine, where an elixir, prepared in the skull of an executed criminal, was known as 'Spirit of the Human Skull'.

See also **screaming skulls**.

CONSULT: Barbara Jones, *Design for Death,* André Deutsch (1967).

## Snake and snake cults

See under **animals and birds**.

## Society for Psychical Research (SPR)

Founded in 1882 by a group of people of largely spiritualistic persuasion, the SPR is today mainly a critical society in Britain that seeks 'to examine without prejudice or prepossession and in a scientific spirit those faculties of man, real or supposed, which appear to be inexplicable on any generally recognized hypotheses'. The society does not hold or express corporate views, and a number of distinguished men have been its presidents, among them Sir William **Crookes,** Sir Oliver **Lodge,** Sir William **Barrett,** the Rt Hon G. W. Balfour, Andrew **Lang,** Camille Flammarion and Sir Alister **Hardy.** The society's lines on **psychical research** have been set out as spontaneous phenomena, **hypnotism,** experimental **telepathy** and physical (**materialization**) phenomena. Under these headings the society has attempted to examine the nature and extent of any influence which may be exerted by one mind upon another, apart from any generally recognized mode of perception; the study of all forms of mesmeric **trance, clairvoyance** and allied phenomena; examination of what appear to be heightened powers of perception; investigation of **apparitions** of the living and the dead, haunted houses and allied phenomena; inquiry into purposeful **dreams,** divining (*see* **dowsing**) and spiritualistic phenomena with attempts to discover their cause and laws.

The society has collected a wealth of material, and there is a fine library on all aspects of psychical research at their headquarters, 1

Adam and Eve Mews, Kensington, London W8. Membership (£12 per annum in 1977) is open to all persons interested in advancing the knowledge of human personality and the exploration of faculties at present imperfectly understood but seeming to be of far-reaching significance. Meetings are held in London and members receive copies of the Society's *Journal* and *Proceedings* and have the use of the library.

CONSULT: Alan Gould, *The Founders of Psychical Research*, Routledge & Kegan Paul (1968); W. H. Salter, *The Society for Psychical Research*, SPR (1948); D. J. West, *Psychical Research Today*, Duckworth (1954).

*The Seal of Solomon hexagram*

## Solomon

Tenth-century King of Israel, the son of David and Bathsheba. Best known for his wisdom, wealth and long and prosperous reign, he was also considered to be a master magician who could control all **demons** with his magic ring (according to legend, he used this power to help him to build the Temple). A number of magical text-books are attributed him, of which the oldest and the most renowned is the **Key of Solomon**, the most famous of all **grimoires**; MacGregor **Mathers** produced an English translation in 1889. A symbolic **hexagram** composed of two interlinked triangles is known as the 'Seal of Solomon'.

CONSULT: S. L. M. Mathers, *The Key of Solomon*, Routledge & Kegan Paul (1972 edition); Kurt Seligmann, *Magic, Supernaturalism and Religion*, Allen Lane The Penguin Press (1971).

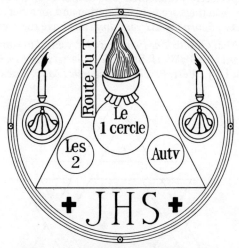

*Magic circle including a triangle of pacts*
*(sixteenth century)*

## Sorcery

The supposed employment of preternatural agencies, and especially such use and collusion with evil **spirits** in the practices of **magic**, **witchcraft** and enchantment. Sorcerers were regarded as priests of Satan and thought to be capable of transforming themselves into animals; they made pacts with the **Devil** and **demons**, performed diabolic and acrobatic dances; had on their persons the **devil's mark**; were capable of controlling the elements and becoming invisible; but their chief function (as the name indicates) was to cast **spells** (or *sors*) over those for whom they wished misfortune. In doing so they invoked the **curse** of **Hell** as a priest calls down the blessings of Heaven.

One example of sorcery is the ancient recipe for enticing a woman. An image (*see also* **sympathetic magic**) must be made in virgin wax mingled with samples of the woman's bodily secretions (saliva, perspiration, ear wax, urine, menstrual blood, etc.); her name must be written on the forehead of the image and the name of her admirer on the breast, both inscribed in **blood** from the third finger of the left hand. Four new needles are placed in the figure at strategic points: back, head, heart and pelvis. A **fire** is then made and lit with paper which contains the handwriting of the woman. **Salt** and mustard seed are sprinkled on to the figure, which is finally placed in the heart of the fire. As the flames consume the waxen image, so the woman's passion for her admirer will, according to the spell, kindle and blossom. To ensure that the right person is affected, the name of the woman is written again in the ashes after the fire has died.

Sorcery in fact became confused with **witchcraft** and with people who were really possessed (*see* **possession**). *See also* **magic circle**.

CONSULT: Émile Grillot de Givry, *Witchcraft, Magic and Alchemy*, University Books, New York (1958).

## Sortilege

The act or practice of drawing lots; **divination** by lots, including the picking of random passages from ancient classical works or the Bible and interpreting the portions elected as a guide for the future. The word is more commonly used today as a term for **sorcery**, and also for **magic** and **witchcraft**. *See also* **bibliomancy**.

## Southcott, Joanna (1750-1814)

English religious fanatic who progressed from dairy-maid to domestic servant before joining the Methodists in 1791; then, a year later, the gifts of **visions** and prophecies 'came upon her', as she says in her book of doggerel verse entitled *Strange Effects of Faith* (1801). Having asserted that her prophecies were the proof of the genuineness of her mission, which was to reveal the true meaning of the Bible, which God had seen fit to reveal through her, it gradually dawned on her that she was in fact Jesus Christ in woman's form. This idea was soon dropped, however, when 'Jesus Christ', in another vision, announced that she was his chosen bride and, although a virgin, would give birth to a male child.

Meanwhile her many writings attracted considerable attention, and when a number of clergymen and others organized a 'trial of her writings' in 1804 and declared them to be of divine origin, enthusiasm reached such magnitude that scores of Southcott societies were founded all over England. Joanna announced that a creative power had mystically entered her body on 11 February 1814, and she duly began to show signs of pregnancy although by then nearly sixty-five years of age. This second 'immaculate conception' was hailed as an indisputable sign and seal of her divine mission, and as the day announced for

*Joanna Southcott (1750–1814), religious visionary*

the birth (19 October 1814) approached, so Joanna's followers became ecstatic and elaborate preparations were made; but the specified date came and passed without any birth taking place, and as one uneventful day followed another, the failure was announced to be the result of 'want of faith' on the part of Joanna's followers. It soon become apparent, however, that the prophetess was seriously ill, and she died on 27 December 1814 of dropsy; her illness having accounted for her appearance of pregnancy.

Joanna Southcott left a box – some say several boxes – that, it was claimed, would save England in an hour of peril; a panacea that would solve all difficulties. But, among a number of other conditions, the box had to be opened in the presence of twenty-four bishops. One box, together with a letter that seemed to authenticate it, was sent to Harry **Price** in 1927, and after examination by X-rays and several attempts at **psychometry**, it was ceremoniously opened (in the presence of one bishop) and found to contain a horse pistol, a purse with a few coins in it and various other innocuous objects. In all there were fifty-six articles as well as a number of books and pamphlets (one book containing annotations by Joanna), and it seems incontrovertible that the box had indeed belonged to Joanna Southcott. Her followers were quite unabashed by the fact that nothing was found that could be considered 'world-saving' and maintained (as they still maintain) that the famous panacea will be found in another box on another occasion.

Among the latter-day Southcottian societies have been the Christian Israelites, the New and Latter House of Israel and the still-surviving Panacea Society, who, after repeated but unsuccessful efforts to have another box opened in the required circumstances, opened it anyway and found that it contained only a lottery ticket and a woman's nightcap. Until a few years ago the Panacea Society had its headquarters in Bedford, where they occupied a number of Victorian villas and sent out their propaganda to all parts of the world with, if requested, a small piece of linen, bought locally, which they claimed was impregnated with spiritual powers that could heal a variety of diseases and soothe anxieties.

CONSULT: Harry Price, *Leaves from a Psychist's Case-Book*, Gollancz (1933).

## Spare, Austin Osman (1886-1956)

Occultist, artist and painter of strange and original art often depicting elementals (*see* **elements and elementals**) and other denizens of unseen worlds. As a child, Spare was befriended by an elderly lady who claimed to be descended from the witches of **Salem** and who taught him to visualize and reproduce **dream** imagery and also how to evoke elemental **spirits** to visible form. He evolved a theory that superhuman powers were latent in the subconscious mind and developed a technique for invoking and harnessing such powers, a process he called the 'Formula of Atavistic Resurgence', or reversion to an earlier type (*see* **atavism**); on one occasion he was apparently so successful in conjuring up 'something' from deep layers of consciousness, at the request of two interested persons, that one of the witnesses committed suicide shortly afterwards and the other went mad. For many years until his death Spare lived as a recluse in a poor part of London with only his beloved cats for company.

CONSULT: Kenneth Grant, *The Magical Survival*, Muller (1972); Osman Spare *The Focus of Life*, Morland Press (1920).

## Speaking in tongues

*See* **glossolalia**; **xenoglossy**.

## Spectre

From the Latin *spectrum* = 'vision'; a phantom, **ghost** or **apparition** of the dead; a disembodied **spirit**; a frightening form, especially an unexpected visitation that appears in a churchyard or some wild and open space; magicians and sorcerers also speak of inadvertently raising spectres who disrupt their activities. *See also* **Brocken spectre**; **hauntings**.

## Spell

A word, or set of words, or procedure of formula that is used as a **charm** or **incantation**, commonly of a relatively minor kind, that is believed to have magical effect; also a condition of enchantment.

The effectiveness of a spell often lies in its associations and method of delivery; often, too, in repetition, when its impact is built up and reinforced. The **grimoires** of the magicians and sorcerers stress the importance of secrecy in casting spells and imply that failure of any spell to work is the result of secret formulas being incorrectly interpreted or misunderstood. Spells were usually used in conjunction with a prescribed and elaborate ritual, though there are also many simple spells, such as peeling an apple in one piece or planting hempseed on All Hallow's Eve (*see under* **festivals**) to conjure up a vision of the person one is to marry.

## Spheres

Division of the **spirit** world according to spiritualist belief. The general opinion, based on alleged communication with the dead, is that there are seven spheres: **Hell**, the Sphere of Desires, the **Summerland**, the Mind, Abstract, the Meeting of the Sexes and the Union of the Sexes. Some spiritualists maintain that the earth is the first sphere (Hell) while others consider it to be the second sphere (the Sphere of Desires). At all events the assumption is that, on **death**, the 'soul' or 'inner self' is transferred to the next sphere where earth-like scenery, harmony, love and kindness help to develop the quality of the soul for higher spheres, which cannot be perceived by spirits occupying the lower spheres, though visitors from the upper spheres do on occasion descend to the lower spheres with information and help. Progression to the upper spheres is accomplished after realization of the conditions and circumstances by a total desire for progress and betterment and an awareness of infinite love, until eventually the boundless seventh sphere is reached: the ultimate abode of the blessed. Other spiritualists have different ideas of the seven spheres, but the principal of progression through experience, reconcilation and desire for improvement (as in the alternative theory of **reincarnation**) is generally accepted.

CONSULT: Nandor Fodor, *Encyclopaedia of Psychic Science*, Arthurs Press (1934); Hewat McKenzie, *Spirit Intercourse; Its Theory and Practice*, Simpkin Marshall (1916).

## Sphinx
Fabulous monster of Egyptian origin, but also figuring in Greek mythology. The Egyptian Sphinx is represented as a lion with a king's head, and the best-known is the Great Sphinx of Giza, situated near the famous pyramids. The Greeks depicted their Sphinx as a winged creature with a woman's head and breasts, a lion's body, feet and tail, and bird's wings. The riddle of the Sphinx is: 'What creature goes on four legs in the morning, on two at noonday and on three in the evening?' The answer is 'Man', who crawls on hands and feet in childhood, walks erect in manhood and uses a stick or staff in old age.

## Spirit
From the Latin *spiritus* = 'breath', 'air'; and *spirare* = 'to breathe'. The principle of life and vital energy, in particular when considered to be separate from the material body; an immaterial, mysterious and apparently intelligent and conscious being ascribed to a divine origin; also an intellectually undeveloped existence, such as an elemental (*see under* **elements and elementals**). The spirit, like the soul, was once thought to be exhaled at **death** and to be composed of a refined substance comparable with breath or warm air. In addition, the wind was regarded as the breath of God, the greatest of spirits and a symbol of the Holy Spirit. A spirit is a being or intelligence with no earthly body; an angel, **demon, fairy, ghost** or **poltergeist**.

Spiritualists believe that spirits have their own hierarchy, a spirit world of ascending **spheres** with, nearest to earth, spirits still attached to their old habits and habitat and ignorant of their true state; then there are spirits who act as intermediaries between the living and those who have passed 'to the world of spirit'; and finally celestial spirits who dwell in a world of light and harmony and are spiritually far in advance of earthly intelligence. Thus spiritualists speak of 'spirit **guides**', 'spirit **controls**' and the 'spirit world'. *See also* **spiritualism**.

## Spirit healing
Also known as spiritual healing or **faith healing**; the apparent

soothing and cure of illness through a medium or healer. In **spiritualism** such healing is said to be the result either of dead doctors working through the medium or of divine power. Absent healing is conducted by a healer in the absence of the subject or patient who often does not know that such healing has been arranged; thus, since no faith on the part of the patient can be involved, spiritualists prefer the term 'spirit healing'.

CONSULT: J. Goldsmith, *The Art of Spiritual Healing*, Allen & Unwin (1960); G. Murray, *Frontiers of Healing*, Max Parrish (1958).

## Spirit hypothesis
The theory that the apparently independent intelligence that communicates and directs the phenomena associated with **mediumship** is a disembodied **spirit**. Opponents of the spirit hypothesis are the scientists with their psychological theories of mental processes; and the Catholic theologians with their dogma of diabolic intervention.

## Spirit photography
*See* **psychic photography**.

## Spiritism
French equivalent of **spiritualism**; associated with the teachings of Allan Kardec. It has also become the accepted word for spiritualistic belief and phenomena in Brazil and other South American countries.

## Spirits
*See* **spirit**.

## Spiritualism
A movement that seeks to prove, by demonstration, survival after **death** and that it is possible to communicate with the **spirit** of someone dead. Spiritualists consider spiritualism not only to demonstrate survival of the human personality, but also to embrace knowledge of the alleged interaction of matter and spirit that implies a comprehension of the intelligent progressive principle which, they believe, underlies the whole of creation, of mankind and of nature in this present life; and of the continuous, individual, progressive, spiritual life in the **spheres** of the hereafter.

Spiritualists maintain that the endeavour to prove the continuity of life or the human personality after bodily death is a science; that science is concerned with the examination of the psychic faculties, both mental and physical; and that since the special activities of the psychic faculties are necessary to obtain proof of the fact of human survival, the scientific findings of this examination have implications which involve philosophy and religion. Therefore spiritualism may rightly be claimed as being fundamentally a combination of science, philosphy and religion.

Organized spiritualism, which Sir Arthur Conan **Doyle** claimed to be 'a religion for those who find themselves outside all religions' but which most spiritualists see as the basis of all religions, began in the United States in 1848 with the experiences of the *Fox sisters* before it spread rapidly to other parts of the world. Psychic powers seem to have been inherent in the Fox family, with the great-grandmother a somnambulist who apparently used to 'attend' phantom funerals of persons still alive and describe people present and every circumstance in great detail; later the description was said to have corresponded precisely with the facts. The house at Hydesville, New York State, occupied by John D. Fox and his family towards the end of 1847, already had an odd reputation, a former tenant having left on account of 'mysterious noises'. Before long the Fox family heard, especially at night, raps, knocks and the noise of furniture being shifted, though nothing was ever found to have been moved that could have accounted for any of the sounds. During March 1848, when two of the Fox girls were aged twelve and fifteen years, the noises became worse, and on the night of the 31st of that month loud outbreaks continuously disturbed the girls' rest.

Mrs Fox thought some of the sounds might be due to rattling window sashes, and Mr Fox got up and shook the sashes to see whether they were loose and whether the noises had any connection with the sounds that continued to disturb the family. Kate, the younger girl, remarked that as often as her father shook the window sash, so other noises seemed to reply, and then little Kate, excited and not at all frightened by the disturbances, began to jump about and clap her hands and it was noticed that sounds followed with exactly the same number of raps. When Kate stopped clapping, the raps ceased; and when Kate clapped again, the raps followed. Devising a code of one rap for 'no', two for 'yes' and three for 'uncertain' or 'unknown', the Fox family became convinced that they had contacted a former inhabitant: a man of thirty-one who had been murdered in the house and whose remains were still buried in the cellar. This information and much more was obtained by means of the 'yes' and 'no' code. Excavation carried out in the cellar and nearby revealed human remains, and much of the 'spirit's' story seems to have been verified. Before long a small band of spiritualists were reporting table-rocking (*see* **table turning**), movement of objects (*see* **psychokinesis**), the playing of musical instruments, psychic touches and raps that seemed to give intelligent answers to questions; thus was born modern spiritualism.

Later the older Fox sister, Margaret became addicted to alcohol, and then to Catholicism, while Lear (another sister) sought to deprive Kate of the custody of her two children. Margaret sided with Kate and the two sought to ruin Lear's reputation; Margaret published a letter in the *New York Herald* denouncing spiritualism, and during the course of interviews and lectures explained and demonstrated her method of producing 'spirit' raps, declaring spiritualism to be a complete fraud. Kate made a similar confession, endorsed her sister's revelations and enthusiastically took part in 'exposure' meetings. Those against spiritualism quickly exploited the disclosures, and Reuben Briggs Davenport seems to have fairly estimated the situation in his book, *The Death-Blow to Spiritualism*. However, within a year, in November 1889, Margaret Fox completely retracted her confession, speaking of financial difficulties and strong psychological pressures.

None of the three Fox sisters long survived the complex affair, Lear dying in 1890, Kate in 1892 and Margaret in 1893. There is evidence to suggest that, during Margaret's last hours, when she was completely incapacitated, knockings and rappings were heard from walls, floor and ceiling of her bedroom.

Other early mediums included *Lizzie and May Bangs* of Chicago, who specialized in 'spirit' or slate writing, painting and drawing (*see* **automatism**), and initially impressed a number of people. During their heyday they gave many public performances where they apparently produced **apports**, were responsible for the disappearance of objects (**dematerialization**) and produced some remarkable chemical effects, such as changing ink into water. One witness of Lizzie Bangs's 'spirit writings' described the use of a typewriter which continued typing messages with the aid of a materialized hand while the machine was held high in the air by four of the male sitters. Dr Hereward Carrington, a distinguished American psychical researcher, exposed the sisters as frauds by means of a small hand-mirror which he held beneath the table. (*See also main entry for* **Bangs sisters**.)

*Florence Cook* (1856–1904) was an early British **materialization** medium, almost exclusively investigated by Sir William **Crookes**. Conscious of **spirits** and voices since childhood, she produced physical phenomena from the age of fifteen while participating in table turning at a tea party. Soon she began to produce mirror writing, and before long she was giving **séances**, during the course of which she became the subject of **levitation**. While in **trance** she appeared to be possessed by a personality calling itself 'Katie King' and claiming to be the daughter of John King, alias Henry Morgan, the buccaneer; an entity that persisted for a number of years. Later 'Katie King' materialized and was photographed many times.

There were a number of alleged exposures, but Florence was always defended by Crookes, who maintained that he was satisfied that 'Katie King' (notwithstanding a remarkable resemblance to Florence Cook) was an independent personality. He affirmed that he had on at least one occasion seen 'Katie King' and Florence Cook at the same time in full light, and, indeed, he produced a photograph of the two together. Crookes also reported that a blister on Florence Cook's neck was not present on the neck of 'Katie King', and that whereas Florence Cook's ears were pierced, those of 'Katie King' were not. After about three years 'Katie King' made her farewells and was replaced by 'Marie', who sang and danced in a professional manner. More alleged exposures followed, including an occasion when Sir George Sitwell grabbed 'Marie' and found that he had captured Florence Cook. Certainly some of the evidence for conscious trickery cannot be ignored.

Crookes maintained to the end of his life that Florence Cook was a genuine medium, but one critic has surmised that he and Florence may have been lovers, and that he cannot therefore be regarded as an unbiased witness; it may be significant, however, that he also vouched for the authenticity of another phantom figure, 'John King', which apparently materialized through another medium, Charles Edward Williams. Florence Cook, later Mrs Elgie Corner, had a sister, Katie **Cook**, who also gave séances as a materialization medium, but who never underwent the scientific tests or achieved the fame – or notoriety – of Florence.

***Madame Elizabeth d'Espérance*** was the pseudonym of Elizabeth Hope (1855–1919), later Mrs Reed, a remarkable private medium who lived at Newcastle-upon-Tyne. She saw 'shadow people' as a child, and once sketched such people that were visible only to her, making drawings later recognized as representing people who were dead. She produced automatic writing and read sealed letters. Before long she was sitting in a cabinet and producing materializations, but after one such figure, a young Arab girl called 'Yolande', was suddenly seized by some sitters, and found to be the medium, Mrs Hope (who maintained that she had suffered agonizing pain and terror during the experience) vowed never again to sit inside a cabinet but always to exhibit herself and her materialization simultaneously.

She was as good as her word, and many sitters asserted that they had seen a materialization – usually 'Yolande', who frequently produced apports – alongside the medium; and it was reported that, as time passed and the medium grew older, 'Yolande' remained young and beautiful. On three more occasions sitters grabbed 'Yolande', and each time the medium was ill. On the last occasion a sitter attempted to violate the phantom girl, and the medium (her hair suddenly turned white, it was said, by the shock) was confined to her bed for two years; but the assault was followed by what was perhaps the strangest incident in the whole of Mme d'Espérance's mediumship: the partial dematerialization of the medium's body. On one occasion her body seemed to disappear completely from the waist downwards, a fact vouched for by responsible witnesses.

**Mrs Helen Victoria Duncan** (1898–1956) was a materializing medium who produced **ectoplasm** in quantity and was the subject of controversy following sittings in 1931 at the London Spiritualist Alliance and under the auspices of Harry **Price**; both published exposures, the former quoting a confession by Mrs Duncan's husband and the latter producing photographic evidence that seemed to show the regurgitation of cheesecloth. The following year, at Edinburgh, Mrs Duncan was sent to prison for pretending to communicate with the dead (under the now obsolete Witchcraft Act) after a 'materialized child' had been seized by a sitter and found to be the medium. Notwithstanding her fraudulent practices on occasions, there were many sitters who remained convinced that Helen Duncan was a very gifted medium.

**Eva C** (c. 1890 – c. 1943) was a French materialization medium whose maiden name was Carrière; she was also known as Marthe Beraud and was the daughter of an army officer and the fiancée of Maurice Noel, the son of General Noel. Maurice died in Africa before the wedding, and the general and his wife thereupon discovered Eva's psychic gifts. They had long been interested in psychic matters and often held séances at their home, the Villa Carmen in Algiers, where the most frequent phantom visitor was 'Bien Boa', a bearded and helmeted figure who regarded himself as the spiritual guide to the family. The conditions under which the white-sheeted 'Bien Boa' appeared were no more convincing than the published photographs, and, indeed, General Noel's Arab coachman declared that he 'played the ghost' at one period and demonstrated how it had been done. Eva is also reported to have confessed to cheating, in the presence of an Algiers lawyer. Later a number of investigators were convinced that she could produce genuine phenomena.

*Mrs Eileen J. Garrett* (1893-1970) was a British trance medium who came into prominence in 1930 over the **R101** séance; she also cooperated in **psychical research** at Duke and other American universities (gradually suspecting that her 'controls' were in reality factors in her own mind); became an American citizen and founded the Parapsychology Foundation in New York. Eileen Garrett became wealthy and world-famous for her exceptional gifts of **extrasensory perception**, her dedication to scientific experimentation, her delightful personality and her books and other writings on the subject of **mediumship**.

*Mrs Samuel Guppy* (*c.* 1860-1917) was a physical medium best known for her alleged 'transportation' (*see* **telepatation**) across London during a séance. According to contemporary evidence, Mrs Guppy was, in 1871, transported from her home in Highbury and precipitated into the middle of a séance at 61 Lamb's Conduit Street, some three miles away. Another levitation and transportation is recounted by Florence **Marryat**, when Mrs Guppy apparently flew from a back drawing-room in Victoria Road to the well-lighted front drawing-room in the full sight of everyone present. Mrs Guppy also specialized in apports and is said to have produced flowers in bloom, complete with fresh earth, during a hard frost one December; and at the same séance to have produced two butterflies. For most of her life she practised her mediumship without financial gain. There are numerous stories of remarkable instances of apports achieved by Mrs Guppy, including live eels, a white cat, three ducks prepared for cooking, showers of butterflies, stinging nettles and sea sand.

*Alec Harris* was a Welsh physical medium who is reported to have produced at one séance twenty fully materialized figures ranging from a six-foot man to a small child. It was reported by Dr Douglas Baker that on occasions the pulse and respiration rates of the forms were recorded and their weights measured. Harris emigrated to South Africa where he continued to give sittings until his death in 1972.

**Daniel Dunglas Home** (1833–86) was probably the most celebrated medium of all time. For nearly forty years apparently inexplicable happenings took place in his presence and in the vicinity of royalty, nobility, scientists and prominent people of all walks of life; he was never exposed or caught cheating and is the only medium to be included in *Encyclopaedia Britannica*. Home's father was an illegitimate son of the tenth Earl of Home, who died in 1841, and he seems to have taken his own son to the United States when the boy was nine, shortly before the disturbances in the Fox household (see above) heralded the birth of modern spiritualism. Home later became the centre of similar strange happenings, and such events were to occur in the presence of 'the prince of mediums' for the rest of his life: in daylight, during séances and just anywhere and at any time. The phenomena reported included raps and taps, inexplicable lights or jets of flame, movement of objects, levitation and **elongation, xenoglossy**, phantom forms, the materialization of a disembodied hand, apports, the ability to handle red-hot coals, the sounds of muffled voices and various other noises, bells being rung and an accordian played.

Home had an air of mystery that repulsed some people, including the poet Robert Browning, who wrote a scathing attack in the form of his poem, 'Mr Sludge, the Medium', but Browning's wife, Elizabeth Barrett Browning, became a Home convert and remained so until her death. Perhaps the best known of Home's many remarkable feats took place in 1868 at 5 Buckingham Gate, London, the home of Lord Adare, when, in the presence of three people – Lord Adare himself, Lord Lindsey and Captain Charles Wynne – he is said to have floated out of a third-floor window and in through another window; an act he repeated through a window that was open only about a third of a metre. From time to time Home complained that the power had left him, but it always returned and he impressed many of the great men of his age, including the Tsar of Russia, the German Kaiser and the French Emperor – although Charles Dickens called him a ruffian and a scoundrel. Home (pronounced Hume) never charged fees for his services, although he accepted gifts. Whatever the explanation, Home never sought converts and did not claim any divinely appointed mission, merely stating that his powers were a 'gift from God'. His strange story stands almost alone as a completely unsolved mystery in the annals of psychical research.

**William Hope** (1863–1933) was a celebrated 'spirit' photographer (formerly a carpenter) who apparently discovered his 'psychic powers' by accident in 1905. He began to sit with some friends in an attempt to develop **psychic photography**. In 1908 Archdeacon Colley, an ardent and experienced psychical researcher, tested Hope, endorsed his 'spirit' photographs and founded the Crewe Circle that attracted many investigators and inquirers, including Harry Price, Sir William Crookes, Sir Oliver **Lodge** and Sir Arthur Conan Doyle. Billy Hope was so often the centre of argument that he became accustomed to accusations of fraud, but he remained the leading exponent of spirit photography to the end of his life. An exposure by Harry Price in 1922 was utterly damning, yet many people continued to believe that Hope had real psychic powers and that he was a genuine medium whose mentality could easily lead to the opposite conclusion on the part of an unsympathetic observer.

**Robert James Lee** (1844–1931) was an English medium who purportedly received spirit messages from the recently deceased consort of Queen Victoria, Prince Albert, in 1861. The Queen arranged for two members of her court to visit the medium anonymously, and within seconds they had been welcomed in the Prince's voice with their precise identities; they were also greeted with an advanced Masonic grip which the medium is unlikely to have known, and a message was written for the Queen and signed with a name only used privately between the Prince and the Queen. Perhaps Lee's best-known psychic excursion concerned the Jack-the-Ripper murders, when he is said to have had several vivid **dreams** of murders before they happened, and in the dreams to have seen the murderer's face. Then one day, the story runs, Lee saw the murderer while travelling on a London bus and followed him to a house in fashionable Park Lane which turned out to be the home of a well-known physician who had connections with the royal family. Lee went to the police with his story, and after talking to the physician's wife, a watch was put on the husband until he was caught leaving the house with a carving knife in a black bag. He was then interned in a mental home for the rest of his life and the murders ceased.

**Eusapia Palladino** (1854–1918) was a celebrated Italian physical medium who submitted to many scientific inquiries, and while some investigators claimed that she cheated, others asserted that she had extraordinary **paranormal** powers. Illiterate and hardly able to sign her own name, Palladino, whose mother had died at her birth and whose father was murdered by brigands when she was twelve, had been taken into the household of a family interested in spiritualism. Before long the little peasant girl was the centre of abnormal happenings, and for the rest of her life apparently paranormal phenomena took place in her presence. She was submitted to one scientific investigation after another, in Paris, London, St Petersburg, Turin, Genoa, Milan and other European cities; and a wealth of literature was published dealing with this remarkable woman and her mediumship.

The phenomena reported at Palladino's séances was that common to most physical mediums: raps and bangs on furniture and walls, while the medium was either securely held or fastened or otherwise restrained and under observation; touchings, movement of objects, the billowing of curtains, partial and fully materilized forms. Some investigators, however, asserted that Palladino would cheat if she had the chance (indeed, she told Professor Cesare Lombroso, 'Watch me or I'll cheat; John King makes me do it' – John King being her alleged **control**); and when one of her hands was freed deliberately so that trickery, if it took place, could be observed, it was so observed.

***Mrs Leonora E. Piper*** (1857-1950) was a remarkable American mental medium who discovered her psychic talents by accident when she lapsed into a trance during a second visit to a blind healer whom she was consulting because of ill-health; while in the trance state she wrote a message for one of the sitters present. From that time (1884), she held sittings privately in her own home and apparently received numerous communications from dead people who included illustrious personages as well as the relatives and friends of local people. Full and detailed records are extant for hundreds of Mrs Piper sittings. During the period 1897-1905, the most interesting of Mrs Piper's communicators, or controls, manifested their presences under the names of 'Imperator', 'Rector' and 'Doctor'. Anyone who had any dealings or contact with Mrs Piper was convinced that she was completely honest, and there is no doubt that the quality of accurate information that came through the communicators is far and away in excess of anything she could have discovered by normal means. Yet most psychical researchers today consider that Mrs Piper's mediumship, remarkable as it undoubtedly was, could have been the result of telepathic communication (*see* **telepathy**) with living people, usually the sitters themselves.

***Stanislava (or Stanislawa) P.*** was a modest young Polish girl whose mediumship was the subject of important experimentation and investigation by the Baron von **Schrenck-Notzing**. She readily submitted to examination of her naked body by a lady doctor and donned a séance costume consisting of black tights and apron tunic. Later a black one-piece costume, fastened down the back, encased the whole of the medium's body, but was sufficiently transparent to reveal the whole surface anatomy; even so, Stanislava P. produced a wealth of physical phenomena in the shape of ectoplasmic flow. In view of her examinations prior to the séances and the fact that after his investigations Schrenck-Notzing was sent a virginity certificate by a physician, it is difficult to suggest how the medium could have secreted the material produced at these séances for which considerable photographic evidence exists. Later, however, at the **Institut Métapsychique International**, Dr Osty photographed Stanislava P. manipulating the séance table with a free hand. (*See* **Crandon, Mrs L. R. G.**, for another remarkable example of ectoplasmic production.)

*Allan (or Alan or Alain) Kardec* (1804-69) was a French doctor, originally a sceptic, who became one of the 'fathers of spiritualism' – which he called **spiritism** – using the term in a general way to include all believers in a continuation of life after death. He became intrigued by 'messages' received at table-rapping sessions and sent out teams of researchers to collect information from people who practised table-rapping throughout France. The results satisfied Kardec that spirits did exist and, convinced that they sought to be contacted, he devoted the rest of his life to questioning them and compiling and collating their answers. He believed that if individual spirits were called upon they would respond; he also accepted **reincarnation**. In South America his teaching, 'There is no death', has found an increasing response, and today there are something like 3 000 Kardec temples in Brazil alone, many specializing in curing or repairing the **aura**, and thereby, it is said, curing the body and the mind.

With the Belfast spiritualist circle that became known as the *'Goligher Circle'* Dr W. J. Crawford conducted lengthy experiments from 1914 until 1920, when he committed suicide. There were four Goligher daughters, who were all mediumistic, with Kathleen (later Lady Donaldson) probably the most psychically gifted. Although poor the family accepted no payment for their séances for the first four years; séances that were held with the aid of a red light at either the Goligher home or Crawford's house. Information was obtained by raps and trance communication, and levitation of the table and so forth seems to have been accomplished by means of ectoplasmic 'rods' or 'cantilevers' which Dr Crawford succeeded in photographing. After Dr Crawford's death, Dr E. E. Fournier D'Albe took over the circle with the intention of confirming Crawford's conclusions, but after twenty sittings he stated that everything he had seen and photographed could be accounted for without recourse to any supernormal explanation. The case thus remains an interesting and well-documented enigma of psychical research.

The history of spiritualism is riddled with fraud and accusations of fraud, and there is some justification for Harry Price's definition of spiritualism: 'At its best a religion, at its worst a racket'; or as the spiritualist Maurice Barbanell puts it, 'Our best is wonderful and our worst is awful.' Many prominent people have embraced spiritualism, including Mrs Harriet Stowe (the author of *Uncle Tom's Cabin*), Alfred Russel Wallace (the naturalist), Sir Arthur Conan Doyle, Sir Oliver Lodge, Hannen Swaffer (the journalist), W. T. **Stead** (the editor and author), Lord Adare and Air Chief Marshall Lord Dowding, while others who have shown more than a passing interest in spiritualism have included Abraham Lincoln, William Makepeace Thackeray, Anthony Trollope, Sir William Barrett and the speed king Donald Campbell. Important spiritualist organizations include the Spiritualists' National Union, the Greater World Christian Spiritualist League, the College of Psychic Studies and the **Spiritualist Association of Great Britain**; while in the United States the National Spiritualist Association of America heads the many smaller societies and associations that cater for the adherents of spiritualism.

*See also* **Schneider brothers** for a classic case of investigation into spiritualist phenomena.

CONSULT: Maurice Barbanell, *Spiritualism Today*, Herbert Jenkins (1969); S. Brown, *The Heyday of Spiritualism*, Hawthorn, New York (1970); C. J. Ducasse, *The Belief in a Life After Death*, Charles Thomas, Springfield, Ill. (1961); J. A. Hill, *Spiritualism: Its History, Phenomena and Doctrine*, Cassell (1918).

## Spiritualist Association of Great Britain

The largest spiritualist association in the world, founded in 1872 as the Marylebone Spiritualist Association. Later it became known for a time as the Spiritual Evidence Society and was formally renamed the Spiritualist Association of Great Britain in 1960. Most of the important names in **spiritualism** have been associated with the organization, from Florence **Marryat**, W. T. **Stead**, Sir Oliver **Lodge** and Sir Arthur Conan **Doyle** to such contemporary figures as Harry

**Edwards**, Ena Twigg, Maurice Barbanell and Air Chief Marshal Lord Dowding. Today the association (housed in a building of historic and architectural interest) has several lecture halls, six **séance** rooms, a restaurant, a bookstall, an absent healing room, a library containing over 4000 books, a chapel, spiritual healing cubicles and rooms for private appointments, psychic development and group séances. It had some 7500 members, a staff of twenty and forty regular mediums; and more than 140000 people a year use its facilities. The association issues a monthly newspaper, *The Spiritualist Gazette*, and a quarterly syllabus, *Service*. Address: 33 Belgrave Square, London SW1.

CONSULT: Roy Stemman, *One Hundred Years of Spiritualism*, Spiritualist Association of Great Britain (1972).

## SPR
*See* **Society for Psychical Research**.

## Stanislava (or Stanislawa) P.
Young Polish medium investigated by Baron von **Schrenck-Notzing**. *See under* **spiritualism**.

## Stead, William Thomas (1849-1912)
Prominent newspaper editor and spiritualist who produced automatic writing (*see* **automatism**) and had considerable experience of the phenomena of **spiritualism**. His **control** was alleged to be a girl named 'Julia', and in 1909 he opened a 'Julia's Bureau' where inquirers could obtain apparent information about the **spirit** world from a group of resident mediums. In many of his lectures and writings Stead drew a picture of a sinking ocean liner with himself drowning as he frantically called for help: he was in fact drowned when the *Titanic* struck an iceberg and sank in 1912.

## Steiner, Rudolf (1861-1925)
Founder of the Anthroposophical Society; a prolific writer and thinker who had a profound effect on education.

Steiner was born in what is now Yugoslavia, the son of a station-master. His early acquaintance with a herbalist and then a Theosophist (*see* **Theosophy**) led to the study of mysticism and progressive social thought. Under the auspices of the Theosophical Society he lectured on **meditation**, teaching that its application could cover and effect the whole spectrum of human life. In 1902 he travelled to London to attend a conference of the Theosophical Society and delivered a lecture which was later regarded as the basis of his teaching of 'spiritual science'. In this he sought to show the connections between the spiritual and the material, between history and nature – bringing them all together and making sense of the amalgamation. Steiner claimed to develop clairvoyant faculties, 'spiritual eyes', and for a time he was connected with mystic and mysterious organizations which practised **sex magic** and other occult rites – indeed, when his wife died in 1911 there were rumours that he had 'strangled her astrally'. Gradually, however, he evolved a mixture that included Theosophist dogma, **karma** and **reincarnation**, European **occultism**, Goethe's scientism, esotericism and a Christian-based religion of his own invention. He called the result Anthroposophy – 'man-wisdom', as opposed to the 'God–wisdom' of Theosophy.

Steiner's teachings that enthusiasm for life must be awakened in every human being; that new organs of perception are developed through one's own efforts; and that this planet is intended to be a world of love and freedom – a training place for love, in fact – evoked a considerable response. The Anthroposophists soon had branches in all the German-speaking countries as well as in Britain. His revelations and ideas covered medicine, farming and physical culture. In education he advocated that a teacher should stay with the same children for eight years; he regarded a child as an incarnation for whom the parents had provided a body.

Today the society Steiner founded runs clinics and mental hospitals; his farming principles (forbidding the use of chemicals and advocating planting in accordance with the phases of the **moon**) have, to a certain extent, been successful and generally accepted. His influence on education can hardly be over-stated: some of the seventy-odd Wardolf Schools run on the lines he advocated throughout the world have no set fees, and the teachers receive no salary, yet they continue and produce vital, self-thinking students of whom Rudolf Steiner would have been proud. He is one occultist whose teaching and original ideas have produced tangible results. His numerous books include *The Philosophy of Spiritual Activity*, *Knowledge of the Higher Worlds and Its Attainment*, *The Course of My Life*, *Occult Science – An Outline*, and *Christianity as Mystical Fact*, all were originally published in Germany and have since been produced in English in many editions by the Rudolf Steiner Press.

CONSULT: A. P. Shepherd, *A Scientist of the Invisible*, Hodder & Stoughton (1954); H. Poppelbaum, *Man and Animal*, Anthroposophical Publishing Company (1960).

## Stella C. (Cranshaw)

Young nurse (later Mrs Leslie Deacon), whose **mediumship** was discovered by Harry **Price** in 1923. She was the subject of a series of remarkable **séances** at the National Laboratory of Psychical Research and produced telekinetic phenomena (*see* **telekinesis**), raps and **ectoplasm**. She was successful in overcoming a number of original and complicated impediments which Harry Price sought to impose on her psychic abilities, and proved conclusively that under test conditions she could still produce phenomena. Dr Eric John Dingwall was one investigator who saw things for which he had no explanation.

CONSULT: James Turner (ed.), **Stella C**, Souvenir Press (1973).

## Stigmata

Wounds, marks or spots that bleed, corresponding with the wounds of Christ; usually on the hands, feet, side and forehead, but occasionally also on the shoulder, wrists, ankles or back, representing the weight of the cross, rope-marks and scourging. While it is difficult to dismiss all the stigmatists over the years, from St Francis (*c.* 1224), to Teresa **Neumann** (1898–1962) (certainly several hundred persons), the modern tendency is to explain the phenomena in terms of auto-suggestion. Practically all cases of stigmatism are associated with members of the Roman Catholic Church, which has long treated with reserve and caution the many instances of hysterical ecstacy and apparent suffering which can follow intense and extended **meditation** on the sufferings of Christ. The wounds of a stigmatist often bleed on Fridays or Holy Days, and then heal with astonishing rapidity, but the history of stigmata is riddled with over-zealous frauds.

CONSULT: Charles M. Carty, *The Two Stigmatists: Padre Pio and Teresa Neumann*, Veritas, Dublin (1956); Herbert Thurston, *The Physical Phenomena of Mysticism*, Burns & Oates (1952).

## Subliminal

Sensations beneath the threshold of consciousness, too slight to be recognized individually; such sensations, thoughts and emotions may form a complex and coherent and continuous chain of memory that could account for much psychical phenomena and obviate the necessity for the **spirit hypothesis** accepted by spiritualists. In particular, subliminal workings of the mind could conceivably account for such activities as **crystal-gazing** and **automatism**, representing a forcing-up of the subliminal mind through the conscious mind of the individual without the amalgamation which normally takes place when unconscious sensations surface to become conscious feelings.

## Succubi

Female **demons** that are said to have sexual connection with sleeping men. Whereas an **incubus** is an unnatural being that appears in corporeal form to torment and sometimes seduce women, a succubus was, or is, the female of the species which can assume human form to cohabit with and sexually drain men. Monks seem to have been particularly attractive to succubi, and Aleister **Crowley** was among those who believed that nocturnal emmission could attract a succubus. In fact it was probably erotic **dreams** and nightmares that gave rise to the belief in succubi in the first place.

The ancients tended towards the idea that succubi were half human and half demon, and the mothers of a number of historical figures, including Alexander the Great, and Robert, first Duke of Normandy, are said to have been succubi. Sorcerers had special formula for dealing with succubi, and Lileth, the demoness of night and queen of the succubi, was considered to be attracted by a copulating man and woman in the hope of obtaining a few spots of semen from which she could create demons and evil **spirits.**

CONSULT: Sinistrari, *Demonality or Incubi and Succubi*, trans. and ed. by Montague Summers, Fortune Press (1927); Benjamin Walker, *Sex and the Supernatural*, Macdonald Unit 75 (1970).

## Summerland

The spirit world, or one of its **spheres**; a land of bliss, rest and harmony, partly a creation of one's own desires – according to Andrew Jackson Davis, who invented the term.

## Summers, Montague (1880-1948)

Roman Catholic priest who taught classics at a public school, wrote or edited more than fifty books with subjects that included a life of St Catherine of Siena (1903), an appreciation of Jane Austen (1919), a history of witchcraft (1926), a book of 'horrid mysteries' (1927), a history of the Restoration theatre (1934) and a bibliography of the gothic novel (1940). He lived largely abroad, chiefly in Italy, and wrote a number of plays and a book of poems. He also founded a society for the production of old plays and himself superintended the production of eighteen as well as a cycle of Congreve revivals; made pilgrimages to famous shrines; researched the worship of saints, liturgies and mysticism; and always enjoyed talking to intelligent dogs — 'That is, all dogs.' But it was his interest in and investigation of occult phenomena that brought him fame after his retirement from the church. His books suggest that he was an expert on **black magic**, **witchcraft** and strange cults and beliefs; and although he was somewhat credulous as a historian, he is best remembered as the author of *The Vampire: His Kith and Kin* (1928), *The Vampire in Europe* (1929) and *The Werewolf* (1933); and as translator and editor of **Malleus Maleficarum** (1928). 'I am,' he once said, 'a firm believer in the supernatural, in miracles and in **ghosts**'; and he certainly believed that the **Devil** and his hoards were as real as anything in this world and that witches and warlocks were literally in the hands of the Devil.

CONSULT: F. M. Guazzo, *Compendium Maleficarium*, Muller (1970 edition); N. Remy, *Demonolatry*, Muller (1970 edition).

## Superstition

Irrational feelings and beliefs that are experienced by the majority of mankind in all civilizations which acknowledge the possibility that ancient beliefs, fears, misinformation and forgotten customs will result in good or bad luck; such superstitions are connected with almost every activity of man, and the superstitious encounter something on which to base an irrational belief in one form or another every day. From birth, when the midwife searches the afterbirth for lumps (indicative of the number of later births that the mother will have), through every stage of life to **death** with its mourning (a disguise to confuse **ghosts**), man, consciously and unconsciously, takes part in superstitions, doing things 'for **luck**' and avoiding other things 'in case of bad luck'. Although we like to think that all superstitions originated with our long-forgotten ancestors, the present age, like all ages, has actually created its own superstitions with motorists' lucky key-rings and licence-holders; and actors and sportsmen in particular remain as superstitious as any of their forebears.

Superstition, a form of personal **magic** used for coming to terms with the unknown, is often the outward manifestation of such deep-seated anxieties as the beliefs that Mediterranean people are sexual athletes and Negro males sexual giants. Yet at the root of every superstition there lies a belief in magic, whatever the superstition may be concerned with: a ladder or a pin, **salt**, wood, lucky **charms**, the number 13, sneezing or a thousand and one other subjects of superstition all over the civilized world.

*See also* **animals and birds**; **trees and shrubs**

CONSULT: E. and M. A. Radford, *Encyclopaedia of Superstitions*, Hutchinson (1961 edition); Eric Maple, *Superstition and the Superstitious*, W. H. Allen (1971); Peter Underwood, *Deeper Into the Occult*, Harrap (1975).

## Swedenborg, Emanuel (1688-1772)

Swedish philosopher, scientist, theologian, mystic, physicist and prophet whose writings on the relationship between the body and the soul, the functions of the brain, and the interpretation of the Scriptures were based on his **dreams**, **visions** and audible experiences. According to Swedenborg, 'heaven was opened' to him and the Lord filled him with His Spirit to teach the doctrines of the New Church; divinely commissioned to do this work, he was convinced that the Lord 'opened the sight of his **spirit**' and so let him into the spiritual world, permitting him to see heaven and **hell** and to converse with angels and spirits for years. The Church of the New Jerusalem, or Swedenborgian Church, was founded after his death. Some of Swedenborg's many writings are available in Everyman's Library (Dent), including *The True Christian Religion*, *The Divine Love and Wisdom* and *Heaven, and its Wonder, and Hell, from things heard and seen.* There is a Swedenborg Society and publishing company at 20 Bloomsbury Way, London WC1.

CONSULT: Harry Boddington, *The University of Spiritualism*, Spiritualist Press (1947); James Webb, *The Flight from Reason*, Alcove Press (1973).

## Symbol

Term for an object representing to the mind something that is not shown but which is realized by association. In **occultism**, the power of symbols lies not in the material object but in the thought that forces attached to it can, in time, form what is considered to be an elemental for good or evil. Early symbols were derived from acrostics of Greek words, others were associated with animals from the Scriptures: the lamb for Christ, the peacock for immortality, the dragon or serpent for Satan. Stars and circles (*see* **pentagram**) became symbols of power, special designs being used for **white magic** and the reverse designs being used in **black magic**. Symbolism has become associated with many articles, but man, both primitive and modern, has tended to accept symbolic connotations in experiences he does not altogether understand; thus **dreams**, religions, sex and art are full of symbolism.

*See also* **phallic worship; totems and totemism.**

CONSULT: J. E. Cirlot, *A Dictionary of Symbols*, Routledge & Kegan Paul (1962); C. G. Jung, *Man and his Symbols*, Aldus/Jupiter (1964).

## Sympathetic magic

The principle that 'things act on each other at a distance through a secret sympathy' (as Frazer, who first coined the phrase, put it); that 'like produces like and that an effect resembles its cause'. A basic assumption of magical thinking exemplified by the wax image pricked and burnt in **witchcraft** when harm is wished on a person so represented; or when a bat is affixed by a **silver** nail to a church porch at the same time that an apparent **vampire** is impaled.

CONSULT: Sir James George Frazer, *The Golden Bough*, Macmillan (1913 edition); Eric Maple, *The Dark World of Witches*, Robert Hale (1962).

# T

## Table turning, or tilting

A crude but simple and popular method of apparent communication with the unconscious self or with extraneous intelligences – possibly **spirits** of the dead.

Those taking part sit around the table, which should be entirely composed of wood, and lightly place their hands upon the table top with palms down and, if possible, fingers outstretched and finger-tips touching to form a circle. Best results seem to be obtained in darkness or near darkness. After a few moments, if any one of those taking part possesses psychic power, the table will be felt to quiver under the sitters' hands; and the vibration will gradually increase until the table is pulsating; then it will often tilt or jerk, seem to stumble, move bodily or undergo **levitation**. At this stage one of the sitters suggests that the table knocks in answer to messages, and after a question has been asked, the letters of the alphabet are called over until the table tilts and raps on the floor when a certain letter is reached. By this somewhat laborious means it has been found possible to obtain, by **typtology**, intelligent messages, often purporting to originate from someone deceased. It has often been reported that, with repeated sittings, the table moves and raps with precision and skill, and that communication with a fresh entity is made apparent by a comparatively clumsy and stolid behaviour of the table. Many sitters assert that a table can express such emotions as humour, hostility and affection. In early days the table had a hole in the centre to enable materialized hands to appear (*see* **materialization**).

## Taboo, or tabu

Something forbidden not by statute or law but by convention; rules of behaviour that govern the human association of people and use of things; a ban or prohibition which has no rational meaning or explanation. Taboo (from the Polynesian, where it implies the threat of a powerful evil influence) is irrational to the outsider, but to the believer needs no explanation. In primitive societies there are taboos upon many aspects of sexual behaviour, food, hunting, birth and **death**, while civilized society is still largely taboo-minded in cultural, artistic, social and religious areas.

CONSULT Ernest Crawley, *The Mystic Rose*, Watts (1932); Franz Steiner, *Taboo*, Penguin (1967).

## Talisman

An object worn or carried that has the power of attracting good fortune or **luck**; something that produces or is capable of producing extraordinary effects; something that acts as a **charm**; a symbol or charm that is reputed to benefit or protect the possessor, especially something that has been magically endowed with the power of exerting a magical or occult influence. Astrological talismans were engraved or otherwise depicted a character or image of a heavenly sign and were said to incorporate and exert the influence of that planet. Although it seems likely that the thoughts of a person wearing or carrying a talisman are constantly dwelling on its purpose and reputed quality, and that such concentration reinforces his own will-power, the records of some healing talismans appear to suggest a certain success that warrants further consideration.

CONSULT: J. E. Lockhart, *Curses, Lucks and Talismans*, Geoffrey Bles (1938); W. G. O. Sepharial, *Book of Charms and Talismans*, Foulsham (1923).

## Tantrism

An Eastern philosophy based on the interplay between the male and female basic forces, Shiva and Shakti; a belief that the generative forces are instruments of the magical power that underlies the entire universe; the Tantrics – the female (Shakti) dominant and the male (Shiva) subordinate – seek salvation through the supreme power of sex. Although the highly disciplined rites of Tantrism involve dancing, domination and sexual activity, the resulting sensual pleasure is regarded as incidental and the principal and practices of Tantrism play an essential role today in many occult societies and organizations; indeed, such activities owe more than the sexual element to Tantrism, where rituals include the use of **grimoires**, candles, incense, **spells**, a **magic circle**, symbolic designs and **names of power**, all used in

Western **ritual magic**. Great emphasis is laid on respiratory exercise and control, exposure of the body to the health-giving rays of the sun and the control of certain bodily functions, including body temperature, pulse rates and sexual climax; and although extensive preparation and training is required to reach such control, there is no doubt that such command can be achieved.

See also **sex magic**.

CONSULT: Agehananda Bharati, *The Tantric Tradition*, Rider (1965); P. Rawson, *The Art of Tantra*, Thames & Hudson (1973).

## Tarot

Set of figured playing cards (*see also* **cartomancy**) that probably originated in Italy five hundred years ago; also, the game played with such cards, which comprise twenty-two 'trumps' and fifty-six other cards.

The Tarot cards, often strange and beautiful in design, have long been thought to form a unique kind of symbolic communication between God, man and the universe, the pictorial cards acting as a stimulus to the imagination that each person interprets for himself. The fifty-six cards are divided into four suits of fourteen cards, each usually known as Wands, Cups, Swords and Pentacles and the Major Arcana – the twenty-two vital cards that are used for **divination** or

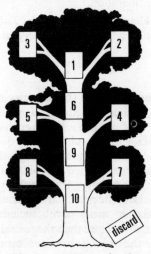

*The Tarot 'Tree of Life'*

fortune telling. There are many interpretations of the Tarot cards themselves, and many ways of using them. It is said that they originated with the gipsies and that they alone know the secret of their meaning; certainly they should always be 'cut' and 'dealt' gipsy-fashion: left-handed. The Major Arcana cards certainly have evocative and emotive subjects and names that lend themselves to many explanations: Justice, the Hanged Man, Death, the Devil, the Tower, Judgement, the High Priestess, the Magician, the Chariot, the Lovers, and, of course, the Wheel of Fortune.

CONSULT: Eden Gray, *The Tarot Revealed*, Inspiration House, New York (1960); S. Mayananda, *The Tarot Today*, Zeus Press (1964); B. I. Rakoci, *The Painted Caravan*, Brucher, The Hague (1954).

## Tasseography
**Divination** by means of tea-leaves.

A little unstrained tea should be left at the bottom of the cup, which should, ideally, have a wide top and a narrow base. The person whose tea-leaves are being told should hold his cup by the handle and rotate it three times, clockwise, causing the tea to reach the rim of the cup and so disturbing the tea-leaves left in the cup. He should then invert the cup completely on its saucer. The person making the divination will then take the cup and look into it and interpret the various shapes and forms made by the tea-leaves on the sides and bottom of the cup.

The leaves that are higher up the inside of the cup, near the rim, represent happiness of the present or imminent future; those further down the cup represent events further and further into the future; and those at the very bottom of the cup represent events of the far-distant future. Particularly clearly defined symbols and shapes are considered to be very lucky, those less clear proportionately less lucky, indecisive and prone to difficulties. There are many books that give excellent interpretations of tea-leaf symbols and it is only possible to give a few representative examples here.

Stars tell of success; triangles of fortune; squares suggest protection of some kind and circles represent frustration. An anchor means the safe ending of a journey or an affair or a deal of some kind; an arrow, a disappointment. A bird-like shape foretells important news and sometimes a journey; a bottle, frustration. A bridge suggests new friends or new business and foreign travel; a butterfly, insincerity. A candle symbolizes a new idea; a castle, an unexpected piece of good **luck** or good news; a cat, domestic difficulties or a disappointment with a female. A church tells of a forthcoming wedding or a serious illness;

clover is a symbol of good fortune while a cross represents bad fortune, ill luck and hard times. A dagger tells of a risk, personal or in business; a dog means friendship. A dot foretells a letter; an elephant, advice from an elderly person; an envelope, news; a fan, unfaithfulness. A flag is always a warning. A gate reveals a forthcoming disappointment; a gun, trouble; a hammer, hard work; a hand, friendship. The sign of a **horseshoe** is lucky and often precedes the successful beginning of a new enterprise. A key symbolizes a favourable time ahead; a knife, a disagreement; a letter, advancement in some form; a man, unexpected help and a visit from a stranger. A mushroom bodes complications at home or work; musical instruments, good companionship; a pipe, the need for taking thought before acting. Scissors augur a quarrel; a snake tells of an enemy; and a tree represents tranquillity, rest and comfort.

CONSULT: Douglas Hill, *Fortune Telling*, Hamlyn (1972); A. M. Miall, *Complete Fortune Telling*, Greenberg, New York (1950).

## Taurus
*See* **zodiac**.

## Tea-leaf reading
*See* **tasseography**.

## Tedworth, Drummer of
*See* **Drummer of Tedworth**.

## Telekinesis
The movement of objects without physical contact; paranormally caused movement of objects; the supernormal displacement of objects. The many physical mediums who have produced telekinetic phenomena under convincing conditions include **Stella C**, D. D. Home, **'Margery'**, Eusapia Palladino and the **Schneider brothers**. Telekinesis is also reported spontaneously in **poltergeist** cases, in haunted houses where furniture is often moved inside closed rooms and in such phenomena as the commonly reported falling of a picture before a **death** in the household. *See also* **spiritualism**; **teleportation**.

## Telepathy
Communication between one mind and another without the use of speech or any of the normal conscious channels. Also known as thought-transference, thought-reading, **clairaudience**, and now included in the comprehensive term, **extrasensory perception (ESP)**.

Telepathy probably plays a part in spiritualist séances when information is often given to a sitter which is within his or her knowledge and could conceivably have been obtained by the medium telepathically. Extensive telepathic tests with special cards (*see* **Zener cards**) have occupied psychical researchers for years, but the elaborate precautions necessary against fraud, conscious and unconscious, have proved formidable obstacles, and the much-sought repeatable experiment seems as elusive as ever: a subject will provide high scores, far in excess of chance expectation, one day, and nothing out of the ordinary the next. Odd irregularities have also been noticed in what started out to be plain one-at-a-time card-guessing experiments, for later examination of the results has sometimes shown a pattern of correct 'hits' just ahead or just behind the target cards.

On the other hand, there exists good evidence for spontaneous telepathy, as everyone knows who has been about to make a remark when the identical words are spoken by someone else; or who has started thinking of someone they have almost forgotten and hear word from that person within a short space of time. Most people have personal experience of such examples of apparent telepathy, but telepathy-on-tap is a different thing, and the astronaut, Edgar Mitchell's attempts to transmit symbols telepathically from space was an interesting idea, though distance on earth has proved no difficulty in world-wide telepathic experiments. The records of the **Society for Psychical Research** and other societies devoted to the study of psychic phenomena are full of material pertaining to telepathy – the universal aunt of **psychical research**.

CONSULT: Whately Carington, *Telepathy*, Methuen (1945); S. G. Soal and F. Bateman, *Modern Experiments in Telepathy*, Faber & Faber (1954).

## Teleplasm
Obsolete name for **ectoplasm**.

## Teleportation
The mysterious and unexplained transportation of human beings, animals and inaminate objects from one place to another, often over great distances and in a fraction of the time necessary under normal circumstances; an intriguing form of psychic happening (if that is what it is) that has been reported throughout the history of mankind. *See also* **telekinesis**.

CONSULT: Nandor Fodor, *Mind Over Space*, Citadel Press, (1962).

## Telesthesia
A word invented by F. W. H. **Myers** to describe the phenomenon of distant perception through psychic *rapport* with a person, place or environment; telesthesia is less than **clairvoyance** in that it is restricted to perception of material things and circumstances. A typical example of telesthesia would be the sensation of a sudden pain (without physical cause) accompanied by the conviction that a loved one is experiencing similar distress caused by an injury of some kind, and later confirmation that actual pain and injury had been experienced by the loved one. Telesthesia is fairly common among identical twins.

## Theosophy
A philanthropic concept that attempts to promote a love of mankind and is religious only in so far as it teaches a spiritual background to existence; a wisdom religion that is claimed to be the substance and basis of all religions and teaches development of latent psychic faculties and the doctrine of **reincarnation**. Theosophy attributes the spirit messages of **spiritualism** to evil **spirits** or astral 'shells' – incomplete beings. Among those influenced by its ideas was Rudolf **Steiner**. *See also* **Blavatsky, Madame; Besant, Annie**.

CONSULT: H. P. Blavatsky *The Key to Theosophy*, Theosophical Publishing House (1889); Annie Besant, *Theosophy and the New Psychology*, Theosophical Publishing House (1904).

## Third eye
Professed organ of occult vision and source of inner enlightenment, apparently situated in the middle of the forehead and visible to **sensitives**; one of the *chakras* or centres of psychic energy in Hindu and Tibetan **occultism**. *See also* **Lobsang Rampa**.

CONSULT: Lobsang Rampa, *The Third Eye*, Secker & Warburg (1956).

## Thought-transference
*See* **telepathy**.

## Thought-forms
Visible thoughts; shapes that owe their existence to the imagination and emotions. Occultists maintain that ideas and desires as well as thoughts take visible form on the **astral plane**.

CONSULT: Annie Besant, *Thought-Forms*, Theosophical Publications

(1969); Nandor Fodor, *Encyclopaedia of Psychic Science*, Arthurs Press (1934).

## Thoughtography
*See* **Serios, Ted**.

## Throngs
Name given to an invisible crowd that is felt to fill a room or throng a roadway, open space or building of any kind.

## Time
An enigma of fundamental importance; one of the two dimensions of our consciousness (the other being space) that has profoundly affected man's views and ideas of life, **death** and belief in gods. J. W. Dunne propounded a new theory of time in 1927 following a series of **dreams** of **precognition** which led to experiments that, in turn, brought him to the conclusion that anyone can duplicate what he did and perceive personal experiences displaced from their correct place in the sequence of time, since what he had stumbled upon was the result of a peculiarity in the structure of time that had been overlooked.

CONSULT: J. W. Dunne, *An Experiment with Time*, Faber & Faber (1927); Sheila Ostrander and Lynn Schroeder, *Psychic Discoveries Behind the Iron Curtain*, Prentice-Hall, New Jersey (1970).

## Tongues, gift of
*See* **glossolalia; xenoglossy**.

## Totems and totemism
A natural object or animal that tribesmen look upon as the hereditary **symbol** of an individual or clan and so regard as an object of worship; any image or picture of such an object or animal.

Totemism is a primitive philosophy, an idea not of the worship of animals or objects but of affiliation with them. The totemic figures of the North American Indians might be individual guardian **spirits** or the spiritual protectors of a group or tribe; such totems were often depicted in the form of an animal or bird, and the Indians did not so much believe in descent from animals as that their early ancestors were in part divine and had the power to change shape from time to time, later generations coming to look upon the totems as their watchful ancestors, protective and comforting. In the study of comparative religions, the worship of totems is regarded as marking a higher level of religious advancement (perhaps the next in succession) to **fetishism**.

CONSULT: Ernest Crawley, *The Mystic Rose*, Watts (1932); Sir James George Frazer, *Totemism and Exogamy*, Macmillan (1935 edition).

*Typical totem pole*

# Trance

A condition of apparent sleep or unconsciousness with certain physiological characteristics; a condition induced by mystical, magical or medical means, resulting in a part of consciousness being split off from the whole; a state suggesting that the soul has passed out of the body; ecstasy, rapture, extreme exaltation. Trance states are also found to be induced as a result of physical causes (a brain tumour or blow on the head); as divine conditions (such as the Delphic Oracle); as the result of physically and emotionally demanding techniques (as with the Whirling **Dervishes** or in the frenzied dancing of **voodoo** worshippers or the demanding dramatic rituals of **occultism** like those employed by Aleister **Crowley**); and as a consequence of using drugs. But the true nature of the trance is unknown. Many spiritualist mediums appear to lapse into a self-induced trance-like state when it would appear their psychic faculties are enhanced and they are in a condition of dissociation of which they have no conscious memory when they return to the normal state.

*See also* **hypnotism; mediumship; spiritualism.**

CONSULT: M. Deren, *Divine Horsemen*, Thames & Hudson (1969 edition); Louis Pauwels and Jacques Bergier, *The Dawn of Magic*, Anthony Gibbs & Phillips (1963).

## Trance personality
*See* **control**.

## Transcendental Meditation (TM)
*See under* **meditation**.

## Transfiguration
Change of appearance or form by abnormal means; a transfiguration medium claims to be transformed into the physical likeness of a deceased or **control**.

CONSULT: Harry Price, *Fifty Years of Psychical Research*, Longmans, Green (1939).

## Transmigration
The passage of the soul after **death** from one body to another; metampsychosis. An idea associated with **reincarnation**, popular in Ancient India and surviving in **Hinduism** and **Buddhism**, and to be found, in various forms, in many other religions.

## Transportation
*See* **teleportation**.

## Tree worship
*See* **trees and plants**.

## Trees and plants
To early man, looking at the abundant primeval forest about him, the origin of trees and plants, their growth and, in some cases, their evergreen foliage must have seemed full of mystery. Compared with the lives of men at that time, trees must have seemed immortal; small wonder that man came to venerate the trees, and tree-worship is evident from the earliest records available. Soon there were sacred trees, trees that protected, trees that healed, trees of **magic**, trees of fertility, trees of evil and trees with oracular powers; equally there were plants with similar magical properties, and today all this is reflected in mythology and **superstition** and the representation of trees and plants in fortune telling or **divination**.

In recent years there have been experiments, particularly in the United States and Scotland, into the effects of talking to trees and plants, and it is claimed that plants loved and talked to, prosper, while unloved and ignored plants, although given the same temperature, light conditions and nourishment, tend to grow less quickly, less strongly and less sturdily. Similar experiments with seeds, some being nourished with water that a healer has held in his hands for thirty minutes and others with tap water, apparently reveal that those seeds which receive water that has passed through the hands of the healer are more fruitful and produce taller and stronger plants. In France, experiments with fungi seem to indicate that the growth of some fungi is influenced merely by the occasional presence of a human being.

Herbs have been used by medical men and spiritual adepts to cure the body and soothe the mind since ancient times. In magic, too, herbs have been used for just as long. Most herbs, in fact, have or have had several uses: angelica, for example, linked with St Michael the Archangel and sometimes called 'the Root of the Holy Ghost', is not only used in medicine and cookery but is also regarded as powerfully protective against **witchcraft**, **spells** and the danger of enchantment. Basil is not only a culinary herb, it is also reputed to breed scorpions; it is regarded by the Italians as a love token and by the Greeks as symbolizing hatred and misfortune, while a leaf of basil on the body of a dead Hindu was thought to ensure his reaching Paradise. Dill, apart from its culinary uses, has long been given to fretful children (its name is derived from the Norse, *dilla* = 'to lull') and it is still used in the practice of witchcraft for working spells and to keep away evil **spirits**.

Toughest and most elastic of British trees, the *ash* has long been regarded as a protection against evil and was once a sacred tree. Pliny wrote of its power against snakes – how snakes avoid even the shadows cast by ash trees, and how a snake would rather perish in fire than crawl over a twig of the tree that is 'the sweetest of our forest fuelling and the fittest for ladies' chambers', as Evelyn puts it, for ash burns even when it is green.

So the belief grew that to carry an ash twig or wear ash leaves in one's hat provided protection from snake bites; a stick cut from ash wood always killed a snake outright; drinking the sap of the ash cured a snake bite; and an ash tree near the door of the house prevented snakes from entering. In Ireland, ash wood was burned to banish the **Devil**, and in Devonshire ash faggots were burned for centuries at Christmastide, partly to protect the inhabitants from the Devil and partly in commemoration of the belief that Mary gave the new-born Christ his first washing and dressing by a fire of ash wood – a belief that may account for many other superstitions linking ash and human birth. In the Scottish Highlands, the nurse or midwife would place one end of a green ash stick in the fire, and while it was burning collect in a spoon the sap or juice that oozed at the other end; this was given to the new-born infant as the first spoonful of liquor to pass its lips, thereby offering the child the strength of the ash tree as well as protection from witchcraft, goblins and other threats present in country beliefs.

A bunch of ash keys was considered a powerful guard against witches; a bunch of ash leaves protected a bed and its occupant; warts could be removed by recourse to the ash; an ash grove secured a house from evil influences; an 'even ash' (a leaf with an even number of leaflets) was considered to be especially lucky, and to find and hold such a leaf ensured that the finder would meet his or her lover before the day was out. Gilbert White, in his *Natural History of Selborne*, describes a row of pollarded ash trees with long cicatrices down their sides, and by way of explanation gives a classic description of how children were cured of rupture by being passed, stark naked, through an ash tree that had been cleft and held open with wedges; afterwards the tree was closed, plastered with loam and 'swathed up'. If the tree healed satisfactorily so would the ruptured child. Ash trees were used in a similar way in Devonshire, where the performances always took place at daybreak and consisted of passing the child through the tree three times and always east to west.

Ash is still the favourite wood for walking-sticks: a reminder of the tree's power and the sacredness of the ashen spear. It was believed that a stick of ash would never injure or harm an animal – in fact, stroking the animal with a branch from the tree was said to cure some ills – and ash was accordingly a favourite herding stick and the proper wood for making shepherds' crooks from time immemorial.

The tall **beech**, widely distributed throughout Europe and also found in Asia Minor and Japan, is one of the strongest of British timbers, and being one of the best for turning, is popular for chair legs, tool handles and various household articles. Beech trees flourished in Britain long before the coming of Julius Caesar, even though he states that the country had no beech trees; Gilbert White considered the beech to be 'the most lovely of all forest trees', and the traditional Yule Log had to be of beech; sometimes a piece of the log would be preserved and placed under the bed to protect the house for twelve months. Charcoal from the log that had burnt all through Christmas Night was pounded and mixed with water to provide a cure for consumption. The beech tree (which never harbours mistletoe) was used in the sacred grove of Diana, where noble Romans embraced it, kissed it, lay under its shadow and poured wine on its trunk. Herbalists have no time for the beech, however, for when brought into the house it was thought to bring with it laborious and difficult childbirth and miserable deaths.

The wood of the slender *birch* is used for plywood veneers, for Russian spoons, Canadian canoes, snowshoes, house roofing; its seeds for food by the Laplanders, bark for candles by the ancient Scots, and also by Northern fishermen who went out spearing fish with the aid of birch-bark torches; and the leaves for making tea. The birch was sacred to the Scandinavian god Thor. It is a symbol of spring and is the tree traditionally used for maypoles: a tree of magic power which is disliked by **fairies,** and at one time its branches were hung over cottage doorways in the west of England to repel enchantment; perhaps even as a passport back to life.

Because of its alleged magic properties, birch was used for arrows, bolts and staffs in olden days, and it was commonly used for besoms (to sweep out evil as well as rubbish) and for birching (to thrash the Devil out of children and wrongdoers). Witches went to their revels on birch broomsticks to meet their master; birch was used to protect cattle and horses from attacks by witches and the forces of evil; and sprigs of birch would be stuck into dung heaps and on the high land where witches were thought to assemble. Birch besoms, dipped in pitch and ignited, were powerful weapons against invisible foes. Villages, houses and farmsteads were also guarded by little birch trees, either set in front of the house or fastened over house-doors, and it was thought that witches who sought to harm men in all manner of ways on Walpurgis Night, must count every leaf of the tree before they could cross the threshold, and while they were still counting dawn would break and their power disappear.

A bundle of birch twigs, tied together and ornamented with pieces of silk and paper ribbons, was used at Eastertide to administer 'Easter Smacks', light blows usually inflicted on the hands and feet of female friends and relatives to drive away sickness and drive health into the body; the beating was thought to bring good luck to the beaten one and to preserve them from flies, vermine and back pains throughout the following year! Afterwards the bundle of twigs would be preserved and used to drive the cattle out to pasture for the first time after their winter confinement. Similar smacks were meted out by young men and women, who beat each other on different days (especially St Stephen's Day and Holy Innocents' Day) with bunches of fresh green birch, and sometimes willow or fir, to benefit the health of the victim and to make him or her fresh and youthful, like the boughs that were used. Birch trees that overhang a house, and especially if they touch the house, are said to bring illness and misfortune to the inhabitants.

Of the two species of *elder*, the dwarf elder, according to legend, grew spontaneously out of the ground where invading Danes had been slaughtered, and its association with **blood** is not altogether unreasonable for it is exceptionally luxuriant and the pithy stem turns red in the autumn. It used to be thought that blood would flow if an elder branch was cut – and very often the next day some old crone would display an arm in a sling. Certainly the leaves and pedicels below the fruit mark the fingers with a dark, blood-like stain, and in the autumn a group of 'Danes' Blood', as the dwarf elder is sometimes called, looks curiously like a ragged regiment, for there is a strange dignity about the plant at this time of the year, a disturbing quality that puts one in mind of a defeated army, bleeding and forlorn. Dwarf elder is used in witchcraft and **occultism**, especially in rites of **sympathetic magic**.

The common elder, 'God's stinking tree' (since in one legend it was used for the Cross) or 'Judas-tree' (since in another legend Judas hanged himself on it), is associated with devil-worship and witchcraft: if it is burnt the Devil will come down the chimney, if you strike a man dead with elder, his hand will come up from the grave and point you out; a boat made from elder will sink; a child that occupies a cradle made from elder will never be healthy, besides falling an easy prey to fairies. Yet, used correctly, elder can be a protection against witchcraft, and **charms** and **amulets** made from the wood protect the wearer against witches and evil spirits. Elder picked on the last day of April and affixed above the doorways of a house will protect the inhabitants from evil for a twelvemonth and the house from being struck by lightning. It was a wood often used for the whips of hearse drivers when hearses were horse-drawn, for they were in great danger from the newly dead. In some parts of England and on the continent a cross of elder was placed upon a grave, and if it flowered the soul of the dead person had gone to heaven; the cross on the grave also provided protection for the corpse since witches and **vampires** disliked the smell of elder, the wood that is sometimes used to form a warlock's crook or a sorcerer's wand.

There is a tradition that *garlic* sprang up where Satan placed his left foot as he departed from Paradise, while the onion grew where he had trodden with his right foot. In ancient times those who gathered powerful herbs for magic and occult purposes forestalled possible dangers from demonic forces they were likely to disturb by, among other precautionary measures, chewing garlic, the odour of the herb being powerful enough to repel such entities. In Italy, garlic was placed in a new-born baby's cradle to protect the child while it was vulnerable between birth and baptism. It is said to be one of the most efficient protections against vampires, and is often employed by present-day witches and practioners of the occult arts.

The *hawthorn*, also known as *may* and *whitethorn*, has long been associated with May Day **festivals,** when, it was believed, witches and fairies were always active, and farm produce, animals, children and womenfolk had to be protected against bewitchment and evil influences. Perhaps because of its many attributes – scent, thorns, delicious flowers and May-time blossoming – the hawthorn has always been considered a supernatural tree, not least with lovers, who laud it in poetry as symbolizing sex and fertility; they see magic in the interweaving of the plant into crosses, coronets and other significant shapes, enhanced by early summer dew – itself a magical substance. Hawthorn was once placed outside the windows of young girls in France so that the stale but sweet scent of the trimethylamine in the flowers, suggestive of sex, wafted up into the windows; it has also been used as an aphrodisiac in **black magic** and occult practices.

Oaths were sworn by hawthorn, and with its purported magical powers, its well-nigh impenetrability, its reputed power against lightning and its popularity as a plant on which to hang the afterbirths of animals in some areas, the shrub was a favourite one for protective hedges. It is said to have been a hawthorn staff that Joseph of Arimathea thrust into the ground at **Glastonbury** to blossom into the Holy Thorn, and some authorities assert that it was the material of Christ's Crown of Thorns. It is still widely believed to be unlucky to bring hawthorn into the house; death comes with it, according to tradition, though in the Victorian language of flowers the hawthorn stood for hope. The thorns have been used to pierce the heart of a sheep in magical practices (as recently as 1964) and to pierce a bat's heart in an act of **sympathetic magic**.

The *hazel* is known as a magical tree with power against all enchantments. It was thought to harbour its own elf (Hind Etin) to guard the nuts, to have particular power against evil spirits and to ward off rheumatism and lumbago (diseases inflicted by malicious elves). In Ireland the hazel is known as the Tree of Knowledge, possibly on account of its protective powers (it is often used for making hurdles), but more likely because of its magic power, which caused it to be one of the four proper woods for **dowsing or divining** the others being rowan, mistletoe and birch. As a medieval symbol of fertility and immortality, it was carried in procession at weddings, and the 'Virgin Branch', a young twig with no side-shoots, was used for ritual flagellation to guarantee fertility, a practice followed by later magicians and occult practitioners for their own purposes. Their **wands** and staffs were often made of hazel wood, as were royal sceptres – an echo of the belief that Mercury was given a hazel rod by Apollo which he used to calm human passions, and that it was the rod of Moses and that of Aaron, originally cut by Adam in the Garden of Eden, taken by Noah into the Ark and handed down to Abraham, Isaac and Joseph. To be specially efficacious, hazel rods should be cut from the eastern side of the shrub on the first night of a new **moon** of Good Friday, St John's Day or Shrove Tuesday, and immediately thrust into the earth so that they catch the first rays of the rising sun.

The *holly* has long been used for protective purposes, and the red berries worn against the **evil eye**, for red is in itself a protection against evil and garlands of the smooth green leaves protect the house from misfortune and the occupants from witchcraft. Children were thought to be cured of the whooping cough if they drank milk from a cup made of holly wood, and a garland around a horse's neck was said to cure the animal of nightmares. Among the traditions associated with holly is the belief that it was one of the woods used for the Cross on which Christ was crucified, and that the thorns and berries commemorate the Crown of Thorns and the drops of blood. Until early in the last century, men and boys of Tenby in South Wales would run through the streets on Boxing Day 'holly-beating' – hitting girls on their bare arms until they bled. This custom is echoed by practitioners of the black arts, who use holly in 'witch's chains' to show unmarried girls their future husbands after ritual flagellation. Holly is one of the objects brought into houses in Scotland and the North of England on New Year's Day soon after midnight: 'First Footing', when a sprig of male holly betokens good luck and the best of life in the year ahead; to carry female holly will bring bad luck.

The evergreen *ivy* was sacred to Bacchus, and it used to be planted outside a tavern to indicate that wine was available within. An earlier name for Bacchus or Dionysus may have been Kissos or Cissos, the ancient name for ivy, and the deity is often portrayed wearing an ivy wreath. In one legend, Kissos is the name of a nymph who danced at a Dionysian festival with such zest and abandon that she collapsed and expired at the feet of the god who, in his grief and melancholy, changed her into the lively and vigorous ivy. As a symbol of fidelity, a wreath of ivy was formerly presented to a newly married couple at Greek weddings; its twining properties symbolized the union of the couple.

Ivy has long had a mournful and magical context, qualities that were combined in the convinctions of the priests of Jupiter, who believed that contact with ivy could put them into prophetic **trances**. The healing properties of ivy include its reputation for curing drunkenness, preventing intoxication, easing corns, skin rashes and a running nose; even ivywood was thought to be advantageous when used for drinking vessels, although ivy is in fact poisonous, and it is probably this which caused ivy to be regarded as a magic plant and its reputation as a protection against evil, as, indeed, it was long before Christmas was celebrated with ivy as a decoration; it could also account for stories of worshippers of Bacchus chewing ivy leaves to cause a state of frenzy, and perhaps also for its reputation as an aid to inspiration.

The *laurel* was sacred to Apollo because Daphne, whom he was pursuing, changed into a laurel tree (according to Ovid); it is a favourite tree for making wreaths for athletic victors, and those who triumph in other fields, and the Greeks regarded the laurel as having oracular powers, while the leaves, either chewed or inhaled as smoke, were believed to assist inspiration. At Delphi a seer would hold a laurel bough, and those seeking to learn what the future held often wore a sprig of laurel. Occultists burnt laurel for its power during **incantations**, and sometimes saw **omens** in the way laurel crackled and burnt. Laurel beneath the pillow at night is said to cause the sleeper to dream of the future. Laurel was also regarded as protective against bad **spirits** and against **sorcery**, and the Greeks not only carried it about with them for this purpose, but also fixed it over their houses to keep away **ghosts**. More recently it was believed to act as a barrier against witchcraft, and its place in the equipment of the sorcerer and white witch is secure so long as superstition lives.

From time immemorial, the narcotic *mandrake* plant has been regarded as possessing many powers: helping women to conceive; restoring the spirits of persons thought to be dying so that they recover; assuaging pain; producing temporary insensibility for medical purposes; relieving convulsions, rheumatic pains, toothache and melancholia. As an aphrodisiac, it is reputed to be unsurpassed by any herb. The mandrake was used by alchemists (as symbols of fecundity). It was a popular ingredient of witches' potions, and was regarded as invaluable as an aid to **clairvoyance**; indeed, the plant was so closely associated with witchcraft that some witches were put to death simply because the plant was found in their possession. It was also said to foretell the future, open locks and discover the whereabouts of gold. The mandrake was thought to have human attributes (during the Middle Ages it was believed to grow from the sperm of a hanged man), and the method of gathering was to tie a dog (which had not eaten for three days) to the plant and then call the dog from a distance so that it drew the mandrake from the soil, whereupon the plant is said to have emitted a human-like cry or shriek, causing the death of the dog; and this was the reason for being some distance away, and stopping the ears as an extra precaution, since it was thought that any living thing that heard the terrible cry would die. It is the semi-human character and physiology of the mandrake that has caused the plant to be the centre of such superstitions. The roots and fruit are still used by herbalists, sorcerers and occultists. In the Victorian language of flowers, the mandrake represented – perhaps appropriately – horror.

The *mistletoe* is a parasitical evergreen flowering in February and March, and most common on apple trees, propagation being effected by birds eating the berries and then wiping their beaks on different trees. The mistletoe, traditionally the wood of Christ's cross (it having become a diminutive plant only subsequently) and of Moses' burning bush, has been used in religious ceremonies since time immemorial: as a healing agency since Saxon times, and as a bough with magical properties for those who kiss beneath it since biblical times. The mistletoe was especially sacred to the **Druids**, from whom we inherit the idea of bringing it into our home at Yuletide, and it was mistletoe, under its old name 'Golden Bough' – derived from Virgil's description of the plant as 'leafy gold', an apt description when mistletoe becomes dry – that gave Frazer the title for his classic work on magic and religion.

The massive, imposing, strong and long-living *oak* has been the chief sacred tree since earliest times over much of Europe. Its rich, luxuriant foliage, its ability to live upwards of a thousand years, its tendency to renew from young shoots from the roots of the old tree so that it may be regarded as perpetual, and its usefulness as the source of genuine turpentine used by the ancients and of a rich, balsamic gum – all these facts have added to the awe and worship that the oak has enjoyed since biblical times and its associations with the Druids and Thor.

The sacred mistletoe grew on the oak; Socrates swore by the oak; oak nymphs were thought to live in oak groves (giving rise to rites still conducted in these places); oak boughs at wedding ceremonies ensured a fruitful marriage. The oak trees were thought to provide protection from lightning (somewhat illogically since the oak is struck more often than other trees), and branches of oak used to be kept in the house for protective purposes (perhaps because it was the 'thunder God's tree'), a habit later replaced by the acorn and preserved symbolically in the shape of today's window blind cord weight; while 'holy oaks', 'gospel oaks' and 'Christ's oaks' are reminiscent of the pagan past, as is the frequent use of oak-leaf decoration in churches. The oak's veneration in the seventeenth century (when Charles II hid in the branches of an oak tree after his defeat at Worcester), its relationship with witchcraft, the festivals that centre round the Green Man, bonfires and superstitions all reflect the deep affinity that still exists between European man and the oak.

Oak wood was used for making idols as well as ships, and the song 'Hearts of Oak' has several interpretations. Jupiter was regarded as the god of the oak, the sky, the rain and the thunder, and early man attempted to exercise the fertilizing functions ascribed to the god in exactly the same way that modern witches seek to use the hidden powers of the oak, and in effect worship and venerate the tree and its produce, although not perhaps to the extent of the pagan Germans, who punished any man who willingly damaged a sacred oak by cutting out his navel, nailing it to the tree and forcing him to walk round and round the tree until his intestines were withdrawn from his body and wound about the trunk.

The *olive* is a slow-growing tree with blue-black oily fruit which can be pickled in brine while green and unripe. Olive oil is extracted from the ripe fruit. Little is known of the olive's origin and rise to importance in Mediterranean civilization, yet it is unlikely that the early peoples (Egyptians, Cretans, Phoenicians, Hellenes, Carthaginians, Arabs, Romans) could have flourished without the olive, symbol of peace and friendship and representing prosperity, beauty, strength and divine blessing. The Garden of Gethsemane was an olive grove, and so long-living is the tree that it is not impossible for some of the present trees there to date from the time of Christ. Athena caused an olive tree to grow on the rock of the Acropolis and gave Athens its name; an olive branch appeared on early Greek coins, and goats (because of the harm they did to olive groves) were favourites for sacrifice to Athena. All the olives on the Acropolis were burnt when Xerxes sacked Athens in 480 B.C., but the tree reappeared miraculously and olives grow there to this day. The olive is also regarded as a protective plant, especially against lightning, witchcraft and all forms of evil, and present-day magicians and occult practitioners employ olive leaves to counteract evil forces.

The *poppy* is the symbol of sleep, death and the soothing of pain, and the red poppy has symbolized remembrance of servicemen killed in two world wars. The white juice of the opium poppy was the source of opium from a time in prehistory, and this fact, coupled with the plant's connection with Ceres, the Roman corn goddess (since poppies flourish in cornfields and corn and poppies together represent life and death), has meant that the poppy and concoctions derived from the plant have always been an ingredient in magical **potions**, brews and mixtures. Some of the magic connotations spring from the former widely held belief that the red poppies of the battlefields of France owed their origin to the blood of fallen soldiers: an example of the time-honoured conjecture that out of blood comes blood.

The poppy in Ancient Greece was the chosen flower of Aphrodite, goddess of vegetation, while in the twentieth century the poppy has been the centre of a number of superstitions and beliefs: smelling poppies is thought to induce a headache (although the poppy is also said to cure headaches); staring at poppies too long causes blindness; to pick poppies causes a thunderstorm (a belief reflected in some local names for the plant: 'thunderbolt', 'thundercup' and 'thunderflower'), although poppy flowers inserted among the roof timbers were thought to ward off damage from storms and lightning.

Sweet-scented and blue-flowered *rosemary* is an evergreen shrub that is regarded as holy and magical; a protection against evil spirits, bad fairies, witchcraft and storms. Rosemary used to be carried at funerals and dropped on to the coffin as it was lowered into the grave as a token of everlasting memory, and a root is still sometimes given to friends who have lost a loved one, to plant as a symbol of remembrance. The practice of dropping a sprig into the wine at a wedding, to ensure faithfulness in love, is echoed by sorcerers and magicians who use rosemary for purification and consecrating purposes, as well as in **sex magic** to ensure undying and all-consuming love.

The *rowan or mountain ash* is said to be a powerful protection against witchcraft and evil of all kinds, and it was one of the trees sacred to the Druids, whose staffs were usually of rowan, consecrated and carved with mystic signs. Apart from planting rowan in one's garden, additional protection against witches and other night-fears could be obtained by nailing branches over the entrances of houses and the doorways of cattle-sheds to protect them – an even surer way of guarding cattle was to tie a cross of rowan-tree wood to each animal's tail with a red thread. In Britain there used to be hardly a churchyard without a sacred rowan tree to ensure that the dead rested in their graves. Divining rods are often made from rowan, and if a witch was touched with a rowan twig, she would be carried off by the Devil. At one time the protective element of the rowan was extended to the use of the wood for chimney crossbeams, water-wheels and farm implements.

**St John's Wort** is an example of a plant reputed to possess magic powers of healing and protection. Associated with St John the Baptist ('wort' being the Old English word for a plant or herb), the festivals of St John's Eve (23 June) and St John's Day (24 June) used to be celebrated with bonfires on which the plant would be smoked; this resulted in a purifying and magically powerful smoke which believers jumped through to be made ceremonially clean and strengthened against the powers of evil. No evil **demon** or wicked spirit was thought to be able to enter a house that contained St John's Wort, a plant that possesses a red juice likened to the blood of St John, the forerunner of Christ. One variety has red dots which can be seen when the leaves are held up to the light, and these are said to be made by the Devil and to appear on 27 August, the day on which John the Baptist was reputedly beheaded, to remind the world of the power of evil by reproducing these marks, reminiscent of wounds. In folk medicine the plant was said to cure depression, melancholy, delusions and madness, and to kill and to help heal wounds; while a salve made from the flowers protected children from illness and caused women to bear children. Furthermore, it was said that a childless woman who walked naked in her garden on St John's Day and picked a flower of the plant before dawn, would cradle a child of her own before the next St John's Day. A maiden picking such a flower and placing it beneath her pillow would, it was thought, dream of the man she would marry.

The graceful *willow* tree or shrub is the traditional emblem of grief, melancholy and forsaken love. Being bitter (because in folk legend Christ was corrected with a withy wand as a child), the willow is indicative of the bitterness of sadness, and it used to be customary to wear a willow sprig or garland to show sorrow. Willows thrive in wet soil, and were therefore considered useful in the treatment of ague and rheumatism. (A bitter infusion obtained from the willow had long been found beneficial against ague, and in the nineteenth century salicin in willow bar was isolated, leading to the discovery of salicylic acid and aspirin.) The great sallow, or groat willow, is considered to possess the power of withstanding enchantment, and it was once common practice to take a 'sally rod' with you when you set out on a journey. The willow is regarded as especially potent when it is touched for **luck**. Willow, like hazel, is popular for making wands used in magical practices, especially divination.

The evergreen *yew*, that lives to an immense age, is coneless, produces exceptionally hard timber, has poisonous leaves and bears red berries. It has a reputation for immortality, and because it was regarded as symbolic of life after death, has long been a favourite churchyard tree. Its strength and protective powers made it magical, and it was thought to protect the house and its owner as soon as it was planted; and when it had grown thick with greenish-black foliage, darker than the darkest night, to provide shelter for elves and goblins, but also to repel witchcraft and restrain the **spirits** of the dead. Strong and supple, it was ideal for bows and spear shafts as well as for magicians' implements and utensils. It was considered very unlucky to damage or cut down a yew tree, though the wood is sometimes used for making rods for dowsing.

CONSULT: C. A. Burland, *Echoes of Magic*, Peter Davies (1972); Sir James George Frazer, *The Golden Bough*, Macmillan (1913 edition); Geoffrey Grigson, *The Englishman's Flora*, Phoenix House (1958); Paul Hawken, *The Magic of Findhorn*, Souvenir Press (1975).

## Trumpet

Cardboard, aluminium or plastic cone-shaped tube with phosphorescent rim that is seen and heard as it floats around in the darkness of a spiritualist circle (*see* **séance**), delivering 'spirit' messages by **direct voice** to the sitters. Mediums specializing in this type of phenomena used to be known as 'trumpet mediums'. It was claimed that the trumpet shape served as a condenser of psychic power and increased the volume of the voice; some mediums used to wet the trumpet before use with the same aim in view.

## Twitchell, Paul

American 'soul traveller' whose followers are taught the doctrines of Eckanker whereby the soul is released from the body in a kind of higher process of **astral projection** and can achieve 'God realization'. Twitchell himself, according to his biography by Brad Steiger, *In My Soul I am Free*, became familiar with the techniques of **astral travel** while a child, and there are many people who claim that he has appeared to them when his physical body has been miles away. Since 1964 he has encouraged the formation of groups of *chelas* ('pupils'), and claims to have followers in every country in Western Europe and in every state in the U.S.A. His many books include *Introduction to Eckanker, The Tiger's Fang, The Far Country, Herbs: The Magic Healers* and *Eckankar: The Key to Secret Worlds* (all published by Lancer Books, New York).

## 'Two Worlds'

Originally a Manchester weekly spiritualist newspaper, founded by Mrs Emma Britten in 1888; now a monthly spiritualist magazine concerned with all aspects of **spiritualism** and the **paranormal**; it is edited by Maurice Barbanell and published from 23 Great Queen Street, London WC2B 5BB.

## Typtology

The name given to the reception of messages obtained through **table turning**.

# U

## Unction

The act of anointing with oil; a religious and magical rite or ceremony to endow a person with supernatural power or grace, or to set them apart. When a member of the Roman Catholic Church is in danger of death, unction administered as a sacrament 'for the health of soul and body' is called 'extreme unction'.

## Unidentified flying objects (UFOs)

'Flying saucers' and other mysterious metallic, usually disc-shaped, 'machines' sighted in the sky that are reported to perform incredible manoeuvres at great speeds and are considered by some people to be vehicles of extraterrestrial origin. Modern sightings date from June 1947, when the pilot of a private aeroplane, Kenneth Arnold, helping in the search for a missing aeroplane that had crashed in the Cascade Mountains, reported seeing nine bright flying objects, disc-shaped and metallic in appearance, that seemed to be travelling at twice the speed of sound. Since then, literally thousands of 'saucer sightings' have been collated from many parts of the world; many unsolicited sightings have shown that 'something' has taken a certain course across half the world, and has been observed by dozens of varied and disinterested witnesses.

Most researchers who have explored the subject of UFOs have been amazed at the quantity and quality of the evidence, much of which has never been made public; and there is no doubt that, in spite of the 'official' view of the scientific world that UFOs do not exist, valid reports of sightings continue and that there is a proportion which it is very difficult to discount. The Condon Report in the United States, and the government action there in closing the Project Blue Book files, should have ended speculation about UFOs, but careful examination reveals that less than a hundred cases were considered, the selection of

them being hardly random and many of the scientists concerned
having definite preconceptions.

Small wonder, then, that book after book has appeared – one by
Professor J. Allen Hynek, the official astronomical consultant to the
US Air Force's Project Blue Book throughout its existence. Some are
undoubtedly far-fetched, for, like the occult, psychic phenomena and
the supernatural, the subject tends to attract the 'lunatic fringe'; but
sane and sensible people have also looked into the subject of UFOs,
and not only has a lot of interesting material been discovered among
the mass of reported sightings (in 1975 it was revealed that, during
three of the American space flights, a cylindrical object with antenna
was logged and photographed); some have also discovered historical
evidence for 'flying saucers' hundreds – some say thousands – of years
ago.

CONSULT: J. Allen Hynek, *The UFO Experience,* Abelard-Schuman
(1972); Jacques Vallée, *Anatomy of a Phenomenon,* Neville Spearman
(1966).

## Urine

In common with other bodily secretions and excretions, urine was
used in **alchemy** and many magical ceremonies since it was thought to
retain some of the vital energies of the body and to provide a magical
link with a body. In **witchcraft**, urine could be used for turning
a witch's **spell** against the witch. Bottled urine was also preserved and
consulted in the absence of a person, for it was believed that, as that
person suffered, so the change would be indicated in the urine. It was
also a favourite ingredient in **black magic**, and may still be.

## Ursuline convent, possession at
*See* **Aix-en-Provence.**

# V

## Vampire

Supernatural resuscitated corpse that sucks the **blood** of the living. The Ancient Egyptians, Greeks, Romans, Assyrians and Babylonians all knew about vampires; some regarded them as **superstitions**, and others considered that they really existed. The same position obtains today, with some people regarding vampires as creations of myth and fantasy, while others have become convinced not only that vampires once existed but that they may still be found.

In China, Persia and especially throughout Eastern Europe there is a persistent belief in vampires, and heretics, outcasts and criminals are thought to become vampires when they die and to have the power to leave their graves at night and prey upon human beings. Much of the present-day interest in the West in vampirism has been prompted by Bram Stoker's classic novel *Dracula* (1897) and its many film versions – a story that he set in then unknown Transylvania, loaded with myth and superstition, mixed in legend and fact, and moulded with fantasy and sexual imagery. Since *Dracula*, the vampire has become a creature that cannot age or die, except it be tracked to its coffin of native earth, which it must occupy during the hours of daylight, and there staked through the heart; some say the head must also be cut off and burnt.

The vampire is a creature that casts no shadow or reflection, a gaunt creature (except when engorged with blood) that has hypnotic powers and superhuman strength, a creature whom all women find irresistible and who, once they have been bitten by a vampire, become vampires themselves. A vampire is said to be recognizable by its piercing eyes, thick lips, foul breath and long and pointed canine teeth, and by such peculiarities as hair in the middle of the palms. The creature is also reputed to have power over wolves, and to be able to change into a bat at will. It shuns garlic and cannot withstand the power of a crucifix or a **silver** bullet.

Modern psychology has revealed a predominance of blood and blood-letting in the erotic fantasies of many people, and the vampire legend (if legend it is) has been described as a kind of repression of incestious, necrophilious, oral and sadistic sexual wishes and guilts. Whatever the reason, the vampire has a strange appeal and attraction for many people, and careful study of the historical and contemporary evidence reveals a wealth of material that, surprisingly, cannot lightly be dismissed.

CONSULT: Montague Summers, *The Vampire: His Kith and Kin*, Kegan Paul, Trench, Trübner (1928); and *The Vampire in Europe*, Kegan Paul, Trench, Trübner (1929); Ornella Volta, *The Vampire*, Tandem Books (1965).

## Versailles visions

The Palace of Versailles has been the scene of a number of apparently supernormal happenings over the years, by far the best-known being the experiences of Miss Anne Moberly and Miss Eleanor Joudain. These they published in 1911 (using pseudonyms) in a book called *An Adventure*.

These two ladies, both distinguished scholars, visited Paris in 1901 and on 10 August went to Versailles and looked round the palace before setting out to see the Petit Trianon, which they had vaguely heard of as the little retreat that Louis XVI presented to his queen, Marie Antoinette, and where she and her ladies had relaxed and amused themselves. When they failed to locate the Petit Trianon, the two ladies, respectively Principal and Vice-Principal of St Hugh's College, Oxford, began to find the gardens depressing; feeling strangers in a strange place they lost their way, and felt lonely and mildly unhappy. Both noticed that, at the same time as they became aware of these feelings, the wind dropped and the landscape and trees suddenly appeared to be flat and two-dimensional, 'as though painted on canvas', as they put it in their book.

They walked on and saw a number of separate people and spoke to some of them. On approaching some farm buildings they met two official-looking persons in uniform green cloaks, whom they took to be gardeners, and when they asked them the way to the Petit Trianon were, rather roughly they thought, directed 'straight on'. They passed a curious plough, at least they thought it curious when they discussed the matter a week later. They passed a cottage where Miss Jourdain saw a woman and child. They encountered a red-faced man in a green cloak – having heard his running footsteps before they saw him – who stopped abruptly in front of them and rapidly but not unkindly gave them further directions. They reached a circular kiosk overshadowed by trees and saw a man wearing a cloak and a large hat who turned and looked at them; he was a most repulsive-looking man, dark-faced and pock-marked. Both ladies were overcome with alarm at the sight of this figure, and feeling that they were in the presence of evil, walked on over a small footbridge beside a waterfall.

They came at last to the Petit Trianon, and there Miss Moberly saw a lady sitting sketching. Thereafter everything became quite normal, and the ladies joined a group of tourists who were being shown over the house and afterwards returned to Paris. It seemed that they had spent an afternoon at Versailles, as hundreds of tourists have done before and since, without seeing anything strange enough to comment upon to each other; yet, a week later, when for the first time they discussed the trip, they discovered something very odd, for while some of the people and surroundings had been seen by both ladies, certain of the figures and objects had been seen by one but not by the other. Miss Moberly, for example, had not seen the cottage or the plough, and her companion had not seen the woman sketching at the Petit Trianon. The more they compared notes, the more puzzled they became, and finally they reached the conclusion that they had 'stepped back in time' and had walked through the gardens of Versailles prior to the French Revolution of 1789, 112 years before. The more they thought about this possibility, the more they thought that it must be what had happened, and they sat down and wrote independent accounts of what they thought they had seen at Versailles a week earlier. But, as Harry **Price** pointed out, they wrote their reports a week too late for these to be of any real value.

*An Adventure* has become a classic, and the fourth edition (1931) carried a preface by Miss Edith Oliver (who had seen similar **visions** herself) and a note by J. W. Dunne, the **time** theorist. The original documents pertaining to the case were deposited in the Bodleian Library, Oxford.

Did the two ladies really step back into the past, speak to people long dead, walk in gardens long disappeared and perhaps see Marie Antionette, and those about her, not long before tragedy overwhelmed them all; or was the whole thing some kind of elaborate hoax? Among the more interesting aspects of the case is the indisputable fact that certain details in the ladies' descriptions of the places they said they had seen was flatly contradicted – even laughed at – by authorities on the period; yet they stuck to their accounts, and later documents were discovered which showed them to have been correct in many details. It may be significant that Anne Moberly was a descendant of Peter the Great, Tsar of all the Russias, who was no stranger to visions and mystical experiences, and she had seen visions and heard voices during her life many times before she went to Versailles.

The story has a perennial fascination, and no convincing answer to the mystery has ever been universally accepted. The book by J. R. Sturge-Whiting, *The Mystery of Versailles,* approached the story from a rationalist angle and set out to prove that everything experienced had a perfectly normal explanation. Incident after incident was examined by Sturge-Whiting, and it seems likely that faulty perception, lapses of memory, an irresistible subconscious urge to accept a supernatural explanation and a certain credulity and subconscious elaboration all contributed to create one of the great popular mysteries of our time. In 1971, Dr Joan Evans, archaeologist and scholar, and the friend and colleague to whom the authors bequeathed the copyright of *An Adventure,* announced that she was 'absolutely convinced that what the ladies saw was a dress rehearsal in eighteenth-century costume arranged by Count Robert de Montesquiou' and that she had decided the only honourable course was to veto further publication of the book. This 'dress rehearsal' story had first been published in France in 1965, but not everyone considers that it can explain all the authors' experiences adequately.

CONSULT: C. Anne E. Moberly and Eleanor F. Jourdain, *An Adventure,* Faber & Faber (4th edition, 1931); Lucille Iremonger, *The Ghosts of Versailles,* Faber & Faber (1957); Peter Underwood, *Hauntings,* Dent (1977).

## Virgo
*See* **zodiac**.

## Vision
An imaginative mental picture; a prophetic sight – especially in a religious context; an experience that would otherwise be regarded as a **hallucination, apparition** or **dream**.

## Voice phenomena
Since 1959, when a Swedish film producer announced that he had obtained voices of dead people on tape, considerable research has been undertaken in an attempt to establish the possibility of the **paranormal** origin of noises and voices sometimes picked up when a

tape recorder is left running in a place unoccupied by human beings. Dr Konstantin **Raudive** and other scientists conducted hundreds of experiments, wrote scientific papers and came to the conclusion that a paranormal explanation was probable.

Alternative theories include the possibility that the subconscious mind of a living person can send out electronic impulses that register as human speech; or that the voices originate from an unknown but intelligent source, possibly from another planet; or that the electro-magnetic tape picks up radio waves or, in some unknown way, registers the past utterances of living or dead people. It is perhaps significant that the voices are often in more than one language, that they appear to be snatches of conversation rather than 'messages', and that the multiplicity of voices has sometimes seemed to depend upon the presence of certain individuals. The usual method used to obtain the voices is to set the machine to 'record' with a microphone 'live' and the volume set to maximum. Better results have been obtained when a diode replaces the microphone.

CONSULT: Peter Bander, *Carry On Talking*, Colin Smythe (1972); Konstantin Raudive, *Breakthrough – An Amazing Experiment in Electronic Communication with the Dead*, Colin Smythe (1971).

## Voodoo, voo-doo, vou-doo, vondou, or vodoun

Derived from the African Ewe tribe word *vadu*, meaning 'gods'. A cult of devil-worship that is particularly prevalent among West Indian and Southern United States creoles, mulattoes and Negroes that involves **hypnotism, possession** and dissociation; **charms**, snake-cults and **witchcraft**; and sometimes cannibalism and human **sacrifice**. In recent years, the full-**moon** rites of Voodooism have been practised in Britain, the United States (where the cult if officially banned) and several European countries. It is also the secret and national religion of Haiti, where, it has been claimed, 95 per cent of the black population is involved in the practice.

The many and varied rites of the cult include 'Voodoo Fire', a kind of sexual sacrifice; 'Congo', a ceremonial dance; 'Cochon Gris', a cannibalistic ritual; 'Hounci', a head-washing initiation ceremony; 'Nine Nights', a formula for dismissing the **spirits** of the dead; and 'Shay Shay', a musical singing and dancing formality where the female parts are played by males. Many Voodoo ceremonies develop into a general carouse and orgy. The snake-dances, for example, involve snakes being placed in the centre of the gathering of worshippers where the serpents remain torpid under the charms of a Voodoo priestess until the atmosphere builds up with music and dancing to a pitch where reality becomes mingled with fantasy; the snakes are then chopped to pieces and eaten, and during the increasing frenzy and excitement, amorous liberties culminate in sexual activities of all kinds. Voodoo priests and priestesses undergo a considerable, difficult and painful apprenticeship.

*See also* **Damballa; hoodoo; obeah.**

Consult: Zora Hurston, *Voodoo Gods*, Dent (1939); Joseph J. Williams, *Voodoos and Obeahs*, Allan & Unwin (1933).

# W

## Waite, Arthur Edward (1857-1941)

American historian of **occultism** who spent most of his life in England. Although he was successively a member of the Theosophical Society (*see* **Theosophy**) and the Order of the **Golden Dawn**, he was influenced all his life by both his mother's faith in the Roman Catholic Church and the themes of ceremony and ritual – the aspect of **magic** which he explored and wrote about in his many books. These included *The Brotherhood of the Rosy Cross* (1924), *The Real History of the Rosicrucians* (1887), *The Holy Kabbalah* (1929), *The Book of Black Magic and of Pacts* (1898) (later revised and reissued as *The Book of Ceremonial Magic*, 1965), *The Hidden Church of the Holy Grail* (1911), *The Secret Tradition in Freemasonry* (1911), *The Pictorial Key to the Tarot* and *Devil-Worship in France* (1896). He designed a set of **Tarot** cards that is still popular, and was a friend of W. B. **Yeats**, Arthur **Machen** and Evelyn Underhill. He is perhaps best remembered as the translator of the books of Eliphas **Levi** on magic, and his theories on occult doctrine have become widely accepted.

CONSULT: Ellic Howe, *The Magicians of the Golden Dawn*, Routledge & Kegan Paul (1972); Francis King, *Ritual Magic in England*, Neville Spearman (1970).

## Walpurgis Night, or Walpurgisnacht

*See under* **festivals**.

## 'Walter'

Alleged **spirit** of Walter Stinson, deceased brother and purported **control** of the American medium Mrs L. R. G. **Crandon**.

# Wand

An indispensable accessory of the magician; a magic 'blasting' or 'thundering' rod; a symbol of authority that can be traced to the staffs of priests, kings and magical healers, even to the rods of Moses and Aaron; an agent of transformation used by **fairies** and conjurers. Wands in the cards of the **Tarot** are connected with energy, enterprise and activity.

The magician, seeking to use the great driving forces of the universe for his own purposes, sometimes made his magic wand of **iron** or used a naked sword; while in **ritual magic** and **necromancy** the wand or rod would be of cypress wood, a graveyard tree and an emblem of **death**. In **witchcraft**, the wand, a phallic symbol, was often made of hazel. Great care was taken by the magician in making this important weapon and symbol of supreme power. The virgin rod would be cut at sunrise, stripped with the magic **athame**, preferably stained with sacrificial **blood**; then, amid prayers and supplications that the wand would enclose great strength, just anger and magical attributes, magnetized caps would be fitted and more calls made to **names of power** to invoke the greatest possible force into the wand. The magician always kept his wand, when not in use, wrapped in silken cloth, of any colour except black or brown; and before use a wand would be purified and consecrated.

# Water divining
*See* **dowsing or divining**.

# Weiss, Ehrick
*See* **Houdini, Harry**.

# Werewolf, or werwolf

From *wer* = 'man', *wulf* = 'wolf': a living person who changes into animal form and becomes a ferocious killer and eater of human flesh. Scientifically known as **lycanthropy**: the magical transformation of man into beast, or the belief that this takes place.

The werewolf tradition is found in most countries of the world and is of very ancient origin. (It was commonly believed that men born on Christmas Eve became werewolves.) The werewolf is, however, essentially different from the other transformation legend, the **vampire**, in that the werewolf is a living person and the change to animal shape only lasts during a lifetime; though the change can be temporary or permanent. In Germanic legend and folklore the change was brought about by donning a wolf's pelt: a practice that is certainly as old as man's pictorial representations of himself and an idea that students of occult mysteries find interesting, especially since it was believed that those who voluntarily took the shape of a wolf were believed to be able to resume the shape of a man at will, while those who underwent the transformation involuntarily were the subjects of malignant **magic**.

In 1521 two Frenchmen were burnt alive at Besançon after one had related how he had taught the other to cover his naked body with a special ointment which caused hair to grow all over the body and claws to sprout, after which they ran on all fours like the wind and ate children. The theme of metamorphosis has been exploited in literature and art, but the occultist looks upon the werewolf as a sorcerer whose **astral body** roams freely where it will while the magician is asleep.

*See also* **Grenier, Jean**.

CONSULT: Sabine Baring-Gould, *The Book of Werewolves*, Causeway Books, New York (1973 edition); Montague Summers, *The Werewolf*, Kegan Paul (1933).

## Wesley poltergeist
*See* **Epworth**.

## Whirling dervishes
*See* **Dervishes, whirling**.

## White magic
Ceremonial **magic** that is used for purposes of good; often healing, curing and treating blemishes, though the methods used are often similar to those employed in the practice of **black magic**,

Ancient Egyptian sorcerers (*see* **Egyptian magic**) were engaged in white magic when they allegedly divided water, so that it stood aside and exposed the beds of rivers, enabling lost articles to be discovered; and so are today's **covens** when they perform **Wicca** ceremonies as an antidote to evil or black magic, or produce helpful medicine. Yet the distinction between black and white magic is often arbitrary since all classifications of magic continually mingle and fertilize each other, with the **Cabala**, for example, being regarded, on the one hand, as sacred writings, and on the other as words of power from the realms of the **Devil**. Again, effigies or images of people are used in both white and black magic, although for different motives, but the basic principle of **sympathetic magic** is common to both systems.

Today white witches often appear in newspaper reports and make headlines with statements proclaiming that they are white witches who practice magic for good purposes, but it is surely significant that there are very few accounts of white witchcraft in the past. White magic may not be practised by sorcerers or satanists, but neither are those who practise it Christians, though some claim to embody a pagan tradition that predates any known religion. White magic is, in effect, an offshoot of black magic. An example of white magic is the ancient formula for laying a **ghost** that involved ceremoniously burying an effigy of the dead person and washing in pure water the person to whom the ghost had appeared – an **exorcism** ceremony that symbolized ritual burial and purification.

CONSULT: Eric Maple, *Magic, Medicine and Quackery*, Robert Hale (1968).

## Wicca
Term used by present-day witches for their **witchcraft**.

## Widdershins
*See* **withershins**.

## Wild Hunt and Wish Hounds
The Wild Hunt is a supernatural and terrifying band of spectral riders, running with black hounds and led by a wild huntsman, that is supposed to career across open spaces, or high in the air overhead, on dark and stormy nights, especially in winter, accompanied by rushing winds, shouts, the blowing of horns and the baying of the hounds. Some people thought the leader was the **Devil** himself, and his hounds the **spirits** of unbaptized children. The belief once commanded considerable force throughout northern Europe, and men and women would go to great lengths not to see the terrifying sight, throwing themselves to the ground, shutting their eyes and holding fast to a tree or something firmly planted in the earth, until the dark rout had passed; for anyone was liable to be seized and carried far, far away and abandoned in some unknown region. Odin (or Woden in Germanic mythology), god of the dead, was another contender for the leader of the Wild Hunt.

Other names for the spectral riders included the Yule Host in Iceland and the Raging Host or Furious Host in Germany; while the names for the wild dog packs included the (often headless) Wish Hounds or Yeth Hounds of southern England; the Gabriel Hounds (with their human heads) of northern England and the Hell Hounds or Night Hounds of central England. The Wild Hunt is one of the most persistent and widespread of all pagan legends, and local or national heroes or **demons** have often come to be associated with the pack of black hounds: Sir Francis Drake on Dartmoor, Tregeagle in Cornwall, King Arthur and King Herla throughout England, King Hugh Capet in France, King Herod, the murderer of the innocents, and even King Wenceslas in Bohemia.

CONSULT: Christina Hole, *English Folk Heroes*, Batsford (1948); Ruth E. St Leger-Gordon, *The Witchcraft and Folklore of Dartmoor*, Robert Hale (1965).

## Willow
*See under* **trees and plants**.

## Wish Hounds
*See* **Wild Hunt and Wish Hounds**.

## Wishing wells
Wells where an unspoken wish is said to be granted, providing a small gift is made: a coin, a pin or even a pebble being dropped into the well as an offering to the **spirit** that dwells therein. Wells have been regarded as the dwelling-places of powerful spirits since time immemorial. Many wishing wells were originally pagan sacred springs and were rededicated by Christian missionaries, their prophetic or therapeutic qualities then being ascribed to a particular saint. Well-dressing is a survival of the pagan belief that each well had its guardian spirit that had to be placated.

## Witchcraft
The occult practices or powers of witches and sorcerers, especially when regarded as the consequence of dealings with the **Devil** or **spirits**; also any claim to produce effects by contract with a supernatural power.

Beliefs in witchcraft has been part of the general pattern of human thought for many centuries and in many countries, but most particularly throughout Europe. There is considerable evidence to suggest that the more important elements of witchcraft were common to Palaeolithic man; certainly there are close resemblances between modern witchcraft and sorcery and that reported in medieval Europe. Witches, in popular conception, have changed little in five hundred

*Three Leicestershire witches of 1619 with their familiars*

years: the 'heyday' of witchcraft lasted from perhaps the middle of the fifteenth century to the middle of the eighteenth century, producing such figures as Matthew **Hopkins**, the 'Witchfinder General', who became extremely powerful and earned himself a fortune at the expense of some 200 people put to death as witches.

Most people picture a witch as a crone who is in league with the Devil, through him being able to control the elements, change shape, cast **spells**, cause illness and bad fortune, transport herself great distances in a short time and ride to the **sabbath** on a **broomstick**; who possesses a '**devil's mark**' and a **familiar** which accompanies her everywhere; and who spends her nights in the company of young men of her choice and from time to time pays homage to the **horned god** himself.

Countless old hags were 'tested' during the witchcraft persecutions, merely because of their physical appearance or some unfortunate minor defect like a twitch, a limp, an eye with a cast or simply a mole or blemish of the skin. As the events in **Aberdeen** or **Salem**, for example, bore witness, there was little hope for anyone arrested on suspicion of being a witch, since they would be likely to be put to some such 'test' as the water ordeal: swimming a witch was a popular pastime and the unlucky woman would be all but stripped, her hands and feet bound crosswise, and a rope tied round her waist before she was thrown far into a pond. If she floated, she was judged to be a witch for the water would reject a guilty person; if she sank, she was innocent, but it was often too late for the knowledge to be of any benefit to her.

Male witches have been known as wizards and warlocks, but it has become common practice to call all who practice witchcraft witches. White witches are those who claim that they only perform their rites for good purposes (*see* **white magic**). A feature of witchcraft, both ancient and modern, is the nude dancing, sometimes wild and exhausting, at other times quiet and reverent.

By 1950 only a few eccentrics would have admitted to practising any form of witchcraft, but today active **covens** are to be found in many parts of Britain and the United States; this revival of the witch-cult is due in no small part to the publication of Margaret Murray's books, the enthusiasm of Gerald **Gardner**, with his witch museum on the Isle of Man, and, more recently, to the **Wicca** activities of such people as Sybil Leek and Alex Sanders.

CONSULT: Christina Hole, *Witchcraft in England,* Batsford (1945); Margaret A. Murray, *The God of the Witches,* Sampson Low, Marston (1931); Jacobus Sprenger and Heinrich Kramer, *Malleus Maleficarum* (trans. and ed. by Montague Summers), Pushkin Press (1948 edition).

## Withershins, or widdershins

From the Anglo-Saxon *wither sith* = 'to walk against'. Withershins is deliberate movement in the opposite direction; in a reversed or wrong way. **Magic circles** are normally drawn clockwise, following the direction of the sun, but in operations consciously evil or dedicated to the **Devil**, the magician works in the opposite direction, withershins – against the sun and therefore unnatural and attractive to evil forces. A black magician will in **black magic** ritual walk round his circle withershins, recite prayers backwards, invert crucifixes, and so forth. In folklore it is considered dangerous to walk round a church or a haunted place withershins, and there are stories of people doing so and odd things happening to them until they correct themselves.

## Worth, Patience
*See* '**Patience Worth**'.

## Wraith

Phantom or **double**, either of a living person who is about to die or who is in serious danger, or of someone recently dead. Also an **apparition** of any kind; a **spectre** or **ghost**.

## Writing, automatic

*See* **automatism**.

# X

## X, faculty
*See* **Faculty X**.

## Xenoglossy, xenoglossis, or xenoglossisia

The name given to the spiritualistic phenomenon of speech in real languages of which the medium has no conscious knowledge; speaking in tongues.

Although the phenomenon is by no means uncommon, good evidence for xenoglossy is somewhat rare; and while at first sight the testimony may seem impressive, it has sometimes been found on investigation that the medium, though consciously unfamiliar with the language or languages, has in fact come into contact with it or them at some time, either verbally or visually; and it seems likely that, in some cases, the subconscious mind can record a great deal of such information quite unconsciously. 'Speaking in tongues', the uncontrollable utterance of unintelligible sounds under the influence of mystical or religious excitement, is reportedly common within fundementalist religious sects. Sometimes the term is used for writing in an unknown language. In medieval times the speaking in foreign or unknown languages was one of the four principal signs of the presence of a **demon**. The Ursuline nuns of **Loudun** apparently spoke in five languages, including a Red Indian dialect, and they confessed to having been possessed by the **Devil**.

Xenoglossy was often encountered in the early days of **spiritualism**, and in recent years has been increasingly reported during attempts at **exorcism**.

CONSULT: George B. Cutler, *Speaking with Tongues*, Yale University Press, New Haven, (1927); M. T. Kelsey, *Speaking with Tongues*, Epworth Press (1965).

# Xenology

The study of the domain between scientifically established **phychical research** and the unestablished and still largely unknown and unexplored areas of psychic and occult phenomena. Xenology aims at the synthesis of all the unexplored or only partially explored regions of science.

# Y

## Yeats, William Butler (1865-1939)

Irish poet, critic and life-long student of **occultism, mysticism** and **magic**. He studied Hindu philosophy, became a member of the Theosophical Society (*see* **Theosophy**), of the Hermetic Order of the **Golden Dawn** and of the **Ghost Club**. He was widely read in philosophy, history and comparative religion; was interested in **spiritualism** and had many psychic experiences. He also made a study of the **fairy** lore of Ireland, the **Cabala, astrology,** Rosicrucianism (*see* **Rosicrucians**) and the **Tarot**. Yeats's poetry and literary compositions were greatly influenced, inspired and coloured by his mystico-religious and occult knowledge and experience, and by the people with whom he came into contact, among them Madame **Blavatsky**, MacGregor **Mathers**, Aleister **Crowley**, A. E. **Waite**, Arthur **Machen** and Evelyn Underhill. His books include *A Vision* (1925), *The Secret Rose* (1897) and *Irish Fairy and Folk-Tales* (1893). He also published many volumes of poetry and a number of plays, including *The Words Upon the Window Pane*, which was based on his knowledge of **séances** and **mediumship**. He was awarded the Nobel Prize for Literature in 1923.

CONSULT: Joseph Home, *W. B. Yeats 1865-1939*, Macmillan (1962 edition); F. A. C. Wilson, *W. B. Yeats and Tradition*, Gollancz (1958).

## Yeti

*See under* **animals and birds**.

## Yew

*See under* **trees and plants**.

## Yin and Yang

The two great opposite and complementary forces in Chinese

philosophy. Yin is female, dark and negative, while Yang is male, light and positive. The Chinese classify all phenomena in terms of 'Yin' and 'Yang', since everything in the universe depends upon the interplay between the two forces. *See also* **Acupuncture** *and* **I Ching**.

*The Yin and Yang: a representation of the Absolute with overlapping negative and positive sections*

## Yoga

A form of **meditation**, an exercise, a religion, a practical discipline, a path to liberation, a voyage of self-discovery: yoga is claimed to be all of these, and much more besides. It is basically a system of Hindu philosophy. There are many kinds of yoga, but all involve breath control and aim at achieving a mystical union between the individual, who undergoes the arduous and carefully planned exercises, and the Universal Soul. Perhaps the best-known branch is **hatha yoga**, the yoga of power, which enables the determined adept, it is claimed, to obtain whatever he desires; but Raja Yoga, the royal path that leads to spiritual perfection, is also of interest to students of the occult and supernatural, for it deals with psychic development.

CONSULT: Mircea Eliade, *Yoga, Immortality and Freedom,* Pantheon, New York (1958); S. Richmond, *Common Sense About Yoga,* MacGibbon & Kee (1971).

# Yoni

Hindu word for the female sex organ, the feminine power in nature; an emblem of pleasure and generation connected with fertility and variously symbolized as a triangle; a V with an additional central line; a stone with a hole through it; a lotus flower or a sea shell. With the **lingam**, the Hindu word for phallus, the yoni was once worshipped in India and elsewhere, and many relics of the cult are preserved in museums throughout the world. *See also* **phallic worship**.

# Z

## Zener cards

Cards specially designed by Dr J. B. **Rhine**, based on an idea suggested by a psychologist, Dr Zener, for statistical and experimental tests in **extrasensory perception**. Zener cards are packaged in bundles of twenty-five, each bundle comprising five cards bearing a simple diagram: a circle, a star, a cross, a square or a set of wavy lines. The cards are shuffled (or 'randomized'), and while the investigator or his assistant (the 'agent') turns the cards face upwards one at a time, the person being tested (the 'percipient') records his or her guesses while screened or otherwise seperated from the agent and the cards. Under such conditions and over extended experimentation it is thought possible to establish the presence of extrasensory perception, after taking chance expectation into account. Zener cards are

*Zener cards: used in ESP tests*

obtainable from the Society for Psychical Research, 1 Adam and Eve Mews, Kensington, London W8; and from the Foundation for Research into the Nature of Man, Durham, North Carolina, U.S.A. CONSULT: S. G. Soal and F. Bateman, *Modern Experiments in Telepathy*, Faber & Faber (1954); G. N. M. Tyrrell, *Science and Psychical Phenomena*, Methuen (1938).

## Zodiac

In **astrology** the zodiac is an imaginary belt in the sky containing all the known planets and the sun and **moon** and many stars grouped into constellations. Divided into twelve named divisions or signs, designed to separate the year into equal parts, each division is marked by the entry of the sun, on its eastward course, into a group of stars; but there are variations between the divisions of the traditional and the **sidereal zodiac**. The position of a planet at the time of a person's birth is said to affect and influence people, as it is events on earth.

*Aries*, the sign for those born between 21 March and 19 April (traditionally), or between 20 April and 20 May (sidereal system), is symbolized by the ram and emphasizes the energy, initiative and aggression that characterizes those born under the sign, usually regarded as the first sign of the zodiac. Arieans are inclined to impetuosity and exaggeration, but are usually self-reliant, born leaders and always full of new ideas. The average Arien invariably thinks first of 'number one', and the only person who really matters to him is himself; with this attitude, and the lack of any real feeling for other people, he is not an ideal marriage partner, though his liking for asserting and exhibiting his masculinity has an undoubted appeal to many partners.

The second sign of the zodiac, *Taurus*, is said to influence those born between 21 April and 20 May (traditionally), or between 14 May and 12 June (sidereal system). The symbol of Taurus is a bull, denoting stability, patience, persistence, reliability and obstinacy. Taureans are the strong and silent ones, the practical people who keep their feet planted firmly on the ground. They are slow to anger, and although they may be capable of violence when finally roused, are faithful and reliable friends. Inclined to be self-indulgent and generous to a fault, they are often sensual and sometimes lazy, but on the whole the Taurean is ambitious and persevering, sincere and plain-speaking, determined yet thoughtful.

*Gemini* is the sign for those born between 21 May and 20 June (traditionally), or between 20 June and 20 July (sidereal system). The symbol of the 'heavenly twins' emphasizes the dual nature of Geminians: they are often very clever, but can be lazy, intelligent but fun-loving, heroic yet frivolous, charming but elusive, quick-witted but stolid. Many physicians are born under this sign, as are many actors and entertainers. Since they are ruled by Mercury, the fleet and timeless messenger of the gods, Geminians rarely look their age. Although they often seem to be making mistakes – even making fools of themselves – their quick minds always find a way out of their difficulties or embarrassment. Invariably bubbling over with new ideas, they are nevertheless capable of great perseverance. Quick to fall in love, they are also quick to find fault, and all too often the enduring love that all Geminians long for eludes them.

*Cancer* subjects are said to be those born between 21 June and 21 July (traditionally), or between about 20 July to 20 August (sidereal system). The symbol of Cancer is generally considered to be a crab, but its pictorial origin is obscure and a lobster, crayfish or other water creature could be the original symbol; at all events, Cancerians are usually changeable, ambitious, devoted and jolly people who appreciate the admiration of others and sometimes tend to say one thing and do another. Yet they are full of imagination, and these emotional and romantic souls often shape their entire lives on one particular person or an idol of their imagination. Original, sociable, luxury-loving and artistic, they are also inclined to be irritable, peevish and sulky when things do not suit them. Many psychic people are born during the early part of the Cancer period, and all Cancerians are the kindest, most hospitable and sympathetic of friends.

*Leo* is the fifth sign of the zodiac for those born between 21 July and 20 August (traditionally), or between 16 August and 15 September (sidereal system). The symbol of Leo is the lion, suggestive of strength, dignity and lordly bearing, though the typical Leo is usually conventional in dress and outlook: his sympathies are far more likely to be with the established order than with revolutionists. Leo subjects are born leaders: self-willed, intelligent, clear-thinking and honest people who have a distinct tendency for plain speaking and blunt frankness. Friendly and good-hearted, they sometimes appear to be haughty and indifferent to the feelings of others, and while they are usually very successful, they do not often have many close friends. In appearance, the typical Leo is taller than average, strong, well-built and active, fair-haired and with blue eyes.

*Virgo* is the sign for those born between 21 August and 20 September (traditionally), or between 16 September and 15 October (sidereal system). Their symbol is the virgin, suggestive of modesty and sympathy, and they are the reserved and undemonstrative ones, though underneath it all they are often shrewd, careful and questioning, the apparent quietness often hiding an inherent nervousness. Courageous in times of danger, and cool and collected when all about them are excited, Virgoans are kind and thoughtful people, inclined to be inquisitive but always willing to see the other person's point of view and to help in any way they can. A common aspect of the Virgoan is a good memory and a genuine 'feel' for history and historical things; indeed, their knowledge of history and historical personages is often quite remarkable, and in connection with their excellent memories they often have an ability to quote from memory long passages from poetry or literature. Often fastidious about their foods, they are inclined to be attracted to 'health' foods and 'patent' drugs.

*Libra* is the seventh sign of the zodiac, and rules those born between 21 September and 20 October (traditionally), or between 16 October and 15 November (sidereal system). The symbol of Libra is the scales or balance, and many astrologers consider this sign, with its emphasis on harmony, powers of evaluation, personal charm and originality, to be one of the more desirable signs to be born under. Librans are always fair in their dealings with others, and often go to great lengths to see the other person's point of view. They possess an inate love of beauty in all natural things, are often artistic and invariably good and fair judges of talent and fashion. Their love of argument makes them difficult to live with at times, but their charm, wit and gift for artistic pursuits usually wins over all with whom they come into contact.

*Scorpio* is the sign for those born between 21 October and 20 November (traditionally), or between 16 November and 14 December (sidereal system). The symbol of Scorpio is the scorpion, suggesting virility, determination and caution, and although some astrologers regard Scorpio as one of the most dangerous signs to be born under, others point to the positiveness, straightforwardness, generosity and understanding of those born under the sign. Such people are usually very energetic and courageous, but inclined to be uninhibited and impatient. To the typical Scorpian, however, nothing is too much trouble, and he is thorough in all that he does. Always (or nearly always) cool and dignified, they have an abundance of wit, humour and good nature; they are observant and often exert (unconsciously) considerable power over others.

*Sagittarius* is the ninth sign of the zodiac and rules those born between 21 November and 21 December (traditionally), or between 15 December and 13 January (sidereal system). The symbol of Sagittarius is the archer – commonly represented by a centaur drawing a bow – and Sagittarians are usually friendly, happy-go-lucky people inclined to be restless but also quick, trustworthy, cheerful and optimistic. They enjoy travel and are often ambitious in one way or another. Generous and successful, Sagittarians seem to have discovered the secret of living, and these uncomplicated but often very attractive people with strong personalities are usually the best of friends and the best of company.

*Capricorn* is the sign of the zodiac occupied by the sun at the moment of birth for those born between 21 December and 21 January (traditionally), or between about 20 January and 20 February (sidereal system). The symbol of Capricorn is a 'sea-goat', mythological creature, part-goat and part-fish, based on the Babylonian god Ea who ruled the region described as 'the waters under the earth'. Capricornians (*capricornius* = 'goat-horned') are usually clear-headed, independent, self-critical people who set a high standard for themselves. Often musically inclined (Mozart, Schubert and Mendelssohn were all born under the sign), they display a clearness, an economy and a brevity in their works that is also evident in those Capricornians who write and who speak in public. They make effective speakers, for they possess an elegant precision in all they say and do and often have distinctive and attractive voices. They also invariably possess a delightful sense of humour and are capable of great devotion and considerable concentration; they are loyal and devoted friends, have a definite business sense and are always fair in their judgements.

*Aquarius* rules those born between 21 January and 19 February (traditionally), or between 12 February and 13 March (sidereal system). Their symbol, a man pouring water from an urn, emphasizes the helpfulness that characterizes those born under this sign. The group of stars that forms the eleventh sign of the zodiac was thought to resemble a water-bearer, and hence the sign. Aquarians are usually sympathetic, kind, understanding, refined, moderate and reasonable; they love peace and quiet and often, characteristically, are noticeable by their quiet dress and gentle voices and manner, although they should never be underestimated for they are intelligent, strong-willed and forceful personalities. Aquarius is a rival with Libra for the title of ideal sign to be born under.

*Pisces* is traditionally the last sign of the zodiac and rules those born between 21 February and 21 March (traditionally), or between approximately 14 March and 12 April (sidereal system). The symbol of Pisces is two fishes, suggestive of tolerance, indolence and patience, and the typical Piscean is genial, pleasant, good-natured and generous. But just because he or she may appear to be somewhat weak-willed and easily satisfied, Pisceans should not be underrated for they often astound people – including themselves – by doing something really remarkable. Kind people who are good talkers and excellent mixers, they often succeed as journalists or actors – professions which are not too close to reality, for Pisceans are inclined to exaggerate and over-state events and experiences. Sometimes they lack self-confidence or are deceitful, and may be inclined either to be taken in by or associated with advertising schemes or bogus 'opportunities'. Yet by and large they are friendly and ambitious people, often with mystic interests. They also love travel and are fascinated by such subjects as astronomy. In appearance, the typical Piscean is inclined to be fleshy, below average in height and possessing short, thick limbs, a pale complexion, a large face and prominent eyes.

CONSULT: Rupert Gleadow, *Your Character in the Zodiac*, Phoenix House (1968); Joan Rodgers, *The Art of Astrology*, Herbert Jenkins (1960).

## Zombies

The living dead of Haiti; bodies without souls; automaton-like creatures brought back from the dead by the rites of **voodoo**. Zombies walk with a shambling gait, downcast eyes, speak gibberish and remain docile as long as they do not eat **salt**, an instant cure for zombification. William Seabrook maintained that several zombies were innocently given salt biscuits by their owner's wife, whereupon they awakened from their stupefaction and, suddenly aware of their true states, hurried to the graveyard and tried to dig themselves back into the earth. Zombies are always treated harshly, and their owners' constant fear is that a zombie released from bondage will revenge itself, either physically or magically, upon his owner. In reality, so-called zombies are probably mental defectives.

CONSULT: Zora Hurston, *Voodoo Gods,* Dent (1939); Frances Huxley, *The Invisibles,* Hart-Davies (1966); Alfred Metraux, *Voodoo in Haiti,* Deutsch (1959).

### Zugun, Eleonore (b. 1914)

A classic case of **poltergeist** phenomena (especially **telekinesis**) coupled with **stigmata**. Also known as the 'Devil Girl', or the 'poltergeist girl'.

The disturbances began when Eleonore was about twelve and went to live with her grandparents at Buhai, a few miles from Talpa, the Romanian village where she had been born. Soon after her arrival showers of stones and broken china smashed several windows in the cottage, and various articles inside apparently moved of their own accord, usually ending up at Eleonore's feet. A priest blessed one stone, marked it with a cross, and threw it far out into the local river from whence it was assumed to have originated since it was wet; within an hour the marked stone was again thrown through one of the broken cottage windows. The affair became the talk of the village and filled the superstitious peasants with dread since they attributed the disturbances to *Dracu*, the '**Devil**' or 'evil one'. An attempt at **exorcism**, incarceration in an asylum and confinement in a convent had no effect on the phenomena, and the girl was becoming something of a problem for her relatives when the Countess Zoë Wassilko-Serecki heard about the case; she had long been interested in **psychical research** and took Eleonore under her wing.

Harry **Price** then heard of the case, and after witnessing convincing phenomena at the countess's flat in Vienna persuaded her to bring the girl to London where he could carry out tests in his laboratory. So, in October 1927, Harry Price and a number of scientists, including Professor William McDougall, Professor Hans Thirring, the Hon. Everard Fielding and Dr Theodore B. Hyslop, witnessed 'spontaneous movements' of objects, telekinetic phenomena and the strange stigmata – weals, scratches and teeth-marks – that regularly appeared and disappeared on the girl's face, arms and hands. Although the teeth-marks were identical to those which would have been the result of her biting herself, and all the marks appeared on those parts of her body which were accessible to her, she was never seen to play any tricks of this description and the marks were certainly painful. The official report stated that the stigmata appeared spontaneously and that

Eleonore was not consciously responsible for them; certainly under scientific test conditions objects moved without physical contact.

The affair came to a dramatic halt when, in 1928, Eleonore had her first menstruation. The girl became perfectly normal almost overnight; there were no more stigmata, and no more moving of objects. Later Eleonore had her own ladies hairdressing business in Czernowitz, Romania, and disappeared from the realm of psychical research.

CONSULT: Harry Price, *Leaves from a Psychist's Case-Book,* Gollancz (1933); Paul Tabori, *Companions of the Unseen,* H. A. Humphrey (1968).